Mental Leaps

* structural diagrams are not really analogies.

They are the result of an analyses which deliberately omits detail/content.
Real analogies offer a richer set of associations.
Seemingly insignificant details may produce something useful/worthwhile.

* in order to understand an analogy the child has to abstract from the example the relevant structural features.

* if instructional analogies are successful, how can they be made so? What is the background cognitively that would make this possible?

* Value of narrative analogies — not static (Maths)

* teddy register analogy

* check out Walkerdine : maths criticism

* Private Myers: remembered better after 2nd time through.
   But which version is remembered?

> * recontextualising of abstract notions/ideas

Mental Leaps

Analogy in Creative Thought

* do multiple reconstruction help

* microworlds / constructionism
↑
contradicts multiple analogies,

Keith J. Holyoak and Paul Thagard

* maths is the analogy not the context. It is a way of understanding a context.

* children constructing analogies. How can I apply this? Need to practice recontextualising. Start with simple examples - create situations, 10 + 2 ?

* developing skills of teaching + learning by analogy are not just add ons. They underpin the two processes. Any enhancement will be to the benefit of both.
Teachers need to develop skills of using multiple analogies and children need to recontextualise their learning.

* write stories with all elements recontextualised.

A Bradford Book
The MIT Press
Cambridge, Massachusetts
London, England

 # numbers are usually used as adjectives.

 # some teachers don't use analogy

 # are all analogies based on the same process? work in AI uses very diff. techniques.

> is Goswami's idea that the ability to use analogy may not develop testable?

First MIT Press paperback edition, 1996
© 1995 Massachusetts Institute of Technology

This book was set in Bembo by DEKR Corporation, Woburn, Massachusetts, and was printed and bound in the United States of America.

Library of Congress Cataloging-in-Publication Data

Holyoak, Keith James, 1950–
  Mental leaps : analogy in creative thought / Keith J. Holyoak and
Paul Thagard.
    p. cm.
  Includes bibliographical references and index.
  ISBN 0-262-08233-0 (HB), 0-262-58144-2 (PB)
  1. Analogy. 2. Creative thinking. I. Thagard, Paul. II. Title.
BD190.H64 1995
169—dc20   94-22734
                                                                CIP

A catalogue of analogues
Analogical complexity + model...

Contents

Preface

Our interests in analogy can be traced back to 1975 when we were in graduate school. Keith Holyoak was studying cognitive psychology at Stanford University, where he was working on the representation of semantic relations in human memory (a topic that he would connect a few years later with the use of analogy in problem solving). Meanwhile Paul Thagard was a graduate student in philosophy at the University of Toronto, where he became fascinated with the creative use of analogy in the work of scientists such as Darwin. After completing our doctoral degrees, we each arrived at the University of Michigan, where Thagard taught philosophy at the Dearborn campus and Holyoak began to work on analogy in problem solving. Richard Nisbett noticed that the psychologist and the philosopher were in different ways dealing with similar issues, and he introduced us in 1980. For the next few years we met regularly with him and John Holland to discuss analogy, along with many other kinds of reasoning. This four-way collaboration culminated in our book *Induction: Processes of Inference, Learning, and Discovery,* which appeared in 1986.

By then, Holyoak had moved to UCLA and Thagard to Princeton University, from which he went to the University of Waterloo in 1992. Nonetheless, we continued a collaboration focused directly on analogy. Our joint research, in which many students and colleagues also participated, produced a series of computer models of human use of analogy, coupled with extensive experimental investigations that provided guidance for the construction of our simulations.

After publishing many technical papers on analogy, we decided to take a broader look at what we and other researchers had learned about the topic over the previous fifteen years or so. Like *Induction,* the book that has resulted is genuinely collaborative; both of us have worked on every chapter. Analogy by its very nature freely oversteps the traditional boundaries between knowledge domains, making it possible to use ideas from one domain to achieve insights in another. But although a number of fine books have reviewed what is known about such specialized topics as the use of analogy by children, by scientists, by poets, and by political leaders, no single book has provided an integrated treatment of analogical thinking across many different domains. This book presents a general theory of analogical thinking, illustrated by applications drawn from the widest possible spectrum. We have not attempted the encyclopedic task of surveying all the valuable research on analogy that has been performed by researchers in many different fields, but have instead tried to show how our own theory can provide a unified explanation of the diverse operations and applications of analogy.

Analogy is a mental tool that everyone uses to some degree. Understanding how we draw analogies is important for people interested in the evolution of thinking in animals and in its development in children; for those whose focus is on either creative thinking or errors of everyday reasoning; for those concerned with how decisions are made in law, business, and politics; and for those striving to improve education. In order to make our discussion as accessible as possible, we have tried to keep technical matters to a minimum. For ease of reading, we have kept the text free of references and footnotes, but extensive reference notes keyed to pages in the text can be found at the end of the book. Throughout the book we emphasize the basic principles that govern the use of analogy. Our major aim in the book is to show how the richness and diversity of analogy in thought can be understood in terms of these principles. Of course, much still remains to be learned. As well as providing a progress report on the scientific analysis of analogical thinking, we hope this book provides some pointers for those who pursue the investigation further.

Acknowledgments

Along the long road that led to completion of this book, we have accumulated many debts. Each author has been involved in a long series of collaborative research projects on analogy, involving many students and colleagues. Keith Holyoak's work on this topic began in 1978 in collaboration with Mary Gick. Their project investigated the use of analogy in problem solving, which became a continuing focus of subsequent research. Later work in Holyoak's laboratories was conducted in collaboration with Dorrit Billman, Richard Catrambone, Ellen Junn, and Kyunghee Koh (at the University of Michigan), Miriam Bassok (at the University of Pittsburgh), and Bruce Burns, Paul Downing, John Hummel, Trent Lange, Eric Melz, Laura Novick, Nina Robin, Bobbie Spellman, Jeff Thompson, Charles Wharton, and Tom Wickens (at UCLA). Bobbie Spellman's contributions to the book were especially wide-ranging, including not only relevant experiments but also discussions of the role of analogy in political decision making, suggestions and legal research on analogical arguments from the law, and critical comments on the entire first draft. Paul Thagard also was aided immensely by a strong group of collaborators who worked with him at Princeton, including Dawn Cohen, David Gochfeld, Susan Hardy, and especially Greg Nelson. At Waterloo, he has similarly benefited from working with Allison Barnes, Lori Buchanan, John Ching, Roy Fleck, Steve Joordens, and Cameron Shelley.

We also learned from many careful reviews and discussions of early drafts of the book. Patricia Cheng was always ready on short notice to help Keith Holyoak grapple with conceptual issues and to give rapid feedback on sections of the manuscript. In addition to reviewing a draft of the book, Graeme Halford provided many stimulating hours of discussion with Keith Holyoak that helped shape the taxonomy of analogical complexity. Others provided useful guidance to the literature in specific areas: Roger Thompson for analogy use by primates, Boaz Keysar for metaphor, and Bill McKellin for treatments of analogy in anthropology. In addition to Halford and Spellman, Ken Forbus, Dedre Gentner, Giyoo Hatano, Elijah Millgram, Erik Steinhart, and several anonymous reviewers provided excellent suggestions for revision in their reviews of a draft of the manuscript. We particularly wish to thank the students who read the first complete draft in the fall of 1993, in a psychology seminar at UCLA and in a philosophy seminar at the University of Waterloo. Tom Bennett, Catherine Fritz, and Davina Klein (UCLA), as well as Craig Beam, John Robinson, and Meg Rohan (Waterloo) provided especially useful comments on the manuscript.

A number of other people provided various types of special assistance. David Shpall generated many of the figures for the book on a microcomputer and aided in other aspects of manuscript production. Other figures were drawn by Robert Bynder and Ben Levin. Art Markman kindly provided us with a camera-ready copy of figure 5.6, and Gay Snodgrass generously allowed us to adapt several of her line drawings to construct the figures that appear in chapter 3 to illustrate match-to-sample tasks. Betty and Harry Stanton, along with Teri Mendelsohn, Sandra Minkkinen, Carol Roberts, and others at MIT Press, deserve special thanks for their careful editorial assistance.

This book would not have been possible without the generous support of several funding agencies. From 1986 through 1992, when the core ideas of our theory were developed, our research was supported by the Basic Research Office of the U. S. Army Research Institute for Behavioral and Social Sciences (Contracts MDA903–86-K-0297 and MDA903–89-K-0179). Special thanks are due to Judith Orasanu for her support as our contract manager. Additional funding for computational work on the project at UCLA was provided by the National Science Foundation (Grant DIR-9024251). During the critical year in which the bulk of the writing for the book was completed, Holyoak was supported by a fellowship from the John Simon Guggenheim Foundation. The National Science Foundation (Grant SBR-9310614) funded research related to the book and provided support to bring the project to completion. Thagard's work on this book has been supported by grants from the National Science and Engineering Research Council of Canada and the Social Sciences and Humanities Research Council of Canada.

We are grateful to the respective publishers for permission to include material published elsewhere:

Thagard, P. (1992) Analogy, explanation and education. *Journal of Research in Science Teaching* 29:537–44. John Wiley and Sons, Inc. (ch. 8)

Thagard, P. (1993). The greatest analogies in the history of science. *Canadian Artificial Intelligence* 31, (Winter), 14–20. (ch. 8)

Thagard, P., and E. Millgram (in press). Inference to the best plan: A coherence theory of decision. In *Goal-directed learning,* edited by A. Ram and D. B. Leake, Cambridge, Mass.: MIT Press. (ch. 6)

Our families provided us with some of the examples in this book, and a whole lot more. The book is dedicated to them.

1

First Steps

A Bird's Backyard

We usually think we see the world the way it actually is. This outlook is comforting and easy to maintain as we follow the rhythms of everyday life, dealing with familiar people and objects in routine situations. Understanding the world around us usually seems simple and effortless. But in fact our conception of the world is in large part a matter of our own creation. Our sense of direct understanding is an illusion, because the apparent simplicity of everyday comprehension arises from the subtlety and complexity of the human mind.

We all have moments when the illusion is shattered. Confronted with unfamiliar or surprising situations that do not readily fit into known patterns, we no longer feel we are seeing the world as it actually is. Instead, everything seems disordered and confused. When a parent is confronted by an unexpected crisis in dealing with a child, when a business finds its old strategies failing in the face of new competitors, or when a country tries to fathom the direction in which its new leader is heading—on such occasions the familiar patterns are broken.

It is then that we become aware of a conscious struggle to see the world as something we can understand. The mind must work to build new patterns. Often it is pressed to work quickly. Novelty can signal danger, a new problem that demands a solution before it is too late. If a primitive hunter is surprised by an unfamiliar large animal in the forest, or the leader of a modern democracy is confronted by the rise of a threatening dictator abroad, action cannot wait for the gradual accumulation of knowledge over hundreds of similar occurrences. In such situations we want a rapid understanding of the situation that brings with it some idea about what to do. Even a rough response will be more useful than a slow, in-depth analysis that requires many more observations than it is possible to make. A good way to proceed is to try to understand the novel challenge in terms of what is already known, even if making the connection requires a mental leap.

When we are young, before most of the familiar patterns of everyday life have been learned, such challenges are the rule rather than the exception. Knowledge of the world awaits construction. For a child the pool of known situations is still small, and novelty is the norm; so much has to be understood in terms of so little. But already the fundamental thought processes that guide the creation of understanding are hard at work. Perhaps it would be more accurate to say they are hard at play, since for a child (as for a scientist), understanding the world often becomes a game driven by natural curiosity.

Consider the following discussion between a mother and her four-year-old son, Neil, who was considering the deep issue of what a bird might use for a chair. Neil suggested, reasonably enough it would seem, that a tree could be a bird's chair. A bird might sit on a tree branch. His mother said that was so and added that a bird could sit on its nest as well, which is also its house. The conversation went on to other topics. But several minutes later, the child had second thoughts about what a tree is to a bird: "The tree is not the bird's chair—it's the bird's backyard!"

In this conversation Neil makes a mental leap, exploring connections between two very different domains. He is trying to understand the relatively unfamiliar world of creatures of the air in terms of the familiar patterns of everyday human households. This small example conveys what we mean by reasoning by *analogy,* or *analogical thinking.* The child's everyday world is the *source analog*: a known domain that the child already understands in terms of familiar patterns, such as people sitting on chairs and houses that open onto backyards. The bird's world is the *target analog*—a relatively unfamiliar domain that the child is trying to understand. Analogical thinking is not "logical" in the sense of a logical deduction—there is no reason why birds and people should necessarily organize their habitats in comparable ways. Yet the analogy is certainly not haphazard. In a loose sense, there is indeed some sort of logic—call it *analogic*—that constrains the way the child uses analogy to try to understand the target domain by seeing it in terms of the source domain.

If we look carefully at Neil's conversation with his mother, we can see the first steps in the use of analogy. As is often the case with children, Neil seems to begin with a question: What might a bird use for a chair?

"Mrs. Nerg." Problem with organisms that are the least like a human.

Life Processes

Chapter 1

This simple example of a four-year-old's analogical thinking gives rise to many surprises and puzzles.

· Preschool children, without any formal training, have a natural capacity to reason by analogy.

· The source and target analogs might never have been explicitly associated before. That is, we have no reason to believe that anyone told Neil that the world of a bird is supposed to be understood in terms of the world of a person.

· Analogical thinking is guided by the goal that triggers the analogy yet can actually give rise to a new goal that changes the way the analogy is used.

· Children evaluate their analogies on the basis of internal criteria that go beyond simple reward and punishment by adults. Neil spontaneously evaluated and revised his interpretation of the tree as a chair, not because his mother disputed this initial suggestion (to the contrary, she voiced her approval), but simply because she introduced a new element into the situation, the role of the nest as a house.

· Part of the evaluation is based on a kind of competition among alternative interpretations. Neil acts as if the tree can be potentially interpreted as either the bird's chair or its backyard, but not both. He gives up the "chair" interpretation not because he finds anything directly wrong with it, but because the rival "backyard" interpretation seems somehow to be more satisfying.

Perhaps the deepest puzzle raised by the example is to explain what led Neil to decide that a tree is not a bird's chair but rather its backyard. After all, by any literal criterion a tree is neither a chair nor a backyard, so why should one interpretation be preferred to the other? The answer takes us to the heart of analogical thinking, which involves establishing a *mapping,* or systematic set of correspondences, between the elements of the source and the target analog. In our example, Neil entertains two alternative possible mappings between the source analog (child's world) and the target analog (bird's world):

Source		Target	Source		Target	
person	↔	bird	person	↔	bird	
chair	↔	tree	chair	↔	?	
			house	↔	nest	*extension*
			backyard	↔	tree	

We can see at a glance that the second mapping provides one more correspondence. In addition, the second mapping is based on a greater number of interconnected facts that relate the two domains to each other. Roughly, the first mapping captures the fact that a bird can sit on

But where does this question come from? Notice that the question contains the seeds of an analogical answer: Neil is looking for something in the world of a bird that corresponds to something in the world of a person. Already the basic connection has been made between the target and source domains. This connection is not at all random. In fact, using knowledge about people as the source analog for understanding non-human domains is so commonplace that it has a name, *personification*. Personification means to treat something that is not a person as if it were one. Such acts of imaginative creation lead into the realm of myth and metaphor, where death becomes not a mere physical process but the name of someone who walks the earth laboring as the Grim Reaper, and the moon becomes a mother who watches over us as we sleep. But personification begins in the minds of children, who from an early age try to understand animals, and sometimes plants and inanimate objects, in terms of people. A bird moves of its own volition, eats and drinks, and nurtures its young as they grow. These basic similarities suggest that a bird is sufficiently personlike to have other properties in common with people, such as needing a place to sit. But of course the child knows perfectly well that birds are not generally found sitting on chairs at the dinner table. So the answer to the question "What do birds sit on?" is not that they sit on chairs but that they must sit on something in their own aerial world that *corresponds* to a person's chair.

The child's initial answer had little or nothing to do with obvious physical resemblances. A tree, after all, does not really *look* like a chair. But it does serve a similar *function*: a bird can alight on a tree to rest, just as a person can sit on a chair to rest. The goal that motivated the child's question—the search for something that functions for a bird the way a chair functions for a person—also provides a basic criterion for identifying a plausible answer.

Yet, most surprisingly, Neil does not simply rest contented with what might seem to be a perfectly sensible answer to his question. Instead, he goes on to examine a different question, apparently triggered by his own answer to his initial query. What is a tree to a bird, really? A tree is a bird's chair in that a bird can sit on it. But a tree is a bird's backyard in that the bird's nest corresponds to a person's house, and the tree is located immediately outside of the nest, just as a backyard is immediately outside of the house. Neil concludes that the latter interpretation is somehow preferable. Even though he began with the question of what is a bird's chair, he arrived at an answer to the question of what is a bird's backyard.

for me it is usually the source, a rich set of relationships, that then latch onto a target

a tree much as a person can sit on a chair; the second mapping captures the fact that a bird lives in a nest, which is situated in a tree, much as a person lives in a house, which opens onto a backyard. Even though both mappings are sensible, the second is in some sense more complete and coherent in the way it relates the bird's world to the human domain. Of course neither mapping provides a full set of correspondences: What is a bird's driveway? Its kitchen? Its mailbox? Clearly, at some point the possible correspondences trail off into incoherent mush. Yet despite the blurry indeterminacies that surround both of Neil's mappings, we sense an underlying analogic that led to his preference for the mapping in which a tree was viewed as a bird's backyard.

Analogic

three constraints: similarity / structure / purpose.

But what is this analogic that makes it possible to understand one situation in terms of another? The child has been taught no rules for thinking by analogy. In fact, there is no reason to suppose that hard and fast rules for analogy are used by either children or adults. Working through an analogy is more like an architect's developing a new design for a building. The architect has some guiding goals, some functions to achieve. There are some materials to work with, some of which have conventional uses that guide their incorporation into the design. The various design decisions have to work together to form a whole. Creating the design is based on laying out the relevant constraints and trying to satisfy them. And just as an architect will build a model that expresses the design for a building, the person uses an analogy to build a model in the mind that can be used to understand something about the world.

analogic

architect

We can see in Neil's analogy the three basic kinds of constraints on analogical thinking that we will encounter again and again as we explore other examples. First, the analogy is guided to some extent by direct *similarity* of the elements involved. The various common properties of birds and people, such as that they have heads and legs and are living things, justify drawing the analogy in the first place.

Second, the analogy is guided by a pressure to identify consistent *structural* parallels between the roles in the source and the target domain. If the tree is going to play the role of the bird's backyard, then the nest (which is located in the tree) ought to play the role of the bird's house (since a house is located within a yard). Structure also involves a *one-to-one* constraint: each element of the target domain should correspond to just one element in the source domain (and vice versa). It is for this reason that when Neil decides that the tree plays the role of a backyard, he no longer accepts it as playing the role of a chair.

Third, the exploration of the analogy is guided by the person's goals in using it, which provide the *purpose* for considering the analogy at all. Thus Neil initially was directed by his entering desire to understand what birds might sit on. But it was apparent that his broader goal was a rather playful quest to understand the bird's habitat in terms of his own familiar dwelling. As we will see in other examples, people generally tend to select especially familiar situations to serve as source analogs.

These three kinds of constraints—similarity, structure, and purpose—do not operate like rigid rules dictating the interpretation of analogies. Instead they function more like the diverse pressures that guide an architect engaged in creative design, with some forces converging, others in opposition, and their constant interplay pressing toward some satisfying compromise. One of our main goals in this book is to show how the human mind creatively uses these constraints together in thinking by analogy.

From Socrates to Velcro and Vietnam

Analogy is not just child's play. There is a common thread connecting the Greek philosopher Socrates, the twentieth-century inventor of Velcro fasteners, and the political leaders of the 1960s who were responsible for the American military debacle in Vietnam during the 1960s. The same thread connects the most famous kite flyer in history, family therapists, and marriage negotiators in New Guinea. All of these, and many others we will also describe in this book, have put analogy to work. The uses they have made of analogy are diverse: generating new ideas, producing inventions, making decisions about war and peace, communicating with other people. Socrates explained his philosophical work by comparing himself to a midwife. Georges de Mestral invented Velcro after noticing the way burrs would stick on his dog's fur. President Lyndon Johnson became convinced that Vietnam was a "domino" in Southeast Asia, the fall of which would cause its neighbors to also topple into the grasp of world communism. Benjamin Franklin conducted his kite experiment to test an analogy he drew between lightning and electricity. Family therapists sometimes try to help troubled families by describing other families with similar relationships and problems. In New Guinea, telling a neighbor a story about betel nuts can be a way to inquire if the neighbor's daughter might marry one's son. On the face of it, these diverse examples might seem completely unrelated to one another; but all of them illustrate the use of analogy as a tool for thinking.

To propose an analogy, or simply to understand one, requires taking a kind of mental leap. Like a spark that jumps across a gap, an idea from the source analog is carried over to the target. The two analogs may initially seem unrelated, but the act of making an analogy creates new connections between them. Nothing ever guarantees that the target will actually behave the way the source suggests it should. Franklin was right: lightning really exhibited all the properties that were predicted by his analogy to electricity. But Johnson was wrong: Vietnam was not a domino whose fall would trigger the spread of communism to Thailand and India. Some of the mental leaps accomplished by analogy have ended in creative triumphs; others have ended in dismal failures. Analogy must be recognized as a source of plausible conjectures, not irrefutable conclusions. The success of an analogy must finally be judged by whether the conjectures it suggests about the target analog prove accurate and useful.

Although making an analogy requires a leap, that leap need not be blind or random. In all its manifestations, analogy is guided by the basic constraints of similarity, structure, and purpose that we saw at work in Neil's analogy of the tree as a bird's backyard. Although often the constraints are only imperfectly satisfied, they still tend to produce ideas that are at least worth considering, even if they ultimately prove to be flawed. By understanding how the human mind naturally draws analogies, we can hope to put this tool for thinking to more effective use.

Indirect Communication

One valuable use of analogy is to allow people to express thoughts indirectly. In the earliest written records of civilization, we see analogy in its many guises that allow such indirect communication—metaphor, myth, fable, parable. For example, in the Old Testament (written before 1000 B.C.), the prophet Nathan tells King David of a rich man who owns many sheep yet nonetheless steals the single beloved lamb of his poor neighbor. David says that this rich thief deserves to die. And then Nathan says to David, "You are the man." For David had arranged the death of one of his most faithful soldiers so that he could have the man's wife, Bathsheba, to add to his own houseful of wives and concubines. The parable is designed as an instructive analogy, in which the mapping between the king and the thief is designed to lure David into an indirect acknowledgment of his own guilt. Similarly, the fables of Aesop (circa 600 B.C.) are stories about animals endowed with human intellect and foibles, whose activities can be mapped onto human situations. Recall the classic story about a fox who cannot reach the grapes he covets and finally pronounces them sour as he gives up trying to reach them. This tale has obvious human analogs, such as the job seeker who fails to obtain a desired position and in the aftermath tells people the job would have been boring anyhow. Indeed, we understand the expression "sour grapes" as the name of this type of situation. For those who remember Aesop, this term is a shorthand for the entire source analog. For those who do not, the phrase will seem more arbitrary, a metaphor cut off from its roots.

It may seem strange that people should speak in parables and metaphors. Why not just come out and say what we mean? It turns out there are often advantages to indirectness. Just as an architect finds it easier to first construct a scale model before going on to build an actual building, it may be easier to express an idea in a familiar source domain before trying to use it to build understanding of the target. The source provides a convenient and tractable model for constructing an explanation or a solution that can then be transferred to the more perplexing target domain.

In some cases it is too dangerous to speak directly. Nathan would have taken a far greater risk if he had simply walked up to David and denounced him as a murderous adulterer; by using his parable, he let the king denounce himself. When living in a repressive society lacking freedom of speech, a political satirist may sometimes reach a broader audience by constructing analogies instead of direct polemics. In the 1960s, when communism still prevailed in what was then the Soviet Union, the Russian novelist Aleksandr Solzhenitsyn wrote the novel *The Cancer Ward*. The book was ostensibly about life in a Soviet cancer ward in the spring of 1955, and the struggle of the patients to maintain their humanity and dignity in the face of the feared and debilitating disease. At the same time, the novel provided a transparent analog to the repression that had faced the citizens of that society under Stalin and their hope for some sort of social and political recovery. In some cultures, such delicate social negotiations as arranging a marriage are carried on by constructing stories that are understood as analogs. Then if anything goes wrong and negotiations collapse, the story can simply be dropped; nothing was ever actually said about a marriage, so no one has lost face if no marriage comes about.

And yet, compelling as these purposes of analogy are, something more fundamental also seems to be at work. There is something inherently pleasurable about finding a mesh between two superficially unrelated situations. Some basic human joy is triggered by the discovery of unexpected connections. To denounce Stalinism indirectly by describing life in a cancer ward is not simply to adopt an expedient disguise; the novel is far more compelling than any literal-minded political diatribe could be. To see one thing *as if* it were another creates a tension between two perspectives: the thing as itself and the thing as something else. To resolve this tension by finding an integrated interpretation is a satisfying achievement. Consider the opening lines of Dante's *Divine Comedy*:

Midway upon the journey of our life,
I found myself within a forest dark,
For the right road was lost.

We understand from this passage that the person's life is like a journey along a road, headed toward some destination. Like a traveler who has become lost in a wood, at midlife the person's life has unexpectedly lost its purpose. George Lakoff and Mark Turner, who have analyzed such poetic metaphors in terms of mappings between analogous domains, note that Dante has built on the fundamental conception of "life as a journey," which permeates everyday thinking. To understand the metaphor we must understand a life to be not only a succession of everyday human activities but also an organized chain of actions directed toward some ultimate goal that provides a criterion by which progress can be measured. The same basic conception of life as a journey helps us to easily understand the meaning of an indefinite number of commonplace expressions, such as "Her career was derailed" or "He lost his bearings after his wife left him." We generally do not feel we are performing a mental synthesis when we understand such conventional utterances; but the possibility of novel variations of the underlying analogical theme keeps the potential for creativity alive.

Ripples in the Air

Another fundamental purpose of analogy is to gain understanding that goes beyond the information we receive from our senses. We hear thunder and see lightning, for example, but how could any amount of sensory experience give rise to the idea that sound and light are transmitted by invisible waves? Indeed, how can we come up with any answers at all to even more basic questions, such as how the human race came into being, or what happens to us after death? To answer such questions our minds must somehow form ideas that go beyond anything we can directly experience.

Analogy provides one powerful mechanism for forming such concepts. Consider, for example, the conceptions of creation, life, and death that form the basis of many people's religious beliefs. The Christian Lord's Prayer begins, "Our Father who art in Heaven." That simple phrase conveys the idea that God is related to people as a father is to his children: as progenitor, protector, and disciplinarian. He exists in a place, Heaven, that is analogous to the earth we know but invisible to us. Many believe that the journey of life ends with a final passage to some other place—Heaven or its less attractive counterpart. God is understood to be more powerful than any human father, and Heaven more spacious and attractive than earth; God and Heaven are not visible to mortal eyes. But despite these differences, the basic conception of the divine sphere is built on an analogy to the social and physical world in which we live. The result is that God and Heaven are not vague abstractions; rather, these concepts are grounded by the analogy to direct experience. Analogy manages to give rise to ideas that take us beyond sensory experience while still maintaining conceptual links to it.

Religion and science are often taken to be entirely different enterprises, but analogy plays an important role in both. Scientific theories, like systems of religious belief, often propose unobservable things like subatomic particles, black holes, and gravity waves. Scientific theories, unlike religions, must eventually be evaluated in relation to observable evidence. For example, even if black holes cannot be observed directly, the astronomical theory that posits them does make potentially testable predictions about, for example, the motion of visible celestial objects. In contrast, faith that "whatever happens is the will of God" may provide us with spiritual comfort, but certainly not with testable predictions. But these differences in how religious and scientific concepts are used should not obscure the fact that the same mental mechanism, analogical thinking, may be involved in the origins of both. (We discuss theological analogies in chapter 7 and scientific analogies in chapter 8.)

The role of analogy in science can be traced back at least two thousand years. The first recorded use of analogy to develop an enduring

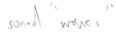

scientific theory produced the idea that sound is propagated in the form of waves. Although we obviously hear sound, we do not have any way of directly perceiving the nature of its transmission. During the reign of the emperor Augustus, a Roman architect and engineer named Vitruvius wrote a set of ten short books on architecture. In these texts he laid out what amounted to the authoritative standards to be followed in extending Roman civilization: how to select a site for a city, how to build the walls, where to situate the temple, how to transport water by aqueducts. In his fifth book he describes how theaters should be built, drawing heavily on the legacy of the Greeks. In his discussion of the acoustic requirements for a theater, Vitruvius describes the nature of sound by analogy to water waves:

Voice is a flowing breath of air, perceptible to the hearing by contact. It moves in an endless number of circular rounds, like the innumerably increasing circular waves which appear when a stone is thrown into smooth water, and which keep spreading indefinitely from the centre unless interrupted by narrow limits, or by some obstruction which prevents such waves from reaching their end in due formation. When they are interrupted by obstructions, the first waves, flowing back, break up the formation of those that follow.

In the same manner the voice executes its movements in concentric circles; but while in the case of water the circles move horizontally on a plane surface, the voice not only proceeds horizontally, but also ascends vertically by regular stages. Therefore, as in the case of the waves formed in the water, so it is in the case of the voice: the first wave, when there is no obstruction to interrupt it, does not break up the second or the following waves, but they all reach the ears of the lowest and highest spectators without an echo.

Hence the ancient architects, following in the footsteps of nature, perfected the ascending rows of seats in theatres from their investigations of the ascending voice.

Notice that Vitruvius not only points out some of the important ways in which sound and water waves behave similarly, such as the parallels between echoes and water waves striking an obstacle, but also some of their differences. He observes that whereas water waves spread out horizontally along a surface, sound waves move in three dimensions. And although too obvious for him to mention, it was doubtless apparent to Vitruvius that sound waves are not wet!

It turned out that the analogy between water and sound waves was fruitful and could centuries later be treated mathematically, moving well beyond Vitruvius's simple qualitative description. One important consequence was that the concept of wave, which now embraced both visible, wet, water waves moving along a plane and invisible, dry, sound waves moving in three dimensions, became much more general and abstract. The mental leap from water to sound was eventually followed in the seventeenth century by another giant bound, when a new analogy was drawn between sound and light. The eventual product of this analogy was a wave theory of light.

In its modern form the wave theory of light is based on highly abstract mathematical concepts, far removed from its ancient link to the observation of ripples moving outward around a pebble thrown into a pond. The concept of *wave* has developed from a specific analog tied to a particular kind of example, water waves, to an abstract category that can be applied to a vast range of situations involving the rhythmic propagation of patterns. The mental representation of a category based largely on similar relations is called a *schema*. As we will see in later chapters, this link between analogy and formation of schemas can be observed not only in scientific developments on the time scale of centuries but also in the way in which ordinary individuals learn from examples.

In chapter 8 we examine a variety of other cases in which analogy has played a crucial role in some of the triumphs of scientific discovery. But it is important to keep in mind that analogy carries with it the potential for traps as well as triumphs. Someone who did not already believe that sound is propagated by waves might well be impressed by the analogy between the echoes that rebound from a mountainside and the way a ball bounces back to us after striking a wall. Indeed, the ancient Greeks did consider the possibility that sound consists of particles, rather than waves. When we examine all the evidence available, it is apparent that sound acts more like water waves than like bouncing balls. But when an analogy is first considered, there is no guarantee that it is the best one possible. Even a fruitful analogy, like that between water and sound waves, is likely to involve important differences between the domains that need to be taken into account.

Creative Connections

The use of analogy in building scientific theories, like its use in writing poetry, connects analogical thinking to the core of human creativity. Figure 1.1 is a sketch of a famous analogy that played a key role in a creative leap in the field of biochemistry. In 1865, Kekulé proposed a new theory of the molecular structure of benzene. According to Kekulé,

Polya / Poincaré / Koestler

 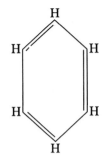

Figure 1.1
The visual analog of a snake biting its own tail contributed to Kekulé's insight that
the molecular structure of benzene is circular.

reverie is an unconscious act.

he was led to the hypothesis that the carbon atoms in benzene are
arranged in a ring by a reverie in which he saw a snake biting its own
tail. This example, like a number of the other great scientific analogies
we will describe in chapter 8, illustrates how visual representations can
contribute to creative thinking using analogy.

George Polya, who wrote extensively on techniques to foster creative problem solving, went so far as to claim that "Analogy pervades all
our thinking, our everyday speech and our trivial conclusions as well as
artistic ways of expression and the highest scientific achievements."
Although we do not believe that analogy is the only cognitive mechanism involved in creative thinking, it does play an important role. It has
often been suggested that creativity is based on some mental mechanism
for combining and recombining ideas in novel ways, where the recognition of viable new combinations depends in part on a kind of aesthetic
judgment that the juxtaposed ideas fit well together. The mathematician
Jules Henri Poincaré described his own creative process on a sleepless
night when "ideas rose in crowds; I felt them collide until pairs inter-
locked, so to speak, making a stable combination." And among the
"stable combinations," he argued, "the most fertile will often be those
formed of elements drawn from domains which are far apart." *

Arthur Koestler developed this idea further, proposing that creative
thinking depends on "bisociation," the interlocking of two domains of
knowledge previously seen as unrelated or even incompatible. He believed that bisociative thinking is the basis not only for major creative
leaps but also for everyday appreciation of humor and metaphor. Figure
1.2 presents an example of how analogy relates to humor. The cartoon

Koestler

cartoon characters are like structural diagrams;

reversal

Figure 1.2
Analogy can be the basis for the humor in a cartoon.

shows a rabbit contorting itself to cast a shadow of a hand on a wall. Why should that seem funny? The reason is that the overt picture is at once both a target analog and a cue that reminds us of a related source analog. Most people are familiar with the magician's trick of holding one's hand so as to cast the shadow of a rabbit on a wall. The humor in the cartoon emerges from the incongruous role reversal between this remembered source analog and the pictured target: the rabbit has become the hand, and the hand has become the rabbit. This "cross mapping" of roles is the product of analogical thinking.

While Koestler recognized the importance of analogy, he also was aware of how difficult it is to understand how analogy is actually used:

Some writers identify the creative act in its entirety with the unearthing of hidden analogies. . . . But where does the hidden likeness hide, and how is it found? . . .'Similarity' is not a thing offered on a plate [but] a relation established in the mind by a process of selective emphasis. . . . Even such a seemingly simple process as recognizing the similarities between two letters 'a' written by different hands, involves processes of abstraction and generalization in the nervous system which are largely unexplained.

As Margaret Boden has observed, writers such as Poincaré and Koestler have raised many of the most basic questions about creativity

Yes eloquent put.

in general and analogy in particular but left them without any satisfactory answer:

Their accounts are highly valuable as descriptions of the phenomena to be explained. They are even useful as the beginnings of an explanation, for they indicate where to start looking in more detail at the psychological mechanisms involved.—How does bisociation . . . actually work, and how are novel analogies recognized? . . . The more recent theories, referring to everyday abilities and expertise, raise further questions about underlying mechanisms.—How is it that people can notice things they were not even looking for? How can people recognize that two different things (two letters 'a', or two apples) fall into the same class? How is it possible for tacit knowledge to be acquired without being explicitly taught, and how can it aid creation?

These are among the questions we will be addressing in this book. In the years since Koestler wrote about bisociative thinking, the scientific discipline of cognitive science has greatly increased understanding of all of the cognitive processes that give rise to human intelligence—perceiving the world, forming and retrieving memories, and expressing thoughts in language. Cognitive science is based on the conviction that answers to questions like those raised by Boden will require integrating the insights of many different approaches to cognition. Our focus will be on what cognitive science has learned about analogical thinking. We will be presenting a very general theory of how a mind can use analogy as a way to extend knowledge in everyday and creative thinking. We call it a *multiconstraint theory,* because we understand analogy in terms of three distinct but interrelated types of constraints, involving similarity, structure, and purpose. This theory is based not only on our own work but on that of many other cognitive scientists. We will be making use of insights provided by cognitive, comparative, developmental, and social psychologists; by philosophers, linguists, and anthropologists; and by researchers in artificial intelligence.

The use of analogy typically involves several steps. Often a problem solver will select a source analog by retrieving information about it from memory (*selection*), map the source to the target and thereby generate inferences about the target (*mapping*), evaluate and adapt these inferences to take account of unique aspects of the target (*evaluation),* and finally learn something more general from the success or failure of the analogy (*learning*). Our theory is intended to apply to all four of these steps. We will see that the constraints of similarity, structure, and purpose apply to each step, but with varying degrees of relative importance.

One of the major ways in which cognitive scientists validate their theories is to see if these theories can guide the construction of computer programs that can show hints of humanlike intelligence. The successes and shortcomings of such simulations of cognitive processes can tell us a great deal about the extent to which our theories are really adequate. A computer simulation is judged successful to the extent that it behaves in ways that mimic human thinking, with its weaknesses as well as its strengths. We are not looking for a superhuman computerized analogical thinker, but rather for simulations that succeed where people tend to succeed and fail where people tend to fail, and that succeed and fail in the same ways as people do. A successful simulation is intended to be a kind of analog of the analogist.

We eventually describe some computer simulations based on our multiconstraint theory, programs that actually find and use analogies to build explanations and solve problems. We also describe other computer models that make use of analogies, a topic that in artificial intelligence is often called *case-based reasoning* (that is, reasoning from past cases when trying to solve a novel problem). However, our focus will not be on the details of particular computer simulations, but rather on the general underlying principles that begin to answer some of Koestler's and Boden's questions about analogical thinking. By understanding how we think using analogy, we can gain some insights into the creative process as well as into the ways we can be informed and misled by analogies in everyday life.

Overview

We develop our theory further in chapter 2 by describing the nature of the constraints of similarity, structure, and purpose. We argue that the human ability to find analogical correspondences is intimately linked to the evolutionary development of the capacity for explicit, systematic thinking. In chapter 3 we look more closely at the evolutionary origins of analogical thought by considering the use of analogies by animals, particularly the chimpanzee. Chapter 4 describes the results of recent research on the development of analogical thinking in children. By examining in some detail when different varieties of analogical thinking emerge, both in evolution and in human development, we hope to gain a better understanding of the constraints that govern the use of analogy by human adults. In chapter 5 we consider psychological studies of analogical thinking in adults that provide a more detailed picture of how analogy operates to make inferences and solve problems.

Chapter 6 discusses how analogies are used to make decisions about courses of action, especially in politics and law. The role of analogy in developing explanations is the focus of chapter 7. We describe how analogy has been used to help address some of the deepest questions that have confronted humanity, such as the nature of God and human minds. Chapter 8 moves on to discuss the explanatory use of analogies in the development of science and technology. We also consider the educational uses and misuses of explanatory analogies. A major concern in chapters 6 through 8 is the normative question of how analogies can be used most effectively, through mindfulness of how the constraints of structure and purpose contribute to the coherence of decisions and explanations. Chapter 9 considers the role of analogy in literature and in oral cultural traditions, highlighting communicative functions that go beyond explanation and problem solving. We discuss several overlapping cultural purposes of analogy: promoting social cohesion, allowing indirect communication, evoking amusement and other emotions, and helping with social and psychological problems. Chapter 9 includes a discussion of the relation between analogy and metaphor.

In chapter 10 we fulfill our promise to provide a more detailed account of how the constraints of similarity, structure, and purpose guide analogy through the stages of selection, mapping, evaluation, and learning. We describe computer programs developed by ourselves and others that suggest mechanisms by which the complex processes of analogical thinking may be performed by computers and, if the simulations provide successful analogies for the mind, by humans. Finally, we summarize our discussion and point to what seem to us to be the major areas in which understanding of analogical thinking needs to be extended and deepened.

Breaking Loose

[handwritten: from sensory experience]

[handwritten: chapter headings; metonomy] *[handwritten: categories]*

Funes in Chains

To see a tree as a bird's backyard, to imagine an echo as a wave rebounding off the shore—these must be counted among the intellectual achievements unique to the human species. What is it about the human mind that allows us to think about analogies, to treat situations that we know to be different as if they were somehow the same? When do these capacities develop in children? To what extent are they anticipated in the mental capacities found in other species? In this chapter we prepare to answer these questions by describing the basic requirements for abstract thinking, the capacities that a mind must have to be able to break loose from sensory experience and create complex models of the world.

The essential requirement for analogical thinking is the ability to look at specific situations and somehow pull out abstract patterns that may also be found in superficially different situations. The reason sound is analogous to water waves is that sound exhibits a characteristic pattern of behavior that corresponds to the behavior of water waves: propagating across space with diminishing intensity, passing around small barriers, rebounding off of large barriers, and so on. The surface elements are very different, but the underlying pattern of relations among the elements is similar. Such abstract patterns of similar relations could not be detected by an organism whose every experience was inextricably tied to vivid sensations of sight, sound, smell, taste, and touch. It is difficult to conceive what the world would seem like to such a creature, but the writer Jorge Luis Borges conveys the flavor in his story *Funes the Memorious*. The fictional character Ireneo Funes is described as having a prodigious memory for every detail of his everyday experiences, for he "remembered not only every leaf of every tree of every wood, but also every one of the times he had perceived or imagined it." But his memory for specific details carried a heavy cost: he was incapable of abstract thought. "Not only was it difficult for him to comprehend that the generic symbol "dog" embraces so many unlike individuals of diverse size and form; it bothered him that the dog at three fourteen (seen from the side) should have the same name as the dog at three fifteen (seen from the front)." For Funes, every situation was perceived in such excruciating detail that any cross-situational commonalities were totally obscured. His mind was shackled by the power of specific sensory experience, unable to break free to see abstract patterns of similarity that we normally take for granted. Instead of enhancing his thinking power, Funes's amazing memory abilities seemed to be cognitive chains, binding him to the particular.

As Funes's limitations of thought suggest, the capacity to see analogies has much in common with the capacity to form and use concepts that represent categories of objects, events, and situations. Funes was unable to see how different events are related to one another, a capacity required for everyday categorization. Consider what it takes to see that Hercules the Great Dane and Fifi the Chihuahua are both members of the category *dog*. This judgment is based on the recognition of some important similarities between two individual objects that are nonetheless seen as distinct from one another. Hercules and Fifi are two very different creatures, only one of which has a growl that is likely to discourage intruders. Despite such differences we know that the two have fundamental biological similarities that allow us to make inferences about their hidden properties. For example, suppose you were told that Hercules has an internal structure called an "omentum" that you had never before heard of. You would then be quite likely to infer that Fifi has an omentum too. The reason is that we believe that internal biological structures are generally common across all members of the same species; so if one dog has an omentum, they probably all do. Our knowledge of biological categories encourages the inference that this internal structure will also be found in animals such as cats and other mammals that are similar to dogs. (As a matter of fact, you have one yourself: an omentum is the thin membrane that holds the intestinal organs in place.) Biological concepts such as *dog* provide powerful tools for thinking, because they guide inferences that go beyond direct observation.

From Reacting to Thinking

The ability to form concepts and think about them, which is present in humans and to a lesser degree in other mammalian species, marked a fundamental evolutionary advance in intelligence. This advance is closely related to the difference between two types of knowledge, *implicit* and *explicit,* that is, between the ability to *react* to something and the ability to think about it. For example, a one-year old child can begin to learn to catch a thrown ball. After some practice, the child will be able to react appropriately to an approaching ball, for example by opening his or her hands. This reaction based on implicit knowledge need not require first thinking about the fact that one's hands have to open to catch a ball—it is enough simply to perform the action in time. But implicit knowledge of how to catch a ball would not be enough to allow someone to recognize that this action is in some way similar to hurrying to the office to "catch" a telephone call. Being able to react to an approaching ball provides even less of a basis for noticing some similarity between catching a ball someone else has dropped and the quick action of a secretary in "catching the ball" after the boss had "dropped the ball" by failing to carry out an important assignment. The ability to recognize such abstract similarities, which is needed to think by analogy, requires explicit representations that can be manipulated and compared to one another. Explicit knowledge makes it possible to focus selectively on specific attributes of objects and on relations between objects, rather than being limited to reacting to global similarities between objects.

We will see in chapter 3 that for animals other than primates, most or all of their knowledge of the world remains implicit. Humans—adults as well as children—also are highly dependent on implicit knowledge, much of which is learned through direct experience. Such complex skills as driving an automobile or doing routine mathematical calculations largely involve implicit knowledge. Implicit knowledge often allows quicker reactions than does explicit knowledge and in some cases is actually more accurate. Moreover, even when explicit knowledge is being manipulated, the process that uses it may itself be implicit. This is true even when we think by analogy. When we compare catching a ball to averting the consequences of an unfortunate mistake by the boss, we are using explicit representations of the two situations being compared. But although we recognize that the cases are similar, we normally do not have any clear idea *how* we do so. In other words, thinking by analogy is an implicit procedure applied to explicit representations. Our goal in this book is to make explicit how that implicit procedure operates.

Although it is not always clear whether the knowledge used to perform some task is implicit or explicit, a number of criteria are useful in distinguishing the two. Explicit knowledge tends to be accessible to consciousness and therefore more readily verbalized by a thinker who has acquired language. When we are conscious of an explicit representation it is because it is active in our working memory—the memory that holds the information we are thinking about at any given moment. Working memory is limited in the amount of information it can handle at once, unlike our long-term memory that can hold an indefinitely large store of knowledge accumulated over a lifetime. Using explicit knowledge often requires noticeable mental effort, whereas using implicit knowledge is generally unconscious and relatively effortless.

If using explicit knowledge is hard work and sometimes more error-prone than using implicit knowledge, why bother? Explicit thinking was a radical advance in intelligence, because it brought with it great flexibility in the way knowledge can be used. Instead of simply reacting to events in the here and now, we can form representations of events that can be stored in long-term memory and later retrieved and used in a different context. Explicit representations can serve as the inputs to procedures that analyze them, reorganize them, and recombine them to form new ideas. And most importantly for us, explicit representations can be compared to one another to discover systematic similarities and differences between them. Some of these similarities and differences may be far removed from the direct products of perception. Analogical thinking, applied to explicit representations of knowledge, can find important commonalities between situations that on the surface appear quite different. Such abstract similarities often provide a basis for intelligent transfer of knowledge—that is, using prior knowledge in new situations—in order to achieve goals. As a result, the ability to use analogy conveys an evolutionary advantage. And the chains of Funes are loosened.

Similarity

To understand explicit representations of knowledge we need to consider how concepts can be formed. To create concepts one needs to be able to detect similarities between situations despite their differences. The very notion of similarity poses many problems, as the philosopher Nelson Goodman has forcefully argued. After all, any two things have indefinitely many common properties, most of which are likely to be trivial; for example, this book and your shoes are both over a million miles from Venus. The hard problem for cognitive science is to explain why particular similarities are used to form concepts, and how concepts in turn alter judgments of similarity. We will not address this deep problem here in any general way, but we cannot avoid examining the basic forms of similarity that guide our making of analogies.

When we recognize that two objects are both apples, this judgment is aided by many shared sensory features, such as their having the same or similar color, shape, taste, and smell. For many purposes it is sufficient simply to react to similar objects in the same way on the basis of their global similarity. If one apple proves tasty, we are likely to expect another similar one also to be good to eat, without necessarily pausing to reflect on exactly which sensory features determine how apples taste. However, the human capacity for analogy depends on more than simply reacting to objects on the basis of some fuzzy sense of overall similarity based on sensory features. In addition, analogy requires concepts that go well beyond immediate perception. We can think about individuals such as Hercules and Fifi, and of categories such as *dog* and *person*. We can think about actions such as *chasing* and more static relations such as *being larger than*. Our store of such concepts forms a vast *semantic network*. Figure 2.1 depicts a fragment of a semantic network that shows a few of the interconnections between everyday concepts stored in our long-term memory system. Many concepts form a chain of increasing generality, ranging from specific individuals through increasingly general categories (e.g., Hercules → Great Dane → dog → mammal → animal → living thing → physical object. Each concept is a *superordinate* of the more specific concepts in this chain. For example, "animal" is a superordinate of "dog." Besides chains of superordinates, the semantic network is interconnected by a number of other very common relations, such as *part of* (e.g., a tail is part of a dog), as well as by more specialized relations, such as *chases* (e.g., dogs chase cats). The semantic connections between concepts provide important building blocks for seeing analogies.

Concepts are needed to understand sophisticated analogies, but analogical thinking also provides part of the answer to the question of how concepts are formed. The first person who noticed that sound behaves something like water waves presumably did not already conceive of *wave* as a category so general as to include both water and sound waves. But seeing the analogy may have paved the way for forming such a category. And once a more abstract concept of wave was established, it played a role in the further extension to light waves. Thus analogy helps to form new and more abstract concepts, which in turn help to see even more remote analogies, which in turn help to form yet more abstract concepts. We will refer to the representations of complex con-

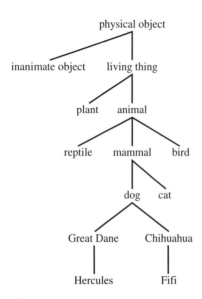

Figure 2.1
Fragment of a semantic network, illustrating superordinate chains. The lines indicate, for example, that a dog is a kind of mammal.

Schemas

cepts such as *wave,* which convey patterns of relations among constituent elements, as *schemas*. For example, the schema for *wave* will represent the fact that wave motion involves the systematic propagation of a form across space, a form that bends around barriers, and so on. This symbiotic interaction between analogies based on small numbers (often pairs) of cases and general schemas for concepts that embrace indefinitely many cases provides direction for many aspects of thinking, including (as we will see in chapter 9) the ability to understand metaphor.

Structure

Although the individual concepts in a person's semantic network are important for thought, the full power of human thinking depends on its capacity to combine concepts to create more complex structures. For example, we can combine representations for Hercules the Great Dane and for the concept of brown to form the proposition that Hercules is brown. This proposition is expressed by the sentence "Hercules is brown," in which the predicate "brown" is applied to the subject "Hercules." Such a proposition can be true, or false if Hercules is some other color; and we can believe it or doubt it depending on the evidence we have. In contrast, it makes no sense at all for someone to believe "that Hercules" without a predicate to form a full proposition.

Our concern is with thoughts, not sentences in English or any other particular human language. Language is a powerful way to express thoughts, but other kinds of representations such as pictures can also convey thoughts. We will often express a proposition in a simple way that makes its structure obvious, using a predicate followed by a subject in parentheses. So the proposition that Hercules is brown becomes

brown (Hercules).

In a simple proposition such as this, the predicate applies to a single entity that fills a single role. That is, the predicate "brown" has one role to be filled, namely that of the thing that is brown. Borrowing terms from knowledge-representation languages in the field of artificial intelligence, we shall refer to a role provided by a predicate as a *slot* and the entity that fills the role as the *filler* of the slot. Thus the concept of brown has the structure

brown (<slot>),   *attribute*

in which an indefinitely long list of possibilities, including Hercules, Jersey cows, and pieces of toast, may fill the slot. A predicate such as "brown" that has just one slot is often called an *attribute,* because such predicates typically refer to an attribute of an object.

The capacity for explicit propositional thought is an essential requirement for the kind of abstraction needed for analogical thinking. For example, suppose we had representations for Hercules the dog and for the Sahara Desert but no way to form propositions with them. Then there would no expressible similarity between the two. However, we can in fact form the propositions

brown (Hercules)

and   *e.g. colour sorting*

brown (Sahara),

which allows us to single out a particular attribute that is common to both Hercules and the Sahara, while at the same time ignoring the huge list of differences between the two. The capacity to focus selectively on a particular attribute of an object, and hence on particular similarities between objects, is an important cognitive advance, because it breaks the dependence on global similarity.

This example can be construed as the basis for an analogy of the very simplest form: we might say that Hercules maps to the Sahara by virtue of a corresponding attribute of brownness, indicated by having the predicate "brown" in the expression of both propositions. That is, we have the mappings

brown ↔ brown

Hercules ↔ Sahara.

This analogy is not very interesting or informative, but it does show how the simplest sort of structure can give rise to analogical connections. A slightly more creative connection would arise if we started with a representation of the Sahara Desert as tan, requiring us to make a slightly greater semantic leap with the mapping

brown ↔ tan.

If all we know about Hercules is that he is a brown dog, any color attributed to the Sahara Desert would be more likely to support a mapping of Hercules and Sahara than would other sorts of properties, such as its being dry or sandy. Brown and tan are linked in our semantic network by both being kinds of colors; they also have a more immediate perceptual link, since we know from sensory experience that they look alike. Thus similarity of concepts comes in degrees.

Notice that in this example we are mapping just one pair of objects considered in isolation from any other objects, which can be done on the basis of the semantic similarity between the attributes that apply to each object in the pair. We will call this type of mapping that takes one pair of objects at a time an *attribute mapping*. Even with such simple mappings based on propositions that concern single objects, we see a way out of the trap whereby Funes was overpowered by the uniqueness of every perceptual experience. With propositional thought, one can still appreciate the richness and diversity of experience yet nonetheless be able to extract and make explicit the similarities that connect distinct situations to one another.

Propositions can be more complex than the examples we have so far considered. Greater structure and power for abstract thought is provided by concepts that have more than one slot to fill, such as *chase,* which requires slots both for the chaser and the chased. Predicates with multiple slots are called *relations* for the obvious reason that they relate the multiple fillers of their slots. The proposition that Hercules chases Fifi can be expressed as chase (Hercules, Fifi).

Here the chaser slot is filled by Hercules, and the chased slot is filled by Fifi, in line with the general structure

chase (<chaser>, <chased>).

Imagine a creature that could form representations of Hercules, Fifi, and chasing, but that could not organize them into propositions structured by slots. Such a creature could not distinguish the proposition that Hercules chases Fifi from the proposition that Fifi chases Hercules. All it would have is an unstructured mental stew of the representations of Fifi, Hercules, and chasing. Fortunately, human thinking uses relations that impose structure on the fillers of their slots, enabling us to have the distinct thought

chase (Fifi, Hercules).

That is, we have the capacity to form new propositions by rearranging the fillers of different slots in a concept.

Having propositions with multiple slots has important psychological implications for our capacity to detect and express similarities between situations. For example, with the two-slot relation *larger than* we can express the propositions:

larger-than (Sahara, Hercules)

larger-than (truck, apple).

From these two propositions we can conclude that the Sahara is related to Hercules in a way that parallels how a truck is related to an apple—in both cases, the former is larger than the latter. Expressed as an analogy, this means that Sahara maps to truck and Hercules maps to apple by virtue of their corresponding roles as slot fillers of the relation *larger than*. We have the mappings:

larger-than ↔ larger-than

Sahara ↔ truck

Hercules ↔ apple.

The two propositions correspond by virtue of the semantic similarity (here, identity) between the relation in each proposition. Although the relation is mapped on the basis of semantic similarity, the other correspondences are not based on any direct similarity between the Sahara and the truck or between Hercules and the apple. These objects are connected only by virtue of filling the same slot in the structure of the two propositions. We have now moved to a more abstract form of similarity: It is the relation between the pairs that is similar, not the attributes of the mapped objects themselves.

Notice that relations create constraints between the mappings of their multiple role fillers. If *larger than* drives the mapping, then Sahara maps to truck if and only if Hercules maps to apple. This is just another way of saying that a two-slot predicate has to map fillers in pairs rather than singly. We call a mapping of two pairs of fillers, based on similarity between a pair of two-slot relations, a *relational mapping*.

You are probably already familiar with relational mappings of the sort required to solve the kinds of analogy problems often used on intelligence tests. These generally involve completing four-term sequences such as, "Hand is to arm as foot is to what?" often symbolized in the form A:B::C:? (for example, hand:arm::foot:?). The answer requires substituting an appropriate D term (here, "leg") to complete the sequence. Such analogy problems are often called *proportional* analogies, because they resemble equalities of proportions (for example, 2:4::3:6). We can view the A:B part as the source, which is mapped to the partially specified target C:?; the mapping is then used to complete the target by generating an appropriate D term. Notice that in such problems the mapping is justified by an identical relation common to both the source and target (here, "is part of"). Basic proportional analogies are thus examples of relational mappings. We mention this fact because in chapters 3 and 4 we will be looking at studies of how apes and children solve proportional analogies, which provide evidence of how analogy ability has evolved across species and how it develops as children grow up. The fact that proportional analogies are relational mappings, rather than the more complex type we will now discuss, means that solving proportional analogies is not sufficient to demonstrate the full power of analogical thinking.

To move beyond relational mapping, we need to consider relations with greater complexity. When Hercules chases Fifi, Fifi runs away, and the chasing is the cause of the running. Naming the propositions for ease of reference, we get:

chase (Hercules, Fifi) *name*: chase–1

run (Fifi) *name*: run–1

cause (chase–1, run–1) *name*: cause–1

The causal relation connects together three slots: the chaser, the chased, and the runner. Predicates such as "*cause*" and "*implies*" that allow one

First order and higher order relations

or more slots to be filled by propositions have been termed *higher-order relations* by cognitive psychologist Dedre Gentner. In contrast, less abstract relations with slots filled by objects, such as *chase,* are called *first-order* relations. Gentner has emphasized the powerful role of higher-order relations in analogical mapping, as sets of propositions interrelated by higher-order relations can be used to help identify correspondences between two analogous structures. In the movie *The Fugitive,* a detective chases the hero, who runs away:

chase (detective, hero) *name*: chase-2

run (hero) *name*: run-2

cause (chase-2, run-2) *name*: cause-2.

Mapping this structure to the preceding one requires putting in correspondence Hercules and detective, Fifi and hero, and the two causal relations between chasing and running.

Ideally, mappings of all sorts should satisfy the two fundamental structural properties of being *one-to-one* and *structurally consistent*. A mapping is one-to-one if every element in the source (object, attribute, or relation) corresponds to a unique element in the target and vice versa. Mapping Hercules to both the detective and the hero would violate this constraint. A mapping is structurally consistent if whenever two relations are mapped their slot fillers are also mapped. In the above example, mapping *chase* to *chase* requires mapping Hercules to detective, because they fill the first slot in the relations. Mapping Hercules to hero or Fifi to detective would be a violation of structural consistency. In our multiconstraint theory, one-to-one mapping and structural consistency are viewed as *soft* constraints, rather than *hard* ones that a mapping must satisfy to contribute to an analogy. That is, satisfying these constraints is highly desirable but not essential. When they are both satisfied, the mapping is an isomorphism. *one-to-one*

Often an analogy does not simply involve putting known fillers into correspondence, but in addition requires finding new fillers to fit into the whole pattern. If you were told that the plot of *The Fugitive* is like that of the book *Les Misérables,* in which a police inspector pursues a convict, you could infer that it is the convict who runs away. You would merely be filling in the question mark in this structure:

chase (inspector, convict) *name*: chase-3

run (?) *name*: run-3

cause (chase-3, run-3) *name*: cause-3.

The basic device for generating inferences by analogy is called "copying with substitution," because it essentially consists of simply copying over propositions known to be true of the source to become inferences about the target, at the same time substituting target elements for source elements in accord with established mappings (such as **hero** ↔ **convict**).

Inferences made by analogy using copying with substitution are never guaranteed to be true. The point to remember is that analogy is a source of plausible conjectures, not guaranteed conclusions. Our claim is simply that *if* two domains are in fact isomorphic in terms of how the objects in each are related to one another, then inferences derived from the source will have some plausibility for the target. In actual practice, the best one can do is select a source analog with sufficient correspondences to the target to justify a tentative mapping, use these correspondences to generate inferences about the target, and then check whether these inferences actually hold up when the target domain is directly investigated.

Indeed, an interesting trade-off emerges between the completeness of an analogy and its usefulness in generating inferences. The more complete the initial correspondences are between source and target, the more confident you can be that the two are in fact isomorphic. But unless you know more about one analog than the other—in other words, unless the initial correspondences between source and target propositions are incomplete—the mapping will not allow any new inferences to be made. A complete isomorphism has nothing to be filled in, leaving no possibility for creative leaps. Incompleteness may well weaken confidence in the overall mapping, but it also provides the opportunity for using the source to generate a plausible (but fallible) inference about the target.

Sensitivity to the structural constraint of isomorphism, coupled with the ability to think explicitly about higher-order relations, provides the basis for moving to a deeper level of analogical thinking. So far the source and target analogs used in our examples have always included similar or identical first-order relations (even though the objects being mapped, such as Hercules and detective, were often dissimilar). However, if the analogs provide a richly interconnected system of relations, it is possible to map them even in the absence of similar first-order relations. For example, suppose the source analog is one of Aesop's fables, the "sour grapes" story in which a fox wants and fails to reach grapes and then says the grapes were sour anyway. Hungering for the grapes caused the fox to try to reach them, and failing to reach them caused him to say that they were sour. We can recognize the analogy between the sour grapes story and the case of a person who tries and fails to get a promotion and in the aftermath concludes the job would have been boring anyway. Desiring the job caused the person to apply for it, and being turned down caused the person to say the job was boring. In this analogy there is little similarity between the corresponding objects, such as grapes and job, and only a modest degree of similarity between the corresponding first-order relations, such as *hunger for* and *desire*. The major similarities involve higher-order relations, most notably *cause*. In addition, the objects and relations are highly interconnected, and we can see that each element in the source maps consistently and uniquely to an element in the target. We will use the term *system mapping* to refer to mappings based on similar higher-order relations coupled with a high degree of one-to-one mapping and structural consistency. In a system mapping like the analogy between the "sour grapes" fable and the case of the disgruntled job seeker, the simpler levels of attribute and relational mapping play secondary roles. Of course many analogies (such as that between the plots of *The Fugitive* and *Les Misérables*) involve similarities at multiple levels of abstraction and hence are based on a mixture of attribute, relational, and system mapping. A mind able to use attribute, relational, and system mappings and which can form analogical inferences by substituting as well as copying is free of the chains that bound Funes to sensory experience.

Models

The causal relations in the sour grapes and job-seeker stories show them to be isomorphic at that level. Isomorphism is not simply an esoteric idea used to describe how analogies work. In fact, it is fundamental to the way we understand the world. Consider an ordinary thermometer, such as one that might hang outside a house. How is it actually related to the temperature of the air? After all, the column of red mercury certainly does not look like air. It is not even the case that, say, one centimeter of mercury is equivalent to ten degrees: thermometers can come in a range of different sizes, so there is no general equivalence between any particular length of the mercury column and any particular temperature. The answer is simply that the relations between different heights of the mercury in the tube are isomorphic to the relations between different air temperatures. For example, if the temperature remains constant, the height of the mercury remains constant; if the temperature rises from ten to twenty degrees Celsius, the change in the height of the mercury will be the same as that which would accompany a rise in temperature from twenty to thirty degrees Celsius. That is, equal temperature changes result in equal changes in the height of the mercury. These correspondences, which will hold for any accurate thermometer, are based on an isomorphism between relations defined on the thermometer's mercury scale and relations defined on temperature changes. Isomorphism is thus a mapping from relations in one system to relations in another that does not require any direct similarity. Even when we speak of the temperature's "rising" or "falling," we are really using a kind of metaphor. Temperature, which as a physical concept can be characterized as the product of the pressure and the specific volume of a gas, is not the kind of thing that literally goes up or down in space. However, it *is* the kind of thing that is isomorphic to something that does go up or down—the column of mercury in a thermometer. The thermometer therefore can provide us with a convenient model of temperature.

Isomorphism is fundamental to all forms of measurement, in which quantities of something are mapped onto units of a scale. It is also fundamental to all simulations and models. When the weather service uses a computer simulation to predict the behavior of a hurricane, we do not expect the simulation to be wet or windy or have any other direct similarity to a real hurricane. What we do expect is that differences in the model's scale of wind velocity over the model's scale of time should correspond to predicted changes in the actual wind velocity of the hurricane over actual time. If the model is indeed isomorphic to the hurricane, it will generate accurate predictions; if the mapping fails the test of structural consistency, predictions will be off the mark. When the weather service constructs such a simulation, it is not building a hurricane but a representation of a hurricane.

Many cognitive scientists agree that people and other animals make predictions by forming mental models, internal structures that represent external reality in at least an approximate way. When you see a dog running or form a mental image of a dog running, your brain exhibits some very complex patterns of electrical and chemical activity. There is no reason to suppose that this pattern in any direct sense looks like a dog running. It may, however, be isomorphic to it in some fashion, so that the change in an image from a dog running to a dog resting would be accompanied by a regular change in the activity of the brain. This neural change should similarly have something in common with what occurs in the brain when an image of a cat running turns into an image of a cat resting.

Analogy takes us a step beyond ordinary mental models. A mental model is a representation of some part of the environment. For example, our knowledge of water provides us with a kind of internal model of how it moves. Similarly, our knowledge of sound provides us with a kind of model of how sound is transmitted through the air. Each of these mental models links an internal representation to external reality. But when we consider the analogy between water waves and sound propagation, we are trying to build an isomorphism between two internal models. Implicitly, we are acting as if our model of water waves can be used to modify and improve our model of sound. The final validation of the attempt must be to examine whether by using the analogy we can better understand how sound behaves in the external world. The basic analogical comparison, however, is not between an internal model and the world but between two different internal models. We will see in chapter 4 that analogical thinking poses special challenges for very young children, because a source analog is both a model of part of the world and the basis for improving another model of a different part of the world, the target.

The idea that analogy is based on finding isomorphisms takes us beyond one of the most influential notions about how prior knowledge is able to influence how we understand new situations. Early in the twentieth century, the psychologist Edward Thorndike argued that transfer of learning depends on the two situations' involving identical elements. Exactly what could count as an identical element was never made very clear, leading to considerable confusion over the years. The idea has often been interpreted, however, as meaning that transfer is only possible when the source and target situations share very specific perceptual properties, such as color, shape, and size. On this interpretation, without such shared properties there is no basis at all for linking the two situations. The view that transfer requires highly specific identical elements has had considerable influence on educational practice, suggesting that what students learn in school will only be useful in tasks that are very similar to those used in teaching the skill. Particularly in our complex modern world, in which most people have to adapt to new job requirements over the course of their careers, the requirement of specific identical elements leads to a rather pessimistic conclusion about the potential usefulness in later life of formal education. But two analogs can be isomorphic even though they do not share any identical (or even particularly similar) elements. In such cases, what is identical across the two structures is not their objects or predicates but rather the overall system of correspondences—the pattern of relations.

We can therefore imagine how transfer might be effected from a source to a target in the absence of identical elements. In later chapters we will explore whether and how this potential is actually realized when people face novel problems. Of course, identical elements can be useful when available even if transfer does not require them. In fact, transfer by identical elements is closely related to the constraint of similarity that we have discussed—the pressure to map elements that are perceptually or semantically similar. And semantic similarity can be based not just on similarity of objects and first-order relations but also on similarity of higher-order relations. Higher-order similarity of relations between relations does not require any identical elements at the perceptual level. The most creative use of analogies depends on both noticing higher-order similarities and being able to map isomorphic systems of relations. These constraints make it possible to map elements that are highly dissimilar, perhaps drawn from very different knowledge domains. We can map elements despite the fact that they are dissimilar in many ways, based largely on the constraint of structure. Because the elements to be mapped will have many differences that must be ignored, this kind of use of analogy is difficult. Nonetheless, it provides the possibility of such creative leaps as recognition of the parallels between motion of sound and motion of water.

Purpose and Cause

Why do people use analogies? The sound/water example is a case of the explanatory use of analogy in which a source is used to explain or develop a new hypothesis about the target. Analogies are also useful for problem solving and planning, when the emphasis is on deciding what to do to accomplish some practical goal, such as finishing an algebra assignment or arranging a vacation. In politics, law, and everyday life, analogies are often used to construct arguments intended to persuade others to adopt a particular course of action. Literary analogies and metaphors can be used to evoke emotional responses, as when Shakespeare compared his lover to a summer's day. In later chapters we will explore all these uses of analogy in much greater detail.

In real-life uses of analogy, the purpose and context of the thinker play an important role in constraining how analogy is used. We would often be swamped if we thought about all our detailed knowledge of the source and target analogs. Somehow, analogy can operate on messy analogs that fall short of the isomorphic ideal we have been stressing. For example, to make any sense of the analogy between water waves and sound propagation, we have to be able to tolerate not only such differences as the fact that water is wet and air is not but also a host of irrelevant but associated relations, such as the fact that water is used to drink and wash clothes, air is needed to breathe, and so on. Mapping will be much easier if we can weed out as many irrelevancies as possible before trying to map the analogs. Since for a novel problem we are unlikely to be entirely certain at the outset exactly what information is actually relevant to its solution, we will need to find a way to identify useful mappings based on a mixture of information that will vary in its importance. It will therefore also be helpful if we can somehow weight information used in the mapping in proportion to how important it appears to be in achieving our goals.

In selecting potential analogs for mapping, in weighting information during mapping, and in evaluating a mapping after it has been obtained, the key is to focus on information that is relevant to the person's goal in using the analogy. If the person wants to solve a target problem by analogy to a source problem, it will be important to consider those aspects of the source that actually mattered to its solution. If the person wants to understand in terms of baseball how cricket is played, the information about the rules of the two games is what matters, not such irrelevancies as the American penchant to drink beer in the bleachers. But notice that what is relevant may vary with the goal. Someone interested in the role of cricket in British social life might well want to see a relation between Americans' drinking beer and cricket players' taking regular breaks for tea.

What often matters to an analogy is the set of *causal relationships* within each analog that bear upon the thinker's goal. Causality is not easy to pin down either philosophically or psychologically. But we all have an intuitive understanding that some regularities in the world are based on the relationship of causes to effects. We perceive some actions as changing the state of the world and some states as enabling or preventing actions from having some effect. In explanatory uses of analogy, what matters are the causal relationships in the source analog that can suggest causes for what is to be explained in the target. In action-directed uses of analogy for problem solving and planning, what matters are the causal relationships that show how to bring about what the thinker desires to happen and to prevent what the thinker desires not to happen.

Causal relations are among the earliest that children are able to recognize, at least at an implicit level. Even six-month-old infants can perceive and react to basic physical causal connections, such as the launching of a billiard ball into motion when it is struck by another. By age two or so, children are able to explicitly represent and talk about particular physical causes, such as cutting and melting, and psychological causes, such as their brother's being mean. We will see in chapter 4 that tasks involving analogies based on well-understood causal relations provide evidence that preschool children are already capable of relational mapping.

However, to think explicitly about causal relations in general, as opposed to particular causal relations, it is necessary to make use of higher-order relations based on causal concepts. It is not enough to be able to represent specific causal regularities, such as the fact that a knife can cut bread; we must also be able to represent more general and abstract regularities, such as the fact that a person can use an instrument to cause a change in an object. A number of concepts are commonly used by older children and adults to describe how one situation is causally connected to another. These higher-order relations include cause, explain, imply, entail, presuppose, facilitate, hinder, and prevent. A thinker who is capable of forming such higher-order relations will be able to use explicit knowledge about causal relations to guide analogical mapping at the system level. Such a thinker can recognize that a secretary intervening quickly to correct the boss's error can be viewed as analogous to a person catching a ball. Despite the lack of similarities between the objects and actions involved in the two situations, they are analogous by virtue of systematic correspondences between patterns of higher-order causal relations.

System mappings bring with them a deeper role for the constraint of structure, along with sensitivity to more abstract similarities of higher-order relations; but they also provide a stronger basis for the constraint of purpose. Once higher-order causal relations can be explicitly represented, they provide a much more direct way of evaluating whether an analogy serves to achieve one's goals. In later chapters we will see that in politics, law, philosophy, science, education, and literature, the same question arises: How can a thinker use analogies productively? Of course, we offer no guarantees, but our general answer is: Work with analogies based on system mappings that can be explicitly evaluated with respect to purpose as well as similarity and structure. In later chapters we will show how this advice can be put into practice.

We can now see how each of our three general constraints on analogy can be used to support an analogy. First, the mapping between attribute → isomorphism

elements of the source and target analogs can be supported by the direct similarity of objects and of concepts. Second, the mapping between analogs can also be supported by taking into account their structure, by showing that each element in the source is uniquely and consistently mapped to an element in the target, establishing an isomorphism. Finally, support for an analogy comes from determining that it satisfies its purpose in producing understanding or accomplishment of practical goals. A target analog must be "sculpted" by transfer from a source analog to suggest a relevant and accurate solution or explanation to the original puzzle that started the whole process.

Ideally, the three constraints will all work together to suggest a single interpretation of how the source is applicable to the target. But in less-than-perfect analogies the constraints can be at odds with each other, for example, when structural considerations support correspondences that are incompatible with object similarities or with the purposes of the analogist. Analogy can still operate, however, provided that there is a cognitive mechanism for balancing the competing constraints and coming up with a coherent interpretation despite some degree of discord. In chapter 10 we describe computer models of analogy that embody such a mechanism.

computer model

We now proceed to use our multiconstraint theory to explain how analogy works on many kinds of tasks in many kinds of individuals. We eventually apply the theory to analogical thinking as sophisticated as that exhibited by the most creative scientists. But the ability to make creative leaps by analogy did not suddenly emerge in the mind of Vitruvius or some other early figure who contributed to the rise of science. The first small but profound steps toward thinking by analogy were taken millions of years ago and are intimately connected to the evolution of cognition. In the next chapter we consider the precursors of analogy use in other animals, especially the closest evolutionary relative of humans that remains on the earth today, the chimpanzee.

Summary

Thinking by analogy requires knowledge to be represented in an explicit form so that systematic comparisons can be made between the source and target. Although sensory and semantic similarities are often useful in analogical thinking, sophisticated use of analogy depends on the constraints of structure and purpose in addition to that of similarity. Finding coherent sets of correspondences involves constructing mappings that are one-to-one and structurally consistent. Mappings can be supported by

Goswami question this
notion

similar attributes, similar first-order relations, and similar higher-order relations. The richest analogies employ system mappings involving relations between propositions. Typically, system mappings involve a set of causal relationships that make a source analog relevant to the purpose of the analogy, which may be problem solving, decision making, explanation, or communication. Analogical thinking operates by attempting to satisfy and reconcile the sometimes discordant constraints of similarity, structure, and purpose.

3

The Analogical Ape

Sameness

The first steps toward analogical thinking require the recognition that two different things can be treated as the same. But Funes was right: the dog at three fifteen has surely changed from the dog at three fourteen. A little older, a new body position—why *should* the two be lumped together under a single shared name? Nonetheless, most of us would cheerfully accept that it was the same dog. Nor do we stop there, for we consider Hercules the Great Dane and Fifi the Chihuahua to be somehow the same, too. At least, two dogs are much more the same than are a dog and a grapefruit.

There is nothing specially human about such reactions to perceived sameness. As far as we know, all other vertebrates (and probably many invertebrates as well) are capable of recognizing the general physical similarity of objects. Of course, nonhuman animals are not able to state their views directly on such matters; in fact, except for mammals there is no evidence to suggest that animals have explicit knowledge of similarity relations. But all vertebrates have implicit knowledge of similarity and can make use of it to react adaptively to their environments. If we observe carefully how animals transfer learned behaviors from one situation to another, we can see how they divide up the world. If a bird snacks once on a noxious monarch butterfly, it will likely avoid any further encounters with insects of that species as well as with harmless viceroy butterflies, a species that has evolved to mimic the appearance of the inedible monarch. Meanwhile the bird will continue to ingest other types of butterflies that look less similar to the one that offended its palate. The bird's pattern of prey selection defines the range of butterflies that it implicitly treats as the same with respect to its goal of getting acceptable meals.

A bird is thus able to react in the same way to objects that share perceptual properties. Furthermore, the perceptual basis for the response may be quite subtle. For example, pigeons can be trained to peck a key for food in response to photographs, taken from different angles, of different people in a wide range of poses. In order to recognize that a photograph includes a person (or a tree or a bird or an example of various other natural classes that pigeons can learn), the pigeon must be attending to complex combinations of features. Even for reactions based on physical similarity, psychological "sameness" can be quite far removed from literal physical identity.

To understand the origins of analogy, however, we have to move beyond implicit reactions to similarities between objects to the evolutionary precursors of explicit thought. Many difficulties arise in discussing the evolution of thinking, because the evidence available is so scant. Thought does not leave fossils behind. Evolution did not follow a simple linear path, and there is no simple rank ordering of animals from less to more intelligent. Various species of birds, for example, display navigational abilities that far exceed those of unaided humans. However, our concern here is not with the evolution of all forms of intelligence, but rather just those forms most related to analogy. After a very brief look at the abilities of pigeons and rats in responding to relational similarities, we will focus on primate species—monkeys, chimpanzees, and humans. Fossil evidence clearly indicates that these species are related and can be ordered by the length of time since each branched off from a common ancestral species. Humans are more closely related to chimpanzees than to monkeys. As we will see, studies of thinking by primates suggest at least a rough sketch of the evolutionary origins of explicit thought.

Analogy depends on sensitivity to relations between objects, and therefore our focus will be on behaviors that appear to reveal such sensitivity. What types of animals can respond to similarity between relations in a way that goes beyond direct similarity of objects? The evidence indicates strongly that all mammals have such capabilities, and birds may as well (although the evidence is more equivocal), whereas fish probably do not. Even in mammals, however, careful tests are required to be sure that the animal is really responding to a relation and not simply to attributes of the individual objects. In 1954, Lawrence and DeRivera performed a classic experiment with rats that demonstrated these animals can indeed respond to similarities between relations. The animals were trained and then tested on a "jumping stand." The rat was placed on the stand facing a pair of gray cards, one above the other. If

A. Training Pairs

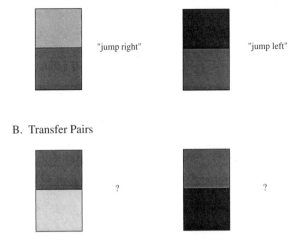

B. Transfer Pairs

Figure 3.1
Examples of pairs of gray cards used in training (*A*) and in transfer tests (*B*) to investigate relational processing by rats in an experiment by Lawrence and DeRivera (1954).

the top card was lighter than the bottom card, the rat was rewarded with food if it jumped to the right; if the top card was darker than the bottom one the rat was rewarded if it jumped to the left. In other words, what the animal needed to do to get food depended on the brightness relation between the two cards.

The experiment included a transfer test to demonstrate that the rats were really responding to the brightness relation rather than to the brightness values of the individual cards. Each card was one of seven shades of gray. During training the bottom card was always the middle gray, and each of the other shades was used as the top card on different trials. Figure 3.1A illustrates two of the training pairs, one in which the top card is lighter than the middle gray (so the rat needs to go right), and one in which the top card is darker than the middle gray (so the rat needs to go left). The crucial thing to notice is how the absolute values of brightness were associated with reward during training. The light gray always signaled "go right"; the dark gray always signaled "go left"; and the middle gray was ambiguous, as it was always present regardless of whether a jump to the right or the left was rewarded.

On the transfer test, Lawrence and DeRivera presented the rats with new pairs of grays, combinations they had never seen during training.

The most interesting test pairs were ones for which the correct reponse could only be made on the basis of the relation, not on what the rat might have learned about the absolute values of individual cards. Two examples are shown in figure 3.1B. Both pairs involve the middle gray; as we saw, this shade had been associated equally often with each response during training, so by itself it provided no information about which way the rat should jump. Unlike in the training pairs, the middle gray is now the top card, rather than the bottom card. In one pair the light gray appears below the middle gray. Since the top card is darker than the bottom card, the correct relational response is to jump left, even though during training the presence of this particular light gray card had always been a cue to jump right. Similarly, in the other pair the dark gray is below the middle gray, so the correct relational response is to jump right. Again, this is exactly opposite to the response that had been associated with the presence of this particular gray during training. These transfer pairs thus pitted the relational response based on relative brightness against the response associated with the level of absolute brightness. The results revealed that on 74 percent of such trials, the rats jumped in the direction cued by the brightness relation.

Rats do not always respond on the basis of the relation. Other similar experiments have demonstrated that rats can respond both to absolute and to relative brightnesses. What is most important, however, is that rats and other mammals are clearly able to perceive physical relations between two objects and sometimes use these relations as the basis for action. But although rats and other mammals below the level of primates can react to relations between objects, their capacity for relational processing appears to fall short of true relational (or even attribute) mapping. Rats can only respond to a limited number of basic perceptual relations, such as relative brightness or size. Although the animals can react to relations, we lack evidence that they can think about them explicitly. That is, although a rat in Lawrence and DeRivera's experiment could perceive that the top card was lighter than the bottom card and react by jumping right, we cannot assume it was explicitly thinking about *the fact that* the top card was lighter, or even about the fact that the top card was a certain shade of gray. Nonetheless, the rat's accomplishment appears to provide a step toward the capacity for relational mapping. In recognizing that different pairs of cards exhibiting the same brightness relation require the same response, the animal is in some fashion responding to sameness of relations rather than only sameness of objects.

Adult humans can readily understand sameness of both objects and relations, and in English (as well as in all other languages, as far as we know) the same word is used for these different varieties of sameness. To understand the evolution of more abstract types of sameness, we need to make more fine-grained distinctions than ordinary language provides. We will call direct physical similarity of objects *O-sameness,* and we will call similarity of the relations between objects *R-sameness.* For simplicity we will generally ignore the obvious fact that similarity of both objects and relations is a matter of degree; for now it will suffice to divide the scale crudely into the binary values of "same" for high similarity and "different" for low similarity.

Just because an animal is able to respond to O-sameness or R-sameness does not necessarily mean that the animal can explicitly think about these concepts, as we do. For example, a bird may respond the same way to a monarch and a viceroy butterfly without being able to explicitly represent the fact that they are O-same as one another. What would be gained if an animal could explicitly represent O-sameness? Such an animal could not only treat two objects as the same, but it could start to think about the fact that the objects are the same and use this knowledge as the basis for action.

A task that can be used to assess whether animals can perceive O-sameness is illustrated in figure 3.2. As depicted in figure 3.2A, the animal is first shown an object, here an apple, which is called the sample. Then the animal is offered a choice between two objects, one that is O-same as the sample (another apple) and one that is O-different (a shoe, for example). The positions of the two alternatives (left and right) are varied across trials; hence O-sameness is defined in terms of sameness of shape rather than position. If the animal selects the object that is O-same as the sample (regardless of its position), a reward is given. (Alternatively, the animal might receive a reward only if it selects the object that is O-different.) This task is called "match-to-sample" for the obvious reason that it requires the animal to match the choice alternatives to the original sample and to select the alternative that matches the sample appropriately. There may or may not be a delay of a few seconds between presentation of the sample and the alternatives. Delay versions of the task test the animal's ability to maintain a representation of the sample in working memory. Here we concentrate on the simplest case, in which the sample and the alternatives are presented simultaneously.

Even pigeons can learn to respond correctly in the basic match-to-sample task. But as in the case of rats learning to respond to pairs of gray

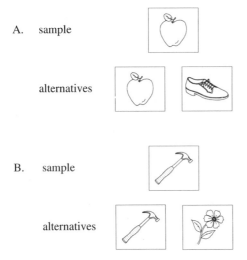

A.   sample

        alternatives

B.   sample

        alternatives

Figure 3.2
(*A*) An example of a match-to-sample problem. (*B*) A transfer problem based on a new set of objects.

cards, there is ambiguity about whether animals are in fact reacting to a relation rather than to the specific objects being related. The simplest possibility is that they might just learn a specific conditional rule, such as

If sample is apple, then pick apple.

The more interesting possibility is that they are learning to respond on the basis of general O-sameness:

If sample is O-same as alternative, then pick that alternative.

The way to test whether the animal is learning a rule based on O-sameness is to see how it behaves on a transfer test, such as that depicted in figure 3.2B. Here the sample is a hammer, and the alternatives for matching are another hammer and a flower. If all the animal had learned was "if apple, pick apple," it would have no basis for responding on this generalized transfer test, since none of the objects have any particular resemblance to apples at all.

On the other hand, suppose an animal is capable of attribute mapping and hence can in at least a crude way think about, rather than simply react to, the category or basic shape of an object. Such an animal could represent the first sample as something like apple (apple-1)

and the apple alternative as

apple (apple-2)

and then react to the O-sameness of the sample and the alternative revealed by their shared attribute. Then on the transfer test the sample would be represented as

hammer (hammer-1)

and the hammer alternative as

hammer (hammer-2).

An animal that had learned to respond on the basis of O-sameness of category or shape would then choose the hammer alternative, because it is O-same as the sample, just as the apple alternative had been O-same as its sample.

Pigeons generally perform poorly on such generalized transfer tests. But for primates, such as monkeys and chimpanzees, the evidence is clear: without any special training or further reward, the animal will transfer what it has learned about matching apples to apples to the new case of matching hammers to hammers. We can therefore be quite certain that primates can react to O-sameness of objects, even though the objects in each pair have no O-sameness to the objects in the other pair. Moreover, if the primate had learned to match an apple to something that was not an apple, then on a transfer test it will match a hammer to something that is not a hammer. Thus the animal is also able to react to the relation of O-difference.

What distinguishes a monkey's performance from that of a pigeon? A pigeon can react to the global similarity of two objects, such as one apple and another. However, it seems to lack the capacity to think explicitly about the physical attributes of objects, as appears to be required in order to perceive a relation that makes the similarity of one apple to another somehow the "same" as the similarity of one hammer to another. In contrast, the primate has evolved to be able to think about attributes of objects and to perceive the relation between sameness of one set of attributes and sameness of another set—that is, O-sameness. The primate can therefore learn to react to O-sameness, rather than to the particular objects that are the same. The result is a major extension in the breadth of transfer across situations.

sample

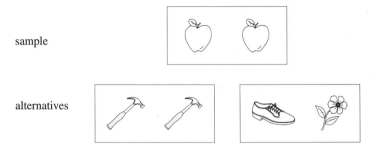

alternatives

Figure 3.3
An example of a pairwise match-to-sample problem in which the sample pair and the correct alternative are each based on O-same objects.

What Sarah Thinks

Nonetheless, even an intelligent chimpanzee turns out to be surprisingly limited in its ability to respond to O-sameness. Figure 3.3 illustrates what appears to be a simple extension of the generalized match-to-sample problem that primates are able to perform so well. The only difference is that the sample and the alternatives are now not single objects but rather pairs of objects. In figure 3.3, the sample is a pair of apples, and the alternatives are either a pair of hammers or a shoe and a flower. Which would you choose? No doubt it is obvious to you that the pair of hammers is the same as the sample in a way in which the shoe-flower combination is not. At first glance, the problem appears to have the same logical form as the generalized transfer test depicted in figure 3.2 (i.e., transfer from the problem in figure 3.2A to that in figure 3.2B), so you might expect any intelligent primate would also be able to succeed on the pairwise match-to-sample task in figure 3.3.

If so, you will be disappointed in the nearest relatives to our own species. No nonhuman primate—not even an intelligent chimpanzee—has ever consistently been able to succeed on the pairwise match-to-sample test without some very special training that we will describe in a moment. No animal other than a human or a chimpanzee has ever succeeded under any circumstances.

Evidently, the apparently innocent step from the task depicted in figure 3.2 to that depicted in figure 3.3 requires another evolutionary leap. Let us look at the two versions of the matching task more carefully. In the single-object version, generalized transfer requires reacting to O-sameness—if the animal has learned to choose the apple alternative that is O-same as the apple in the sample (figure 3.2A), then it will also choose the hammer alternative that is O-same as the hammer in the sample (figure 3.2B). However, although this performance may require explicit representations of the attributes of objects, it does not require an explicit representation of the relation of O-sameness. That is, although the animal is using O-sameness, it does not know that it is using it. It may be using O-sameness implicitly, without having constructed an explicit representation.

The trouble is that an implicit reaction to O-sameness is not sufficient for success on the pairwise version of the task, because this task does not allow an immediate reaction to O-sameness. Instead, it is necessary first to explicitly represent the fact that the sample consists of one object that is O-same as another, for example,

O-same (apple-1, apple-2).

This representation must be "held in mind" while the animal processes the two sample pairs, which could be represented as

O-same (hammer-1, hammer-2),

O-different (shoe-1, flower-1).

Only after forming such explicit representations could the animal compare the relation in each alternative to that in the sample and select the alternative that is described by the same relation as that used to represent the sample. In other words, the pairwise task cannot be solved by reacting to O-sameness of two objects; rather, it requires the ability to react to R-sameness of two relations. To perceive R-sameness, it is necessary for the animal to have an explicit representation of the relation of O-sameness, which can link pairs of apples, pairs of hammers, pairs of frogs, and so on.

It turns out that although chimpanzees do not ordinarily form explicit representations of O-sameness, they can learn to do so. The first nonhuman animal to solve the pairwise match-to-sample task was an African-born chimpanzee (*Pan troglodyte*) named Sarah. Sarah's life was very different from that of any other chimpanzee who lived before her. She spent nineteen of her first twenty years in a laboratory directed by psychologist David Premack, attending a kind of school five days a week since she was about five years old. Much of her school time was spent studying a form of artificial "language." The "words" of this language were colored plastic tokens in various shapes, sizes, and textures, which Sarah was trained to put together into ordered strings to represent propositions, such as "apple is red," "blue is on yellow," "round shape of apple," and so on. Over the course of training, the strings and corresponding propositions increased in complexity, including, for example, "red on yellow, if then, Sarah take chocolate," and "Sarah take apple in red dish, banana in blue dish." These examples are given in English but with the word order that Sarah learned.

One of Sarah's words is especially important to our story: she learned to build propositions with a token for "same." She could use "same" to relate two objects of the same type, as in "apple same apple," and also to relate two strings that both expressed the same proposition, as in "apple is red, same, red color of apple." If Sarah had in fact acquired an explicit representation of the concept of O-sameness, then perhaps she would be able to succeed in the pairwise match-to-sample task illustrated in figure 3.3.

And succeed she did. Not only did she select the alternative that matched the sample by also exemplifying O-sameness when given a problem like that depicted in figure 3.3, but she also solved problems in which the sample and the favored alternative both exemplified O-difference. Figure 3.4 shows a problem of the latter sort. The sample consists of a bottle and a bell; the alternatives are identical to those in the problem shown in figure 3.3. For the problem in figure 3.4, Sarah would select the shoe-flower pair rather than the pair of hammers. Furthermore, she did not need any special reward in order to make these choices. She simply expressed her preference for whichever alternative exhibited the same relation as that exhibited by the sample.

sample

alternatives

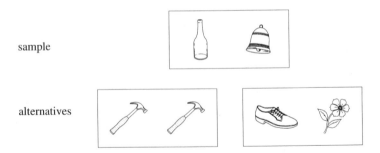

Figure 3.4
An example of a pairwise match-to-sample problem in which the sample pair and the correct alternative are each based on O-different objects.

How did Sarah solve the pairwise match-to-sample problems? The task can be viewed as an analogy problem that can be solved by relational mapping, with the sample serving as the source analog and each alternative serving as a possible target analog. Figure 3.5A illustrates how a sample consisting of two apples maps consistently to an alternative consisting of two hammers, but not to a sample consisting of a shoe and a flower. The two O-same relations are identical, producing a mapping by pairs between the first apple and the first hammer and between the second apple and the second hammer. The hammer-hammer alternative is thus analogous to the apple-apple sample, whereas the shoe-flower alternative is not (because the relation in the latter alternative differs from that in the sample). Figure 3.5B illustrates how the preference will reverse when the sample consists of two different objects, a bell and a bottle. The sample would now be represented by

O-different (bell-1, bottle-1),

and the alternatives would again be

O-same (hammer-1, hammer-2),

O-different (shoe-1, flower-1).

Now it is the shoe-flower pair that exhibits the same relation, O-different, as does the sample, whereas the hammer-hammer pair exhibits a

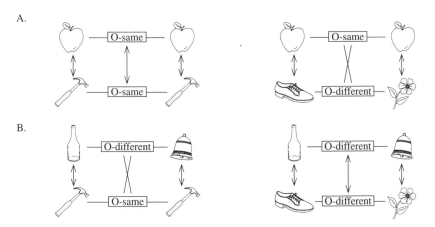

Figure 3.5
Relational mapping in the pairwise match-to-sample task. (*A*) Only the first alternative (*left*) has the same relation, O-same, as the sample. (*B*) Only the second alternative (*right*) has the same relation, O-different, as the sample.

relation different from that of the sample. Relational mapping will therefore favor selection of the shoe-flower pair.

Notice that relational mapping of the sort depicted in figure 3.5 amounts to an implicit response to R-sameness between the relations in the sample and in the preferred alternative. That is, the similarity constraint on relational mapping—the tendency to map similar relations to each other—leads to a preference for the alternative with a relation that is R-same as the relation in the sample. However, we need not assume that Sarah actually formed an explicit concept of R-sameness. As the diagrams in figure 3.5 make clear, it is possible to respond on the basis of the similarity between relations without explicitly representing the higher-order relation of R-sameness. We will see later that the apparent absence of such explicit higher-order relations from the conceptual repertoire of the chimpanzee places bounds on their analogical ability.

The obvious question, given her superior performance on the pairwise version of the matching task, is what made Sarah special? Was she simply smarter than other chimpanzees that failed the pairwise task? This does not seem to be the case. Sarah was certainly bright, but by many measures some of the other chimpanzees that lacked her special training—and failed the pairwise matching task—were also bright. The best evidence that her specialized experience was crucial in some way is provided by further tests that Premack performed using other chimpanzees who were considerably younger than Sarah. Two young language-trained chimpanzees succeeded on the pairwise matching task, whereas four otherwise comparable animals that did not receive language training failed. It is therefore clear that something about the special training with symbol manipulation was responsible. Moreover, the impact of the training on the animals' reasoning abilities was quite selective. For example, the language-trained animals (Sarah included) were no better than the others in tasks that required making inferences about the spatial locations of hidden objects.

Is it necessary for an animal to have a language to solve pairwise match-to-sample tasks? Premack himself has disavowed any claim that what Sarah and the others learned was really comparable to human language. What exactly ought to be considered a language is a highly controversial issue; fortunately, it is not an issue that is relevant here. What is clear is that the training did encourage Sarah and her younger fellow students to use explicit propositional representations to control their actions. And of special importance, the animals were taught to make responses on the basis of an explicit concept of sameness. It appears that Sarah was the first nonhuman animal ever to have acquired an explicit relational concept by learning.

What kinds of knowledge must an animal already have in order for language training to generate an explicit concept of O-sameness? This is a difficult question to answer. However, later work provided evidence that even infant chimps will react in some fashion to R-sameness, without any special training at all. David Oden, Roger Thompson, and Premack adopted a technique that is often used with preverbal human infants to test what they see as the same or different. The technique is based on the fact that chimpanzees, like human infants, get bored more quickly when an experience seems much the same as one they have already undergone recently. Four infant champanzees were presented with a pair of objects, such as two pieces of garden hose (O-same), or a plastic block and a metal bracelet (O-different). The animal being tested was first allowed five minutes to familiarize itself with the sample pair of objects by handling it or otherwise interacting with it. After a fifteen-second interval, the animal received a second pair of objects. These were always different objects from those given on the familiarization trial, but the relation between the objects in the new pair was varied. Examples would be a pair of plastic chain links (O-same), or a bottle cap and a strip of wood (O-different). The experimenters then measured how long the animal handled the new pair of objects over a further five-minute period. The entire procedure was repeated twelve times in each of three four-hour sessions, with a week separating each session.

The results of this experiment are shown in figure 3.6. The graph plots the difference between the average time the animal handled the first and second pair of objects. The higher the bar, the sooner the chimpanzee became bored with the second pair—in other words, the more it seemed like the "same thing" as the first pair. As you can see, the results show that the chimpanzees found the second pair more boring when it was R-same as the first pair. The effect appears more robust when both pairs were O-same, but the basic pattern also held when both pairs were O-different. It is as if the infant chimpanzees found it boring to deal with O-sameness repeatedly or with O-difference repeatedly.

Because infant chimpanzees without any training of the sort Sarah received are able to react to R-sameness, you might suppose that with a bit of direct training they could go on to solve the pairwise matching task. But these animals could not consistently select the alternative that

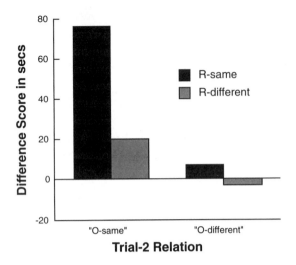

Figure 3.6
Trial 1 minus trial 2 differences in handling times for O-same and O-different pairs that are either familiar (R-same) or novel (R-different). Adapted with permission from Oden et al. (1990).

exhibited the same relation as the sample, even when they were repeatedly rewarded when they chose correctly. (Other evidence suggests, however, that such training can produce success if it is extended for one or more years.) It thus appears that chimpanzees react to a relationship that they are unable to readily use. Their reaction to R-sameness seems to be spontaneous, acquired early in life, and almost certainly not learned from experience. Furthermore, the ability to react to R-sameness sets chimpanzees apart from less intellectually advanced primates. Further experiments with monkeys, using the same procedure that shows chimpanzees react to R-sameness, have failed to find any evidence that monkeys see any similarity between what makes one pair of objects the same and what makes a different pair of objects the same. Human infants, on the other hand, also react to R-sameness, at least by the age of seven months. So chimpanzees, like humans but unlike monkeys, apparently have the inborn capacity to react to R-sameness.

While infant chimpanzees and humans apparently react to R-sameness, do they really perceive this higher-order relation? Not necessarily. It may be possible to explain the infants' pattern of handling pairs of objects solely in terms of implicit reactions based on O-sameness and O-difference. All we need to assume is that these infants implicitly perceive O-sameness and O-difference of objects and that they find repeated perception of either one of these relations to be boring. Although we can describe this pattern as "reacting to R-sameness," it is not clear that the infants are actually even perceiving R-sameness, far less that they are explicitly thinking about it as a concept. Nonetheless, their innate ability to perceive O-sameness and O-difference is undoubtedly important in giving them the potential to acquire explicit concepts of O-sameness and O-difference and then to perceive R-sameness of such relations.

How Thought Evolved

It is worth pausing to reflect on what has happened over the course of the evolution of relational mapping, culminating in Sarah's solution of the pairwise match-to-sample task. To put it in more general terms than apples and hammers, we will use letters to stand for objects of a certain recognizable kind. For example, any example of an apple might be designated by "A," and "A_1" would stand for some particular apple. An animal capable of simply reacting to global physical similarity can match A's to A's and B's to B's and respond accordingly. But although such an animal can respond to all A's in one fashion and to all B's in some other fashion, it does not necessarily perceive any commonality between the bases for these separate judgments. Such an animal is roughly at the mental level of a pigeon: in a match-to-sample task where the sample is an A, it can learn "if A, then pick A," but it will be at a loss as to how to respond if then given a transfer task in which the sample is a B instead of an A.

To be able to generalize to new objects, the animal would need to have the ability to perceive the common basis for matching objects according to a shared category or shape, namely, O-sameness. To perceive O-sameness the animal needs an explicit representation of the attributes of objects. With this additional mental machinery, which is available to primates, the animal will be able to transfer what it has learned about picking an A to match an A—to select the alternative that is O-same as the sample—and apply this knowledge to pick a B to match a B. However, because it is responding to O-sameness on an implicit basis, the animal is limited to making an immediate response to a pair.

Here is where the special training of Sarah and the other language-trained chimpanzees triggered another mental leap, up to the level of relational mapping. To do relational mapping, the animal must first be able to translate correspondences obtained by attribute mapping, such as

$A_1 \leftrightarrow A_2$

and (in a separate attribute mapping)

$B_1 \leftrightarrow B_2,$

into representations that at least approximate propositions expressing *the fact that* the mapped objects are related. Furthermore, the relation used in these propositions must be general enough to apply to different kinds of objects that can be grouped on the basis of attribute similarity. The necessary relation is provided by an explicit concept of O-sameness. Armed with this concept, the animal can recode the above attribute mappings into the propositions

O-same (A_1, A_2)

O-same (B_1, B_2)

for any pair of examples of A's or of B's. An animal that can form such propositions has taken a giant stride toward abstract thought. For now it is prepared to map not simply objects one by one, but objects taken in pairs—mappings driven not by direct physical similarity of objects but by similarity of the relation between the objects. By mapping two propositions of the above sort, an animal like Sarah can arrive at the correspondences

O-same $\leftrightarrow$ O-same

$A_1 \leftrightarrow B_1$

$A_2 \leftrightarrow B_2$

based on mapping objects in pairs. These mappings are not justified by direct similarity between A's and B's. Instead, the mapping is justified by the fact that A's and B's can play parallel roles with respect to O-sameness: the A's are O-same as each other just as the B's are O-same as each other. An animal with this much mental equipment is able not only to solve the basic match-to-sample task and perform well on generalized transfer tests with completely different objects, but also to solve the pairwise version of the task. Apples may be freely replaced by hammers, and the problem will still be seen as the same.

The remarkable progression in abstract thought that we have just outlined required several million years of biological evolution. With Sarah's final step, the progression moved from the timescale of evolution to that of learning. Her feat in solving the pairwise version of the match-to-sample task was the mental equivalent of the first flight of the Wright brothers—only a short wobbly hop, but one that we can look back on as the dawn of space travel.

If we look carefully, we can see that the progression from reacting to physical similarity to performing relational mapping is based on a general strategy for deepening the abstraction of thinking, moving beyond direct sensory experience into the realm of concepts. Of course, by calling it a "strategy" we do not mean that it is deliberate or purposeful—it is simply a general description of how abstract thought appears to have evolved. The strategy might be sketched this way:

Step 1: Based on whatever means of mapping elements the animal already has at its disposal, it finds correspondences and identifies sets of elements that map consistently. The earliest basis for mapping was global physical similarity of objects.

Step 2: Explicit concepts are formed to capture the basis of the mappings.

Step 3: The strategy cycles back to step 1. It will now be possible for the altered animal to map elements on the basis of the new concepts that have been formed. Armed with this new way to justify mappings, steps 1 through 3 are repeated.

The full power of the strategy lies in its call to "repeat." What exactly does that mean? The intellectual developments roughly bounded by a pigeon and Sarah appear to have required two cycles through the strategy. In the first cycle, step 2 provided the capacity to represent attributes of objects explicitly. For example, instead of just reacting in the same way to different apples because they look alike, the animal could now think about the basis for the similarity of different apples, expressed as a concept that applies to any apple, as in

apple (apple-1),

in which "apple" serves as a shorthand for those attributes generally shared by apples. Roughly speaking, this evolutionary move takes us from the pigeon to the monkey, which returns from step 3 armed with the ability to perform attribute mapping. In the second cycle, this more sophisticated animal is able to form mappings by reacting to the relation of O-sameness between attributes of objects, which allows it to solve the generalized match-to-sample task with single objects. At step 2, the basis for these mappings is coded as the explicit concept of O-sameness. This move required both evolution (roughly, from the level of the monkey to that of the chimpanzee) and the special training that Sarah received.

Sarah represents an animal that could return from step 3 to step 1 with the novel capacity to perform relational mapping. She can now map elements in pairs based on similarity between different occurrences of her new relational concepts, such as O-sameness, which allows her to solve the pairwise version of the match-to-sample task.

The case of Sarah is especially striking, because for the first time our strategy operated in part by learning within an individual animal, rather than solely by evolution of new species. What would a third cycle of the strategy bring? We have already hinted at how an animal might go beyond Sarah's level of relational mapping. The basis for a relational mapping (step 1 repeated) is the sameness of a relation in the source to a relation in the target—in other words, R-sameness. An animal that could form an explicit concept of R-sameness (step 2 repeated) would have a new and more abstract basis for mapping. Before we consider animals capable of this deeper level of abstraction, let us look more carefully at the thinking of our nearest evolutionary cousins.

The Analogies of Apes

Sarah's training allowed her to become the first nonhuman animal to solve analogy problems in the proportional format used on human intelligence tests. As we mentioned in chapter 2, a proportional analogy has the form A:B::C:D ("A is to B as C is to D," as in "A can opener is related to a can as a key is related to a lock"). The problem solver might have to judge whether A:B is the same as or different than C:D, or to choose the best completion for an analogy from a set of alternatives, as in A:B::C:? in which the answer is the best "D" term. We can treat the A:B pair as the source analog and C:D as the intended target analog. Taking the "can opener" problem as an example, the obvious representation of the source would be

open (can opener, can),

and the representation of the target would be

open (key, lock).

The source and target form a relational mapping based on the R-sameness of the two relations.

The resemblance to the form of the pairwise match-to-sample task should be apparent. In the pairwise matching task, although the problem solver is not directly asked to map the sample to the alternatives, this is in fact how the task can be performed. The analogy format simply makes the requirement explicit. In general, an analogy problem can use any relation to link the objects in the source and in the target ("open" in the above example). In the pairwise matching task, the relation happens to be O-sameness. The higher-order relation of R-sameness, however, is special. In a basic proportional analogy, the justification for mapping the source and target is always that the relation in the source analog is R-same as that in the target, regardless of what specific relation is used in each analog. However, a relational mapping only requires an implicit reaction to R-sameness rather than an explicit representation of the concept.

Analogy problems in which a missing term has to be generated, as in A:B::C:? pose yet another cognitive requirement—the ability to consider a question. The idea of a question is one we take for granted, but like the idea of sameness of relations, it in fact represents a considerable cognitive achievement. Notice that understanding or formulating an explicit question requires representing a missing slot filler in a proposition. For example, the question "What is the color of an apple?" has the logical form

color-of (apple, X?),

in which "X?" represents a missing slot filler. The answer to the question is some definite value, such as red, that can fill the empty slot denoted by "X?" to generate a complete proposition that is true. Similarly, "How old is Neil?" has the form

age-of (Neil, X?),

where the answer is some particular age, say four years, that could replace "X?"

The mental representation of a missing slot filler such as "X?" that holds a slot open for something that might fill it can be termed a *query marker*. Our English words for types of questions—"who," "what," "where," "when," "why," "how"—pick out different types of fillers for the empty slot: "what" typically calls for an object of some sort, "who" for a person, "where" for a place, and so on. Questions can be thought of as incomplete propositions in which a query marker holds open a slot that needs a filler.

The language training Sarah and the other chimpanzees received gave them a great deal of experience in answering questions. Early on, Sarah was taught that a special token acted as a query marker, just as

Problem A   **Problem B**

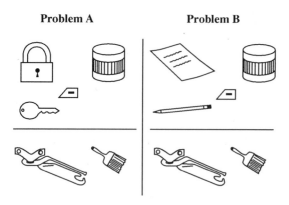

Figure 3.7
Examples of functional analogy problems that Sarah solved. (*A*) When shown a closed lock and a key and a closed painted can, she selected the can opener (rather than the paint brush) as the appropriate completion to make the two relations the "same." (*B*) When shown a marked paper and a pencil, and the same closed painted can, Sarah selected the paint brush as the better completion. From Gillan et al. (1981). Copyright (1981) by the American Psychological Association. Reprinted by permission.

"X?" does in the above examples. If Sarah had already learned the tokens for "color of" and for "apple," and was being taught the token for "red," she would be shown a string of tokens representing "X? color of apple" and receive a reward if she correctly replaced the "X?" with the token for "red." Sarah and the other language-trained chimpanzees caught on quickly as to how the query marker was to be interpreted, suggesting that chimpanzees may have some natural concept of this sort. With a query marker, an animal can start to think about what it does not yet know, not just about what it currently does know. Along with her experience working with a token for "same," Sarah's experience with the question token provided an important way for her to answer analogy questions.

Premack and his colleagues were able to test Sarah on analogies involving other relations besides O-sameness. She proved proficient in solving analogies based on functional relations, in which each analog involves an instrument that can operate in some specific way to change the state of another object. Figure 3.7A shows the key–can opener analogy on which Sarah was tested, along with the pair of alternatives she had to choose between to fill in the missing term in order to make the source and target the "same." (The shape with an equal sign in figure

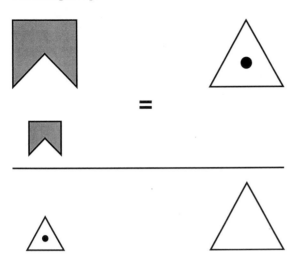

Figure 3.8
Example of a geometric analogy problem that Sarah solved. When shown a large, dark sawtooth and a small, dark sawtooth, and a large, white triangle with a dot, she selected the small, white triangle with a dot (rather than the large, white triangle with no dot). From Gillan et al. (1981). Copyright (1981) by the American Psychological Association. Reprinted by permission.

3.7 represents Sarah's token for "same," which was actually a yellow, plastic rectangle.) The can in the picture was both closed and painted, and the incorrect alternative was an object closely associated with a painted can, namely a paintbrush. Nonetheless, Sarah selected the can opener as the object that best completed the analogy.

Besides the relation of opening, as in the key–can opener analogy, Sarah could map analogs on the basis of "marking." In fact, as the display in figure 3.7B indicates, it was possible to design a marking analogy that reversed Sarah's choice between the same two alternatives. Given pictures of a marked paper and a pencil as the source pair ("pencil marks paper") and a picture of the painted can, she now selected the paintbrush ("brush marks can") as the better completion, rather than the can opener.

Notice that these analogies cannot be answered in any obvious way on the basis of direct physical resemblances. Not only does a can opener not look like a key, nor a can like a lock, but also the motion of opening a can with a can opener actually has very little physical overlap with the motion of opening a lock with a key. The fact that we call both these actions opening—just as Sarah learned a single token that applied in both cases—calls attention to their commonalities. But these commonalities have less to do with physical appearance than with their similar functions: both openings are actions that achieve access to a space that was initially blocked. As we will see shortly, Sarah's problem solving, like her analogy solutions, showed that she was able to represent the purposes of actions.

Using various matching tasks, Premack and his colleagues were able to show that Sarah could solve other analogy problems. These included geometric analogies, such as that depicted in figure 3.8. These problems were based on arbitrary forms that could vary in shape, color, and marking (either unmarked or with a black dot). In this example, when shown a large dark sawtooth form and a small dark sawtooth form and a large white triangle with a dot inside, Sarah selected the small white triangle with a dot rather than the large white triangle with no dot. That is, she was able to pick the form that created the relation "larger than" between the two target forms, the relation that was illustrated for the source pair.

One of Sarah's tasks required her to respond on the basis of a mapping between proportional relations. For example, Sarah was shown a "sample" of a half-filled glass cylinder. Then she had to choose between half of an apple or three-quarters of an apple as the better match to the sample. Sarah consistently solved problems of this sort correctly, revealing that she was sensitive to the fact that a half-filled cylinder is relationally similar to half an apple, even though the objects themselves are very dissimilar. Sarah's success on the proportions test indicates that chimpanzees can perceive something akin to part-whole relations.

Another interesting example of Sarah's ability to match on the basis of abstract relational similarities involved same/different judgments between pairs of three-item sequences. The sequences were composed of physically dissimilar nonsense shapes. Each sequence of three was presented twice, and Sarah was required to judge whether the order was the same in the two presentations. In a challenging form of the test, the first presentation consisted of the three objects' being presented one at a time, in serial order, whereas the second presentation consisted of the same three objects' being presented simultaneously in a certain spatial order. To compare the two sequences, Sarah had to map an ordering based on time to an ordering based on space. (On other trials, the first sequence was spatial and the second was temporal.) Although her performance was imperfect on this matching task, it was well above chance. It therefore appears that Sarah was able to recognize that order of objects in time is relationally similar to order of objects in space.

In several types of analogy tests, then, Sarah's language training gave her a qualitative advantage over chimpanzees that lacked language training. Her apparent mastery of explicit concepts for relations appears to be the most important factor that helps explain what Sarah's successes have in common with each other. In later work, Premack and his colleagues trained other chimpanzees in a similar fashion, systematically testing their performance on analogy problems at different steps in the training process. The crucial event appeared to be the introduction of plastic words for "same" and "different." Moreover, it was actually sufficient simply to teach the use of "same" and "different" as they apply to objects (e.g., two apples were called "same," but an apple and a banana were "different"). Without further direct training, the chimpanzees were then able to apply their tokens for "same" and "different" to relations as well as objects. In contrast, the researchers found that neither teaching tokens for words nor teaching sentence-like strings of tokens was sufficient to produce success on an analogy task.

In fact, studies that Premack has performed reveal that chimpanzees will eventually learn to respond on the basis of relational similarity after one to three years of "dogged training," even without being taught tokens for "same" and "different." For example, the animals will eventually learn to match samples on the basis of like proportions (e.g., matching a quarter of an apple to a quarter of a glass of water). Furthermore, unlike arbitrary learned relations, such as "if the light is red, turn right," chimpanzees do not have to be rewarded for making correct match-to-sample choices. Eventually they simply seem to notice, for example, that a certain proportion of one object is similar to that proportion of another object and begin to respond on that basis. But without an explicit name for "same," the animals do not transfer what they learn to new relations. Thus, having learned to match samples of like proportions does not lead to success in forming analogies on the basis of other relations. In contrast, animals who have acquired tokens for "same" and "different" are able to handle any of a wide range of tasks that depend on reacting to sameness of relations. Teaching tokens for "same" and "different" helps the animal to break loose from the immediate training context and solve a much wider variety of relational problems.

We are still left wondering how training with symbolic tokens for "same" and "different" allows explicit relational concepts to provide new mental tools for guiding the behavior of chimpanzees. One possibility that Premack has suggested is that various parts of Sarah's training, which were directed specifically at the generation of propositions based on explicit concepts for relations, caused her to shift greater attention to this more abstract level of description. Sarah and her fellow students spent a great deal of time in situations in which they were encouraged to treat relations expressed in propositions as more important than the particular items filling slots at any particular time. This is a very different regimen from that which confronts an ordinary chimpanzee living in the wild, whose experience is likely to encourage a decidedly more practical bent. In the wild, it is the salient perceptual properties of objects and relations between objects that are usually most important to survival. Consequently, although they also may perceive the deeper relations, untrained chimpanzees presumably generally ignore them. In contrast, Sarah was encouraged to pay less attention to surface properties of objects, and instead to focus on deeper relations. Indeed, Premack found that she sometimes experienced a surprising degree of difficulty solving simpler problems that required attention to more primitive object similarities. There may be an inherent trade-off between attention to abstract and to concrete aspects of mental representations. The focus on the abstract at the expense of the concrete, apparent in the thinking of the first chimpanzee intellectual, may also characterize the thinking of the human variety.

The Invention of Problems

Let us step back a moment. Sarah's accomplishments may seem like so many puzzles invented by clever psychologists—amusing to us, perhaps even to Sarah, but having nothing to do with the real world of a chimpanzee. But this would be a gross underestimation. There is reason to think that Sarah's abilities and those of other apes are telling us about the dawn of the kind of intelligence that makes us human. Let us look again at the capacities for analogy that have been revealed in the minds of chimpanzees. Without specialized training, we find evidence of

· explicit attributes representing object categories based on physical similarity
· the ability to perceive O-sameness as well as more concrete physical relations.

At least when chimpanzees are given training in the manipulation of a symbol system, we find in addition

· explicit representation of O-sameness as a concept
· relational mappings based on similarity of relations without similarity of objects
· explicit representation of query markers
· perception of relational similarity, R-sameness.

What advantages might these capacities convey for an animal in its natural habitat?

While spending the period of the First World War on the island of Tenerife, the psychologist Wolfgang Köhler conducted a series of studies demonstrating that chimpanzees can systematically solve problems by using simple tools. If the animal was presented with food that was in some way inaccessible—out of reach overhead, or outside the cage—it would take advantage of objects in its cage to obtain the food. For example, if the food was outside of the cage, the chimpanzee might take a long stick and use it to draw the food within reach. Simple problem solving of this sort has also been observed in the natural behavior of chimpanzees in the wild.

It therefore appears that the higher primates have, in at least some crude sense, invented tools. But actually this statement skips a crucial step: it would be more accurate to say primates have invented problems. This may seem like a surprising claim, since problems seem to be part and parcel of what it means for any animal to be alive on this planet. There is no doubt that a laboratory rat, for example, miserable with hunger as it scours the experimenter's maze searching for food, is confronting what we would all recognize as a problem. But we have no good reason to suppose the rat is thinking about, rather than simply reacting to, its state of deprivation. A problem is the recognition of a gap between the present state of affairs and some desired goal state. To represent *the fact that* it has a problem, an animal needs some explicit representation of what is absent—a solution that would fill the gap. Only then will the animal be able to reason about how the problem might be solved or recognize that some object provides a means to close the gap—that is, recognize that an object might be used as a tool.

This description of what it means to have a concept of a problem should sound familiar. We have already talked about what it takes to represent a gap in knowledge: a query marker. A problem is really just a kind of question to oneself. It has the basic form, "How can the current state of affairs be transformed into a state in which my goal is achieved?" or

transform (<solution?>, <initial state>, <goal state>).

The symbol "solution?" represents the missing knowledge of how to accomplish the desired transformation. The solution is generally an action or sequence of actions, and a tool is an object that is used to help perform the required actions. A tool, then, is more than just an object used to do something: it has to fill a special slot that is defined by its role in the overall schema for a problem.

With the invention of some simple version of the concept of a problem, it becomes possible to solve a problem by recognizing that it involves objects and relations similar to those involved in previous experiences. In other words, the capacities for analogy can become mental tools for problem solving. Let us imagine a fanciful, but perhaps not entirely implausible, scenario for the invention of a tool by a chimpanzee living in the wild. Suppose that one day it playfully bangs a rock against a nut, and the nut happens to break open. With a basic capacity for recognizing causal sequences and for storing explicit propositions in memory, the chimpanzee might code the initial state of the nut as

closed (nut-1) *name*: closed-1,

its own action of striking the nut with the rock as

strike (self, nut-1, rock-1) *name*: strike-1,

the final state of the nut as

open (nut-1) *name*: open-1,

and the causal connection between the action and the change in the state of the nut, from closed to open, as

break-open (strike-1, closed-1, open-1) *name*: break-open-1.

Now let us suppose that on some future occasion this chimpanzee is hungry. It finds a nut (nut-2) but is at first unable to open it. A rock (rock-2, different than the earlier one) is lying within its view. The animal may be able to formulate its problem as wanting to take this closed nut,

closed (nut-2) *name*: closed-2

and have it open,

open (nut-2) *name*: **open-2,**

by opening it somehow,

make-open (action?, closed-2, **open-2**) *name*: make-open-2

The boldface on **open-2** signifies that the animal must be able to understand this to be a desired goal state—it can imagine the nut to be open, even though at this moment it remains closed. In addition, the symbol "action?" serves as a query marker for the (so far unknown) action that would accomplish the desired physical transformation.

If the animal can succeed in formulating its problem along the above lines, its basic analogical tools can be brought into play. Physical similarity of elements may be sufficient for the present problem to cue the animal's prior experience in opening nuts. It will then be straightforward to establish the mappings:

nut-2 ↔ nut-1

closed-2 ↔ closed-1

open-2 ↔ open-1

self ↔ self.

Furthermore, the animal may be able to detect that its present goal of opening nut-2 is relationally similar to breaking open nut-1, so that

make-open-2 ↔ break-open-1.

Now the animal can make some inferences by analogical substitution. By trying to complete the mapping of make-open-2 to break-open-1, matching corresponding slot fillers, the chimpanzee finds that

action? ↔ strike-1.

Its final step is to construct a specific description of "action?" using the established correspondences. By performing copying with substitution, the basic device for generating analogical inferences, the animal should now be able to formulate a much more specific description of its problem—how to break the nut by striking it with something:

strike (self, nut-2, object?) *name*: strike-2.

At this point the animal has a new question: what can be used to strike the nut? Given that all other slots have been mapped from strike-2 to strike-1, consistency requires that

object? ↔ rock-1.

If the chimpanzee had not noticed already, this should be enough to allow simple attribute mapping to find a filler for the query marker "object?" namely

rock-2 ↔ rock-1.

The last gap has now been filled. The original query marker, "action?" has been replaced by a plan for action:

strike (self, nut-2, rock-2) *name*: strike-2.

This may seem like a lot of mental work just to figure out that a rock can be used to crack a nut now, just as on another day some other rock was used to crack some other nut. However, the "just" reflects our own proficiency in such routine tasks. If this kind of problem keeps recurring, and the animal has some basic learning ability, the plan for a solution may eventually be recast as a direct rule, something like "If I want to break open a nut, strike it with a handy rock." But the situation is quite different for an animal at the dawn of problem solving or a child first learning about its world or for any of us when faced with a novel problem for which we have no prestored recipe for reaching the goal. Analogy provides a way to fill the gaps in a novel problem by mapping it to a past experience involving similar objects and relations.

Given our earlier discussion of the actual evidence about their mapping ability, have we credited our hypothetical wild chimpanzee with more mental skill than is justified? After all, our wild chimpanzee did not have Sarah's schooling, but we have assumed it could explicitly represent relations and query markers, imagine possible states, and detect R-sameness. However, in many ways our scenario is not that demanding. The only relations required are ones that express frequently used physical actions, such as those required to open nuts, that are closely tied to achieving the animal's basic goals. There is good reason to suspect that coding of causal connections based on one's own physical actions is at the evolutionary leading edge of cognitive sophistication. Coding causal relations is essential for explicit problem solving, a mental skill that surely had survival value for the primate ancestors of both humans and chimpanzees. Furthermore, the mappings that we assumed were heavily guided by similarity of objects, such as nut-1 and nut-2, as well as similarity of relations, such as break-open-1 and make-open-2. Much of the work required for mapping the source and target situations could be done by attribute rather than relational mapping.

Analogy and problem solving may well have evolved together. Sarah is certainly proficient at both analogy and problem solving. We already mentioned that analogies based on functional relations, such as the "can opener to the can," are among the problems on which she excels. It is also clear that she can perceive causal relations of considerable complexity. When shown a videotape of a human actor struggling to escape from a locked cage, Sarah would select a photograph of a key, the instrument for a solution. (At least she would if the actor was someone she liked. If she disliked the person in the videotape, she would often pick a photograph showing some "bad" outcome!) In other tests she demonstrated that she understood the roles that actions play in transforming objects. For example, she was taught actions that had opposite causal effects, such as marking versus erasing a piece of paper. She was also taught to read sequences from left to right. Then she was given sequences such as

blank paper ——————— marked paper

and the reverse,

marked paper ——————— blank paper,

along with three alternative instruments, including pencil and eraser. After preliminary training, she could reliably choose the correct instrument that would effect each change (i.e., pencil in the first example, eraser in the second). This performance shows that Sarah did not simply know that blank paper, marked paper, pencils, and erasers go together in some loose, associative way. Rather, she knew what slot each state or instrument fills in the relational structure that represents a causal event sequence, in which an instrument is used to change an initial state into a final state. Sarah's ability to distinguish between causal sequences with reversed initial and end states resembles the human ability (discussed in chapter 2) to distinguish such pairs of propositions as "Hercules chases Fifi" and "Fifi chases Hercules."

Animals without language training failed even simpler versions of such tests. But notice that what Sarah was asked to do was considerably more complex than figuring out that if one rock can crack a nut, another rock might open another nut. It seems that Sarah's understanding of causal sequences, like her ability to recognize relations between relations, builds on mental skills that in simpler forms are exhibited by untutored members of her species. Present-day apes may well have the kind of mind that was once possessed by the long-vanished evolutionary ancestors of humans.

Hitting the Wall

The performances of Sarah and other similarly trained apes reveals that the basic constraints postulated by our multiconstraint theory of analogy—similarity, structure, and purpose—are already in place in the chimpanzee. Sarah is able to detect and represent similarities between objects and relations. By mapping similar relations, she can place pairs of objects in correspondence on the basis of their structural roles. For example, by mapping the relation of opening a can to the similar relation of opening a lock, Sarah can determine that a can opener is to a can what a key is to a lock, even though a can opener does not look like a key nor a can like a lock. Sarah is thus capable of relational as well as attribute mapping. Moreover, Sarah's skill in the use of analogies is matched by her proficiency in understanding causal relations and the purposes of actions. She is able to understand questions that depend on such functional relationships as that linking a desired state with a means of attaining it. The cognitive tools that the chimpanzee has available to represent queries and relations between objects appear to be sufficient to allow simple problem solving by analogy.

And yet something is still missing. Sarah was a bright chimpanzee with the benefit of the best education. She broke new intellectual ground for her species, but she never became a rocket scientist. Not only did she never discover the wave theory of sound (a small complaint—not many people have either), but she would never have been able to make the slightest sense of it. It is always a bit dangerous to draw negative conclusions from what an animal fails to do. Perhaps her training was somehow less than ideal after all, and the sheer time and effort required obviously made it impossible to attempt teaching her everything. But it is clear that at some point the chimpanzee "hits the wall" and can follow the path of human intelligence no further.

One striking failure that Sarah exhibited in her understanding of causal relations is instructive. She was shown a videotape in which a human actor discovers a small fire of paper burning on the floor; he looks concerned as if he wishes to put the fire out. Sarah was then shown three alternatives (matches, knife, clay) and trained to associate a token with the likely cause of the fire (matches). In addition, she was shown three other alternatives (water, tape, eraser) and trained to associate another token with the instrument that could provide a solution to the actor's problem (water). After being trained to make the appropriate choices, Sarah was tested on her ability to use the tokens appropriately on tests with other problems. For example, suppose she saw videotape of a scene in which a person is concerned because a piece of paper has been cut. Would Sarah associate the cause token with knife, and the solution token with tape? Premack reports that the answer is "no." Thus even though Sarah can clearly understand what is the specific cause of a specific outcome (burning paper or cut paper), she seems unable to acquire the more abstract concept of cause itself, abstracted from any specific causal scenario.

It is certainly not surprising that chimpanzees are incapable of full human intelligence. To begin with, the gross neurological differences between chimpanzees and humans are massive. The human brain is over three times larger in volume than that of the chimpanzee. Most of the increased size of the human brain involves the cerebral hemispheres, the site of advanced cognitive functioning; and the greatest changes of all involve the frontal lobes that lie just behind our brows. Clearly, these changes point toward some major advances in cognitive capacity. Furthermore, chimpanzees are considerably weaker than human children at a number of tasks involving representations. For example, although chimpanzees can be taught to match pictures of objects to the objects themselves, they find this task very difficult. In the course of learning, they are prone to match pictures with pictures and objects to objects, regardless of their content. Thus when shown a banana as the sample and forced to choose between a picture of a banana and an actual shoe, the animal is likely to pick the shoe. Interestingly, similar errors are made by severely retarded children.

Earlier we sketched a general strategy for deepening the abstraction of thinking by generating new concepts that explicitly represent the common basis for certain analogical correspondences. O-sameness, we argued, was a concept that explicitly represents the basis for attribute mappings that depend on physical similarity. Armed with this relation, an animal like Sarah can now map pairs of objects in which the two items are O-same as each other. We suggested that this process of progressive abstraction could be extended. What should the next intellectual move be? To follow our strategy, the animal (either altered by evolution or guided by its own learning capability) should now use its new mappings to aid it in forming new concepts that explicitly represent the basis for the mappings.

What would this mean? For Sarah, it would mean forming explicit concepts of R-sameness and R-difference to express the basis for her relational mappings. These concepts are higher-order relations between relations and hence would allow Sarah to move from relational to system mappings. We can illustrate an analogy requiring system mapping by further generalizing the match-to-sample task. Sarah can solve problems in which the sample is a single object or a pair of objects; now let us consider a version based on a sample of four objects, such as the problem in figure 3.9. Which of the two alternatives would you choose as the best match? There is no real right answer, but there is a deeper answer. Notice that both alternatives involve entirely different objects than the sample. The first alternative (the left one in figure 3.9) also involves different relations than the sample: in the sample, both pairs are O-same

sample

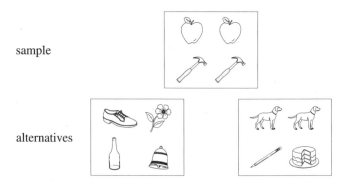

alternatives

Figure 3.9
A match-to-sample problem based on quadruples of objects, which can only be solved by system mapping.

as each other, whereas in the first alternative both pairs are O-different. In the second alternative, the top pair is O-same, but the bottom pair is O-different. The second alternative thus has more overlap with the sample at the level of first-order relations than does the first.

However, as is illustrated in figure 3.10, only the first alternative is truly isomorphic to the sample. If we represent the explicit concept of R-sameness, we can see that the two O-different relations in this alternative are R-same as each other, just as the two O-same relations in the sample are R-same as each other. That is, an implicit reaction to R^2-*sameness,* the higher-order sameness of relations between relations, supports consistently mapping the relation of R-same in the sample to R-different in the alternative. This system mapping provides a basis for choosing the first alternative as the better match to the sample.

We conjecture that Sarah would be unable to appreciate the deeper match in the quadruple version of the match-to-sample task, because chimpanzees are unable to form mappings at the system level. If this conjecture is correct, chimpanzees will have other related cognitive limitations. For example, an animal capable of system mapping might be able to represent the fact that the relations of marking with a pencil and erasing with an eraser are R-different in a special way: the slot fillers for the initial and final states are reversed. That is, given

mark (pencil, blank-paper, marked-paper) *name*: mark-1

erase (eraser, marked-paper, blank-paper) *name*: erase-1,

the mappings are

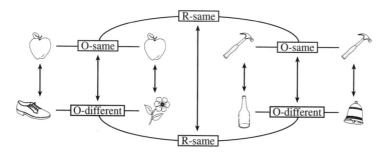

Figure 3.10
The mapping between the sample and the first alternative in figure 3.9, which share only the higher-order relation of R-sameness.

mark ↔ erase

pencil ↔ eraser

blank-paper ↔ marked-paper

marked-paper ↔ blank-paper.

Let us call this special kind of R-difference between mark-1 and erase-1 "R-reverse," since it basically is the mapping between actions that reverse each other's effect. So we have

R-reverse (mark-1, erase-1) *name*: R-reverse-1.

Notice that the relation of R-reversal depends on finding a mapping between two triples of slots, where the slot fillers cannot be mapped on the basis of element similarity (note that blank paper maps to marked paper rather than to blank paper, opposite to the obvious attribute mapping) nor on the basis of perceptual similarity between actions (since marking and erasing do not look that much alike). Forming an explicit concept for the higher-order relation of R-reversal thus depends on the capacity to perform a system mapping, exploiting the structural constraint of isomorphism.

Now, it happens that the relation of R-reversal is the basis for other mappings. For example, consider examples of cutting and joining:

cut (knife, whole-paper, cut-paper) *name*: cut-1

join (tape, cut-paper, whole-paper) *name*: join-1.

These two actions can also be mapped, resulting in correspondences that satisfy R-reversal, which can be summarized as

R-reverse (cut-1, join-1) *name*: R-reverse-2.

Now we have two examples of the higher-order relation R-reverse, which we might say are R^2-*same* as each other—that is, we have sameness of relations between relations. As in the system mapping required to solve the quadruple version of the match-to-sample task, we have moved another notch up the abstraction hierarchy.

Now suppose the animal not only could respond implicitly to R^2-sameness but was able to formulate an explicit concept to represent the way in which the relation between marking and erasing, reversibility of a transformation, is R^2-same as the relation between cutting and joining. Such an animal would understand the explicit concept of "reversible transformation" and could potentially use this concept to think about such issues as what properties of transformations are required for them to be reversible. Our strategy for deepening the abstraction of thought would have been repeated yet again.

As far as we can tell, neither Sarah nor any other chimpanzee could ever be this insightful. Evolution did not innately provide the chimpanzee with the concept of sameness of relations between relations; nor did it provide the learning capability that would enable an individual chimpanzee to form such concepts. A creature that was born with, or that could learn, such concepts would be able to move beyond the simple relational mappings at which Sarah excels, to perform more complex system mappings. Rather than being satisfied by having solved a problem by analogy, it might go on to ponder the basis for the analogy, internally reorganizing its knowledge in a quest for hidden regularities. In addition to seeing correspondences between known objects and relations, it might elaborate partial mappings by positing hidden causes—God in Heaven, invisible ripples of sound in the air.

Evolution did not endow the chimpanzee with these capacities. But it so favored another species that walks this earth today. Taking another leap, we arrive at ourselves.

Summary

Analogical thinking is the product of evolutionary changes in the way animals represent knowledge of relations. All vertebrates are able to respond implicitly to similarity between relations in a way that goes beyond direct similarity of objects. However, only in primates do we find clear evidence of explicit knowledge of relations. Evidence from match-to-sample tasks reveals that monkeys can perform simple attribute mapping based on explicit representations of sameness of objects. But monkeys are unable to solve similar problems that would require explicit representations of sameness of relations, rather than just sameness of objects. In contrast, chimpanzees have the capability to explicitly think about sameness of relations; however, this capability is only fully revealed after special training in the use of symbols for "same" and "different." The development of explicit knowledge of relations appears to be related not only to the use of analogy but also to the kind of deliberative thinking needed to reason about how to solve problems. Chimpanzee intelligence is nonetheless bounded in ways that suggest this species is incapable of system mapping, which is required for more abstract forms of analogical thinking. Although chimpanzees can think explicitly about first-order relations, they do not seem to be able to think explicitly about higher-order relations, such as cause. This limitation restricts their ability to use structure to guide analogical thinking and also their ability to think about the purpose of analogies.

4
The Analogical Child

Lori's Magic Carpet

A little girl named Lori, just four years old at the time she participated in a psychological experiment, made a mental leap that surpassed any analogical achievement by the apes discussed in the last chapter. The experimenter read Lori a picture-book fairy tale about a magical genie. In the story (see box 4.1), the genie decides to move his home from one bottle to another. He is faced with the problem of safely transferring a number of precious jewels to the new bottle. The genie's solution (each step of which was clearly depicted in a series of colored pictures) was to command his magic carpet to roll itself into a tube, place it so as to form a hollow bridge between the two bottles, and then roll his jewels through it.

After making sure that Lori understood the story (that she knew what a genie is, for example), the experimenter posed a problem for her to solve. Two bowls were set about three feet apart on a table. One bowl contained a number of small round balls, and the other was empty. Lori was seated beside the filled bowl. She was asked to remain seated and so could not reach the empty bowl. A variety of other objects were available on the table, including an aluminum walking cane, a large rectangular sheet of heavy paper, children's scissors, tape, paper clips, and rubber bands. Lori's task was to devise as many ways as possible, using the materials provided, of transferring the balls from the filled bowl to the empty bowl. The experimenter did not mention any connection between this problem and the fairy tale Lori had just heard.

At this point one of Lori's first reactions was to say, "Let's pretend they're real jewels" (referring to the balls). After considering a couple of the objects on the table, she looked at the sheet of paper and said, "That will be a magic carpet." She then laughed as she picked it up, rolled it,

Box 4.1   The Magic Carpet Story (from Holyoak et al., 1984)

Once upon a time there lived a magical genie. He was a very old, wise, and rich genie indeed. One day while he was polishing his home, which was actually a bottle, he decided he would like to find an even bigger and better home to live in. So he began searching far and wide for another bottle. Finally he found the perfect home. It was larger, prettier, and not too far away from his old bottle. The genie was very excited and began moving his belongings right away. But now the genie had a problem. He had a great many beautiful and very precious jewels in his old home. He had to somehow get all the jewels from his old bottle to the new bottle without dropping or losing a single jewel. After thinking a bit, the genie came up with a wonderful idea.

He searched for his magic carpet. Then he commanded it to roll itself up into a long hollow tube. Next the genie commanded his flying carpet to place one end at his new home so that it formed a sort of hollow bridge between the two bottles. Then, the genie very carefully took one jewel from inside his old home and placed it into the opening of his new carpet. At once, the jewel began tumbling and rolling through the carpet tube until it reched his new home and plopped safely inside. The genie grinned happily and began rolling all his jewels through the carpet and into his new home. In fact, I'm sure you can still find him sitting in his new, bigger, and better bottle with all his jewels and smiling contentedly even today!

and asked the experimenter to help tape it. "That's the way the genie did," she exclaimed as she rolled the ball through her newly constructed tube. "I did it just like the genie!"

Here we see a clear example of solving a problem by analogy. Because Lori was not told to use the fairy tale to solve the problem, we must credit her with spontaneously selecting the genie story as a source analog to apply to the target problem of transferring balls. Lori then explicitly makes the mappings:

balls ↔ jewels

sheet of paper ↔ magic carpet

Lori ↔ genie.

Notice that none of these mappings seem to be based on overwhelming perceptual similarities between the corresponding objects. The jewels were colored differently than the balls and, unlike the balls, were described as being of great value; the sheet of paper did not look especially like a carpet, far less a magical one; and Lori was not by any means a genie. There are resemblances of course—the balls were small and round like jewels; the sheet of paper was a broad rectangular shape, flexible enough to be rolled, as was the carpet; and Lori, like the genie, was a purposeful humanoid agent with a problem. What is remarkable is that these resemblances, unlike the hosts of differences between each mapped pair, happen to be highly relevant to Lori's purpose in applying the analogy: she, like the genie, manipulates a flexible object to form a hollow tube, through which small round objects will roll. It is the purpose for which the analogy is used that determines which similarities of perceptual attributes are important.

The two situations have more similarity at the level of first-order relations, which connect multiple objects. For example, both the jewels and the ball were to be transferred from one location to another. But the relational mappings are not entirely straightforward. For example, the genie (unlike Lori) also transferred himself from one location to another. Rolling the jewels is relationally similar to rolling the balls; but notice that Lori was not told she could roll balls—this was an inference derived from the mappings, not a basis for making the mappings in the first place.

The main guides to Lori's mappings seem to lie at the more abstract level of similarity between higher-order relations, coupled with the constraint of structural consistency. What the genie story and Lori's task have in common is a similar goal structure. The genie wants to move the jewels from one bottle to another, just as Lori wants to move the balls from one bowl to another; the genie wants to avoid dropping any jewels, just as Lori wants to avoid dropping balls. Lori appears to have achieved a system mapping, based largely on higher-order relations such as "want" that interconnect several source objects (the genie, the jewels, the carpet, the two bottles) that form consistent correspondences with the higher-order relations connecting several target objects (Lori, the balls, the paper, the two bowls).

Not only does Lori manage to find a system mapping, but she goes on to make use of it to generate a solution plan by copying with substitution. The genie rolls his magic carpet into a tube, so Lori rolls her paper similarly; the genie places the tube so that it reaches from one bottle to the other, so Lori similarly places her paper tube between the two bowls; the genie rolls his jewels through the tube to his new bottle, so Lori rolls the balls through her tube to the far bowl. Moreover, Lori actually goes beyond the analogy by adapting her solution to the unique constraints of the target problem. It is all very well for a genie to

"*higher order*" *debate.* "needs a chapter on the

command his magic carpet to roll up, but rolling a sheet of paper poses additional complications. Lori was able to select the tape as a tool to hold her paper tube together, even though the tape did not correspond to anything in the source.

From her first expression of seeing the analogy—"Let's pretend they're real jewels"—this episode of problem solving is strikingly similar to children's pretend play. When a three-year-old girl pretends to be her mother, she is likely to imitate her mother's behavior (using the mother as a source analog, with herself the target), perhaps talking like her mother on a toy telephone. Lori's solution has a similar analogical quality but is less dependent on similarities between corresponding attributes and first-order relations. Even though Lori uses the analogy in direct service of solving an explicit problem that has been set for her, she shows an element of playfulness reminiscent of Neil's insight that a tree can be seen as a bird's backyard (see chapter 1). Like most children at different ages who were observed to solve the ball problem by analogy to the genie story, Lori's verbal and other behaviors evidenced clear signs of excitement and triumph as she developed her solution. A good analogy is not only understood; it is also felt.

attributes

Toward System Mapping

Lori was one of the youngest children who participated in a series of experiments on the use of analogies to solve the ball problem, reported in 1984 by Keith Holyoak, Ellen Junn, and Dorrit Billman. If a child seemed to run out of ideas without seeing the analogy on his or her own, the experimenter would provide two progressively more specific hints: "Does anything in the story help?" and "What did the genie do, and could you do anything like that?" Lori was by no means a representative four-year-old with respect to her use of analogy, any more than Neil was. In fact, Lori was the most insightful subject to be tested in the age range of four to six years. Only about one in ten children at this young age was able to come up with the paper-rolling solution after reading the genie story, even after both hints had been given. However, the overall success rate of four- and five-year-olds went up to about 50 percent when the source story used more familiar cartoon characters, especially if the children were given two different examples of rolled-tube solutions before attempting the ball problem. (Snoopy, the dog made famous in the comic-strip "Peanuts," was portrayed rolling his blanket into a tube to transfer a bird's eggs to a new nest; Miss Piggy, of the television show *The Muppets,* was shown rolling a carpet to transfer her jewels to a safe.)

Young children were also more successful in transferring a different solution illustrated in another version of the genie story, in which the genie used his magic staff to pull the new bottle next to his old one. After hearing the magic staff story, all the young children tested produced the analogous "cane" solution (using the aluminum cane to draw the far bowl toward them so they could simply drop the balls into it). About half the children gave this solution without any hint, and the others produced it in response to the experimenter's later questions. Notice that the high perceptual similarity between the child's cane and the genie's staff (compared to the lesser similarity between the piece of paper and the magic carpet) makes the cane solution considerably less dependent on the ability to construct a system mapping using higher-order relations.

What did children actually do when they failed to notice the possibility of the analogy or were unable to use it? Often they tried other, nonanalogous solutions. Some of these were crude, such as throwing the balls (they always missed or bounced out of the bowl); some were more creative, such as using the tape dispenser as a scoop; many were overly optimistic, such as using a paper clip as a catapult. The remarks of children in the age range of four to six who failed to generate the rolled-paper solution, even after the experimenter's hints, proved especially revealing. It was not that the children had simply forgotten the story: when prompted to use the story, many children could retell it, mentioning the important elements. Rather, many children seemed simply unable to figure out how to map the story to the ball problem. One child responded to the suggestive question "Could the story help?" by retrieving two pictures that had been used to illustrate the story and using them to push the balls around. This child seems to have completely missed the possibility that the meaning of the story could be related to the ball problem, instead focusing on the story's pictures as physical objects that might serve as tools somehow. Another child repeated that Miss Piggy rolled up the carpet to make a tube but denied that he could do anything like that. Another responded to prompts by saying he could roll a blanket up but that there was no blanket on the table. The idea that something might correspond to the blanket—even though nothing really looked like a blanket—seemed to have eluded this boy.

Such reactions point to a specific problem that many of the young children appear to have had—difficulty in deriving system mappings in the absence of more direct attribute and relational similarity. Another sign of this problem is that even the successful transfer found for this age group for the "cane" solution could easily be disrupted if the mapping was made more difficult. In one experiment, some children heard the original magic staff version of the genie story, while others were told an otherwise identical version that introduced an extra character—a friend of the genie, who helped him find a new bottle. To an adult, this small change seems simply irrelevant, and it remains obvious that the genie's use of his staff to move the bottle is analogous to using the cane to move the bowl. For five- and six-year-olds, however, the change often seemed to obscure the underlying analogy so as to block transfer of the solution. Although all of the eight children who received the original magic-staff story produced the cane solution (at least after a hint), only one of five children who heard the story with an extra character was able to do so. Apparently the extra character, which added an element to the source that lacked any match in the target problem, seriously disrupted the children's ability to work out the systematic correspondences between the analogs.

It seems, then, that children from about four to six years of age are in transition as they acquire the capability to deal with system mappings. Thus we find the occasional precocious four-year-old like Lori who can cope with complex analogies that require mappings based on higher-order relations and structural correspondence, but many slightly older children who are unable to see that far "below the surface," especially when the source and target are only messy approximations to the iso-morphic ideal.

By later childhood, at age ten to twelve, the transition is complete. Translating the genie's rolling of his carpet into the child's rolling of a piece of paper is almost trivially easy. Of ten children tested, every one succeeded in generating the rolled-paper solution, although seven required a hint to use the story. The older children thus still had difficulty in selecting the analog without guidance, but working out the mapping posed no problem for them. As we will see in chapter 5, the greater difficulty of selecting superficially dissimilar source analogs than actually using them is also characteristic of adults when they solve problems. Not only did the older children easily generate the rolled-paper solution, but four of them also tried to turn the aluminum cane into a tube by removing the stoppers from its ends. No child who had not heard the magic carpet story ever attempted this solution. The older children were thus sometimes able to select the source analog on their own and were always able to map its elements and adapt the solution to fit the unique constraints of the target problem. In addition, it seems some of them were able to use the story analog and the ball problem to abstract a general principle, something like "make a tube out of some suitable material." Once they learned this schema for "tube solutions," they were able to generate other variations of such solutions, such as modifying the cane.

First Relations

The capability of finding system mappings, which begins to develop at about age five, is a major cognitive transition separating human intelligence from that of any other species. We will have more to say about this transition later in this chapter. But first we need to look at the development of the ability to find and use simpler attribute and relational mappings. These earlier transitions, which make possible the first steps in analogy use, can be traced back to infancy. When we compare the relative intelligence of various primate species at a series of different ages, beginning with the newborn, we see a striking reversal of fortune. At age six months, based on their early sensory and motor skills, the ordering of intelligence is very clear: the leader is the monkey, followed by the chimpanzee, with the human trailing behind. The monkey is born with virtually all its adult brain weight, the chimpanzee with about 60 percent, and the human with less than 30 percent. Relative to newborns of other species, the human infant has sometimes been described as a premature neonate, and the slow development of its brain forces a long period of dependence on adult caretakers.

And yet before it is even a year old, the human infant has made its move to the lead among developing primate intellects. Indeed, by the second year of life the cognitive differences between the human and other primates are so marked that the different species can scarcely be compared. For example, a two-year-old given a set of blocks of different colors, randomly intermixed, will often spontaneously pull out the blocks of a particular color, say red, setting them aside to form a cluster of same-colored blocks. Such spontaneous sorting depends on attribute mapping. Moreover, the child is not simply responding in the same way to similar objects based on reward and punishment (like the bird that learned to avoid eating monarch butterflies and their mimics). Rather, the child is exploiting the ability to do attribute mapping to restructure the world, forming clusters that "go together" simply because it is intrinsically rewarding to do so. Such sorting behavior, like virtually all of the ensuing spontaneous advances in human cognitive competence, simply never spontaneously occurs in the chimpanzee or monkey. The chimpanzee, given extraordinary training, can acquire some of the human child's skills; the monkey is far less capable. Sarah, the most schooled chimpanzee in history, has (if we ignore the gap in language ability) reached roughly the intellectual competence of a three-year-old human child. The road beyond is blocked for her: no matter how well schooled, the chimpanzee will never acquire the cognitive skills of a five-year-old child.

Even in infancy the human child is able to make inferences on the basis of perceptual similarity. Suppose an infant eleven months of age is given a novel toy that has some interesting property, such as a can that produces a wailing sound when tilted. The baby is allowed to explore the object for thirty seconds, after which it is taken away and the baby is given a second toy. The second toy looks similar to the first, but it does not produce the interesting sound. The infant is likely to spend time trying to make the second toy produce the sound (for example, tilting it one way and another as if trying to make it wail). Such reactions are far less frequent if the second toy does not look like the first one. The baby thus uses salient visual properties of objects, such as the cylindrical shape of the can, to infer specific functional properties, such as producing a wailing sound when tilted. These expectations guide the infant's actions in exploring similar-looking objects and lead to surprise if the expectations are violated. A single initial example is enough to generate very specific expectations about the links between perceptual attributes and functions of objects.

Human infants respond not only to perceptual attributes of single objects but also to basic relations between objects. As we mentioned in chapter 2, six-month-old infants are already sensitive at an implicit level to physical causal relations, such as one object's striking another and appearing to set it in motion. Over the following year of life, the capability to use explicit knowledge undergoes substantial development. By the time they approach two years of age, children are able to manipulate simple tools and use them to solve problems. With the support of perceptual similarity between objects, children can transfer similar relations—actions performed with tools—from a source to a target. Furthermore, children focus on perceptual similarities that are causally connected to the functions of tools.

Ann Brown had one- and two-year-old children solve a problem in which they had to choose a tool that would make it possible to pull a toy closer so they could reach it. Examples of the available tools are

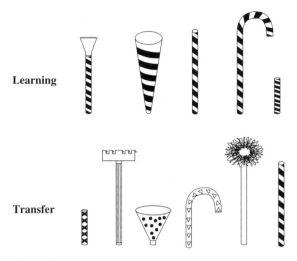

Figure 4.1
The learning and transfer tools available to children trying to reach a toy across a distance. From Brown (1989). Reprinted with the permission of Cambridge University Press.

shown at the top of figure 4.1. All the tools were painted with distinctive red and white stripes. Either on their own or with their mother's help, the children learned that one of the tools—the cane—could be used to pull the toy within reach. The children were then given a new version of the problem, in which they had to select a tool to reach the toy from a different set of alternatives, as illustrated at the bottom of figure 4.1. One of the alternatives was perceptually similar to the cane in that it was long and striped; another had the same hook shape but was too short to reach the toy. However, almost all of the children rejected both of these alternatives, instead picking the transfer tool that was long enough to reach the toy and had a head that enabled pulling (a black rake). The children thus were not misled by superficial perceptual similarities that were irrelevant to the purpose for which they intended to use the tool. Instead, their mapping was guided by just those similarities that were based on attributes that enabled the same basic action of pulling to be performed.

Early Relational Mapping

Although even infants can detect some relational similarities, and two-year-olds can transfer identical relations from one problem to another when the corresponding objects have relevant perceptual similarities, this does not mean that full relational mapping has been achieved. More sophisticated analogical reasoning requires the capacity to view the source analog both as itself and as a possible model of the target analog. This duality of the source involves an insight that is not generally available to children until about age three. Judy DeLoache performed an intriguing series of studies in which children had to find a hidden toy based on information provided by a scale model. The physical layout used in the experiments is shown in figure 4.2. The experimenter would take a child into the smaller room, where the child would watch while a toy dog, Little Snoopy, was hidden behind a piece of furniture in the scale model, such as the miniature couch. Then the child was asked to find a larger Big Snoopy, which had been hidden in "the same place" in the larger room. This task requires mapping identical spatial relations between objects, where corresponding objects are identical except for a size transformation. Three-year-old children made few errors on this task; the child would promptly go to the full-size couch in the larger room and retrieve Big Snoopy. In contrast, children just a few months younger—aged two years, six months—almost always failed. They did not search systematically in the larger room, appearing to be unaware that seeing where Little Snoopy was hidden in the model provided any clue as to where Big Snoopy might be. It was not that they had forgotten what they had seen, as they could easily go back to the smaller room and retrieve Little Snoopy. It was simply that they failed to appreciate that the scale model was really an analog for the larger room. Not only could the younger children not find a hidden object, but in another experiment they were unable to imitate the experimenter by hiding Big Snoopy in "the same place" in the larger room as they had observed Little Snoopy hiding in the model. The same dramatic differences between the performance of the two age groups were observed when the child saw Big Snoopy hidden in the larger room and then had to search for Little Snoopy in the model.

Another similar study provided even more compelling evidence that the difficulty of the younger children is tied to the dual status of the source analog. In this experiment, some of the children were first convinced that the experimenter had a machine that could expand (or shrink) objects. (The children first saw a puppet go into the experimenter's machine,. which was then closed so the puppet was hidden; after lights on the machine had blinked for a moment, it was opened to reveal that the puppet had changed in size. Of course, the experimenter had secretly switched the original puppet for one that was identical

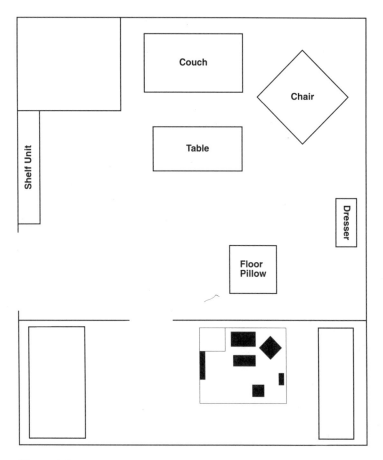

Figure 4.2
Layout of the two rooms used in studies of children's understanding of scale models. The large room is at the top, with labeled items of furniture. The scale model is at the bottom; darkened areas in the scale model correspond to the items of furniture in the large room. Room dimensions were 4.80 m × 3.98 m × 2.54 m. Model dimensions were 71.1 cm × 64.8 cm × 33.0 cm. From DeLoache (1989). Reprinted by permission.

except for its size.) The children were then shown Snoopy being hidden in a small model of a space. This entire model was then placed in the "size-transforming" machine, and the children saw a much bigger version of the space emerge when the machine was opened. The children were then asked to locate Snoopy in this larger space.

Notice that this task is just like the usual one in which an object was hidden in a small model and then had to be located in an analogous but larger space. However, there is a crucial difference: the children in the "size-transformation" condition were led to think that the small and large spaces were actually the *same* places rather than one's being a model of the other. Sure enough, even the two-and-a-half-year-olds were able to find the hidden Snoopy when they thought the small and large spaces were one and the same, except for the size having changed. So we can be sure the children did not have any simple problem with spatial perception or memory. Rather, the young children had difficulty only when they had to think of the source in two distinct ways: both as itself and as an analog of a separate target.

Notice that a scale model is a toy in its own right, and children are interested in where Little Snoopy is hiding within the model. Perhaps the very richness of the three-dimensional model interferes with children's ability to see it as something else—an analog of the larger room. If so, DeLoache reasoned, the younger children might actually perform better if the information about the hiding place was provided by two-dimensional photographs of the larger room, rather than by a scale model. Children at age two and a half years already appreciate that photographs are interesting not for what they are (stiff pieces of colored paper) but because of what they represent (real, three-dimensional objects). In another experiment, the experimenter pointed to a location in a photograph and told the child that Big Snoopy "is hiding there." Now the younger children were highly accurate in finding the hidden toy.

It therefore seems that young children are capable of transferring spatial knowledge from a source to a target. They can readily do so when the source is a photograph, in which case even children under three years of age can map identical spatial relations from small objects to otherwise identical large objects. They can also transfer spatial knowledge when they think a single object has simply undergone a change in size. The problem for children at this age is that they fail to appreciate that a scale model—an interesting object in its own right—can also represent something else. Insight into the dual status of source analogs, at least for spatial models, appears to emerge quite abruptly at about age three.

Spini: abstracts from word proportion

DeLoache's task does not require true relational mapping, since the corresponding objects in the room and the scale model are perceptually similar. However, other evidence suggests that relational mapping emerges around age three or four. One example came about when a father was reading a book about stringed instruments to his oldest son, three-year-old Daniel, who was extremely interested in music. The book described the violin family, consisting of the violin, viola, cello, and bass, all of which Daniel knew well. His father remarked that the violin family has four members, just like Daniel's family, and then asked him who in his family was the "bass." Daniel immediately said "Daddy" and also identified Mommy as the cello. At first Daniel thought he was the violin, but then he quickly realized that his younger brother Adam was the violin, leaving himself to be the viola. This episode shows that a three-year-old can use a common relation, here "bigger than," to map objects that lack similar perceptual attributes.

Experimental work has revealed that by about age four children begin to be able to solve simple relational analogy problems of the sort at which the chimpanzee Sarah has also succeeded (see chapter 3). In some experiments children of various ages have been presented with analogy problems using pictures like those illustrated in figure 4.3. Here the analogy requires mapping the causal relation of "produced by cutting" across perceptually different objects. The child was shown pictures of a loaf of bread (A) and a slice of bread (B), followed by a whole lemon (C). The child was then asked to select the best picture to replace the question mark on the space for the fourth picture. The analogical completion was a slice of lemon (D). The other pictures were distractors, including a slice of cake representing the appropriate causal transformation (cutting) applied to the wrong object (E), two squeezed lemon halves representing the wrong causal transformation (squeezing) applied to the correct object (F), a yellow balloon that looked similar to a lemon (G), and a lemon identical to the C picture (H). The experimenter would give the child feedback after each trial. The child was told which answer was correct and why: "Look, over here you have a loaf of bread, and that matches a slice of bread that has been cut off. So when I put down a lemon over here, you know you need a slice of lemon that has been cut off." The experimenter's explanations thus focused attention on the identical relation that held between both the A and B terms and the C and D terms of the analogy problem.

Three-year-old children are generally correct only at about a chance level in selecting the analogical completions for problems like that illus-

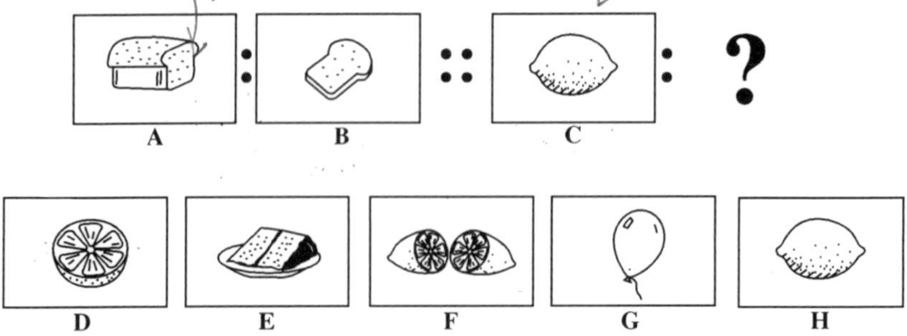

Figure 4.3
Example of an analogy problem used with young children. When shown a loaf of bread and a slice of bread, and a lemon, the correct analogical completion is the slice of lemon. The other pictures are distractors. From Goswami and Brown (1989). Reprinted by permission.

trated in figure 4.3, in which only the relation and not the mapped objects is similar. However, four-year-olds perform well above chance, and six-year-olds almost always select the completion based on relational similarity. As the proportion of analogical responses increases across this age range, the tendency to select an alternative based on direct similarity to the C object correspondingly decreases. Other studies have shown that the majority of four-year-olds can also reliably select the analogical completion based on other familiar relations, such as "lives in" (e.g., "bird is to nest as dog is to kennel"), avoiding such associated but nonanalogical distractors as "bone." These results indicate that by the age of four, children are able to perform relational mapping even when the corresponding objects are dissimilar.

Given a modest amount of instruction and a supporting context, preschool children can learn general schemas and strategies from experience with analogies. Ann Brown and Mary Jo Kane found evidence that even three-year-olds, with guidance from a teacher, can use analogies and learn from them. Children were told a series of stories about animals, accompanied by pictures. Each story presented a problem concerning animal defense mechanisms, accompanied by information about animal habitats, their appearance, their food-gathering habits, and so on. Much of this information was actually irrelevant to solving the problem. Children received six story problems, divided into three pairs. Two stories involved animals (the hawkmoth caterpillar or the crested rat) that defended themselves from a predator by mimicking a more dangerous animal. In two other stories, an animal (the arctic fox or the chameleon) camouflaged itself by a color change, and in the third pair an animal (the walkingstick insect or the pipefish) camouflaged itself by a shape change. The crucial information about the animal's strange markings, or its ability to change color or shape, was always embedded in irrelevant information, and the connection to defense was not explicitly mentioned in the story. For each problem the question to the child involved how the animal could avoid being eaten, for example, "How could the hawkmoth caterpillar stop the big bird that wants to eat him?" (Answer: "Look like a snake.")

Brown and Kane used a training procedure in which the children attempted the problems one at a time. Whenever they failed to give the appropriate answer, the children were guided to the solution by the experimenter. The two problems in a pair were given in succession. The crucial transfer test was the second problem in the third pair. Brown and Kane found that about 75 percent of the children succeeded in solving this problem after receiving the five earlier stories, as compared to only about 10 percent of children who did not receive the first two problem pairs. It is important to note that all the children received the first story in the final pair, so all of them had at least one source analog available. However, strong transfer required more extensive prior experience with the first two pairs of stories. These results reveal that very young children can be led to focus on relational structure and to extract common relational patterns or schemas from multiple analogs.

The ability to map similar relations even though the related objects are dissimilar manifests itself in less sober activities than solving problems. As Koestler emphasized in his discussion of bisociative thinking, humor often depends on the juxtaposition of incongruent interpretations of events. We saw in chapter 1 how analogy can play a role in making a cartoon seem funny. A similar basis for a joke is the possibility of making a conceptual slip by confusing corresponding elements in an underlying analogy. Michael Waldmann gave children ranging from four to eight years of age a series of jokes and collected various measures of how humorous the children found the jokes to be. An example of a joke he used is "Otto and his mother get caught in a thunderstorm. Suddenly there is lightning. He says, 'Look, Mom, we've been photographed.'" For an adult, the humor depends on appreciating Otto's apparent confusion of lightning with a camera flash. That is, instead of simply mapping lightning to a camera flash because of the similar relation they are involved in (illuminating an object), Otto actually thinks the lightning *was* a camera flash. Of course, children might laugh at the joke without

Important difference with Gosmani, as well as higher order relations

seeing its analogical basis, simply because "being photographed" is incongruous in the context. To control for this possibility, Waldmann also presented incongruous "clunkers" that lacked any analogical basis, such as "Otto and his mother get caught in a thunderstorm. Suddenly there is lightning. He says, 'Look, Mom, we've been painted.'" Notice that the two versions are identical except for the last word.

The results were very clear. Children at all ages, including the four-year-olds, found the real jokes funnier than the matched clunkers. They rated the real jokes as funnier and were more likely to laugh or smile at them. However, the younger children were far less able than the older children to explain why the jokes were funny. Also, the younger children were slower to laugh at the real jokes than were the older children (even though time to laugh at the clunkers was roughly constant across the age groups). Waldmann's results suggest that four-year-olds spontaneously notice incongruities based on relational mappings. What develops later is greater processing speed and more explicit understanding of the mapping process itself.

knowledge plays a role here

Personification

clear difference. How would x cope with this?

So what about new learning

The analogies of young children reveal the way in which familiarity of source analogs guide their selection and use. Perhaps the earliest domain that children actively use as a source analog to help understand the world is based on their familarity with themselves and other people. Dedre Gentner asked four-year-olds as well as older children and adults where various body parts would be if they existed on inanimate objects, such as trees or mountains. Even the four-year-olds performed well on this task. When asked "If a tree had a knee, where would it be?" some of the young subjects looked down at their own legs before answering. They seemed to be explicitly mapping spatial relations between their own body parts onto the target analog.

Personification—the use of knowledge of people as a source for understanding where a knee would be on a tree, why a tree might be a bird's backyard, how God can be conceived as a father in Heaven or death as the mother of beauty—may well be the most powerful analogical tool in the mental repertoire of children. The developmental psychologist Jean Piaget was the first to systematically study and describe the characteristics of what he called "childhood animism." He found, for example, that a six-year-old might explain that the sun was hot because it wants to keep people warm, attributing humanlike intentions

Animism → not something we grow out of?

to inanimate objects. Although Piaget's interpretations of his findings have been questioned, the phenomena he described are certainly real. More recent research has clarified when and how children use knowledge of people as the source analog for analogical inference about targets that are not human. It turns out that their uses are actually quite systematic, in ways that support our multiconstraint theory of analogy.

It is certainly not the case that children indiscriminately treat all objects—humans, animals, and inanimate objects—as if they were like people. Even three-year-olds know that a person, a cat, and a doll have eyes, but a stone does not; and that a person and a cat can walk on their own, but neither a doll nor a stone can. Thus children are not blindly animistic. If they have the opportunity to observe whether or not an object has a certain property, they certainly use that information. Rather, children (and adults) tend to rely on the source analog of a person when they do not already know the facts about the target analog and when the target is viewed as similar to a person in ways that are relevant to the question. Susan Carey taught children of various ages and adults that people have a previously unknown internal organ and then asked them to predict whether various other animals, plants, and inanimate objects would also have this kind of organ. For four- and six-year-olds the unfamiliar organ was a spleen; for ten-year-olds and adults the new organ was the even more obscure omentum, which we mentioned in chapter 2. Given the bare fact that people have a spleen (or omentum), to what other sorts of things would the organ be attributed? For all age groups the percentage of "yes" responses declined across the animals as their similarity to people went down (people, mammals, birds, bugs, worms). The four-year-olds sometimes claimed that nonanimals (flowers, the sun, clouds, vehicles, and tools) also would have a spleen, whereas the older groups almost never extended the organ to objects that were not animals. In general, Carey found that four-year-olds were most heavily influenced by the analogy to a person, with more sophisticated knowledge about biological categories playing an increasingly large role for older children and adults. Her findings indicate that analogical transfer is triggered when the target is not yet well understood (which is most likely the case for young children) and is constrained by the similarity of the source and target analogs.

Carey found that people provide an especially potent source analog for young children. For an adult, a dog is an excellent example of a mammal, at least as good as a person is. But for four-year-olds, a person is the example par excellence of animals in general. In one experiment

Carey asked children and adults if aardvarks, an unfamiliar type of animal, have a spleen (or omentum), after being told that either people or dogs have one. For four-year-olds, the frequency of attributing a spleen to aardvarks was 76 percent if the source analog was people, but only 29 percent if the source was dogs. By age six and thereafter, dogs and people proved about equally effective as source analogs. Carey also found a large asymmetry in transfer for four-year-olds: if they were taught that people have a spleen, 71 percent agreed that dogs have a spleen too; but if they were taught that dogs have a spleen, only 18 percent agreed that people have a spleen too. This asymmetry was weaker for six-year-olds and was not found for the older groups.

It appears, then, that the youngest children relied most heavily on the familiar source analog of a person to guide their analogical transfer to other animals. Presumably young children know about their own internal organs (both from being told and from having direct sensations, such as hearing their heart beat and stomach growl) and generally assume (usually correctly) that other animals have the same sorts of organs as people do. Accordingly, four-year-olds have great confidence that some new organ that people have inside them will, like hearts and stomachs, also be found in other animals that resemble people in important ways. As children acquire more knowledge about biology, they become more willing to accept other good examples, such as dogs, as source analogs to make predictions about other animals. Although knowledge about people is especially likely to be used as a source analog by children, the more general principle is that any especially familiar domain is favored as a source. For example, Kayoko Inagaki found that Japanese children who kept pet goldfish were more likely than children who did not to use knowledge about goldfish to make inferences about frogs.

Children's use of their knowedge of people as a source analog also reveals their sensitivity to a basic constraint that guides the evaluation of analogical inferences—checking inferences against what is already known about the target. The purpose of the analogy is generally to make plausible conjectures about unknown aspects of the target. If the person analog suggests an inference that is known to be false or highly suspect, the analogy will be rejected. Notice that Carey's questions were about an unknown internal organ, which could not be observed. Because the youngest children had no independent way to assess the likelihood that aardvarks have spleens, for example, they were very likely to rely on the person analogy in making their judgments. Kayoko Inagaki and Giyoo

Hatano asked Japanese kindergarten children various questions about how a person, a rabbit, or a tulip would react in novel situations, such as being given too much water day after day, or being in danger of being struck by a car. They found that the children often made incorrect personifications about unobservable properties, such as mental states, claiming, for example, that a tulip would feel pain. But they almost never made errors about observable properties; they would not say, for example, that the tulip would run away from an oncoming car or call out for help.

In general, then, inferences triggered by analogy to people tend to be accepted only when the target is perceived as similar to a person (thus human properties are more likely to be extended to a rabbit than to a tulip) and the target property cannot clearly be rejected on the basis of other knowledge or direct observation (thus humanlike mental states are more likely to be overextended to other objects than is humanlike overt behavior). Children use their knowledge of people not only to make inferences about other animals but also to try to understand those aspects of human existence that are beyond their experience. A young child is likely to view death as a kind of sleep and hence potentially reversible. Because of this inference based on the analogy with living people, the child might interpret the hushed silence at a funeral as the result of concern not to wake the dead person, who is simply resting.

It is striking that the child's conception of death as sleep has much in common with the prevalent religious beliefs of adults regarding the afterlife and hope of resurrection. Because such beliefs concern unobservable states of being and are not clearly incompatible with other beliefs the person may have (such as knowledge based on science), they often straddle the gray boundary between understanding of reality and metaphorical appreciation. Indeed, some adults believe (much as children do) that plants have mental states. In one study, for example, about 15 percent of adults (presumably somewhat lacking in biological knowledge) agreed that a tree can feel happy. Even adults who have acquired firm knowledge of the biological limits on attributions of mental states will still use the person analogy to point out relational correspondences. The ocean, for example, might be described as a living thing with the moods of a person. Such a claim would not mean that the adult believes the ocean is really alive, any more than a four-year-old believes that a tree really has a knee. Drawing analogies to people is a basis both for inferences about facts about the world and for metaphorical understanding that goes beyond our conventional adult categories.

The Next Steps

It is now clear that the basic components of analogical thinking are already present in preschool children. The highly sophisticated analogical skills of three- and four-year-olds have important implications for our understanding of how children think about the world. Some psychologists, faced with clear evidence that such young and unschooled children already seem to have very general conceptions about how the world operates, often without apparent direct experience, have assumed that much of this knowledge is simply innate. For example, one extreme view is that children have innate ideas about how living things differ from inanimate objects (for example, that growth is inevitable for living things). There is no way at present to rule out the possibility of such specific innate knowledge, but we can certainly point to an alternative: the three-year-old child already knows a great deal about what it is like to be a person and is equipped with a general ability to form plausible conjectures by analogy. When this analogical capacity is applied using knowledge of people as the source analog, the child will be able to make mental leaps to answer novel questions about other living things, such as "Could we keep a tulip the same size forever by not giving it water?"

Given the well-established analogical skills of four-year-olds, what is left to develop in later childhood? What are the next steps toward becoming an analogical adult? Part of the answer, of course, is simply the gradual accumulation of additional knowledge. New knowledge provides the potential for finding new source analogs, which can be applied to appropriate targets to extend the range of potential analogical inferences. Increased knowledge also helps in evaluating the plausibility of analogical inferences. However, it seems that development of analogical thinking involves more than simple accretion of knowledge. As we suggested earlier in this chapter, a more qualitative change seems to occur beginning at about age five: the ability to form system mappings. The impressive range of demonstrations of analogical transfer prior to that age invariably depend on finding mappings based on similar or identical relations, such as "produced by cutting," even though the elements that are related may differ. To transcend this dependence on relational similarity the child must be able to map on the basis of similarity of relations between relations, using the isomorphism principle to place elements into correspondence.

The development of system mapping appears to go hand in hand with the development of the capacity to think explicitly about higher-order relations. By about age five, children begin to be able to make analogical inferences that seem to depend on explicit knowledge about such higher-order relations as "cause." As is generally the case, the leading edge of analogical development involves the use of highly familiar source domains, such as knowledge of people. Here, for example, is how a five-year-old Japanese girl explained why flowers need just the right amount of water: "Flowers are like people. If flowers eat nothing [that is, are not watered], they will fall down of hunger. If they eat too much [are watered too often], they will be taken ill."

At a slightly later age, children become able to use system mapping reliably to solve more arbitrary analogy problems with less familiar types of content. An important limitation of typical analogy problems as tests of system mapping is that their very form involves mapping only two slot fillers at a time: in a problem of the form A:B::C:D, A:B is the source (two slot fillers) and C:D is the target (two slot fillers), and the solution depends on the mappings

$A \leftrightarrow C$

$B \leftrightarrow D.$

In general, the only possible basis for establishing these mappings is the similarity of a relation between A and B to that between C and D. For example, given the analogy

loaf of bread:slice of bread::lemon:slice of lemon,

(which four-year-olds can often solve), the mapping is based on the relation of "produced by cutting" that links both the source and the target pair. A system mapping is not required.

It is possible, however, to construct analogy problems in the proportional format for which system mapping can play a role in the solution. A proportional analogy will involve higher-order relations when each term is itself based on a set of interrelated parts. Consider the solved geometric analogy depicted in figure 4.4. How would you describe the relationship between the A and B terms? Both shapes have several components and could be described in a variety of ways, with the number of psychological elements varying depending on how the components are grouped into chunks. One natural description would be that the A term consists of a pattern (pattern$_A$) made up of the six small components, surrounded by a square border (border$_A$). Similarly, the B term consists of pattern$_B$, which is O-same as pattern$_A$ and border$_B$, which is a circle rather than a square. The source A:B could then be

It's the difference that counts

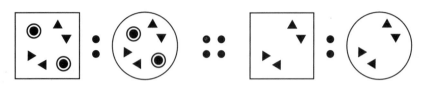

Figure 4.4
A geometric analogy in which the border on a pattern is changed. Adapted from Goswani (1989). Adapted by permission.

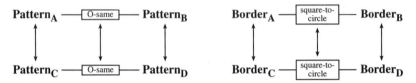

Figure 4.5
The mapping between the A:B and C:D parts of the analogy problem shown in figure 4.4.

described as changing the border from square to circle, keeping the pattern the same. This description when applied to the C term will generate the D term to complete the analogy. Figure 4.5 depicts the basis for the mapping. Each analog is based on two relations rather than only one, and both relations must be mapped between the source and the target. This problem is thus more complex than the simpler relational mappings in which only a single relation must be mapped. However, notice that the two relations could be mapped separately on the basis of semantic similarity (O-same to O-same, circle-to-square to circle-to-square) without necessarily processing both relations at once or representing a higher-order relation between them. Thus this analogy problem does not demand a full-blown system mapping.

Now consider the analogy problem in figure 4.6. Like that in figure 4.4, the source A:B could be described in many different ways. One natural way is to view each term as a distinct pattern, each with two parts, the white and the black sections. The source might then be characterized by the description, "change the circle into a rectangle, keeping the proportion of the pattern that is black constant." As figure 4.7 indicates, this problem is complex because the source and target involve different proportions (one-half and one-quarter, respectively), so that semantic similarity of first-order relations is not enough to determine the appropriate mapping. Rather, the mapping depends on representing

Goswani's claim:

re higher order

the fact that the proportion of A that is black (one-half) is R-same as the proportion of B that is black, just as the proportion of C that is black (one-quarter) is R-same as the proportion of D that is black. In other words, what is the "same" in the source and the target is neither the particular patterns nor the particular proportion relations; rather, it is the higher-order relation of "sameness of proportions." Thus the analogy problem in figure 4.6 requires not only mapping multiple relations (as does the problem in figure 4.4) but doing so on the basis of a higher-order relation. The problem in figure 4.6 thus appears to have the complexity of a system mapping.

If children are usually not capable of performing a true system mapping until age five or six, we would expect four-year-old children to perform very poorly with problems like that illustrated in figure 4.6. This indeed seems to be the case. In one experiment only 27 percent of four-year-olds were reliably correct more often than the chance level. In the same study only 37 percent of four-year-olds scored above the chance level on the simpler type of problem shown in figure 4.4 (which also involves mapping multiple relations). In contrast, by age six 88

Figure 4.6
A geometric analogy in which one pattern is changed into another, holding constant the relative size of two parts of each pattern. Adapted from Goswani (1989). Adapted by permission.

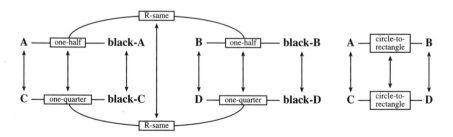

Figure 4.7
The mapping between the A:B and C:D parts of the analogy problem shown in figure 4.6.

percent of children scored above chance on both types of problems. Like the developmental pattern observed in children's ability to generate the "rolling" solution to the ball problem that we discussed earlier, these changes in performance on geometric analogy problems support the claim that system mapping is an important development that occurs in middle childhood.

More generally, as Dedre Gentner and Graeme Halford have argued, it appears that the development of analogical thinking is closely tied to a series of relational shifts as children become sensitive to increasingly abstract relations. In accord with the progression of abstraction we described in chapters 2 and 3, children are first able to react implicitly to similarity of objects (infancy), later to similarities based on explicit attributes (about age one), then to similarities based on first-order relations (about age three), and later still to similarities based on higher-order relations (about age five). Gentner attributes these shifts to increases in children's knowledge, whereas Halford proposes that the shifts are fundamentally maturational, linked to increases in the capacity of working memory. It seems very likely that both of these views are correct: maturation of cognitive capacities enables the child to form more abstract representations of knowledge, which in turn allows the child to acquire new forms of knowledge. As we foreshadowed in chapter 3, the shift to higher-order relations and system mapping is especially significant, because this is the step at which human analogical thinking definitively advances beyond the capacity of any other species.

Dedre Gentner and Cecile Toupin performed an experiment that illustrates ways in which analogical reasoning changes during childhood, as well as ways in which it stays the same. These investigators presented two groups of children, aged four to six and eight to ten, with simple stories. An example of a story would be one in which a cat was friends with a walrus, who in turn played with a seagull. The cat was reckless and got into danger, at which point the seagull saved it. Some children received unsystematic versions much like the above, in which the various actions were not clearly related to one another. Other children received systematic versions that included simple motives and other causal relations. In our example, the systematic version included the information that the cat was jealous because the walrus played with the seagull, so the cat got angry, which is why it was reckless. In the end, because the seagull saved the cat, the two became friends.

After the child had acted out a story using some props to represent the characters, the experimenter asked the child to act out the same story

— get this research

Table 4.1
Mapping Conditions for a Story Used by Gentner and Toupin (1986)

Source/Target	Similar objects/ similar roles	Dissimilar objects	Similar objects/ dissimilar roles
dog	cat	camel	seagull
seal	walrus	lion	cat
penguin	seagull	giraffe	walrus

with different characters. Gentner and Toupin varied the similarity of the characters who played parallel roles. As the example in table 4.1 indicates, similar characters might play similar roles (for example, dog mapping to cat), all characters could be dissimilar (dog mapping to camel), or similar characters could play dissimilar roles (dog mapping to seagull instead of to cat). In terms of our multiconstraint theory, the latter "cross-mapped" condition created a conflict between similarity based on the attributes of individual objects and that based on the structural constraints imposed by the relations. Because identical relations were to be transferred from the source to the target, acting out the second story could always be accomplished using relational mapping. However, if attribute mapping was also used, "similar characters in similar roles" would make the task easier. And if the children were able also to perform system mapping using higher-order relations, then the systematic stories would be easier than the unsystematic ones.

In fact, Gentner and Toupin found that performance at both age levels declined from the condition with similar characters in similar roles to that with dissimilar characters and to the cross-mapped version in which similar characters played dissimilar roles. For the older children, providing the higher-order relations in the systematic version improved performance, especially for the cross-mapped condition, suggesting that the children were also capable of system mapping. The younger children, however, did not seem to be helped as much by higher-order relations.

Gentner and Toupin's results provide further evidence that children's ability to perform system mappings develops during middle childhood. Importantly, however, their results also indicate that the simpler bases for mapping, including similarity of the attributes of objects, continue to be used as well. As these investigators argued, the propensity to focus on relations, rather than the objects being related, may increase with age. Indeed, as Halford has argued, the very capacity to think about higher-order relations may develop as the child matures. But this overall

relational shift should not obscure the fact that the analogical child—indeed, the analogical infant—continues to be a part of the analogical adult. As we will see, adults have the potential for creative mental leaps that break the bonds of simple similarity, yet they also continue to be guided—and sometimes beguiled—by surface resemblances.

Summary

Analogical thinking increases dramatically in sophistication during the preschool years, and the multiconstraint theory explains the nature of the fundamental transitions that children undergo. Based on implicit reactions to perceptual similarity, infants use analogy to form expectations about what novel objects may do. By eighteen months of age, children are capable of attribute mapping. They focus on those attribute similarities that are tied to the purpose of the analogy and can use analogy to select similar objects to solve problems. Relational mapping begins to develop around age three. At this age, children explicitly understand that one domain can be taken as a model for another, and their use of analogy is sensitive to similarity of relations as well as of attributes. By age four, children can solve proportional analogy problems of the standard A:B::C:D form as long as the problems are based on a familiar relation (for example, a physical transformation, such as cutting) that holds both between A and B and between C and D. At the same age, children can appreciate humor based on analogical mappings. Analogies with people, based on a highly familiar source analog, are spontaneously used to make inferences about a wide range of unfamiliar situations. Use of analogies to people is constrained by similarity of the source and target analogs, as well as by other knowledge that can be used to evaluate the plausibility of analogical inferences.

Beginning at around age five, children make the further transition to system mapping. At this age they begin to reason explicitly about higher-order relations, such as cause. They become able to transfer solutions across problems with similar goal structures even in the absence of similar first-order relations and objects as long as they are told to consider the source analog when trying to solve the target problem. By about age six, children can solve complex proportional analogy problems based on relatively unfamiliar content, finding mappings on the basis of similar higher-order relations. With the achievement of system mapping, human analogical thinking surpasses that of any other species in terms of its capacity to transcend perceptual similarity.

5

The Construction of Similarity

Making Saddam into Hitler

As we suggested in chapter 1, our conception of the world is in large part a matter of our own creation. By now it should be apparent how analogy helps to build understanding, molding the way the person thinks about the target analog into a pattern taken from the source analog. As the parts of the two situations are aligned in accord with the constraints that govern the use of analogy, and information is copied from one to the other, further similarities between the two are actually created. The result is that the target is increasingly seen as another example of "the same kind of thing" as the source is understood to be. But the resulting sameness is much more complex than the direct perceptual or semantic similarity that comprises an immediate constraint on analogizing, because the constraints of structure and purpose have also affected the judgment of how similar the source and target are. The construction of full similarity depends on all of the basic steps in using analogies: selecting a source analog, mapping the source to the target, evaluating the analogical inferences to assess whether they need to be adapted (or rejected altogether), and learning something more general using the source and target as examples. And the basic constraints on the use of analogy—direct similarity, structure, and purpose—guide each of these steps.

The power of analogy to create similarities makes it a tool for many purposes—for solving problems, constructing explanations, and creating evocative metaphors. It also makes it a tool for argument and persuasion. When coupled with mass communication, analogy can be used as an instrument of propaganda, even as an incitement to war. A striking historical example of the role of analogy in shaping public opinion, which illustrates how similarity can be constructed, was provided by the Persian Gulf conflict of 1990–91. In August of 1990, Saddam Hussein (known simply as Saddam to friend and foe alike) sent an invading army from Iraq to occupy the neighboring country of Kuwait. Saddam claimed, without justification by international law, that all of Kuwait— rich in oil and virtually defenseless—was actually a lost province of Iraq. His army then proceeded to loot Kuwait and terrorize its people. For the United States and its allies, the invasion of Kuwait created an unanticipated crisis. The loss of access to Kuwaiti oil was a serious concern; but worse, it was feared that Saddam could move on to gain control of neighboring Saudi Arabia and the other small states of the Persian Gulf region, countries that were the primary sources of oil for the industrialized countries of North America, Europe, and Asia. At the same time, armed intervention to stop Saddam presented many military and political hazards.

When the crisis began in the summer of 1990, the entire situation was poorly understood, with many conflicting elements that generated considerable uncertainty in most Americans (including policy makers). Most Americans had previously been only dimly aware that Kuwait existed; they were now told that it was not a democracy but had oil that America needed. They knew little about Saddam but might have remembered that the United States had recently supported him in a war between Iraq and Iran. People understood that Iraq might be threatening Saudi Arabia; but they also learned that Saudi Arabia (like Kuwait) was an absolute monarchy and an Islamic society in which women were not allowed to drive automobiles—not at all the picture of a kindred democracy sharing American values. Such confusing beliefs either did not support any clear policy decision or provided support for conflicting policies.

Shortly after the invasion of Kuwait, President George Bush launched a vigorous campaign to generate domestic and international support for military intervention to free Kuwait. His argument focused on an explicit comparison of Saddam to Adolf Hitler, and of the Persian Gulf crisis to events that had led to World War II a half century earlier. The World War II analogy, which was widely discussed in the media, helped to impose coherence on people's understanding of the Gulf situation. A commonsensical mental representation of World War II, the source analog, amounted to a story figuring a villain, Hitler; misguided appeasers, such as Neville Chamberlain; and clear-sighted heroes, such as Winston Churchill and Franklin Delano Roosevelt. The countries involved in World War II included the villains, Germany and Japan; the victims, such as Austria, Czechoslovakia, and Poland; and the heroic defenders, notably Britain and the United States. By drawing the analogy between Saddam and Hitler, President Bush encouraged a reasoning process that led to the construction of a coherent system of roles for the players in the Gulf situation. The popular understanding of World War II provided the source, and analogical mapping imposed a set of roles on the target Gulf situation by selectively emphasizing the most salient relational parallels between the two situations. Once the analogical correspondences were established (with Iraq identified as an expansionist dictatorship like Germany, Kuwait as its first victim, Saudi Arabia as the next potential victim, and the United States as the main defender of the Gulf states), the clear analogical inference was that both self-interest and moral considerations required immediate military intervention by the United States. Aspects of the Persian Gulf situation that did not map well to World War II, such as the lack of democracy in Kuwait, were pushed to the background as the analogy took hold. President Bush was able to convince most of the American public, as well as members of Congress and leaders of other Western nations, that the World War II analogy was sound. As a consequence, he was able to put together a multinational coalition to repel the Iraqis from Kuwait. After a massive military buildup in Saudi Arabia, in January and February of 1991 the allied forces bombed Iraq and drove its army from Kuwait.

During the first two days of the counterattack against Iraq in January 1991, Barbara Spellman and Keith Holyoak asked a group of undergraduates at the University of California, Los Angeles, a few questions to find out how they interpreted the analogy between the Persian Gulf situation and World War II. The two situations were by no means completely isomorphic; in fact, the analogy was messy and ambiguous. Similarity at the object level favored mapping the United States of 1991 to the United States of World War II, simply because it was the same country, which would in turn support mapping Bush to Roosevelt. On the other hand, the United States did not go to war until it was bombed by Japan, well after Hitler had marched through much of Europe. One might therefore argue that the United States of 1991 mapped to Britain of World War II, and that Bush mapped to Winston Churchill (because Bush, like Churchill, led his nation and Western allies in early opposition to aggression). However, other relational similarities supported mappings to the United States and Roosevelt; for example, the United States was the major supplier of arms and equipment for the Allies, a role parallel to that played by the United States in the Persian Gulf situation. These conflicting pressures made the mappings ambiguous.

Leaders and countries in both analogs found themselves in a complex web of relations; for example, Churchill was not simply the leader of Britain, but also the person who inspired the British people, led the drive for the country's military buildup, and so on. It follows that the pressure to maintain structural consistency—a central component of our multiconstraint theory—implies that people who mapped the United States to Britain should also tend to map Bush to Churchill; whereas those who mapped the United States to the United States should instead map Bush to Roosevelt. Notice that this is not a logical requirement—a person might think the United States should map to itself, but Bush should map to Churchill, because each was the dominant leader of the war effort. For that matter, nothing prevented people from giving both mappings as answers. However, the multiconstraint theory predicts that people should prefer one-to-one mappings—Bush to either Churchill or Roosevelt, but not to both—and mappings that maximize structural consistency, by keeping leaders and countries together.

At the same time, the multiconstraint theory allows the possibility of mappings that violate the one-to-one constraint when enough evidence favors multiple mappings. For example, several European nations (Austria, Czechoslovakia, and Poland) were targets of German aggression prior to the outbreak of World War II, and Kuwait might be mapped to more than one of them. Similarly, Saudi Arabia played a role somewhat similar to that played by Britain in World War II (staging area for the counterattack, target of missile attacks) and also somewhat similar to that played by France (under threat from Germany at the time Britain responded to the invasion of Poland).

The undergraduates were asked to suppose that Saddam Hussein was analogous to Adolf Hitler. They were then asked to write down, regardless of whether they thought the analogy was appropriate, the most natural match in the World War II situation for Iraq, the United States, Kuwait, Saudi Arabia, and George Bush. For those students who gave evidence that they knew the basic facts about World War II, the majority produced mappings that fell into one of two patterns, as depicted in figure 5.1. Those students who mapped the United States to itself also mapped Bush to Roosevelt; these same students also tended to map Saudi Arabia to Britain. Other students, in contrast, mapped the United States to Britain and Bush to Churchill, which in turn (by the one-to-one constraint) forced Saudi Arabia to map to some country other than Britain (usually France). The mapping for Kuwait (which did not depend on the choice of mappings for Bush, the United States, or Saudi Arabia)

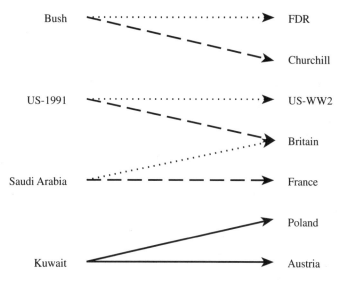

Figure 5.1
A bistable mapping: If Bush is FDR (Franklin Delano Roosevelt), then the US-1991 (United States during the Persian Gulf War) is the US-WW2 (United States during World War II) and Saudi Arabia is Great Britain (*dotted lines*); if Bush is Churchill, then the US-1991 is Great Britain and Saudi Arabia is France (*dashed lines*). In either case, Kuwait maps to Poland and/or Austria (*solid lines*). From Spellman and Holyoak (1992). Copyright (1992) by the American Psychological Association. Reprinted by permission.

was usually to one or two of the early victims of Germany in World War II, usually Austria or Poland (or to a grouping, such as "countries Hitler took over").

The analogy between the Persian Gulf situation and World War II thus generated a "bistable" mapping: people tended to provide mappings based on either of two coherent but mutually incompatible sets of correspondences. Spellman and Holyoak went on to perform a second study, using a different group of undergraduates, to show that people's preferred mappings could be pushed around by manipulating their knowledge of the source analog, World War II. Because many undergraduates were lacking in knowledge about the major participants and events in World War II, it proved possible to guide them to one or the other mapping pattern by having them first read a slightly biased summary of events in World War II. The various summaries were all historically correct, in the sense of providing only information taken directly from history books, but each contained slightly different information and emphasized different points. Each summary began with an identical passage about Hitler's acquisition of Austria, Czechoslovakia, and Poland, and the efforts by Britain and France to stop him. The versions then diverged. Some versions went on to emphasize the personal role of Churchill and the national role of Britain; other versions placed greater emphasis on what Roosevelt and the United States did to further the war effort. After reading one of these summaries of World War II, the undergraduates were asked the same mapping questions as had been used in the previous study. The same bistable mapping patterns emerged as before, but this time the summaries influenced which of the two coherent patterns of responses students tended to give. People who read a Churchill version tended to map Bush to Churchill and the United States to Britain, whereas those who read a Roosevelt version tended to map Bush to Roosevelt and the United States to the United States. Even summaries that had been written to support a crossed mapping (for example, making Churchill the most important leader but the United States the most important country) tended instead to produce one of the two patterns in which the mapping kept the leader and his country together. It appears that even when an analogy is messy and ambiguous, the constraints on analogical coherence produce predictable interpretations of how the source and target fit together.

These results suggest one way in which analogies can be used to systematically influence people's inferences—the source can itself be massaged to encourage a desired mapping. This strategy is often employed when an analogy is being used to win an argument or teach new information. For example, a lawyer may be selective in describing a precedent case so as to foster a desired mapping to the case being appealed; a teacher may review an earlier example so as to highlight correspondences with new material being introduced. People do not always make mental leaps by analogy on their own; more often the leaps are initiated and guided by someone else.

The use of World War II as a source analog did not begin with the Persian Gulf War. Four decades earlier, President Harry Truman discussed how the events leading up to World War II influenced his decision to send American forces into Korea: "This was not the first occasion when the strong had attacked the weak. I recalled some earlier instances: Manchuria, Ethiopia, Austria. I remembered how each time the democracies failed to act it had encouraged the aggressors to keep going ahead. Communism was acting in Korea just as Hitler, Mussolini, and the Japanese had acted. . . ." The World War II analog, whenever it is raised, is presented as an argument for military intervention. After a long-drawn-out military intervention in Vietnam in the 1960s and early 1970s ended in a humiliating defeat for the United States, a very different source analog entered American discourse on foreign policy. In many subsequent arguments about foreign crises, the Vietnam analog provided an argument for a hands-off policy.

As we will discuss further in chapter 6, the World War II and Vietnam analogs afford prime examples of how analogical thinking can be dominated by source analogs that are highly familiar. In the late twentieth century, these two source analogs provoked debate in relation to every international crisis for which military intervention by the United States was considered. In 1981, social psychologist Thomas Gilovich reported an experimental demonstration that even superficial similarities between political situations could selectively evoke one of the two then-dominant source analogs and thereby influence foreign-policy recommendations. He gave students in a political science course (dealing with conflicts from World War I on) a description of a hypothetical crisis. The crisis involved a threatened attack by a large totalitarian country, A (see the map in figure 5.2), against a small democratic country, B. The subjects were asked to select an option for the United States to follow ranging from extreme appeasement of country A to direct military intervention.

Two versions of the crisis were constructed, which were intended to cue either the World War II or the Vietnam analogy. The World War II version referred to the impending invasion as a "blitzkrieg," whereas the Vietnam version referred to it as a "quickstrike." The World War II version described how minority refugees were fleeing from country A in boxcars of trains to country C (intended to be reminiscent of the transport of minorities in Nazi Germany). In contrast, the Vietnam version indicated that minority refugees were fleeing from country A in small boats that sailed up the "Gulf of C" (intended to make the geography depicted in figure 5.2 more similar to that of the Indochina peninsula).

These differing cues are ones that most people would think have no relevance to deciding how the United States ought to react to the crisis. After all, why should it matter whether refugees are fleeing in boxcars or in small boats? Nonetheless, when they first read the crisis description, the students who received the World War II version made more interventionist recommendations than did those who received the Vietnam version. It appears that the details influenced which source

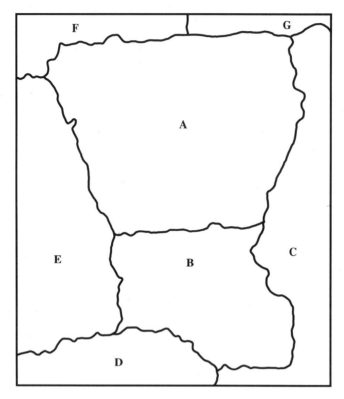

Figure 5.2
Map of the "crisis area". From Gilovich (1981). Copyright (1981) by the American
Psychological Association. Reprinted by permission.

analog was initially activated in memory and selected for comparison to
the target crisis. The selection stage, which governs which analogy will
be drawn, will be open to such biases whenever salient similarities
irrelevant to the purpose of the analogy guide memory retrieval. In
contrast, when Gilovich asked the students (at the end of the experiment)
to rate how similar the crisis was to World War II and to Vietnam, these
details had no influence on their ratings. When both analogs were being
considered together, the students appeared able to focus on the underlying causal relations.

    In 1990, the World War II and Vietnam analogs squared off against
each other as rival precedents for understanding the Persian Gulf crisis.
Proponents of the Vietnam analog pointed out that Iraq had a formidable

army, Kuwait was inhospitable and unfamiliar terrain for American soldiers, and some countries might support Iraq. This was the familiar Vietnam recipe for quagmire and defeat. The arguments from the Vietnam analog were countered in part by casting doubt on these claimed similarities between Vietnam and Iraq. The capability of the Iraqi military was questionable; the Kuwaiti desert was a harder place to hide in than the Vietnamese jungles; and it was unclear that Iraq had any friends willing to come to its aid. In the war of analogies Vietnam was the loser, and World War II prevailed. Given the quick attainment of American military objectives that ensued—the greatest triumph in Bush's presidency—the Vietnam analogy looked even worse in hindsight.

In an ironic twist to history, President Bush's analogy between Saddam and Hitler proved even more potent than he probably intended. Saddam had already committed acts of genocide against Iraqi minorities before the Persian Gulf War; he killed with greater fury in the aftermath of his defeat in Kuwait. Evidence mounted that he had been secretly attempting to build an atomic bomb as well as lesser instruments of mass destruction. Why, some then asked, had President Bush stopped the war before removing Saddam from power? That was no way to treat a Hitler. Revelations followed that the United States had continued to provide weaponry to Iraq even after its war with Iran had ended (while Bush had been vice president) and that the Iraqis had actually made use of American weapons in capturing Kuwait. The analogy between Bush and Churchill weakened. George W. Ball (a knowledgeable commentator, who three decades earlier had provided insightful analyses of analogies to the Vietnam situation, as we will discuss in chapter 6) made these observations in August of 1992, just three months before the next American presidential election:

If Hussein is a second Hitler, the President, in pursuing the war, might well have followed the lesson learned by the Allies in 1945. Not only should the Iraqi forces have been expelled from Kuwait, but their fighting power should have been destroyed and Iraq occupied. Their criminal government should have been deposed, its adherents purged from major positions in public and private life and its leaders tried as war criminals.

By the fall of 1992 the glory of Bush's victory over Saddam had been tarnished; meanwhile, the festering domestic problems of the United States had captured the voters' attention. Bush lost the election that November.

The Tumor and the Fortress

The fact that people can impose coherent interpretations on messy, ambiguous analogies like that between World War II and the Persian Gulf situation testifies to the power of the interacting constraints that guide the use of analogy. (It also illustrates the influence of analogy on politics, about which we will have more to say in chapter 6.) However, although political analogies can be complex, they are by no means the deepest analogies ordinary people are capable of understanding and using. The analogy between World War II and the Persian Gulf situation is founded on some initial similarities at every level of abstraction: the abhorrent personal qualities of Hitler and Saddam (level of attribute mapping); similar relations between countries, such as "invading" (level of relational mapping); and similar higher-order relations, such as "preemptive intervention" (level of system mapping). More abstract analogies span very different domains of knowledge, linking systems of objects on the basis of similar higher-order relations and structural consistency, despite lack of salient similarities between either mapped objects or first-order relations. In chapter 8 we will describe examples of system-level analogies that have provided the basis for creative scientific discoveries.

First, however, we will examine the strengths and weaknesses that ordinary intelligent adults, such as college students, display when they have an opportunity to solve a problem using a cross-domain analogy. You can begin by testing your own ability. Read the problem in box 5.1. In this "tumor problem," a doctor has to figure out how to use rays to destroy a stomach tumor without injuring the patient in the process.

Box 5.1   The Tumor Problem (from Gick and Holyoak, 1980)

Suppose you are a doctor faced with a patient who has a malignant tumor in his stomach. It is impossible to operate on the patient, but unless the tumor is destroyed the patient will die. There is a kind of ray that can be used to destroy the tumor. If the rays reach the tumor all at once at a sufficiently high intensity, the tumor will be destroyed. Unfortunately, at this intensity the healthy tissue that the rays pass through on the way to the tumor will also be destroyed. At lower intensities the rays are harmless to healthy tissue, but they will not affect the tumor either. What type of procedure might be used to destroy the tumor with the rays and at the same time avoid destroying the healthy tissue?

Box 5.2   The Fortress Story (from Gick and Holyoak, 1980)

A small country fell under the iron rule of a dictator. The dictator ruled the country from a strong fortress. The fortress was situated in the middle of the country, surrounded by farms and villages. Many roads radiated outward from the fortress like spokes on a wheel. A great general arose who raised a large army at the border and vowed to capture the fortress and free the country of the dictator. The general knew that if his entire army could attack the fortress at once it could be captured. His troops were poised at the head of one of the roads leading to the fortress, ready to attack. However, a spy brought the general a disturbing report. The ruthless dictator had planted mines on each of the roads. The mines were set so that small bodies of men could pass over them safely, since the dictator needed to be able to move troops and workers to and from the fortress. However, any large force would detonate the mines. Not only would this blow up the road and render it impassable, but the dictator would destroy many villages in retaliation. A full-scale direct attack on the fortress therefore appeared impossible.

The general, however, was undaunted. He divided his army up into small groups and dispatched each group to the head of a different road. When all was ready he gave the signal, and each group charged down a different road. All of the small groups passed safely over the mines, and the army then attacked the fortress in full strength. In this way, the general was able to capture the fortress and overthrow the dictator.

Most people find it hard to think of a satisfying solution. The crux of the problem is that it seems that the rays will have the same effect on the healthy tissue as on the tumor—high intensity will destroy both, low intensity neither. How can the rays be made to impact selectively on the tumor while sparing the surrounding tissue? Some people consider sending the rays down the esophagus, an open passage to the tumor. However, since the esophagus is not straight, this possibility does not seem practical. Few people are able to think of a solution that might actually work.

Now consider the "fortress story" in box 5.2. On the surface this story would seem to have nothing to do with treating cancer. A general is trying to capture a fortress controlled by a dictator and needs to get his army to the fortress at full strength. Since the entire army can not pass safely along any single road, the general sends his men in small groups down several roads simultaneously. Arriving at the same time, the groups join up and capture the fortress.

Can you use the fortress story as a source analog to help solve the radiation problem? Many people are able to use the analogy to generate a convergence solution to the tumor problem, one that parallels the general's military strategy: instead of using a single high-intensity ray, the doctor could administer several low-intensity rays at once from different directions. In that way each ray would be at low intensity along its path and hence harmless to the healthy tissue, but the effects of the rays would combine to achieve the effect of a high-intensity ray at their focal point, the site of the tumor.

When Mary Gick and Keith Holyoak asked college students to solve the tumor problem, only about 10 percent of them produced the convergence solution in the absence of a prior analogy. In contrast, about 75 percent succeeded when they first read the fortress story and were told to make use of it in solving the tumor problem. Some of the students were asked to talk out loud as they solved the problem, and a few of them explicitly mentioned the analogical mappings: "Like in the first problem, the impenetrable fortress, the guy had put bombs all around, and the bombs could be compared to the destruction of healthy tissue. And so they had to, they couldn't go en masse through one road, they had to split up so as not to destroy the healthy tissue. Because if there's only a little bit of ray it doesn't damage the tissue, but it's focused on the same spot." One of the students even thought of another analog he had come across prior to the experiment: "I remembered reading an ad at one time on one. Some company has really expensive lightbulbs, and when the filament breaks inside it's really expensive to replace the lightbulb, so what they do is take lasers from all different angles and, like shooting through they don't disturb the glass but when they concentrate they fuse the filament."

The analogy between the fortress story and the tumor problem is quite complex and abstract. The major mappings between objects, such as

fortress ↔ tumor

army ↔ rays

general ↔ doctor,

connect objects with little or no similarity based on their attributes. There are some similar first-order relations, especially those describing the spatial relations (the fortress is in the center of the country, the tumor is in the interior of the body). However, the major similarities between the two analogs involve higher-order relations that describe the goals

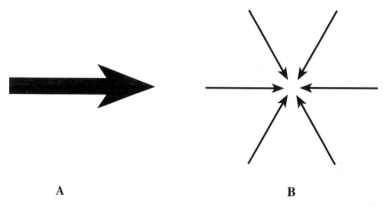

A   **B**

Figure 5.3
A visual analog of the tumor problem. The single large arrow (*A*) can be mapped
to a single high-intensity ray; the multiple converging arrows (*B*) can be mapped
to multiple converging low-intensity rays. From Gick and Holyoak (1983). Reprinted by permission.

and constraints in the two situations—causal connections, such as providing a reason, being a desire, or preventing or enabling an action. The
analogy is thus primarily at the system level of abstraction, the level that
allows older children and adults to think explicitly about relations based
on goals and causal relations. In addition to simply being abstract, the
analogy is also incomplete. For example, the multiple roads leading to
the fortress have no counterpart in the tumor problem (at least until the
analogy itself leads people to invent the possibility of sending rays along
more than one path). Also, in the fortress problem the entire army would
be endangered if it were sent along one road, whereas sending high-
intensity rays along one path would not make the rays "blow up"—it is
the patient who would suffer, not the rays. And of course, the tumor
problem is initially incomplete, because it lacks a solution. But adults
generally cope with these difficulties quite well, finding the appropriate
mappings between dissimilar objects and generating the analogous convergence solution.

The source analog need not be presented verbally. If people first
study the diagram in figure 5.3 and then are told to use it to help solve
the radiation problem, about 70 percent are able to generate the convergence solution. They can see the large arrow as a visual representation
of the single large force and the smaller converging arrows as a representation of the way in which the flawed procedure (apply a single strong
ray) can be made to work (apply multiple converging weak rays). As we

will see in chapter 8, visual analogies have often contributed to scientific creativity.

Some people even suggest sensible adaptations of the analogous solution. People sometimes suggest using multiple ray machines to generate several low-intensity rays, thus adapting the convergence solution to the unique constraints of the target problem. Experiments with the tumor problem have certainly demonstrated that a remote analog can be the source of a creative solution to a new problem in a very different domain.

But before people can use a remote analog, they have to be able to find one. And it is the stage of selecting a source analog, especially by retrieving it from memory, that is often the hurdle that blocks the process. Consider what happens, for example, when college students first read a series of three stories in the guise of a test of story understanding. After reading each story, the students are asked to recall it from memory. One of these stories (the second in the series) is the fortress story; the other two are similar in style but are not analogous. When they are done with the story tasks, the students are given a short break for about five minutes and then begin the second part of the experiment. Their next task, it turns out, is to solve the tumor problem. However, the students are not told anything about the story task's being relevant to solving the tumor problem. Will they spontaneously notice the analogy with the fortress story? For most people, the answer is "no." Typically, only about 20 percent of college students will produce the convergence solution without a hint to use the analogous story. If the same people are then given a simple hint—"you may find one of the stories you read earlier to be helpful in solving the problem"—most of them quickly come up with the analogous solution. In other words, people often fail to notice superficially dissimilar source analogs that they could readily use. They also fail to notice the relevance of the diagram in figure 5.3 if they are not specifically told to use it.

The difficulty of retrieving remote analogies is not really surprising when we think about what it involves. When a benevolent teacher points out a useful source analog, the students can focus attention directly on it and compare it to the target. But when people are trying to solve problems on their own, anything in their memory might potentially be relevant. A person's memory is an immense storehouse of information; finding a remote analog would seem much like searching for the proverbial needle in a haystack. Not only that, but the target problem is likely to cue other information of more obvious relevance. People trying to solve the tumor problem are likely to try to remember what they know about cancer treatment, rather than about military strategy. It is perfectly sensible, of course, to search for knowledge directly related to the problem at hand. But the cost of searching close at hand is that remote analogs may easily be missed.

Finding a source analog in memory requires finding some semantic connection between the target and the analog. As we saw in chapter 2, memory is organized so that concepts similar in meaning are linked. Even relatively remote source analogs can have semantic links to the target if the representations of each contain similar higher-order relations, which is why some people do succeed in spontaneously accessing the fortress story when solving the tumor problem. If the source analog has additional semantic connections based on similar objects or relational connections, spontaneous access is much more common. Suppose, for example, that the lightbulb-repair scenario that one student mentioned is turned into a source story and presented to a group of college students, who then are asked to solve the radiation problem. The laser used to repair the filament is similar to the rays. Even though the rest of the lightbulb story is still quite remote from cancer treatment, about two-thirds of the students tested noticed the analogy and used it to generate the convergence solution to the tumor problem.

In an extreme demonstration of the impact on retrieval of similarity between objects, another study used as the source analog a story about a surgeon who used converging rays to treat brain cancer. Almost 90 percent of the students immediately transferred this solution to the tumor problem. Clearly, access to a source analog is strongly aided if the source and target have similar objects. Yet people can successfully map analogs (after retrieval) across a vast range of differences between objects. Whether the source is a story about a surgeon using rays to treat brain cancer or the tale of the general attacking the fortress, the vast majority of people successfully generate the convergence solution to the tumor problem once they receive a hint to use the source story.

Similarity of objects is not the only factor that influences selection of a source analog—more abstract similarities between goals and constraints are also very important. In one study, the lightbulb-repair story was modified slightly so that it was less isomorphic to the tumor problem, even though it involved the same elements as before. The sole change was in the reason given for why it was impossible to use a high-strength laser to repair the broken filament. The structurally parallel version stated that high-strength lasers would break the fragile glass surrounding the filament (analogous to the risk to the healthy tissue around the tumor). In the less parallel version, the constraint instead was simply that the lab did not have a high-strength laser. Both versions then went on to describe how multiple low-strength lasers were successfully used in lieu of a high-strength laser. Only about half as many people spontaneously generated the convergence solution to the tumor problem when the less parallel insufficient-intensity version of the lightbulb story was substituted for the original fragile-glass version. Both structural parallelism and similarity of elements appear to guide access to source analogs.

Experiments with other types of analogies besides the tumor problem and its analogs have contributed to our understanding of how people use analogy to construct similarities between situations. We will briefly consider some other important findings about the stages of selection, mapping, and adaptation, and then return to work on the tumor problem that sheds light on the final stage—learning more general schemas as a consequence of solving problems by analogy.

Selection

The selection of source analogs highlights one of the most intriguing qualities of human memory: its capacity to allow novel experiences to bring to mind relevant prior knowledge, even though objects and events in the new situation have never been directly associated with those involved in the remembered ones. For example, a person who sees the movie *West Side Story* for the first time is likely to be reminded of the play *Romeo and Juliet,* despite the displacement of the characters in the two works over centuries and continents. The two stories are analogically connected, because they systematically correspond in the relationships among their actors, actions, plans, goals, and themes. *West Side Story* and *Romeo and Juliet* involve young lovers who suffer because of the disapproval of their respective social groups, causing a false report of death, in turn leading to tragedy. It is these structural parallels between the two stories that make them analogous, rather than simply that both stories involve a pair of young lovers, a disapproval, a false report, and a tragedy.

We saw that such structural parallels can help induce people to access and use source analogs in solving problems. Work on story reminding confirms the importance of structure, as well as similarity of concepts, in selecting analogs from memory. In addition, story reminding illustrates how the competitive nature of memory retrieval influences selection of analogs. Charles Wharton and his colleagues performed a series of experiments in which college students tried to find connections between stories that overlapped in various ways in terms of the actors and actions in each story (levels of attribute and relational mapping) and the underlying themes (level of system mapping). In one such experiment, the students first studied about a dozen target stories presented in the guise of a study of story understanding. After a brief delay, the students read another list of stories and were asked to write down any story or stories from the first session of which they were reminded.

Each cue story could be related to an earlier story at the relational level, the system level, both, or neither. For example, consider the "target," "near-cue," and "far-cue" stories in the left column of box 5.3. All these stories are examples of a theme often called "sour grapes," after one of Aesop's fables that we mentioned in chapter 1. In each story the protagonist tries to achieve a goal, fails, and then retroactively decides the goal had not really been desirable after all. The three stories in the right column are closely matched to those in the left column in terms of characters and actions but are organized so as to represent a distinctly different theme, which might be called "self-doubt"—the failure to achieve a goal leads the protagonist to doubt his or her own ability or merit. Because such themes depend on higher-order causal relations, stories with similar themes can potentially be mapped on the basis of shared patterns of higher-order relations. But whereas the target and the near cue involve similar objects and first-order relations (people trying to get a job), the target and the far cue involve dissimilar objects and first-order relations (a person trying to get a job versus a king trying to suppress a war). Half of the cues that any single person saw were far analogs (same themes, dissimilar actions) or far disanalogs (different themes, dissimilar actions) with respect to the previously studied target stories. The other half of the cues were near analogs (same themes, similar actions) or disanalogs (different themes, similar actions) with respect to the previously studied targets. Near analogs thus mapped at both the relational and system level, whereas far analogs mapped only at the system level; near disanalogs mapped at the relational level but not the system level, and far disanalogs did not have clear mappings at any level.

Besides varying the relation between the cue and target stories, the experiment also varied the number of target stories that were in some way related to a single cue. Cues in the "singleton" condition were each

Box 5.3 Examples of Target Stories and Near and Far Cues for Two Different Themes (from Wharton, 1993)

Theme 1: "Sour Grapes"

Target: John was very confident about himself. He did a lot of homework in order to get good marks. John had only a B+ GPA in his first year in high school. He was sure he could do better. Earlier, a counselor had arranged for him to meet with the recruiter from Yale. When he got home from class, he opened the thin rejection letter from Yale. Later, that night he had mentioned to his father how he believed that people from Ivy League schools were pretentious.

Near cue: Lisa spent long hours trying to make her corporation successful. She was very sure about herself. Lisa had broken up with her fiancé a year ago. She wanted to meet someone new. A coworker set her up to go out with someone he knew well. She waited at the fancy restaurant until 8:30 and then left without ordering dinner. She told her friend that she thought that her date probably wasn't that handsome and that investment bankers are really boring, anyway.

Far cue: Elle was a unicorn who wanted to see what was on the other side of the river. She thought the lands over there were enchanted and rich with meadows and fruit trees. One day she set out to cross the river. Unfortunately, the water was very fast and too deep. Elle swam as hard as she could but after twenty minutes she had to turn back because of fatigue. Elle decided that the stories about the land on the other side of the river were just false rumors and that there was probably nothing of worth over there.

Theme 2: "Self-Doubt"

Target: Derrick had failed to make the gymnastics team last fall. He practiced a lot in order to make the team. He wanted to try again. Derrick was positive he had a lot of potential. His PE teacher had gotten him a try out with the gymnastics team coach. The gymnastics team coach watched him perform and then told his PE teacher that he didn't want him on the team. Derrick confessed to his teacher that the coach undoubtedly thought he, Derrick, didn't have the talent for gymnastics.

Near cue: Jennifer worked hard attempting to create a new business venture. She had divorced her husband some time before. She wanted to start socializing again. A friend fixed a blind date for her with one of his friends, Henry, from work. Jennifer was very excited. She waited alone at the entrance of the museum for two hours. She confessed to her friend that her date thought she wasn't that attractive and that software engineers aren't interesting.

Far cue: Elle was a unicorn who wanted to see what was on the other side of the river. She thought the lands over there were enchanted and rich with meadows and fruit trees. One day she set out to cross the river. Unfortunately, the water was very fast and too deep. Elle swam as hard as she could but after twenty minutes she had to turn back, exhausted. Elle decided that she wasn't worthy of being in the magic lands.

related to only one target story, which might be either a far or near analog, or a far or near disanalog. Cues in the "competition" condition, on the other hand, were related to two target stories. The two targets were either both far or both near, and one was an analog and the other a disanalog.

How often would each type of relationship between cue and target lead to successful reminding? If similar first-order relations are used as retrieval cues, then the near targets should be retrieved more often than far targets. If similar themes at the system level also can serve as retrieval cues, then analogs should be retrieved more often than disanalogs. The most interesting comparison is between far analogs and disanalogs. If far analogs are reported more often than far disanalogs, it means that similarity of higher-order relations, coupled with structural correspondence, is at least sometimes enough to trigger reminding.

In addition, the comparison between the singleton and competition conditions can tell us how reminding is influenced by the alternatives available in memory. In the singleton condition, only one target has any overlap with the cue. Even if that target is a disanalog (especially a near disanalog), it will be the best game in town. That is, people may tend to be reminded of the best match to the cue, even if that match is not especially good. In the competition condition, however, the same disanalog target will no longer be the best match in memory—its paired analog target will have the same similarity at the attribute and relational level and greater similarity at the system level. If human memory retrieval is fundamentally competitive, as we have reason to believe, then reminding for any target will depend not only on its own similarity to the cue but also on the similarity of any competing targets. The disanalog targets will suffer the most from competition with analog targets. This means that we would be more likely to find an advantage for the analog targets over disanalogs when these stories must compete to be retrieved.

Figure 5.4 shows the proportion of targets of each type that people accessed. In the singleton condition (left panel), we can see that analogs were not accessed reliably more often than disanalogs. However, near cues (either analogs or disanalogs) produced more remindings than far cues. This means that if a cue and target share similar first-order relations, then even a target based on a different theme is likely to be accessed when there is no better candidate in memory.

The results were quite different in the competition condition (right panel). Now both similarity of first-order relations (near versus far cues) and structural parallels at the level of themes (analogs versus disanalogs)

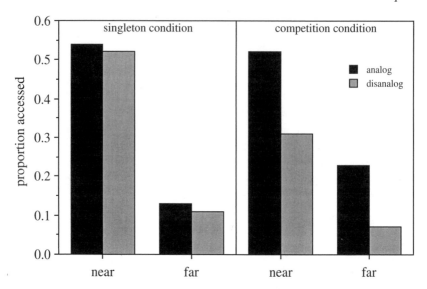

Figure 5.4
Proportion of target stories accessed in singleton condition (*left panel*) and competition condition (*right panel*) for near and far cues that were either analogous or disanalogous to the target. From Wharton (1993). Reprinted by permission.

contributed to reminding. In particular, notice that people were sometimes reminded of the far analog, reliably more often than the far disanalog. So it seems that similar higher-order relations that provide a clear underlying theme are at least sometimes enough to bridge between a cue and an analog in memory.

Although it is interesting that people can access memory on the basis of such abstract cues (most theories of memory retrieval fail to explain how this could happen), this capacity would have little practical value unless it holds up over longer delays than a few minutes. In another experiment, Wharton tested the different types of cues in a competition condition but delayed the reminding test for either five minutes, a day, or a week. Figure 5.5 shows the results. Although the overall frequency of reminding declined somewhat between the one-day and the one-week delays, the basic pattern stayed the same. The near cues produced more remindings than the far cues, and the analogs—even the far analogs—produced more remindings than the disanalogs.

These experiments, like the studies of solving the tumor problem, illustrate how the selection of analogs is controlled by the constraints of structure and similarity. The purpose of the analogy is also undoubtedly important. It is because people are interested in the underlying themes

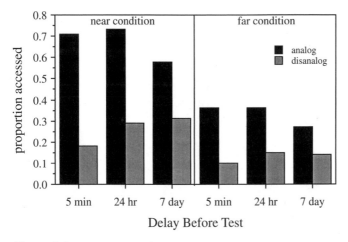

Figure 5.5
Proportion of target stories accessed in competition condition for near cues (*left panel*) and far cues (*right panel*) that were either analogous or disanalogous to the target, after three different delays. From Wharton (1993). Reprinted by permission.

of stories that they use them as retrieval cues. Probably the most important finding to emerge is that finding a remote analog in memory, although difficult, is by no means impossible. Especially when many different memories are related to a cue—the kind of situation typical of everyday experience—higher-order relations that form structured patterns can lead people to make a mental leap to a remote but deep analog. This ability is likely to be a key contributor to creative thinking.

Mapping

After a source analog has been selected—either by active retrieval from memory or by having someone point it out—mapping can guide the construction of similarities between the source and the target. Take a look at the pictures in figure 5.6, used in experiments conducted by Art Markman and Dedre Gentner. What object in the bottom picture best goes with the woman in the top picture? At first glance, especially when this single mapping is considered in isolation, people tend to say that the woman in the bottom picture goes with the woman in the top picture. This, of course, is a simple attribute mapping. But now examine the scenes more carefully. What is really going on? In the top picture, a man is bringing groceries from a truck and giving them to the woman, who

(a)

(b)

Figure 5.6
A pair of scenes in which attribute and system mappings conflict for an object. The woman in the picture is receiving food from a man, while the woman in the bottom picture is giving food away to a squirrel. Attribute mapping encourages matching the woman in the top scene to the woman in the bottom scene, but system mapping encourages matching the woman in the top scene to the squirrel in the bottom scene. From Markman and Gentner (1993). Reprinted by permission.

is thanking him. In the bottom picture, the woman is taking food from a bowl and giving it to the squirrel. Once we understand the relations, the woman in the top picture may seem to go not with the woman in the lower scene but with the squirrel. If people are asked to match not just one object but three (for example, the woman, man, and groceries in the top picture to objects in the bottom picture), they are led to build an integrated representation of the relations among the objects and of higher-order relations between relations. Consequently, people who map three objects at once are more likely to map the woman to the squirrel on the basis of their similar relational roles than are people who map the woman alone. Active mapping of multiple objects seems to encourage people to process relations, which in turn changes the apparent similarities of individual objects.

Figure 5.7 provides an even more striking illustration of how mapping can generate similarities. When people are asked to say how the A and B shapes are similar, they often say something like "they both have three fingers." Yet when asked to say how shapes B and C are similar, people are likely to say "they both have four fingers." How does B come to have both three *and* four fingers? The answer is that people are mapping the perceived parts of the objects in order to generate some of the similarities that they report. When they map B to A, the three clear prongs on B match the three prongs in A, so the ambiguous right extension of B tends to be left unmapped (because of the preference for one-to-one mappings). The ambiguous region is simply assimilated to the lower "palm" portion of B, which matches the palm portion of A. In contrast, when people map B to C, the ambiguous extension on B can map to the rightmost prong on C—and suddenly B has a fourth finger! A major similarity between B and whichever object it is compared to is actually created by analogical mapping. In fact, any time the

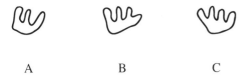

A   B   C

Figure 5.7
The *B* shape seems to have three fingers when it is mapped to *A*, but four fingers when it is mapped to *C*. From Medin, Goldstone, and Gentner (1993). Copyright (1993) by the American Psychological Association. Reprinted by permission.

representation of one situation is fleshed out by analogy with another, similarities between the two are being constructed.

Douglas Hofstadter and Melanie Mitchell have placed particular emphasis on the way in which the representations of the source and target can emerge as part of the mapping process, so that different mappings create different similarities. They have constructed a computer model called Copycat, which solves analogies based on changes in letter strings. An example is the problem, "If the string *abc* is changed into *abd,* then how could *kji* be changed in the same way?" This problem is a kind of proportional analogy in the familiar form of A:B::C:D. But since each term can be represented in terms of its internal structure (for example, the A term, *abc,* is an ascending sequence), the problems can involve mappings at multiple levels of complexity, including the system level.

These problems have no right answer as to what counts as changing the second string in "the same way" as the first. Both people and Copycat generate a range of responses, which vary in the complexity required for the underlying representations of the strings. For the "change *kji*" problem, there are different possible answers based on the levels of attribute, relational, and system mapping. At the attribute level, one could propose the completion *kjd.* This answer would follow if the change from *abc* to *abd* was simply described as "replace the rightmost letter with *d.*"

A more sophisticated response would be the completion *kjj.* This answer is based on a relational mapping: if the change from *abc* to *abd* is described as "replace the rightmost letter with its successor in the alphabet," then mapping the "successor" relation to itself suggests changing *kji* to *kjj* (since *j* is the alphabetic successor of *i*). The "same" change is now defined in terms of a relational role, rather than the identity of the substituted letter.

A yet more complex representation of the strings can suggest the completion *lji.* Suppose *abc* is viewed as an ascending sequence of three letters, whereas *kji* is represented as a descending sequence. Both ascending and descending sequences are transitive orderings, but they go in opposite directions. An isomorphic mapping can be created in which the rightmost letter in the ascending sequence (*c* in *abc*) maps to the leftmost letter in the descending sequence (*k* in *kji*), because each is the highest in its sequence. The change from *abc* to *abd* can then be described as "replace the highest letter with its successor in the alphabet." This complex system mapping supports generation of the answer *lji.* The varied answers to this deceptively simple letter-string analogy problem demonstrate how humans can interpret "sameness" at different levels of abstraction. Different mappings between concepts in turn can lead to different constructed similarities.

The research we have described so far demonstrates the impact of both structure and similarity on mapping. What about the purpose of the analogy? It is true that people seek and use analogies to achieve their goals. But we can still ask whether the purpose can actually change the mappings that people generate, rather than just the initial selection of a source or the later adaptation of a solution. One way to investigate this issue is to have people draw analogies between situations for which the mapping is ambiguous, and then see if the people's goals will alter their preferred mappings. Spellman and Holyoak performed an experiment of this sort, in which college students were asked to map the characters in two soap-opera plots. The students were told to pretend that they were writers of a successful new soap opera and that they were in court trying to prove that writers from another soap opera had stolen their ideas. Each soap opera involved the entanglements of multiple characters. In the first soap opera, set at a university, an ex-alcoholic professor named Peter was in love with his research assistant, Susan, and had cheated his brother out of his inheritance. These characters were connected by three types of relations: professional (Peter was Susan's boss), romantic (Peter was in love with Susan), and inheritance (Peter cheated his brother). The second soap opera was set in a city and involved two fairly distinct sets of characters. The lawyer set included Leslie, an ex-addict entertainment lawyer, and Mark, a young lawyer working at her firm. The doctor set included David, a prominent physician who had suffered a nervous breakdown, and Felice, his intern. Leslie and David were half-siblings and Mark and Felice were cousins. Both pairs had aging relatives ready to leave them money in a will. In one version of the story Leslie and Felice (the women) cheat David and Mark (the men), respectively, out of their shares of the inheritance, and in the other version the men cheat the women out of their shares. Thus the same three types of relations—professional, romantic, and inheritance—were also involved in the second soap opera.

To manipulate the purpose of using the analogy, the students were told that the judge in the plagiarism trial wanted them to predict what would happen in the next episode of the city soap opera. If they could figure out who would do what to whom in the episode, this would be solid proof that the writers of the city soap opera had plagiarized ideas from the university soap opera. Half the students were told that the

Table 5.1
Optimal Mappings for the Main Source Characters, Based on Goal-relevant Relation (Professional or Romantic) and Gender of Cheater (from Spellman and Holyoak, 1993)

Professional plot extension			Source characters	Romantic plot extension		
Male	Female	Role		Role	Male	Female
David	Leslie	Boss	Peter	Pursuer	Mark	Felice
Felice	Mark	Underling	Susan	Pursued	Leslie	David

crucial episode was "just like" what had happened in an episode of the university soap opera in which Peter had tried to steal credit for Susan's ideas. For these students, the professional relations between the characters were therefore most important for the plot development. The other half of the students were asked to predict an episode "just like" one in which Peter had tried to seduce Susan, in which case the romantic relations were critical. The inheritance relations did not play any direct role in either of the two episodes. After they had written extensions of the plot, all the students were directly asked to select the best match for each character in the university soap opera from among the characters of the city soap opera. Thus the experiment measured people's preferred mappings both indirectly, by which characters were used to extend the plot, and directly by the mapping task.

So, which characters in the city soap opera correspond to Peter the professor and Susan his assistant? Without taking the goal into account, the mapping is actually four-ways ambiguous, as schematized in table 5.1. The basic ambiguity is that Peter is somebody's boss, as are David and Leslie, and he pursues someone, as do Mark and Felice. But consider how the mapping would be expected to shift if people place greater weight on the relations most central in extending the plot to predict the crucial new episode. If the episode hinges on the professional relations, then Peter will seem more like David or Leslie (the bosses) than like Mark or Felice (the underlings). Suppose that we are dealing with the version of the city soap opera in which the women cheat the men out of their inheritances. If people place at least some weight on the incidental inheritance relations, the mapping of Peter to Leslie will be preferred over the mapping to David (because Leslie, like Peter, cheated someone out of an inheritance). To be consistent with this mapping for Peter, Susan would then be mapped to Mark.

Now consider the situation from the point of view of someone who had to predict the plot focusing on the romantic relations. Peter would now map best to either Mark or Felice, who shared the role of pursuer. Of these two possibilities, the mapping to Felice will be preferred if people are sensitive to the inheritance relations as well as the romantic relations. Consistency would then make Susan tend to map to David.

By seeing how the students actually mapped Peter and Susan as a pair, we can determine whether their mappings were sensitive to the students' purpose in using the analogy. Those students who gave greater emphasis to the type of relation that was important for extending the plot (either the professional or the romantic relations) would give one of the two mappings consistent with the goal-relevant relations. In addition, those students who also gave at least some weight to the inheritance relations—even though these was not relevant to the plot extension—would select a mapping in which Peter mapped to a cheater.

The left panel of figure 5.8 displays the results for the plot-extension task. The great majority of the students developed a sensible plot extension in which Peter and Susan mapped consistently to one of the two character pairs that matched on the important type of relation. Of these two possibilities, there was a weak preference for the pair that also matched on the incidental inheritance relations. The goal clearly had a strong influence on people's choice of characters.

The right panel of the figure displays the results for the explicit mapping task. This task, unlike the plot-extension task, did not actually require people to focus on the type of relation needed to write the new episode. Nonetheless, people may continue to give greater weight to whichever type of relation had been relevant to their goal. And as you can see, people preferred to map Peter and Susan on the basis of the goal-relevant relation (left two bars) rather than the opposing relation, although this preference was weaker than it had been in the plot-extension task. In addition, people tended to prefer a mapping that was consistent with the inheritance relations.

Notice that in both the plot-extension and the explicit mappings tasks, the majority of the students mapped Peter and Susan to some consistent pair of characters (that is, two people who interacted with each other), rather than splitting the mapping in some way (the "other" responses, indicated by the bar at the right of each panel). This experiment thus shows that people are sensitive to all three of the basic constraints we have been talking about—structure (making consistent

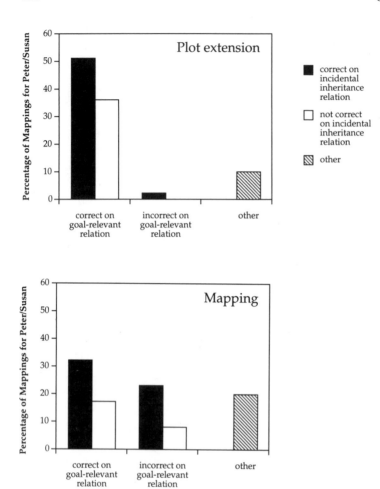

Figure 5.8
Percentages of students in the plot–extension task (*top*) and the explicit mapping task (*bottom*) who mapped Peter and Susan on the basis of the goal-relevant relation (either professional or romantic) and on the basis of the incidental inheritance relation. From Spellman and Holyoak (1993). Reprinted by permission.

mappings for the pair of characters), similarity (mapping professional relations to professional, romantic to romantic), and purpose (resolving ambiguous mappings on the basis of whichever type of relation is most relevant to the person's goal in using the analogy).

The examples we have described in this chapter, from the messy analogies between political situations to the even more ambiguous analogies between soap opera plots, reveal that people are extremely good at finding sensible mappings even when the analogs are far from isomorphic. Are any mappings really difficult for adults to work out? Problems can certainly arise when the constraints to which people are sensitive conflict with each other. For example, Brian Ross gave college students examples of probability problems, to illustrate the application of equations, and then asked them to solve a new problem. He found that the students often made errors in setting up the required equation when similar objects played different roles in the source and target analogs (for example, if the first problem involved assigning computers to offices and the second involved assigning offices to computers). These difficulties were especially remarkable because the students had the necessary formula right in front of them. This is the kind of cross-mapping situation we discussed in chapter 4, in which attribute similarity and relational similarity are pitted against one another. Adults (at least when they are novices in solving the type of problem) experience the same difficulties with cross mappings as young children do. People with greater expertise in a domain are better able to focus on deeper structural relations while ignoring more superficial types of similarity.

Mapping can also be extremely hard when people are asked to map concepts that have very different internal structures. Consider the mathematical concept of a rate, which is itself built from a relation between more basic concepts. Velocity, for example, is defined as a rate of change in distance per unit of time. Other rate concepts have an analogous structure. For example, typing rate can be defined in terms of the number of words typed each minute. In contrast, other superficially similar quantities are not usually thought of as rates. The salary a person earns in a year, or the number of potatoes harvested in a day, are usually thought of simply as amounts, rather than as rates, even though they also make reference to time intervals. Rates and amounts differ in their mathematical properties. Amounts are strictly additive. For example, if a person earns a salary of $10,000 for six months of work and $20,000 for the following six months, we would say the total salary for the year is $30,000. In contrast, adding rates is often meaningless. If a train traveled at fifteen miles per hour for half an hour and then twenty-five miles per hour for the next half hour, we could not claim that its "total speed" was forty miles per hour.

It turns out that people find it extremely difficult to map rates onto amounts, even in contexts in which it would be mathematically appropriate. Miriam Bassok taught high school students how to solve problems involving changes in velocity (i.e., acceleration). For example, if one knows the initial velocity of a train and how much its velocity increases each second, a simple equation can be used to calculate the train's final velocity after ten seconds. After the students had learned how to solve such velocity problems, they were asked to solve novel problems in other domains. These problems could potentially be mapped to the earlier velocity problems, so that an analogous equation could be transferred over. Some of the new problems also involved rates. For example, the student might have to calculate the final typing rate of a typist, given the initial typing rate and the increase in typing rate that occurred each minute the typist was warming up. The students were often successful in using the analogous velocity equation to solve such isomorphic rate problems.

They were far less successful, however, for new problems that involved amounts rather than rates. In principle, the velocity equation could also be mapped over to solve a problem in which a bank teller has an initial salary and receives a constant raise each year, and the goal is to calculate the teller's final salary after some number of years. But to make such a mapping it would be necessary to map a rate (velocity) onto an amount (salary). But because these two types of concepts have different structures (a rate is inherently a ratio, whereas an amount is a simple quantity), this mapping is extremely difficult, at least for novice problem solvers.

It is important for educators who wish to use analogies to aid in teaching to understand such limitations on human mapping ability. People are certainly capable of finding mappings between very different problem domains (such as train velocities and typing rates), but the teacher has to take into account the way in which the student thinks about the underlying concepts in each domain. If the student represents supposedly corresponding concepts in terms of radically different structures, such as rates versus amounts, analogical transfer across the domains is likely to be blocked.

Evaluation

Once two situations have been mapped and the source has been used to generate inferences about the target, one might suppose that the job is done. In fact, this is the stage at which analogies become most dangerous. If the mapping seems coherent and the inferences are not obviously implausible, then people are likely to feel that they truly understand the target domain. But there is an ever-present threat: despite what the analogy suggests, the target domain simply may not behave in a way that parallels the source domain. In other words, despite its intuitive appeal, the inferences generated by an analogy can turn out to be wrong or seriously incomplete. The essence of analogic is that if the target domain is sufficiently isomorphic to the source domain, then the mapping can be used to fill in gaps in knowledge of the target. The catch is that for complex realistic situations, the isomorphism between the source and the target domains will be approximate at best. As we have stressed in earlier chapters, the inferences generated by analogy must be evaluated, adapted to the unique requirements of the target, and possibly abandoned.

To some extent the earlier stages of analogy can prevent the generation of erroneous inferences. If a plausible source analog is selected, and if the mapping is guided by the purpose of the analogy as well as by structure and similarity, then the inferences made about the target are more likely to be accurate. But to the extent that the isomorphism between the source and the target domains is imperfect, it will be impossible for the source to provide a complete and accurate model of the target. Nonetheless, the output of the mapping stage can itself provide some guidance in evaluating the implications of differences between the source and target. Differences are of two basic types, those that are mapped and those that are unmapped. A mapped difference is based on a correspondence between nonidentical elements. In mapping Vietnam to Kuwait in order to predict whether military intervention would be feasible in the Persian Gulf War, the jungle of Vietnam might be mapped to the desert sands of Kuwait, because each is the basic terrain of its country. Once this mapping is made, one can evaluate whether the difference between jungle and desert is causally related to the prognosis for defeating the enemy by air strikes. One might then decide that although air power proved ineffective against guerrillas hiding in the Vietnamese jungle, it might well be more effective (as proved to indeed be the case) in smashing the Iraqi army as it sat exposed in the Kuwaiti desert. Other differences will be unmapped, involving elements of one analog that have no apparent parallel in the other. For example, the role of the neighboring state of Saudi Arabia, which sided with the United States in coming to the aid of Kuwait, had no obvious parallel in the Vietnam situation.

Mapped differences are more salient than unmapped differences, and mapped differences are the easiest to think of when two objects are compared. Markman and Gentner asked students to list differences between pairs of objects and found that they generated more mapped than unmapped differences. Moreover, mapped differences were identified most easily for objects that were relatively similar. For example, it is easy to think of differences between cars and motorcycles (such as the fact that cars have four wheels, motorcycles only two) because such similar objects have many such mapped differences. It is harder to list differences between such dissimilar objects as cars and grapefruits, since virtually all their differences will be unmapped. Paradoxically, it is easier to think of differences between similar objects than between dissimilar objects, even though dissimilar objects obviously must be more different. The reason is that similar objects produce a clearer mapping, which makes the mapped differences explicit. Unmapped differences, which the mapping process drops rather than highlights, are the most likely to lead to unexpected failures of analogy-based inferences about the target domain.

The seriousness of generating erroneous inferences about the target (or failing to generate correct ones) will depend on the cost of making a mistake. In some situations it will be possible simply to test the inference and find out if it is correct; if an error is detected, little or no harm is done. But if it is difficult to test the inference, or if mistakes can not simply be "taken back," then inferences need to be evaluated carefully before an irrevocable action is taken. For example, suppose a political crisis is seen as a parallel to developments leading up to World War II, leading to the inference that military intervention is essential. If the basis for the analogy turns out be ill founded, the consequences of the mistake are likely to be grave.

If an analogy is ill chosen in the first place, erroneous inferences are inevitable. Too often people—including politicians and teachers—make use of superficially appealing analogies to highly familiar source analogs, which actually miss most of the important causal relations in the target. In 1991, people who argued that American involvement in freeing Kuwait would be analogous to the disastrous American experience in

Vietnam often ignored major relevant differences. For example, Vietnam involved a civil war between rival Vietnamese factions, whereas Kuwaitis unanimously viewed the Iraqi invaders as an army of occupation. There was therefore no reason to expect the Iraqis to benefit from the support of large numbers of the local population, as the enemy that the United States faced in Vietnam had been able to do. Of course, once the Iraqi army disintegrated within weeks of American intervention, the inference to stagnation and American defeat that had been supported by the Vietnam analogy proved blatantly false.

Analogies should enhance thinking, not substitute for it. People sometimes latch on to a salient analogy and focus on it to the neglect of deeper thought about the relevant problem, decision, or explanation. But how can we tell that an analogy is inadequate? Answering this question depends on close attention to the purpose for which the analogy is intended as well as to constraints of structure and similarity. Chapters 6, 7, and 8 respectively address the evaluation of analogies used in decision making, inference to explanatory hypotheses, and teaching.

Evaluation of an analogy can yield one of three verdicts: the source can be applied to the target, it should not be applied to the target, or it can be applied to the target with modifications. The last verdict requires that the solution offered by the source be adapted so that it can be used to provide a solution for the target problem. Operation Desert Storm, the successful attack on the Iraqi army in the Persian Gulf War that avoided the main Iraqi fortifications, was modeled in part on the 1863 Civil War campaign at Vicksburg, where General Grant sent his troops around the Confederate front line and attacked from the side and rear. Obviously, however, the enormous differences between the armies and the environments in the two situations implied that the solution to the historical problem could only be applied very roughly to the contemporary one. Adaptation was needed, bringing to bear all the problem-solving resources available, including general knowledge of the domain of military strategy.

Artificial-intelligence researchers have identified a number of strategies for adapting previous cases to apply to new ones. One of the most powerful is Jaime Carbonell's idea of *derivational* adaptation, which uses the whole planning sequence that went into a solution of a source to generate a new planning sequence for producing a solution to a target. For example, adapting a computer program in the language PASCAL to produce a program in LISP can best be done not by blindly translating PASCAL into LISP, but by noticing how the plan to produce the

PASCAL program can be modified to generate a plan for producing a LISP program. Another adaptation strategy used in case-based reasoning when a piece of the retrieved solution does not apply to the problem at hand is *abstraction and respecialization:* Look for an abstraction of the problematic part of the solution that does not pose the same difficulty, and then try applying other specializations of the abstraction to the current situation. For example, using the New York City subway solely on the basis of knowledge of the San Francisco subway can get you into trouble, since the latter but not the former has only ticket machines. To pay in New York City, however, one can invoke more general knowledge about how tickets are purchased and apply it to the new case. Case-based reasoning programs also sometimes include special-purpose adaptation heuristics useful in particular domains. For example, the CHEF meal-planning system inserts a defatting step into any recipe that includes duck.

Learning

The difficulty of evaluating analogies does not mean that they are useless for acquiring expertise—far from it. People who map two superficially different situations that share analogous causal relations relevant to achieving a goal have the opportunity to do more than simply solve the target problem. In addition, they can potentially learn about the important similarities between the analogs. If the analogous solution in fact works for both situations, the two analogs can be seen as examples of a common category—a kind of problem that allows a certain kind of solution. The common aspects of the analogs—which may be patterns of higher-order relations—can be abstracted to form a schema representing the new category. The differences between the two analogs, which involve domain-specific details that were not crucial for achieving the analogous solutions, can be deemphasized. The resulting schema will therefore lay bare the structure of the analogs, stripping away the specifics of the individual examples. Once a schema has been learned and stored in a person's semantic network, interrelated with other concepts, it will be relatively easy to access it and apply it to novel problems.

One way to build a schema from analogs is to present the learner with multiple examples and encourage processing of their common structure. Gick and Holyoak used this technique to investigate transfer of the convergence schema from multiple examples to the tumor problem. In addition to studying the fortress story, some students also studied

a story about a firefighter who extinguished an oil-well fire by using multiple small hoses. The students wrote summaries of each story and also were asked to write descriptions of the ways in which the stories were similar. The idea was that in order to find similarities the students would have to map the two analogs to each other, which would encourage abstraction of a schema. After a brief delay, the students were asked to solve the tumor problem. Those students who received two source analogs were more than twice as likely to produce the converging-rays solution to the tumor problem, without requiring any kind of hint, than were students who received just one source analog.

In addition, a striking relationship was observed between a measure of the quality of the schemas people learned from the two source analogs and their success in transferring the solution. Some of the students wrote descriptions of the story similarities that focused on the critical causal structure of the problems. For example, one student wrote, "Both stories used the same concept to solve a problem, which was to use many small forces applied together to add up to one large force necessary to destroy the object." Students whose descriptions suggested they had formed good schemas, ones that captured the essence of the shared structure, produced the convergence solution to the tumor problem without a hint over 90 percent of the time. In contrast, other students wrote descriptions that basically missed the point. One such description was, "In both stories a hero was rewarded for his efforts." Although perfectly true, this similarity was quite irrelevant to how the protagonists solved their problems and why the convergence principle was successful. Students whose descriptions suggested they had formed poor problem schemas, or no schema at all, were able to generate the convergence solution to the tumor problem only 30 percent of the time. What matters is not only how many examples are provided but what is learned from them.

Schemas can be learned not only from multiple initial examples but also by successful use of analogy to solve problems. That is, if a person studies a single source analog and then uses it to solve a target problem, a schema may be acquired as a byproduct of mapping and generating inferences about the target. As a result, the person will be yet more successful in transferring the solution procedure to other analogous problems.

In general, any kind of processing that helps people focus on the underlying causal structure of the analogs, thereby encouraging learning of more effective problem schemas, will improve subsequent transfer to new problems. For example, both schema quality and transfer were

detailed experiment

improved when the diagram in figure 5.3 accompanied presentation of the two source analogs. The abstract diagram helped the students focus on the common structure, divorced from the details about fortresses and oil well fires. The same sort of improvement was obtained when each story stated the convergence principle abstractly: "If you need a large force to accomplish some purpose but are prevented from applying such a force directly, many smaller forces applied simultaneously from different directions may work just as well." Importantly, neither the diagram nor the verbal principle benefited transfer when added to a *single* source analog. These aids were only effective in augmenting performance when *two* source analogs were provided, because only with two examples is it possible to map them to generate a schema.

Even with multiple examples that allow novices to start forming schemas, people may still fail to transfer the analogous solution to a problem drawn from a different domain if a substantial delay intervenes or if the context is changed. An abstract schema, much like a specific analog, can easily become a needle in a haystack. But as novices continue to develop more powerful schemas, even long-term transfer in an altered context can be dramatically improved. Richard Catrambone and Keith Holyoak gave students a total of three source analogs to study, compare, and solve. The students were first asked a series of detailed questions designed to encourage them to focus on the abstract structure common to two of the analogs. They were given parallel facts about the fortress and fire stories and asked to write a more general statement that captured what both meant. For example, the two facts might be

The fortress is difficult to capture, because a large army of soldiers can not attack it from one direction.

The fire is difficult to put out, because a large amount of water cannot be thrown at it from one direction.

An appropriate answer, which the students were told after they gave their own answer, would be

A target is difficult to overcome, because a large force cannot be aimed at it from one direction.

After this abstraction training, the students were asked to solve another analog from a third domain (not the tumor problem), after which they were told the convergence solution to it (which most students were able to generate themselves).

Finally, a week later, the students returned to participate in a different experiment. After the other experiment was completed, they were given the tumor problem to solve. Over 80 percent came up with the converging-rays solution without any hint. As the novice becomes an expert, the emerging schema becomes increasingly accessible and is triggered by novel problems that share its structure. Deeper similarities have been constructed between analogous situations that fit the schema.

The message, then, is simple. Analogy is not a surefire shortcut to expertise, far less a substitute for careful thinking and detailed study of a new domain. But when it is used carefully—when a plausible analog is selected and mapped, when inferences are critically evaluated and adapted as needed, and when the deep structure of the analogy is extracted to form a schema—analogy can be a powerful mental tool. At its best, analogy can jump-start creative thinking in a new domain and through successive refinements move the novice along the path to expertise.

[handwritten marginal note: deep-structure]

Summary

When we think analogically, we do much more than just compare two analogs on the basis of obvious similarities between their elements. Similarity at a more general level emerges as the result of applying the constraints of structure and purpose. These constraints apply at all stages in analogy use: selection, mapping, evaluation, and learning. When analogs are selected from memory, the constraint of similarity plays a large role, but structure is also important, especially when multiple source analogs similar to the target are competing to be selected. For mapping, structure is the most important constraint, but similarity and purpose also contribute. Mapping highlights differences between mapped elements, but tends to obscure differences between elements that do not participate in the mapping. Unmapped differences are the most likely to lead to unexpected failures of analogy-based inferences. In evaluating an analogy, its success in accomplishing the purpose of the analogy is naturally the most important concern, but satisfying this constraint is intimately connected with the structural relations between the analogs. When a source analog is evaluated as being relevant to a target, even if the inferences it provides are only partially valid for the target, it may be possible to adapt the analogical inferences to provide more useful transfer to the target. Finally, learning can occur when schemas are formed from the source and target to capture those patterns of relational structure in the analogs that are most relevant to the purpose of the analogy.

6

What Is to Be Done?

Howard's Dilemma

The field of mathematical decision theory attempts to use algebraic methods to optimize choices between alternative actions. Although such decision-making methods can be useful when all the options are known and the relevant considerations are clearly understood, in everyday life people are often forced to make decisions despite major gaps in their knowledge. The person trying to decide what to do may not be sure what actions are possible or how to weight the costs and benefits of different options. Even decision theorists must cope with the uncertainties that plague everyday decision making. According to one story (perhaps apocryphal), an eminent philosopher of science once encountered a noted decision theorist in a hallway at their university. The decision theorist was pacing up and down, muttering "What shall I do? What shall I do?"

"What's the matter, Howard?" asked the philosopher.

Replied the decision theorist: "It's horrible, Ernest—I've got a terrific job offer and I don't know whether to accept it."

"Why, Howard," reacted the philosopher, "you're one of the world's great experts on decision making. Why don't you just work out the decision tree, calculate the probabilities and expected outcomes, and determine which choice maximizes your expected utility?"

With annoyance, Howard replied: "Come on—this is serious."

Serious decision making in politics, business, and everyday life often finds us in situations in which we know very little about the probabilities or utilities of various possible outcomes. Indeed, we often lack a very good idea even of the possible actions open to us and the kinds of consequences they might have. Small wonder, then, that decision makers often resort to analogical thinking. The question "What did we do last time?" is not always the best way to reach an optimal decision, but it can have cognitive advantages over an attempt to quantify ignorance. If Howard can remember the results of previous moves, whether by himself or by people he knows, he can start to get a rough idea of the impact moving might have on his own life. Previous decisions can serve as source analogs, helping him with his impending target, the decision whether to move. The analogs, such as a colleague thriving at the new institution or another whose marriage suffered from relocation, might support decisions in either direction. We will see that analogy can contribute to more creative and effective decisions by suggesting possible actions to take and what goals to take into account, as well as in forecasting the potential effects of the actions on the goals.

In previous chapters we were able to base our judgments about the adequacy of our theory of analogical thought on an array of controlled psychological experiments. In the next four chapters, which concern the use of analogy by politicians, philosophers, scientists, poets, and other people faced with complex decisions and difficult problems, we have to be much more anecdotal. But we will show how a great many analogies in various domains can be understood in terms of the constraints of similarity, structure, and purpose. Moreover, we will expand our concern with how people use analogies to consider how people *should* use analogies, considering normative questions as well as descriptive ones. Although the common use of analogy in decision making, explanation, education, and literature is easy to document, not everyone is happy about it: critics have claimed that analogies more often corrupt thought than aid it. Distinguishing effective uses of analogies from disastrous ones is part of the normative project of providing guidance as to how analogies ought to be used.

Coherent Decisions

The purpose of the analogies discussed in this chapter is decision making. Evaluation of the effective use of analogies requires comparing how decisions are actually made to how they ought to be made. As our Howard anecdote illustrates, mathematical decision theory is not easily applied to the kinds of complex, indeterminate situations in which analogies are normally used. At the same time, there is certainly more to everyday decision making than using analogies. To understand the role of analogies in making decisions, as well as the potential risks involved, we need to place the use of analogies in the context of a flexible, qualitative theory of decision making.

Thagard and Millgram have proposed a theory that construes decision making as the product of a set of interacting constraints. Although these constraints are not identical to those that govern the use of analogy, they have the same quality of operating as interacting pressures that may converge or conflict. In addition, analogy can itself provide some of the constraints used to guide decisions. When people make decisions, they do not simply choose a single action to perform; rather, they adopt complex plans on the basis of a holistic assessment of various competing actions and goals. A choice is made by arriving at a plan involving actions and goals that are coherent with other actions and goals to which one is committed.

Consider poor Howard, distressed by the question of whether to accept his job offer. Why are such decisions so difficult? Important life choices like this one involve many different, and sometimes intensely conflicting, goals. Perhaps Howard is attracted by the new position because it offers increased salary and prestige, as well as new opportunities to advance science, but he is concerned that moving would involve considerable dislocation and loss of established relations with colleagues. Moreover, he may have a family with roots in his current community. He thus has to deal with a plethora of interconnected, and possibly ill-specified, goals that are relevant to his choice. How can he trade off prestige against security? What is the expected balance between the desire for novelty in his intellectual environment and the established comfort he has already achieved? How can he assess the relative importance of his own happiness compared to that of his family, who would move with him? How should a spouse's career and social relations and the schools and friendships of children enter into the calculation? How can he balance the short-term loss of intellectual productivity induced by moving against the projected gains from being at a more high-powered institution? How does increased salary balance against the various reasons for staying put? Small wonder that Howard was annoyed by Ernest's suggestion that he apply to his own case the techniques he taught to his students.

Thagard and Millgram proposed a set of principles designed to specify the kinds of relations that exist among actions and goals. These relations give rise to coherence estimations, which determine not only choices of actions to perform but also revisions of goals. Goals will include not only positive states one wants to achieve, such as the goal of having a more prestigious job, but also negative states one wants to avoid, such as the goal of avoiding separation from friends. No sharp distinction can be made between actions and goals, since what in one context is best described as an action may be best described in another context as a goal. For example, if someone's main goal is to travel from Waterloo to Los Angeles, the traveler will set the subgoal of getting to the Toronto airport; but this subgoal is itself an action to be performed.

What determines whether a set of actions and goals constitutes a coherent plan? Several simple qualitative principles are important. First, some goals (but not all) must have intrinsic importance, triggering the search for a plan to achieve them. Different goals may have different inherent priority, which can be based on sources such as biological needs, indoctrination, and social comparison. The point is that intrinsic desirability is independent of the coherence considerations that govern acceptability of actions and subgoals, although coherence can have some effect on the ultimate impact of intrinsic goals too. An ascetic may have the same intrinsic need for food and sex as anyone else, but adoption of more spiritual goals may lessen the impact of physical goals on decision making.

Second, if a set of actions together facilitate the accomplishment of a goal, then each action in the set coheres both with the goal and with each other action in the set. Such positive coherence relations involve mutual facilitation. For example, if the action of getting to the Toronto airport facilitates the goal of getting to Los Angeles, then the action and the goal cohere with each other. But actions and goals can also be incoherent. So a third principle is that actions or goals will be incoherent with each other to the extent that they are incompatible, that is, are difficult or impossible to accomplish jointly. The "best plan," as viewed by the decision maker, will consist of the set of actions and goals that most strongly facilitate each other and inhibit their rivals. In chapter 10 we will describe how coherence of plans, or *deliberative coherence,* can be efficiently assessed by computational models similar to the ones we use to model analogy.

Let us consider how these principles might apply to Howard's dilemma. We assume that Howard has explicit representations of actions and goals, along with knowledge about which actions can be used to accomplish which goals. One of Howard's goals might be to further the scientific understanding of decision making. He might consider that a good way to do so would be to start a new institute for studying decision making, and perhaps moving to the new job would make possible such

an institute. Then the action of taking the new job facilitates establishing the institute, which facilitates the scientific understanding. Establishing the institute can be described equally well as an action to be taken and as a subgoal to the basic goal of increasing understanding. People can represent multiple layers of actions, goals, and subgoals, as in this structure:

increase scientific understanding
    ←start institute
    ←take job

The backward arrows signify that each lower subgoal corresponds to an action that can achieve the goal above it (e.g., starting an institute is a way to increase scientific understanding). Typically, a number of actions will together be jointly necessary for accomplishing a goal or subgoal. For a new institute to facilitate scientific understanding, it is necessary to do more than simply open it: at the same time it will be necessary to find funding and office space. So the actual facilitation relations might be something like the following:

increase scientific understanding
    ←open institute and fund it and house it
    ←take job

All of these actions will tend to cohere with each other as well as with the overarching goal of increasing scientific understanding, which they jointly facilitate.

But Howard has other goals, and some of these are not entirely compatible with the above plan. Moving may facilitate his career goals but be incompatible with goals related to preserving important social relationships. It is difficult, although perhaps not impossible, for life to be both exciting and comfortable.

The global coherence of a plan is partly affected by the decision maker's overall system of beliefs about what facilitates what. For example, Howard may believe that being at the more elite institution will make him happier. But this belief may be undermined if he does a systematic comparison of people he knows and discovers that the people at the most elite institutions are not any happier than those at moderately elite ones. Moreover, actions are chosen not in isolation but as parts of complex plans that involve other actions and goals, with goals being partly revisable, just like choices of actions. On this account, a decision maker needs first to construct a complex structure of actions and goals connected by relations of facilitation and incompatibility, and then to derive from this structure a set of actions and goals that comprise a coherent plan. The overall procedure can be broken down into the following steps:

Step 1: Identify relevant actions and goals.
Step 2: Identify facilitation and incompatibility relations among the actions and goals.
Step 3: Choose a coherent plan involving actions and goals.

The last step involves evaluating both the desirability of actions and the importance of goals.

Analogy can help in both steps 1 and 2. Sometimes a decision situation is simple enough to make obvious what is to be accomplished and the possible means for accomplishing it (step 1). But in more complicated situations, analogies can be very useful for getting ideas about what matters and what can be done. Moreover, it will often be useful to consider not just a single analog but many. Concentration on a single analog may lead one to focus on a narrow set of goals and a narrow course of action, but use of multiple analogs can suggest many possible things to do as ways of accomplishing multiple objectives. As we will see shortly, multiple analogs have sometimes been used to reach decisions about what to do in political crises.

Analogies can also be very useful in step 2 in helping to identify the relations among actions and goals. Actions do not wear their consequences on their sleeves; determining the potential results of a possible action is often very difficult. Historical analogies are often useful for divining the possible consequences, both good and bad, of actions under considerations. As we saw in chapter 5, proponents of American military intervention to thwart Saddam Hussein's invasion of Kuwait pointed to how war successfully overcame Hitler's aggression, but critics used the Vietnam analogy to argue that the deployment of American troops could lead to pointless loss of life.

More generally, we can contrast two methods of using analogies to make decisions:

1. In a problem situation, find the one previous situation that best matches the current one, and do whatever worked then and avoid what failed then.
2. Use any number of relevant previous situations that correspond in different ways to the current one, and use information about them to construct and choose a coherent plan.

The second method is clearly preferable, since it will generate a much more informed decision about what to do. The role of analogy in assessing coherence of plans shows why multiple analogies are important: what matters is not just similarities and differences but picking up on the possible actions, goals, and facilitation relations. Thus in decision making, analogy needs to be considered within a broader framework of forming and evaluating plans. We will argue similarly in the next chapter that arguments about which explanatory hypotheses to believe should never be purely analogical, but that analogy can nevertheless make important contributions to choosing good theories. Analogy is indispensable, but it does not stand alone.

The normative question that arises when analogy is used in decision making is this: how should an inference based on analogy be justified? This question lies at the heart of the evaluation stage of analogical reasoning. In chapter 5 we saw that people are quite facile at finding mappings between complex situations but can be misled if the mapping supports inferences about the target that are in fact erroneous. Informal logic books often include a section on the use and misuse of analogies, but the treatment is usually superficial, concentrating on argument rather than on the diverse roles of analogies in thought. They provide advice about choosing analogs that have similarities and lack differences and usually insist that the similarities be relevant, but they say little more about how to assess relevance.

Viewing analogical thinking in the context of coherence-based decision making provides a deeper approach to the normative question, one which fits well with our multiconstraint theory. To make effective use of multiple source analogs in assessing the coherence of decisions, it is essential to find system mappings based on such higher-order relations as "facilitates" and " is incompatible with." In using analogies to evaluate options in the Persian Gulf crisis, for example, it was necessary for President Bush to consider both that attacking Iraq might facilitate the goal of stopping an aggressor, just as attacking Germany did, and that an attack might be incompatible with the goal of avoiding unacceptable American casualties, as proved to be the case in Vietnam. The structure of Bush's decision involves relations among propositions:

attack (U.S., Iraq) *name*: attack-1

stop (U. S., Iraq) *name*: stop-1

facilitate (attack-1, stop-1) *name*: facilitate-1

avoid (U.S., casualties) *name*: avoid-1

incompatible (attack-1, avoid-1) *name*: incompatible-1

Since no one source analog is likely to provide all the relevant higher-order relations, it is often useful to construct multiple mappings to different source analogs, which can provide information about different options and their possible consequences. Then the structure of the analogs can fully serve the purpose of analogizing, through the system mappings made possible by higher-order relations such as "facilitates."

Furthermore, analogies do not have to be taken as indivisible wholes. In chapter 5 we described evaluation as an important part of the use of analogy: the inferences about a target are not simply to be accepted uncritically; rather, they ought to be evaluated and adapted as necessary. For example, the American military leaders in 1991, while employing the analogy between Hitler and Saddam to justify attacking Iraq, also used the analogy with Vietnam in recommending a massive initial attack, rather than the incremental involvement that developed in Southeast Asia in the 1960s. A single analog can seldom provide a complete basis for a decision; but aspects of several analogs can often provide part of the basis for developing a coherent plan. Although analogy-based inferences never guarantee optimal decisions, they derive the strongest possible justification when multiple source analogs are mapped to the target at the system level, with the results of these mappings being used as part of an overall evaluation of decision coherence.

There is no circularity in saying that the evaluation of decisions depends in part on the evaluation of analogies, at the same time that the evaluation of analogies depends in part on the evaluation of the decisions that they encourage. Both decision making and analogy involve simultaneous satisfaction of multiple constraints. In chapter 10 we show that it is possible to build computer simulations of the process of satisfying multiple constraints at once, both for decision making and for analogy. Although it is more difficult to model interactions of the two different sets of constraints, we will provide some suggestions about how this might be accomplished.

Houses and Baseball Players

Certain types of decisions are particularly dependent on the use of analogy. In general, analogies will be especially important when the decision maker is unable to base a decision on simple rules or principles.

Such situations arise when the basis for the decision is changing dynamically and when each case is unique in some important way. In domains with these characteristics, analogy is not simply a way for a novice to get started—it is also a basic form of reasoning by domain experts.

One such class of situations involves real estate appraisal. During periods when the market is changing rapidly, housing prices will be volatile. In addition, as every realtor knows, the most important factor that governs real estate prices is location, and no two properties are located in exactly the same place. An expert appraiser must use recent sales to determine a reasonable price for a house. Moreover, the situation is fundamentally adversarial, with a seller obviously looking for the most expensive analogs and a prospective buyer looking for the analogs with lower prices. In addition to location, relevant factors include size and condition. The appraiser estimates a value by finding the most similar recent sales and making adjustments for the differences between the houses.

Similar reasoning occurs in decisions about the salaries of major-league baseball players. In major-league baseball, salaries can be volatile, and each player is unique. In arbitration hearings, a player suggests to an arbitrator what his salary should be, and the management of the team he works for suggests a lower figure. After hearing the arguments of the player and the team, the arbitrator must choose one of the figures as the fairer salary for the player. The arguments are largely analogical, with both sides describing other players in the league who are similar to the player whose salary is being determined. Naturally, the player looks for similar players with higher salaries, while the team cites similar players with lower salaries, and the arbitrator must decide which players are most similar. Steve Mann describes the case of Texas Rangers first baseman Rafael Palmeiro, who requested a 1992 salary of $3,850,000, while the team offered $2,350,000. Palmeiro's agent compared his batting performance favorably to very highly paid performers, such as Wally Joyner, who made $4,200,000 annually; but the team claimed that his record was comparable instead to John Kruk, who had just signed for $2,400,000. The arbitrator had to decide whether Palmeiro was more like Joyner and the other examples cited by the player's agent, or more like Kruk and the other examples cited by the team's representative.

The perspective of each adversary here is much like that of the rival attorneys in legal disputes, which we discuss in the next section. Selection of cases (similar players) is based both on the extent to which the analog matches the player under discussion and also on how well the analog fits with the desire of the arguer for a higher or lower salary. The role of the arbitrator, like that of a judge, is more difficult in that it requires evaluating the similarities between each of the rival cases raised by the two sides and the case to be decided. Adversaries can choose their cases using a purpose-driven system mapping, but the arbitrator has to take both sides into account, just as a judge has to select from among the legal precedents presented by opposing lawyers, or a political leader has to choose from among the historical precedents presented by aides favoring different decisions.

During the Great Depression of the 1930s, the famous baseball player Babe Ruth was once told that his salary had grown higher than that of the president of the United States, Herbert Hoover. He replied, "I had a better year than he did." This joke highlights the need for salary judgments to be based on factors deemed relevant to the case at hand. No university professor is going to be able to use Palmeiro's salary as part of an argument for an increase in faculty salaries. In baseball, there are quantitative measures, such as batting average and slugging percentage, that enable the arbitrator to make a somewhat objective match. Implicit in the evaluation is the higher-order relation that batting average, for example, should help determine the salary of a player. From the perspective of the team, part of the case could therefore be represented as

Target	Source
influence	influence
bats-in-1991 (Palmeiro, .302)	bats-in-1991 (Kruk, .291)
gets-paid (Palmeiro, ?)	gets-paid (Kruk, $2,375,000)

The arbitrator must estimate the similarity of Palmeiro and Kruk with respect to batting average and weight the appropriate influence of that factor, while simultaneously taking into account more qualitative factors, such as overall contribution to team performance. The basic principle is that a player's performance should determine his salary, but since there are no clear principles specifying how this determination should work, an arbitrator can do no better than consider relevant analogies.

Complaints about the complexity and messiness of using analogical reasoning in such contexts must be balanced by an obvious fact: often, there is not much else to go on. On the brighter side, attention to the structure-purpose connections afforded by system mappings can make the process of analogical decision making much less arbitrary than it would be if it were based only on overall similarity.

Courtroom Analogies

One of the most important domains in which analogy is routinely used to guide decision making by domain experts is the law. And like the situations in real estate appraisal and salary arbitration, the use of analogy in the law takes place in an adversarial context. According to law professor Cass Sunstein, "[R]easoning by analogy is the most familiar form of legal reasoning." In law school, much of what students are taught consists of important cases that provide precedents for making legal decisions. Kevin Ashley, a law professor and artificial-intelligence researcher, has noted that "lawyers have no choice but to argue from cases." In Anglo-American law, a holding by a court in a previous case is virtually binding on the same court or a lower court in a similar case. Courts are obliged to decide a case in accordance with the most analogous precedent. Even in cases in which there are relevant legal principles, application of the principles is rarely clear-cut and therefore depends on citing previous cases in which the principles have been applied. Precedents are especially important in establishing that a case deserves to be heard by the court (because the case is like other cases that have been heard) and in appealing an adverse decision to a higher court (because the decision was at odds with decisions in other cases).

Ashley describes the quandary of a fictitious attorney who needs to construct an argument on behalf of a client. The client wishes to sue a former employee who profited from the use of ideas and computer software developed while employed by the client. The attorney must write a memorandum justifying the client's desire to begin a lawsuit against the former employee. According to Ashley, a legal argument can cite four main kinds of authorities: legal cases, court-made rules or principles, provisions of statutes and constitutions, and secondary authorities, such as legal treatises. Citing a legal case is an argument from analogy, asserting that the current dispute bears relevant similarities to the cited case. Citing rules, statutes, and principles might seem to involve a simpler kind of argument, in which a ruling about the current dispute is simply deduced from the general prescription. However, attorneys typically cite particular cases in which a statute was applied, to better show how the statute applies to the current case. But what determines whether a previous case is relevant to a current dispute? This question raises the same basic problem that inevitably arises in justifying decisions by analogy—deciding which similarities and differences between the source and the target are relevant to the decision. Sunstein poses the basic problem that arises when analogies are used in legal settings:

The method of analogy is based on the question: Is case *A* relevantly similar to case *B*? Is a ban on homosexual sodomy like a ban on the use of contraceptives in marriage, or like a ban on incest? Is a restriction on abortion like a restriction on murder, or like a compulsory kidney transplant? To answer such questions, one needs a theory of relevant similarities and differences. By itself, analogical reasoning supplies no such theory. It is thus dependent on an apparatus that it is unable to produce. In short: Everything is a little bit similar to, or different from, everything else.

Ashley provides a practical approach to grappling with this deep problem by pointing out several criteria that can be used to select relevant precedents. The precedent should generally involve the same claim and the same decision as is desired in the current dispute. The attorney's basic aim is to find the precedents that best support the client's aims. Of course, the attorney should also be alert for precedents that might be used to support the opposing side. Ashley says that attorneys aim to find precedents that are most "on point," sharing the strengths and weaknesses of the current dispute. Finally, precedents are stronger if they come from higher courts of relevant jurisdiction and have never been questioned. Attorneys on both sides of a conflict attempt to put together the strongest overall argument they can by compiling relevant (on-point) precedents.

To help them retrieve potentially relevant cases, attorneys rely on various aids, such as indices and computer databases. However, they have to depend on their own abilities to select cases that are relevant to the current case, as well as to map and adapt the precedents to the dispute at hand. Our multiconstraint theory implies that they do so by cognitive processes sensitive to similarity, structure, and purpose. Ashley's emphasis on finding cases that are on point shows that mere similarity of objects or relations is not going to get an attorney very far in selecting precedents. Rather, a precedent makes a good source analog only if its structure enables it to be used for the purpose of whoever wants to use it. Legal analogies will be most effective if they are based on system mappings that highlight structural correspondences between the precedent and the new case.

Ashley has written a computer program, called Hypo, that automates finding and evaluating relevant cases using the criteria he describes. In Hypo, relevance is determined by storing with each case a list of "dimensions," which are factors that courts have described as important to their decisions. Whether one precedent is more on point than another does not depend on comparing just any similarities and differences, but only those that involve dimensions—factors that are known to have influenced previous decisions. Hypo thus makes use of the same sort of combination of structure and purpose that is generally important for using analogies well in decision making. In analogical decision making, the optimal system mapping depends on having matching facilitation relations between the source and the target analogs: it is important to find cases in which similar actions facilitated similar goals. In the search for precedents to influence legal decisions, the crucial relation is influence: what aspect of the previous case influenced the judicial decision? Implicit in the understanding of precedents is a higher-order relation of the form

support (dimension, decision).

The dimension and the decision are themselves complex relations, such as (in Ashley's case of the former employee) the fact that a computer program was developed for one company and used by another.

Ashley's approach seems very appropriate for the kind of legal purpose he considers, finding precedents that can make a difference to the client. Judges face the more difficult task of evaluating the different precedents presented by opposing sides in a dispute. In making their decisions, judges will often need to consider multiple analogies that have discrepant implications, because the influence relations will lead in different directions. As long as the judge is simply weighing precedents from previous court cases, balancing different analogies will be a difficult, but still fairly constrained, problem. The importance of having multiple analogs contribute to the judge's decision shows one of the advantages of the adversarial nature of legal proceedings, since attorneys on opposing sides will be strongly motivated to suggest different source analogs. In real disputes, however, there are various other factors that judges take into account: legal principles, empirical facts, social needs, and so on. Analogy is certainly not the only component in judicial decision making.

When analogies are used in arguing very difficult ethical issues, such as abortion and restrictions on free speech, it is crucial to get beyond the mere swapping of alternative analogs. (See "Intuition Pumps," at the end of chapter 7.) The key question to ask is: what is it about the analog that makes you intuitively reach a certain conclusion? This question should help to bring out the higher-order relations that help to determine relevance to the case. It is not enough to say that abortion is bad because it is like infanticide, which is bad: you need to ask what factor makes infanticide bad and whether or not abortion involves the same factor.

This process will not, however, always produce rules that can be easily applied, since there will usually be cases in which intuitively a rule seems to fail. In practice, the law has some fluidity, as the give-and-take between these cases and rules leads to continuous adjustments. The political philosopher John Rawls suggests that we keep adjusting our principles on the basis of our intuitions about particular cases, and our intuitions about cases on the basis of our principles, until we have a set of intuitions and principles that fit well together. He calls such a state "reflective equilibrium." Reflective equilibrium seems to depend on the kind of coherence-guided decision making we have been emphasizing.

It might seem that once legal principles and intuitions of justice converge at some reflective equilibrium, the use of analogy in the law could be abandoned. However, Sunstein provides a number of reasons why eliminating analogy is neither possible nor desirable. First, reasoning by analogy puts much less demand on the time and capacities of lawyers and judges, who can seek a solution to particular disputes without having to take a stand on large, difficult, and controversial general issues. Second, reasoning by analogy can allow people to reach agreement on particular issues without having to reach accord on general principles. Third, the use of analogical reasoning may be more flexible in the long run than reflective equilibrium, allowing the evolution of legal and moral ideas over time. Someone who actually reaches reflective equilibrium may find it difficult to adapt to new information and arguments. Finally, the use of analogical reasoning in law allows treating the precedents as fixed points with which even those who disagreed with earlier decisions have to deal. Treating precedents in this way imbues the legal process with considerable conservatism, but it is easy to imagine what would happen in already crowded courts if every dispute became a philosophical debate.

Even though precedents have a privileged status in the law, they can be reexamined and reinterpreted in light of new cases. This continued scrutiny of analogies is closely related to the evolution of legal principles. At one time, for example, an American legal principle held that a person could only be sued in a state in which the person was physically present. Many cases were decided on the basis of this principle, creating a body of precedents. Eventually, however, the principle and the interpretation of the precedents were challenged by new actual and hypothetical cases that arose as the result of innovations in transportation and commerce. On the one hand, it violated natural intuitions that a woman on a transcontinental flight aboard a commercial airliner, quite unaware that she was passing through the air space of Iowa, should at that moment be exposed to a lawsuit initiated in that state. On the other hand, suppose a man residing in California were to set up a small business in Iowa, with an office and employees situated there. In some circumstances it would seem reasonable for him to be sued in Iowa (for example, in a case based on an injury someone suffered at the Iowa office), even though the man had never personally set foot in the state. Such new examples triggered a deeper analysis of the basis for the decisions made in apparent precedents, looking for distinctions between those situations and the newer ones. The new cases eventually led to a revision in the relevant legal principle, which became what is termed "minimum contact": in order to be sued in a state, the person must have some minimum contact with the state that conveys the benefit of protection by that state. Thus the airline passenger has no such minimum contact and therefore can not be sued in Iowa; in contrast, the Californian businessman could be sued, because his Iowa office benefited from that state's police, regulation of utility companies, and so on.

A similar example of the reexamination of principles and precedents arose in the early 1990s with the growth in electronic bulletin boards, on which computer users could post messages that would be broadcast to other subscribers. A lawsuit was filed involving an electronic information service that ran hundreds of bulletin boards devoted to specialized topics, with a total of over two million subscribers. One of these bulletin boards, called "Money Talk," was devoted to discussion of financial investments. One subscriber posted a series of messages denouncing a certain company as a bad investment, making such claims as, "My research indicated company is really having a difficult time. No cash, no sales, no profit, and terrible management. This company appears to be a fraud. Probably will cease operations soon!" The company in question was not amused and retaliated with a lawsuit against the man who had posted the message, claiming that his messages had caused the value of the company's stock to decline by 50 percent and alleging libel and securities fraud.

The ensuing legal arguments consisted largely of debates over the relevance of rival precedents that might be mapped to the new technology of electronic bulletin boards. Bulletin boards were compared to books, bookstores, newspapers, telephones, billboards, radio talk shows, and even the town crier. The legal problem was that none of these source analogs provided an entirely convincing match. The defense suggested that a computer message was essentially the same as a personal telephone call and could not constitute libel. But the offended company countered

(handwritten annotation: "In analogy, books → computers is often used")

that it was one thing to transmit misinformation to a friend over a telephone but quite another to transmit it simultaneously to thousands of people over a computer network. The company claimed the proper analog was a newspaper, in which case the author of the message would be subject to libel laws. However, the new electronic technology of bulletin boards clearly differed in many significant ways from conventional newspaper publishing. The information service (fearing it would also be sued) argued against the publishing analogy, on the grounds that the service did not and could not exercise editorial control over messages that were composed and transmitted almost instantaneously by thousands of users. This case had not yet been decided as this book was completed. In an earlier case, a judge had likened an electronic information service to a bookseller, who is not held legally responsible for the contents of every book in the bookstore. In this example, like the various cases involving liability to suits within a state, we see the evolution of law being guided by a deepening examination of the similarities and differences among a set of related cases that provide the bases for judicial decisions.

Such examples, as well as Sunstein's arguments, suggest a general reason why analogies must be taken seriously. Someone might argue that there is no reason ever to reason by analogy, since an analogy will be valid only if there is some general principle that makes the analogy redundant. But general principles are often very hard to establish, and principles may themselves require revision in light of new cases. As the legal philosopher H. L. A. Hart pointed out, "there is no authoritative or uniquely correct formulation of any rule to be extracted from cases." As new cases arise, the entire set of cases may suggest different rules. Given the limited basis for reasoning entirely from rules or principles, arguing from case to case is often the best that we can do. But such arguments need not be feeble if they involve representations of the cases rich enough to bring out how the structure of each case is relevant to the purpose for which the analogy is to be used.

Legal reasoning is often a matter of reaching explanatory conclusions, not just making legal decisions. In a murder trial, for example, a jury will have to decide matters of fact, such as whether the accused really did kill the victim. As we will see in chapters 7 and 8, this kind of inference involves evaluating the explanatory coherence of competing accounts of what happened, and analogy can play a role in determining the relative coherence of the cases of the prosecution and the defense.

Lessons of the Past

At the beginning of the last chapter, we described the massive impact of the analogy between Saddam Hussein and Adolf Hitler on decisions leading up to the Persian Gulf War of 1991. The arena of foreign affairs and war provides the most dramatic domain in which, for better or worse, analogy has made a strong contribution to decisions. One might suppose that historical lessons for current concerns could take the form of generalizations based on the whole previous course of human history. But the trouble is that the environment in which history is perpetually being made is dynamic. Nations and their leaders rise and fall, alliances and international bodies are ever in flux, monetary systems and patterns of commerce vary, new technologies change the ways in which wars are fought and peace is maintained. The space of possible foreign crises is so huge and so fluid that the actual events of history constitute no more than a minuscule sample of what might have been in the past and what may be in the future. It is virtually impossible to conduct anything like controlled experiments to determine the impact of decisions on history. For all these reasons it is difficult to glean strong generalizations from the historical record and use them to set current policy. Instead, like the routine decisions of everyday life, political and military decisions with enormous human consequences are often based on qualitative assessments of the coherence of plans, with analogies providing a major source of information feeding into the decision process.

Richard Neustadt and Ernest May have chronicled many instances of political decision making affected by historical precedents.

World War II

The action of Prime Minister Neville Chamberlain in signing the Munich Agreement with Germany in 1938, acquiescing to Hitler's move into Czechoslovakia, has ever since World War II been synonymous with the negative connotations of the term "appeasement." But the failure to stop Hitler in his tracks at Munich can be understood more charitably when we realize how salient the carnage of World War I was for the British and the French. Not wishing to repeat that horrific episode, leaders leaned heavily toward avoiding war. Moreover, in 1938 Britain was militarily unprepared for war with Hitler. Chamberlain viewed his situation at Munich as analogous to that which preceeded World War I.

Korean War

In 1950, South Korea was invaded by North Korea, and President Harry Truman had to decide how to respond. Although South Korea was not thought to be of significant strategic value, Truman was struck by analogies to the incidents that had preceded World War II: the Japanese invasion of Manchuria, the Italian attack on Ethiopia, and the German annexation of Austria. (See the quotation from Truman in chapter 5.) Just as George Bush worried about Saddam Hussein's invasion of Kuwait, Truman feared that the invasion of South Korea was just the beginning of a chain of aggressive acts like those that led to World War II.

Cuban Missile Crisis

In 1962, President John F. Kennedy and his advisors faced the decision of how to respond to evidence that Russians were building launch sites for medium-range nuclear missiles in Cuba, just ninety miles off the coast of the United States. In the early attempts to explain what the Russians were up to, an analogy was drawn to the 1956 Suez crisis, which had served as a distraction for the Russian invasion of Hungary. By analogy, some advisors predicted that the Russians were using the missiles in Cuba as a distraction from a planned move on Berlin. Some advisors urged an air strike on missile sites in Cuba, but Robert Kennedy and others compared such a strike to the infamous Japanese attack on Pearl Harbor in World War II. Another crucial influence on the decision of the president to move fairly cautiously was his reading of a book on the outbreak of World War I; he did not want to duplicate the stumbling of leaders into a disastrous war that no one wanted.

Swine Flu Scare

In 1976, a new strain of flu turned up at a U.S. army base. The strain was caused by an influenza virus common among pigs but not found in people for decades. Medical specialists feared that there could be an epidemic as serious as the 1918 influenza epidemic that killed more than half a million Americans. Based in part on that frightening source analog, President Gerald Ford approved a massive immunization campaign. However, no serious flu ensued, and the swine flu vaccine caused serious medical problems in some of those who received it.

Much of our emphasis in this book is on the creative possibilities of analogies, particularly when they involve leaps across domains. But analogies can be stultifying as well. Most political analogies seem to be restricted within a single, narrow domain. The source analogs chosen

[handwritten: war they prepare for "the last one."]

are extremely salient, as when politicians could not avoid thinking of the beginnings, conduct, and aftermath of World War I as they were drawn toward World War II. It is often said of military leaders that the war they prepare for is the last one: in the 1930s, horses were still a part of British military strategy, because tanks had not worked that well in World War I. It often seems as if some single source analog dominates the decision making of a generation of leaders, who apply it profligately and uncritically to whatever crises arise on their watch. Such use of single analogs is scarcely more sophisticated than that of the young children we described in chapter 4, who use the familiar source analog of people to understand other living things.

Although most political analogies are based on analogs that can be found within the political domain, there is one cross-domain analogy that continually plays a major role in political decision making. May says that "when thinking of international relations, most of us visualize nations as rational unitary actors, defining objectives, laying plans, and following sequences of coherent actions in pursuit of their ends." But there are many respects in which organizations that are filled with parochialism and internal conflict do not behave like individuals. The analogical conception of the nation as a person can be seriously misleading. Indeed, given the complexity of human thought, it may be more useful to think, conversely, of a mind as a social entity rife with conflict as well as cooperation. *[handwritten: metaphor]*

Historians are aware that governmental decisions are often made with historical precedents in mind, but many think that politicians and administrators do not use history well. According to historian James Banner, "most historians have come to believe that the use of historical knowledge by policymakers is seriously defective." It is certainly notable that those who have written about the use of analogy in political decisions have concentrated more on failures than successes. In contrast, those who have written about the use of analogy in science have documented successes rather than failures (see chapter 8). Perhaps the contrast indicates that science has had more successes and fewer failures than politics; or perhaps it is simply that we care most about (and therefore pay more attention to) the dramatic successes of science and the even more dramatic disasters of international relations. In any case, there is reason to heed the warning of Gilovich: "[T]hough there is certainly a great deal of truth to Santayana's maxim that 'those who do not remember the past are condemned to relive it,' one might also be cautioned that those who do not forget the past can be led to misapply it."

No More Vietnams

What is to be done? Can the use of analogy in political decision making be improved so as to avoid catastrophic errors? Various suggestions have been offered. Neustadt and May recommend compiling a list of like-nesses and differences between the target problem and the historical source and then dividing what is believed about these situations into three categories: known, unclear, and presumed. But although making such distinctions should help ensure that analogies are not used unreflectively, they provide only part of what is required for effective use of analogy. A more radical proposal for aiding policymakers in their use of history was made by Banner, who urged the creation of a council of historians, which he termed the "History Watch," or "Historical Analogy Police." Some kinds of historical policing would be straightforward enough, such as correcting politicians' garbling of dates. But analogies are much more complicated, and Banner does not say how the analogy police would separate the valuable uses of historical analogies from the dubious ones.

Perhaps the best way to fully appreciate the grave dangers that accompany analogical decision making and the difficulty of combating flawed use of source analogs is to examine the lessons of Vietnam. Yuen Foong Khong has made a careful historical analysis of the role that analogy played in the fateful decisions made by American leaders in the early 1960s—decisions that determined how the United States pursued the first war that it was to lose. The origins of the Vietnam War can be traced to the aftermath of World War II, when the French attempted to reassert their prewar colonial domination. From 1946 to 1954, the French fought a Vietnamese nationalist and communist movement led by Ho Chi Minh. After eight years of war, the French army was decisively defeated near the village of Dien Bien Phu. A conference in Geneva then produced a peace agreement under which Vietnam was to be divided temporarily at the seventeenth parallel, with the forces of Ho Chi Minh controlling the northern sector and the French and their Vietnamese allies controlling the southern sector. Elections were to be held in 1956 to unify the country under one government. By then the French had left, and South Vietnam was controlled by Ngo Dinh Diem, a staunch anticommunist backed by the United States. Diem refused to hold the elections, which authoritative observers on both sides agreed would have been won by Ho Chi Minh. Over the next few years, Diem's authoritarian regime persecuted, and in some cases executed, Ho

Chi Minh's southern supporters and alienated other sectors of the society. In 1959 North Vietnam authorized military action against the Diem government by guerrillas based in the South. The second Vietnam War began: The country was to be reunited not by the ballot box, but by blood. Before the war ended, with the capture of the South Vietnamese capital in 1975, hundreds of thousands of Vietnamese were dead on both sides, and more bombs had fallen on their soil than on all the countries combined in World War II. The United States, which began to send troops to support South Vietnam in the early 1960s, eventually suffered over three hundred thousand casualties, with fifty-eight thousand dead.

Khong traces the multitude of analogical influences on American decisions about what to do about Vietnam. The Vietnam War was played out against the backdrop of the Cold War, the forty-year period of tension and hostility between the United States and its allies on one side and the communist nations of Russia and China on the other. During the final years of the French war, the United States was paying most of the costs of the French military efforts, motivated by the fear of expanding communism. But when the French were nearing defeat in 1954, President Eisenhower, after much debate among his political advisors, refrained from sending American troops to rescue the French. The slogan "no more Koreas" was often heard at that time, shortly after the end of the Korean War. For many this phrase had a precise meaning: the United States must never intervene unilaterally too close to the Chinese border. Lacking support from America's allies, and too recently stung by the Chinese entry into the Korean War in support of North Korea, Eisenhower's anticommunist leaning was outweighed by the lesson he had learned from Korea.

By 1961 the Diem regime was already doing badly in the war, and it was the turn of President Kennedy to consider American options. Some of his advisors, including Secretary of Defense Robert McNamara, advocated massive direct military intervention. But Kennedy, like Eisenhower before him, opted for a more cautious approach. Kennedy perceived the ambiguity of the situation in Vietnam, as there had been no clear invasion comparable to the invasion of South Korea by North Korea. Setting aside the Korea analogy, Kennedy was guided by the analogies offered by relatively successful anticommunist resistance efforts in Malaya, the Philippines, and Greece. His decision was to increase covert action to contain the communist insurgency in South Vietnam.

In an insightful memo written in October of 1961, Lyman Lemnitzer, chairman of the Joint Chiefs of Staff, directly criticized the Malaya analogy. Lemnitzer noted that the two situations differed in that the British had been directly in control of Malaya, whereas the United States did not control South Vietnam; and that the borders of Malaya had been secure, whereas the guerrillas in South Vietnam had access to sanctuaries in Laos and Cambodia. And indeed these relative weaknesses of the situation facing the United States in Vietnam contributed to the eventual failure of the program of covert action that Kennedy initiated.

President Ngo Dinh Diem was assassinated in November 1963 in an American-backed coup, to be succeeded by a series of governments that were authoritarian, unstable, and generally incompetent, and which grew to be increasingly dependent on the United States. Three weeks after the death of Diem, Kennedy was himself the victim of an assassin's bullet, and President Lyndon Johnson inherited the Vietnam problem. The war was going badly for the South, and by 1965 the regime was in danger of falling. Johnson and his advisors, including Secretary of Defense Robert McNamara, Secretary of State Dean Rusk, and national security advisors William and McGeorge Bundy, were most heavily influenced by the analogies of Korea and of World War II. As Eisenhower had done in justifying the Korean War, and as Bush would do in justifying the Persian Gulf War, Johnson turned to the Munich analogy to publicly justify his decision in 1965 to send American combat troops into Vietnam: "Nor would surrender in Viet-Nam bring peace, because we learned from Hitler at Munich that success only feeds the appetite of aggression. The battle would be renewed in one country and then another country, bringing with it perhaps even larger and crueler conflict, as we have learned from the lessons of history."

But although the Munich analogy was often cited, especially in public, the main analogy on which Johnson and his advisors relied was that of Korea. The Korea analogy that in 1954 had deterred Eisenhower from intervening in Vietnam, and in 1961 had been found unsatisfying by Kennedy, became in 1965 a major basis for the decision to commit one hundred thousand American ground troops to that very same place. What had changed? Different people were making the decisions, of course, and history had moved on. Johnson's advisors were willing to agree that the French had been a colonial power; but they believed the United States was fighting for a nobler cause. In their view, colored by the escalation of warfare in Vietnam over the years, North Vietnam had in fact invaded South Vietnam, just as North Korea had invaded South Korea. Aggression must not be rewarded, and American forces could achieve victory as they had in Korea. At the same time, the moderating impact of the Korean analogy—the specter of intervention by China on the opposing side—had not been altogether lost. This aspect of the Korea analogy weighed especially heavily on Dean Rusk, who still regretted his own failure to forecast China's entry into the Korean conflict. In 1965, Johnson first authorized strategic bombing of North Vietnam and then a few months later ordered a large increase in ground troops. Although these moves were major escalations in American involvement, they represented much less than a full commitment of the vast military capability of the United States. It appears that the residual restraints were largely intended to reassure China that American military objectives remained limited to the defense of South Vietnam, rather than extending to the conquest of North Vietnam or a threat to China itself.

There was one other analogy that was discussed with great heat by Johnson's advisors in their private meetings, but which was almost never mentioned in public. This was the analogy of Dien Bien Phu—the final defeat of the French in Vietnam. A young American named George Ball had worked as a lawyer for the French government during its period of grief in Vietnam, and he never forgot that historical source. Ball was now serving as undersecretary of state in the Johnson administration; outranked by most of the other participants in the Vietnam decisions of that era, he became the lone proponent among them of de-escalation and a negotiated American withdrawal. In a prescient series of memos written in late 1964 and in 1965, Ball argued against applying the Korea analogy to Vietnam. He pointed out a number of crucial differences: the United States in Vietnam lacked a mandate for intervention from the United Nations and had no major allies; there had not been a real invasion by the North, but rather an escalating civil war; and South Vietnam lacked a strong leader and stable government. For these reasons the Vietnam War was neither as justifiable as the Korean War nor as likely to be won by the United States. The more apt analogy, Ball went on to argue, was the French experience in Vietnam. The United States was still fighting the fiercely nationalistic supporters of Ho Chi Minh and in their eyes had simply inherited the colonialist mantle of the French. The French eventually ended the war when domestic support eroded, and Ball predicted that domestic support for the Vietnam War would similarly erode.

Ball's predictions based on the French analogy proved strikingly accurate. His gloomy prognosis about the impact of deeper American military involvement on public opinion at home was especially insightful, given that in 1965 Johnson actually enjoyed a high level of domestic support. At that time over 60 percent of the American public supported Johnson's handling of the Vietnam situation. In the previous year the United States Congress had, by a margin of 512 to 2, passed a resolution that effectively gave Johnson full discretion to pursue military options. But in the late 1960s war protests were to grow increasingly widespread, and in the face of growing unpopularity Johnson declined to run again in the presidential election of 1968.

The most unusual aspect of Ball's analysis was that he actually proposed an experiment to put his French analogy to the test. In 1965, shortly before Johnson made the decision to send more American troops to Vietnam, Ball raised the possibility of increasing the troop level to one hundred thousand (from its current seventy-five thousand), but no more, for a period limited to three months, to see how the American forces would actually fare against the Vietnamese enemy. Such a "controlled commitment," Ball argued, would "prevent the momentum of events from taking command," and "on the basis of our experience during that trial period we will then appraise the costs and possibilities of waging a successful land war in South Viet-Nam and chart a clear course of action." Ball believed the test would reveal that military victory for the United States was unlikely. Asked twenty years later how he could justify risking one hundred thousand lives to test his prediction of failure, Ball noted that his proposal was a final effort to dissuade Johnson from making his imminent decision to commit even more American troops to the war on a open-ended basis.

George Ball and his Dien Bien Phu analogy lost the battle for the heart and mind of Lyndon Johnson in 1965; it was vanquished by Rusk, McNamara, and the two Bundys, all of whom strongly disputed the "French defeat syndrome." These other advisors provided analyses of why the situation in Vietnam was like that in Korea and unlike the French experience in Vietnam. As Khong notes, the lessons of Vietnam are not encouraging for those who have offered cognitive reforms in the use of analogy to make political decisions. Johnson's advisors in many ways seem to have anticipated Neustadt and May's recommendations for serious evaluation of analogies, collectively providing systematic lists of similarities and differences, focusing on the underlying causal structures of the various analogs, and thoroughly debating the merits of alternative sources. But in the end, the wrong decision was made.

Is there anything to be done to ensure that analogy brings us no more Vietnams? Or is analogy inevitably the source of political tragedies, to be balanced against its role in scientific triumphs? Profound difficulties clearly arise in the use of analogy to make political decisions like those that faced Johnson. Unlike the case in science, controlled experiments are virtually impossible in the arena of foreign policy. Ball's proposed experiment in controlled commitment, never conducted, serves to remind us that the exigencies of war are hard to reconcile with the requirements of experimental design. In the absence of controlled tests, feedback regarding the success or failure of analogical predictions is generally ambiguous. In such situations, the human apparatus for assessing the coherence of decisions can be dangerously resistant to corrective external guidance. Dean Rusk, for example, believed that Vietnam was analogous to Korea and made policy recommendations on that basis. Rusk fully expected that, as had been the case in Korea, American forces in Vietnam might suffer substantial losses and early setbacks but would finally prevail. This prediction could not have been disconfirmed by Ball's three-month trial war, no matter how badly it went for the American side. In addition, the Korea and Munich analogies carried with them the predictions that defeat for the United States would have extremely adverse consequences. The deeper the American commitment became, the more plausible such adverse consequences became, strengthening the coherence of the pro-interventionist analogs in the minds of their believers.

The lesson of Vietnam, however, is not that analogy is inevitably misleading in foreign policy decisions. George Ball's analyses of the Korea and Dien Bien Phu analogies, like Lyman Lemnitzer's earlier criticisms of the Malaya analogy, are now generally regarded as fundamentally correct. Even though Ball's views did not prevail in 1965, some of his opponents eventually were persuaded by the course of subsequent events. By 1967 McGeorge Bundy, who in 1965 had been a keen critic of the Dien Bien Phu analogy, had come to see considerable merit in it. Bundy was able to examine the negative trends apparent both in the course of the war and in domestic opposition to it, and use that feedback to modify his assessment of the coherence of his own earlier decisions.

George Ball, who history must now credit as the greatest American political analogist of his time, seems to have followed the method of analogical decision making that we recommended earlier: using multiple analogies, selectively and often in piecemeal fashion. He was able to contrast the situations in Korea and Vietnam without entirely dismissing the Korean precedent. He focused on specific causal factors linked to the outcomes in each situation, such as the contrast between the stable government and strong leader of Korea and the shifting, unpopular figures who headed the government of South Vietnam. Ball's opponents in the debates often seemed to confuse the causal relevance of similarities and differences. For example, many argued that Vietnam was the moral equivalent of Korea because North Vietnam was attacking South Vietnam; they went on to predict that the United States would win in Vietnam as it had in Korea, eliding from the issue of whether the war was moral to whether it was winnable. In contrast, Ball acknowledged the core ambiguity of the Vietnam War—whether it was an invasion of one nation by another or a civil conflict. He pointed out that even if the war could indeed be considered an invasion, this did not mean it was winnable. Ball argued that the North Vietnamese viewed the conflict as a civil war, a war required to expel another colonial power and thereby unify their nation, and for that reason would fight relentlessly whatever the cost, just as they had done against the French. Moreover, they would be able to persuade many countries that might otherwise have allied themselves with the United States that the Vietnam conflict was actually a civil war, in which other nations had no business. Whether or not the United States was truly on the high moral ground, Ball linked the widespread *perception* of moral ambiguity (or worse) to his dismal but correct prognosis for the American cause.

We have already seen evidence of Ball's selectivity in the use of source analogs. During the Vietnam policy debates, he never favored the Munich analogy. In the previous chapter, however, we quoted his admonishment a quarter century later to President Bush, criticizing Bush's failure to draw the full consequences of his own comparison of Saddam to Hitler. Ball never considered Ho Chi Minh to be Hitler but was willing to accept that Saddam was at least a reasonable facsimile. This sort of selectivity in the use of diverse historical precedents contrasts with the simplistic application of some single salient historical case to whatever new crises may arise.

Ironically, American foreign policy debates in the late twentieth century were in fact largely dominated by a single salient historical case—Vietnam. In the 1970s and 1980s other countries' misadventures were likened to that of the United States in Vietnam. Thus Afghanistan became "Russia's Vietnam"; in an especially ironic twist, a Vietnamese incursion into Cambodia was sometimes described as "Vietnam's Vietnam." A major reason that Bush did not drive Saddam from power in 1991 in the aftermath of the Persian Gulf War was that he feared that United States forces could become embroiled in an ensuing civil war, as had happened in the context of the civil war belatedly recognized to have gone on in Vietnam. Saddam might be Hitler, but Iraq must not become Vietnam.

The lessons of Vietnam, like the war itself, are fraught with ambiguity. To previous lessons we can add one more, which is to avoid forcing any single historical analog to fit every future crisis that bears some superficial resemblance to it. In this sense, as in so many others, may there be no more Vietnams.

Summary

This chapter has shown the relevance of analogy to many different kinds of decision making: personal decisions, baseball arbitration, legal reasoning, and international affairs. The same lessons apply in all cases. Analogies are ubiquitous in decision making, but their most effective use requires the presence of higher-order relations, such as facilitating and supporting, which make possible system-level mappings that put the structure of the analogs at the service of the goals of the analogist. A decision maker should avoid fixating on a single source, especially one that involves only a superficial attribute or relational mapping, and should instead seek multiple sources to contribute to a decision about what to do. The decision will typically include the balancing of a variety of conflicting constraints involving how actions facilitate goals, as well as how some goals and actions can be incompatible. Analogical thinking in personal, legal, and political decisions is too important to be abandoned, but decision makers need to be aware of the need to evaluate analogies as part of the process of choosing plans.

need to evaluate analogies

Wondering Why

Gods Like Us

When strange and surprising things happen, people naturally search for explanations. Why do sounds echo? Why did the dinosaurs become extinct? Why is Daddy grumpy today? One powerful way of producing explanations is to use analogy, making a leap from one's understanding of some familiar happening to understanding of a surprising occurrence. The last two chapters described analogies as they are used in complex human problem solving and decision making. Now our focus shifts to another role of analogy, that of fostering explanation and understanding.

For at least as long as written records exist, analogy has contributed to human explanations of the world—how it was created, why events unfold as they do. This chapter and the next describe some highlights of the use of analogical explanations in philosophy and science. Many different cultures have found it natural to explain puzzling aspects of the world by talking of gods who created the world and influence it in various ways. Despite their enhanced powers, these gods are in many important respects often remarkably similar to people. The reason is simple: people create gods in their own image. We will trace a strand of explanation that began with the ancient Greeks and continued to be developed through to the nineteenth century, when thinkers made explicit analogical arguments for the existence of the Judeo-Christian God. We will also trace two other strands of analogical explanation—one concerning the nature of knowledge itself and the other concerning the knowledge we have of other minds.

Sometime before 700 B.C., the blind poet Homer wrote *The Iliad* and *The Odyssey*, epics telling the story of a group of Greek warriors before and after the fall of Troy. The characters in this story included not only human heroes, such as Achilles and Odysseus, but also the Olympian gods, who were regular participants in the events described by Homer. G. E. R. Lloyd remarks that "the world of the Homeric hero is in a real sense governed by and controlled by the gods. They often influence physical phenomena, such as the sea, the winds, storms, thunder and lightning, either directly or indirectly, and they have power over men too, affecting their physical strength, their morale, even their thoughts and desires." But how did the Greeks of Homer's day create their pantheon of gods?

Zeus, Athena, Apollo, Aphrodite, Hermes, and their cohorts had powers that exceeded those of humans. Yet these gods were like humans in their appearance and relationships and were capable of being both amorous and belligerent. Lloyd reports, "Not only are the Olympians generally conceived in the form of men, but the whole Homeric description of the gods—of their life, their behaviour and the motives which govern it, even of their rudimentary political organisation—faithfully reflects Homeric society itself." Thus, much of what happens in *The Iliad* and *The Odyssey* is understood to be the result of actions of members of a parallel society, the gods who mingle with humans and help to direct the course of their lives.

What the Homeric Greeks thought about the Olympians was clearly an analogical extension of what the Greeks thought about themselves. Like the Greeks, the gods had a powerful king, Zeus, who directed, and came into conflict with, other gods. Also like the Greeks, the various gods had quarrels and alliances. Like humans, but more powerful, the gods had control over physical objects and even the weather. We could thus draw out a detailed mapping between the attributes and social structure of the gods and those of the Greeks.

Much happened to Homer's heroes that no one could understand: physical disasters, strange dreams, surprising births, and so on. Introducing the gods into the picture knit together many of these happenings with explanations that people could comprehend, because these explanations were similar to those they used in their everyday lives. The gods loved and fought and schemed just like people. Centuries later, the Romans also had a society of gods analogous both to the Greek complement (for example, with Jupiter the counterpart of Zeus) and to their own society. The Greek philosopher Xenophanes had noted hundreds of years earlier the tendency of different peoples to credit the gods with their own particular characteristics. He remarked that if cows had gods, the gods would look like cows.

Monotheistic religions, such as Judaism, Christianity, and Islam, have no such room for social mappings between the affairs of humans and the affairs of a multitude of gods. But analogy has been frequently discussed in the Christian theological tradition. Writing in the thirteenth century A.D., St. Thomas Aquinas worried about how he could have knowledge of an infinite immaterial being so different from humans. He thought that God not only must be of a different genus from humans but must transcend all natural categories. Medieval discussions of analogy often focused on questions of ambiguity. For example, when a term such as "powerful" is applied to both humans and to God, the term was considered unavoidably ambiguous, since it was being applied to such different kinds of being. Nonetheless, Aquinas concluded that we could infer by analogy to humans that God is in some sense a being with knowledge and will.

Theological analogizing is clearly a tricky business, because it is difficult to decide which characteristics of humans ought to be transferred to God or a set of gods. Unlike Christian theologians, Greek mythologists attributed human weaknesses as well as strengths to their gods. Aquinas used analogy to reach conclusions not only about the nature of God, but also about his very existence. Aquinas provided five arguments for the existence of God, of which the fifth is essentially an argument from analogy concerning the design of the world. We will discuss this argument later in this chapter.

Plato's Cave

Writing a few centuries after Homer, Plato inaugurated systematic philosophy in his brilliant dialogues. Plato made frequent use of analogies in developing his political and psychological ideas, for example, drawing comparisons between the cosmic order and the social/political order. Here we want to focus more narrowly on Plato's epistemological analogies—the analogies he used to promote his view of the nature of knowledge. Then we will describe how later thinkers concerned with the philosophy of knowledge used alternative analogies.

In book 7 of the *Republic,* Plato used an extended analogy to try to undercut the commonsense view that knowledge is derived from sense perception. Plato imagined a long cave in which some people spend their whole lives fettered to one spot, unable to turn their heads. All they can see is shadows cast on a wall by the light of a fire burning higher up the cave. The shadows are of various puppets and implements that, unknown to the prisoners in the cave, are carried in front of the fire by those above. Plato argued that the knowledge we receive from our senses is like the beliefs that the people in the cave have about these shadows. The prisoners assume from their limited experience that they are achieving knowledge of reality, when in fact they are only perceiving a dull projection of the outside world.

Plato's own view was that genuine knowledge comes only a priori, independently of sense experience. In his middle dialogues, Plato's spokesman Socrates helps other thinkers to see the limitations of their knowledge, as he urges them to achieve knowledge by apprehending the abstract forms, the innate concepts that encapsulate knowledge. In the dialogue *Theaetetus,* Socrates describes his own role as analogous to that of a midwife. Just as midwives help women to bring children into the world, Socrates helps people to bring good ideas into the world. In the same dialogue, Socrates compares memory to the imprint on a block of wax and also likens knowledge to wild birds in an aviary.

Many philosophers since Plato have used analogies to help explain the nature of knowledge, but the analogies have varied with their epistemological positions. Whereas Plato gave sense experience a minor role in producing knowledge, his wax analogy was taken up by more empirically minded philosophers. Plato's student Aristotle compared the impact of the senses on the mind to the imprint of a metal ring on a wax tablet, identifying the mind as a blank slate. Centuries later, John Locke took experience to be the sole source of knowledge and denied any innate ideas; updating Aristotle's writing technology, he compared the mind to a white paper on which the senses can leave impressions. Gottfried Leibniz countered empiricist analogies with another, saying that the mind is more like a block of veined marble that can be sculpted in only a limited number of ways. Noam Chomsky used a battery of very different analogies in a more recent defense of the innateness of grammar and concepts. He claimed that learning a language is like undergoing puberty—something you are designed to do at a particular time. Chomsky also suggested that teaching should be compared not with filling a bottle with water, but rather with helping a flower grow in its own way.

As these arguments suggest, traditional epistemologists have been concerned to establish knowledge with foundations in either sense experience (the empiricist tradition of Locke and Hume) or reason (the rationalist tradition of Plato, Descartes, and Leibniz). Francis Bacon rejected this dichotomy, using a lovely trio of analogies:

Those who have handled sciences have been either men of experiment or men of dogmas. The men of experiment are like the ant, they only collect and use; the reasoners resemble spiders, who make cobwebs out of their own substance. But the bee takes a middle course: it gathers its material from the flowers of the garden and of the field, but transforms and digests it by a power of its own. Not unlike this is the true business of philosophy; for it neither relies solely or chiefly on the powers of the mind, nor does it take the matter which it gathers from natural history and mechanical experiments and lay it up in memory whole, but lays it up in the understanding altered and digested. Therefore from a closer and purer league between these two faculties, the experimental and the rational (such as has never been made), much may be hoped.

Using a more modern metaphor commonly employed in cognitive science, we would say that Bacon appreciated that the origin of knowledge is neither totally bottom-up (based on sense experience) nor totally top-down (based on prior knowledge); rather, knowledge is acquired by the systematic integration of inputs of both types.

The empiricist and rationalist search for foundations for knowledge presumes an analogy that compares knowledge to buildings that need to rest on a solid base. Twentieth-century analogies for knowledge present a more dynamic picture that undercuts the desire for foundations. W. V. O. Quine, following Otto Neurath, compared philosophy and science to a boat that needs to be repaired at sea. Faulty planks can be replaced, but there is no way the whole structure can be taken apart. Quine described the structure of knowledge as a "web of belief" and as a "fabric of sentences":

The lore of our fathers is a fabric of sentences. In our hands it develops and changes, through more or less arbitrary and deliberative revisions and additions of our own, more or less directly occasioned by the continuing stimulation of our sense organs. It is a pale gray lore, black with fact and white with convention. But I have found no substantial reasons for concluding that there are any quite black threads in it, or any white ones.

Quine's epistemological views have had great influence on contemporary philosophy, an influence due in part to the aptness of his analogies.

Other contemporary theorists, such as Donald Campbell, comparing the development of knowledge to the development of biological species, advocate an enterprise they call *evolutionary epistemology*. Just as new species arise from previous ones by genetic changes and the pressures of natural selection, so ideas arise by a kind of mutation process and then undergo a kind of selection. Thagard has argued that biological analogies for the development of knowledge are misleading and weak compared to epistemological analogies that have their source in the domain of computation. We will pursue the analogy between thinking and computation further in the next chapter.

Designing the World

Let us return to the analogies used to comprehend God. St. Thomas Aquinas and many other thinkers, including the eminent early scientists Robert Boyle and Isaac Newton, thought that the world displays evidence of having had a designer. This line of argument hit its peak in 1802, with William Paley's *Natural Theology*. Paley contrasted the case of discovering a stone while crossing a heath with discovering a watch. One could easily explain the presence of the stone by supposing it had been there forever, but the presence of the watch would require a very different explanation. For the watch is a complex, intricate device, requiring the inevitable inference that the watch must have had a maker. Similarly, Paley contended, the eye and many other complex structures found in nature are evidence of design, and hence of a designer, namely God. Paley and other thinkers in the first half of the nineteenth century devoted volumes to describing the complexity of the natural world as evidence for the work of a designer.

The analogy between human artifacts, such as a watch, and the natural world is a sophisticated analogy based on a system mapping. The watch has complexity that is the result of a design, and so does the world. Simplifying, the source and target analogs are:

Source	Target
design (watchmaker, watch) *name*: design-1	design (God, world) *name*: design-2
complex (watch) *name*: complex-1	complex (world) *name*: complex-2
cause (design-1, complex-1)	cause (design-2, complex-2)

That is, the watchmaker's designing the watch caused the complexity of the watch, and similarly God's designing the world caused the complexity of the biological world.

Paley and other natural theologians worked out such analogies in excruciating detail. However, a pure analogical argument is far from convincing. David Hume had already argued in his *Dialogues concerning Natural Religion* that it was dubious to compare things in the world to the world as a whole, and suggested that human intelligence might not be the right model for the cause of the whole universe. Hume contended that the world is more like an animal or vegetable than like an artifact produced by an intelligent being and that the presence of evil in the world did not suggest a designer who was benevolent and omnipotent.

These theological debates suggest some of the limitations of analogical inference. In general, a single analogy considered in isolation does not provide a very convincing form of argument. In explanation, as in decision making, it is often wise to work with multiple analogies. And as is the case for problem solving, where analogical thinking may suggest a solution but does not itself show that the solution will work, so in explanation analogical thinking is more useful for suggesting possible explanations than in justifying their acceptance.

Nevertheless, an analogy, such as the argument from design, can provide part of a justification for the inferred conclusion. The complex and intricate nature of the world cries out for explanation, and one could contend that the best available explanation derives from the hypothesis that God designed it. Inference to the best explanation is a reasoning pattern common in science and in everyday life: we accept a hypothesis on the grounds that it provides a better explanation of the evidence than alternative hypotheses. Analogy can contribute to showing the explanatory power of a hypothesis if the hypothesis supports explanations analogous to those provided by accepted theories. The analogy between the world and objects designed by humans supports inference to God as the best explanation, since we can better appreciate the design of the world by God through comparison with design of artifacts by people. The inference to the hypothesis that God designed the world gains credibility not just from the analogy itself but also from the contention that it explains more about the natural world than any other available hypothesis.

The explanatory superiority of divine design could be readily defended in 1802, despite Hume's complaints about the quality of the analogy, because of the lack of alternative explanations of natural complexity. The situation changed dramatically, however, in 1859, when Darwin published *On the Origin of Species*. For the first time, a rich alternative hypothesis became available to explain the origins of complex aspects of plants and animals: variation and natural selection. As we will see in the next chapter, Darwin's discovery and development of his theory of evolution itself relied heavily on nontheological analogies. Unlike pure analogical reasoning, inference to the best explanation is explicitly comparative, requiring that alternative hypotheses be considered before a hypothesis can be selected as part of the best explanation.

Darwin provided an alternative hypothesis that did not exist in Paley's day, undermining both Paley's claim that divine design was the best explanation of the complexity of the biological world and his analogy with artifacts.

✳   In chapter 6 we argued that the best analogies used in decision making employ system mappings, based on explicit higher-order relations, to aid in judgments of deliberative coherence. Similarly, an analogy used in defending a hypothesis, such as the existence of God, should employ a system mapping that can contribute toward a judgment of explanatory coherence, showing that the hypothesis supported by analogy is part of the best explanation of the evidence. According to Thagard's account, hypotheses gain explanatory coherence by virtue of explaining evidence, being explained by higher-order hypotheses, and being analogous to accepted explanatory hypotheses. These contributions to coherence can be thought of as soft constraints analogous to those governing analogy and decision making: we want a theory to explain a lot, to do so simply, to be compatible with what is known, and to be itself explainable. For analogy to contribute to coherence, there must be similar hypotheses explaining similar evidence, with the explanation relations in the two analogs making a system mapping possible. The argument from design clearly uses a system mapping, as shown by the presence of the higher-order "cause" relation in both the source analog (watch/watchmaker) and the target analog (world/God). So there is indeed an analogical explanation that makes the hypothesis of divine creation a legitimate candidate to be evaluated by inference to the best explanation. This hypothesis must compete, however, with Darwinian and other scientific explanations of the world.

In explanation, we should be most impressed by analogies with a structure that fully serves the explanatory purpose. The crucial part of the structure will be higher-order relations, such as "explain" and "cause," that are intended to carry over from the explanatory source to the target to be explained. As in decision making, in which analogies and decisions can be simultaneously evaluated, evaluating the explanatory coherence of hypotheses goes hand in hand with evaluating the quality of the analogies that provide part of the support for the hypotheses. Thus we may decide that the analogy between the world and a watch is weak, not because of any inherent analogical flaw, but because it does not fit with Darwinian explanations, which (as we will see in chapter 8) were supported in part by a different set of analogies.

Other Minds

An eminent philosopher was once asked, "Are there other minds?" He replied; "Not many." This is an unorthodox answer to an old philosophical question that arises because of the apparent discrepancy between the knowledge that individuals have of their own minds and the knowledge that they have of the minds of other people. I know that I have a mind, because of direct awareness of my thoughts and feelings. But how do I know that you have thoughts and feelings at all like mine? How do I know there are any minds other than mine?

Since David Hume, at least, many philosophers have sought a solution to the problem of other minds by using analogical reasoning. You and I are alike in many ways: we have similar bodies and similar behavior. So by analogy I can conclude that since I have thoughts and feelings, so probably do you. This analogical transfer is performed by the process that in chapter 2 we called "copying with substitution." The source is "I," and the target is "you"; the analogs include such information as the following:

Source	Target
have (I, body) *name*: have-1	have (you, body) *name*: have-2
perform (I, actions) *name*: perform-1	perform (you, actions) *name*: perform-2
think (I) *name*: think-1	
feel (I) *name*: feel-1	

The target can be completed by copying the predicates "think" and "feel" over to the target and substituting "you" for "I," thereby creating the inferences that you think and you feel.

This use of analogy seems like a reasonable way to form the conjecture that you have a mind like mine, but how convincing is it on its own? From my individual perspective, there remain the obvious differences between my familiar mental experiences and yours, which I cannot experience. As with the argument from design, as long as we are only comparing similarities, it is hard to reach a very confident conclusion when there are clear differences as well. As with the argument from design, however, we can advance further by recasting the argument as an inference to the best explanation, with analogy incorporated as part of the explanatory structure. The mapping between the source and the target above is merely a relational mapping, putting similar predicates and objects into correspondence with each other. But if we pay attention to the explanatory structure of the source and target, we can identify a richer system mapping that can feed into a judgment of explanatory coherence.

Why do I perform the actions that I do? Part of the commonsense explanation of my behavior is that my thinking causes my actions. Ordinary explanations say that I perform an action because of my beliefs and desires: I have a desire and a belief that the action will tend to accomplish it. Cognitive psychology gives a more sophisticated kind of explanation than this by postulating mental structures and processes that lead to action. Either way, I explain my own actions in terms of my mental experiences. Similarly, the best explanation I can give of your actions depends on postulating that you have mental experiences like I have. This hypothesis can be formed from the proposition "think-1" in the above source, to produce, by copying with substitution,

think (you) *name*: think-2.

Schematically, we can portray the explanatory analogy as involving higher-order relations, such as,

Source	Target
explain (think-1, perform-1)	explain (think-2, perform-2)

That is, just as my thinking explains the actions I perform, so the hypothesis that you think can explain the actions you perform. Once the explanatory relations in the source and target are identified, we have a system mapping in addition to a relational mapping, and with it comes the beginnings of an argument to the best explanation. How else could I explain why you perform the actions that you do? Perhaps you are a robot or a member of some nonhuman species with mental processes totally unlike mine. But neither of these hypotheses has any independent plausibility of the sort that the analogy between you and me gives to the hypothesis that you do what you do because you have a mind like mine.

Alvin Plantinga argued that the analogical argument for other minds had the same flaws as the analogical argument for the existence of God, and he drew the conclusion that if my belief in other minds is rational, so is my belief in God. (This is an analogical argument about analogical arguments!) If the two arguments are understood purely as analogies based on relational mappings, his conclusion is valid: both analogies can be sufficiently undermined by relevant differences to make them unconvincing. But if we recast the arguments as involving inference to the best explanation, with an analogical component, then a relevant difference between explaining the complexity of the biological world and explaining the behavior of other people emerges. In explaining the complexity of the biological world, design by God must compete with a strong alternative hypothesis, that of evolution by natural selection. In explaining the complex behavior of others, however, no credible alternative has yet been proposed to compete with the hypothesis that other people have minds.

Understanding that analogy is part of inference to coherent explanatory theories takes care of the traditional general problem of other minds: we are justified in supposing that other people have minds, because that is part of the most explanatorily coherent account of complex human behavior. But a difficult psychological and epistemological problem remains. Granted that other humans have minds basically like yours, you still face the problem of understanding particular aspects of other people's minds. Analogy, and even analogy-based inference to the best explanation, might get you in trouble here—for example, if you are dealing with a member of the opposite sex. According to Deborah Tannen, men and women unconsciously have very different conversational styles. Men are more likely than women to use language to try to compete and impress, while women are more likely to try to reach consensus. A man who explained a woman's public verbal behavior by analogy to his own behavior would risk making a serious mistake, and vice versa, since the correct explanations of the speech patterns of the man and the woman may well be quite different.

Despite such pitfalls, analogical inference is a powerful and useful way of understanding other people, particularly when it brings an emotional appreciation of someone else's situation. This appreciation is what we mean by "empathy." When you see someone crying over the loss of a loved one, you can understand the person's grief by imagining yourself in that situation and experiencing similar feelings. Alvin Goldman has argued that this kind of simulation of the situation faced by another is a common way of understanding others. Simulation and empathy do not require either an implausible attribution of rationality or a well worked out psychological theory: we just imagine ourselves in someone else's situation and draw out the factual and emotional consequences.

As Allison Barnes has argued, empathy is a form of analogical inference. I notice similarities between myself and you and infer your mental state by transferring my projected state to you. What makes empathy different from other varieties of analogical thinking is that what gets transferred can be an emotional state. The products of analogy include not only propositions but also feelings. Empathy can even play a role in legal decision making, sometimes leading to acquittals that go against legal principles. Jurors may put themselves in the shoes of an accused (for example, someone who killed a spouse after years of being abused) and realize that they would have had the same emotions as the accused and therefore might well have done the same thing.

Analogy can also be useful in understanding your own mind. The traditional philosophical problem of other minds takes for granted the knowledge one has of one's own mind, but that is often very limited. People are sometimes perplexed by their own actions and can seek explanations of them by analogy to why other people behaved as they did in similar situations. Chapter 9 describes how psychotherapists use analogies to help people understand their problems. Ideally, people should employ analogies that contribute to the best explanation of their problems; however, personal goals, such as maintaining self-esteem, may sometimes make us to choose analogies that cast an unrealistic but flattering light on our behavior.

Intuition Pumps *simplistic ethical arguments*

Analogy plays an important role in arguments for the existence of God and for other minds, as we have seen. It also figures prominently in smaller-scale philosophical arguments. Philosophers often use analogical thought experiments to show that there is something wrong with a view they contest. John Searle attacked the view that computers have cognitive states, by telling a story that involved his being locked in a room and given a large batch of Chinese writing. He knows no Chinese but is given a set of English rules for correlating elements of this batch with elements of other batches. Unknown to him, the rules are such that when someone gives him a batch of Chinese symbols that constitutes a question, he is able to hand back a batch of Chinese symbols that constitutes an answer to the question. Searle claims he is just like a computer program, taking input and producing output. His analogical argument is that just as he does not understand Chinese, so a computer that has internal rules that enable it to manipulate symbols does not really understand language either.

The Chinese room

Like the crude form of the argument for other minds, Searle's case depends on copying with substitution: Searle maps to the computer;

since Searle does not understand Chinese, the computer does not understand language. Many people have pointed out that Searle's argument is defective, but seeing it as an argument by analogy provides a different way of identifying the defects. The crucial question is: what is to be mapped to what? Searle places in correspondence (a) himself in the room manipulating Chinese symbols and (b) the computer that is claimed to understand language. But the **Searle ↔ computer** mapping is misleading in several respects. First, the kind of computer he envisions is like the ones used in the late twentieth century for simulations of artificial intelligence. Such computers are clearly dependent on human input. However, the kinds of computers for which it may some day be possible to make plausible claims about their capacity to think will be much more autonomous entities. These computers will have robotic connections to the world and the ability to learn from their interactions with it. They will be much more than simple input-output devices. So Searle has mischaracterized the target analog. Second, he gets the mapping wrong, since what corresponds in Searle's story to the complex computer hypothesized to understand language is not just Searle, but Searle plus the rules for manipulating symbols. The fact that Searle does not understand Chinese provides no support for the conclusion that the whole system— comprised of Searle together with all the rules and the ability to use them to answer Chinese questions—does not (at some implicit level) understand Chinese. Searle's simplistic analogy serves as an "intuition pump" to provoke unreflective judgments about a substantive issue, whether computers could think.

Intuition pumps are widely used in ethics when philosophers debate moral issues such as abortion. Judith Jarvis Thomson defended the permissibility of abortion, not by denying that a fetus is a person, but by comparing a woman with an unwanted fetus to the following case. Suppose you wake up in the morning and find yourself attached to a famous violinist, who is unconscious. You have been kidnapped because your blood type is the same as the violinist, and your circulatory system has been connected with his to enable your kidneys to clean his blood. To unplug you would be to kill him, but after nine months his kidneys would be strong enough to let him live on his own. Are you obliged to stay connected to the violinist? This story is intended to be analogous to the situation of a woman with an unwanted pregnancy, and it pumps our intuitions to conclude that even if the fetus is a person, the woman has no moral obligation to bring it to term. We are encouraged to do an analogical transfer of our moral judgment concerning being bound to the violinist to the situation of carrying a fetus. This form of argument is similar to President Bush's comparison of Saddam Hussein to Adolf Hitler (chapter 5) in that accepting the analogy is tantamount to accepting a prescription for action.

The problem with such intuition pumps is that someone who wants to reach a contradictory conclusion can generally concoct another related case that pulls one's intuitions in a different direction. James Humber proposed that you imagine yourself being involved in a shipwreck and tying yourself to a large piece of flotsam. A nonswimmer grabs your arm and asks you for help to get onto the flotsam, which could support both of you. You reply that the nonswimmer has no right to the use of your body, and you let him drown. Most people would regard this action as immoral, and Humber wants to conclude analogically that a pregnant woman has an obligation to complete her pregnancy. Ethicists toss such stories about in an often fruitless game of "my intuitions are stronger than your intuitions."

Our general stance about what makes for good analogies shows why such intuition pumps are always going to be inconclusive. The basic problem is that we lack any independent way to evaluate whether the inferences about the target domain generated by such analogical mappings are in fact justified. How are we to decide whether the differences between the source and target can be safely ignored? Consider the two competing analogies to an unwanted pregnancy. In the case of the attached violinist, the inference that he can be justifiably unplugged seems to hinge in part on the fact that someone (whoever attached the violinist) might have first sought our consent but failed to do so. In addition, the burden of being attached to the violinist in this artificial way appears to be severe. In the case of the unfortunate nonswimmer, the opposite inference, that we have a moral obligation to provide aid, seems to trade on the fact the nonswimmer did seek our consent and that the cost of helping him onto the flotsam appears slight. Which case, then, is more like an unwanted pregnancy? It is easy to argue that neither source matches well on these crucial causal factors. The fetus does not ask for the mother's consent but surely is excused, since it is unable to do so; neither source captures this nuance. And how does the burden of carrying a fetus to term compare either to being attached to an adult by a machine for nine months or to offering one's arm to someone for a moment to help them? The comparisons are murky, to say the least; many people might feel that the burden of pregnancy falls somewhere between the two source cases. It may in fact help clarify our moral intuitions to work through what drives our judgments about a family of interrelated analogies. But none of these intuition pumps can conclusively tell us what is right for the target case.

Like decision making and explanation, the development of ethical judgments should exploit and evaluate multiple analogies. But ethical intuition pumps are unable to contribute to judgments of deliberative or explanatory coherence, because neither of these types of coherence can be clearly related to ethics. Perhaps a different kind of coherence is required to evaluate ethical conclusions. As we saw in chapter 6, John Rawls employs a kind of coherence criterion when he discusses the need to reach a "reflective equilibrium" that strikes a balance between our ethical principles and our ethical judgments about particular cases. We are not about to propose a methodology for reaching ethical conclusions but rest with the point that analogies alone are unable to transcend the inherent subjectivity of intuition pumps.

Asian Analogies

Our examples so far have been drawn from Western culture, but analogy has also been important in the religious and philosophical writings of ancient India and China. Consider two passages from the Upanishads, written before 400 B.C. One passage uses analogies to describe the Hindu view of the cyclic nature of existence:

The world is the wheel of God, turning around
And round with all living creatures upon its rim.
The world is the river of God,
Flowing from him and flowing back to him.
On this ever revolving wheel of being
The individual self goes round and round
Through life after life.

or are these metaphors

Another passage uses an analogy to characterize the relationship between the individual self and pure consciousness:

As a lump of salt thrown in water dissolves
and cannot be taken out again, though
wherever we taste the water it is salty, even
so, beloved, the separate self dissolves in the
sea of pure consciousness, infinite and immortal.

The Chinese provided examples of highly sophisticated argument based on analogies. The Chinese philosopher Mencius (Meng-tzu), an important disciple of Confucius, wrote around 300 B.C., not long after Plato. He shared Confucius's belief that people are inherently inclined to be good, and he engaged in an argument with a philosopher named Kao Tzu, who maintained that people were inherently neither good nor bad. The argument unfolds around two rich analogies, the first of which is intended to show that dutifulness can be imposed on people, but only unnaturally:

Kao Tzu said, "Human nature is like the *ch'i* willow. Dutifulness is like cups and bowls. To make morality out of human nature is like making cups and bowls out of the willow."

"Can you," said Mencius, "make cups and bowls by following the nature of the willow? Or must you mutilate the willow before you can make it into cups and bowls? If you have to mutilate the willow to make it into cups and bowls, must you, then, also mutilate a man to make him moral? Surely it will be these words of yours men in the world will follow in bringing disaster upon morality."

Here Mencius rejects Kao Tzu's analogy, on the grounds that moral education is not mutilation. A second analogy, however, is turned by Mencius to his own advantage:

Kao Tzu said, "Human nature is like whirling water. Give it an outlet in the east and it will flow east; give it an outlet in the west and it will flow west. Human nature does not show any preference for either good or bad just as water does not show any preference for either east or west."

"It certainly is the case," said Mencius, "that water does not show any preference for either east or west, but does it show the same indifference to high and low? Human nature is good just as water seeks low ground. There is no man who is not good; there is no water that does not flow downwards.

"Now in the case of water, by splashing it one can make it shoot up higher than one's forehead, and by forcing it one can make it stay on a hill. Now can that be the nature of water? It is the circumstances being what they are. That man can be made bad shows that his nature is not different from that of water in this respect."

Mencius argues that the inclination of human nature is like water's inclination for lower ground, and he enriches the analogy by comparing people becoming bad to water being forced upward against its nature. Regardless of how plausible one finds his reasoning, there can be no doubt that we have here a highly sophisticated system analogy: just as splashing water causes it to go against its nature, so circumstances can cause humans to go against their nature. Thus the ancient Chinese, like the ancient Greeks, practiced complex analogical thinking.

Analogies are even more a part of the mystical Taoist tradition than they are of the rational Confucian tradition. Writing a bit later than Mencius, the Taoist thinker Chuang Tzu used multiple analogies to suggest how to tutor an unruly prince. The tutor must harmonize with the prince, not simply lecture him: "Don't you know about the praying mantis that waved its arms angrily in front of an approaching carriage, unaware that they were incapable of stopping it? Such was the high opinion it had of its talents. Be careful, be on your guard! If you offend him by parading your store of talents, you will be in danger." Chuang Tzu proceeds to compare the tutor to a successful tiger trainer who understands and follows along with his tigers, not going against them, and to a horse lover who is careless about hurting his horse.

Chinese philosophers in the third century B.C. not only used analogies but were aware of the significance of their use, as we see in this ancient story:

Someone said to the King of Liang, "Hui Tzu is very good at using analogies when putting forth his views. If your Majesty could stop him from using analogies he will be at a loss what to say."

The King said, "Very well. I will do that."

The following day when he received Hui Tzu the King said to him, "If you have anything to say, I wish you would say it plainly and not resort to analogies."

Hui Tzu said, "Suppose there is a man here who does not know what a *tan* is, and you say to him, 'A *tan* is like a *tan,*' would he understand?"

The King said, "No."

"Then were you to say to him, 'A *tan* is like a bow, but has a strip of bamboo in place of the string,' would he understand?"

The King said, "Yes. He would."

Hui Tzu said, "A man who explains necessarily makes intelligible that which is not known by comparing it with what is known. Now Your Majesty says, 'Do not use analogies.' This would make the task impossible."

The king agreed. In chapter 8 we mention scientists and educators who doubt the value of analogy; it is interesting that both these doubts and the appropriate counters to them have been around for more than two thousand years.

Of course, Chinese use of analogy did not end in the third century B.C. The Maoist slogans of the 1960s, "Let a hundred flowers bloom" and "Women hold up half the sky," made political points more effectively than more prosaic admonishments would have. In chapter 9 we will discuss other analogies that are important in several Asian cultures.

Philosophers are not the only thinkers who use analogies in trying to gain a systematic understanding of the world. In the next chapter we describe analogies that have made noteworthy contributions to science and technology.

Summary

We have seen that analogies have played an important role in several of the central branches of philosophy: metaphysics (God, other minds), epistemology (Plato's cave, Neurath's ship), and ethics. (The development of theories in logic has also employed analogy: George Boole explicitly modeled his early work in propositional logic on algebra, and so did Charles Peirce.) Analogies have contributed to religious and philosophical thought in India and China as well as in Europe and America.

Just as evaluation of analogies in decision making is in part a matter of deliberative coherence, so evaluation of analogies in explanation is in part a matter of explanatory coherence. The most powerful analogies are ones based on system mappings with higher-order relations, such as "explain" and "cause," which afford the analogies a structure that directly contributes to their explanatory purposes. Like decision making, explanation can benefit from use of multiple analogies; and evaluation of competing analogies is part of the process of evaluating competing hypotheses.

evaluating competing analogies

8

The Analogical Scientist

Great Scientific Analogies

Several years after he carried out his famous kite experiment, Benjamin Franklin responded to a query concerning how he came to propose it, by quoting from a journal that he had kept at the time:

Nov. 7, 1749. Electrical fluid agrees with lightning in these particulars: 1. Giving light. 2. Color of the light. 3. Crooked direction. 4. Swift motion. 5. Being conducted by metals. 6. Crack or noise in exploding. 7. Subsisting in water or ice. 8. Rending bodies it passes through. 9. Destroying animals. 10. Melting metals. 11. Firing inflammable substances. 12. Sulphureous smell. —The electric fluid is attracted by points. —We do not know whether this property is in lightning. —But since they agree in all the particulars wherein we can already compare them, is it not probable they agree likewise in this? Let the experiment be made.

The kite experiment was thus inspired by the analogy Franklin noticed between lightning and electrical phenomena, such as sparks.

Historians, philosophers, and psychologists of science have documented many instances of analogical thinking. This chapter presents a collection of many of the most important analogies that scientists have used, and it provides an account of the main mechanisms required for analogical thinking in science. The various contributions of analogy to the discovery, development, and evaluation of scientific theories have involved a number of different ways of representing, constructing, and using analogies. Analogies are also important in teaching science, as well as other topics. We draw some conclusions concerning the educational use and misuse of analogies.

It would be easy to compile a list of hundreds of analogies that have been used by scientists, but our goal is to identify the analogies that qualify as most important according to two criteria. First, the analogy

vital contribution to scientific thinking + theoretical advance.

must have clearly contributed to some vital stage of a scientist's thinking, whether it was the discovery or development of an idea or the later argumentation in its defense. Second, the scientist's thinking that involved the analogy must have contributed to a major theoretical advance. The theory to which the analogy contributed need not be accepted today, but it must have been important in its own time and context.

Because additional candidates may well be defensible, the following list is not definitive. However, it suffices to provide a broad sample of highly significant analogies for analysis and generalization, presented here in chronological order. As we saw in the last chapter, rich analogies abound in the writings of Plato, Aristotle, and other Greek thinkers. But we have identified only one scientific analogy of enduring significance before the modern era.

1. Sound/water waves   The analogy between sound and water waves was discussed in chapter 1. Water waves were first used to suggest the nature of sound by the Greek Stoic Chrysippus around the second century B.C., but our knowledge of his views is fragmentary. In the first century A.D., the Roman architect Vitruvius, in the course of explaining the acoustic properties of Greek amphitheaters, explicitly compared the sound of voices to water waves that can flow out and bounce back when obstructed, just as sound spreads and echoes. Here we have the ancient origins of the modern wave theory of sound.

2. Earth/small magnet   In his landmark work *De Magnete,* published in 1600, William Gilbert described important experimental investigations of the nature of magnets, and he proposed for the first time that the planet earth is a giant magnet. The basis for his hypothesis was a systematic comparison between the properties of the earth, such as how it affects compasses, and the properties of the small spherical magnets on which he had performed many experiments. The earth is like these objects in many respects, so, according to Gilbert, we should infer that the earth acts like a magnet, engendering the magnetism of the objects that were part of it. Indeed, since the common properties of the earth and small magnets define what it means to be a magnet, the earth not only acts like a magnet, it is a magnet.

3. Earth/moon   Galileo's *Dialogue concerning the Two Chief World Systems,* published in 1630, contained two analogies that made important contributions to his contention that the earth moves. First, Galileo compared the earth to the moon, both of which are spherical, dark, opaque, dense, and solid, with similar expanses of light and dark and of land and sea. Since the moon was known to move in an orbit, he argued it was reasonable to suppose that the earth does too.

4. Earth/ship   Galileo used a different analogy to rebut an argument that the earth does not move. Opponents of his theory argued that if a rock is dropped from a tower, it lands at the base of the tower, suggesting that the tower, and hence the earth, is not in motion. Galileo countered this argument with a ship analogy, comparing the tower to the mast of a ship that is moving. He pointed out that a rock dropped from the top of the mast will fall and land at the base of the mast even though the ship is moving.

5. Light/sound In his 1678 *Treatise on Light,* Christiaan Huygens used an analogy between light and sound in support of his wave theory of light. That theory was eclipsed for more than a century by Newton's particle theory but was revived in the early nineteenth century by Thomas Young and Augustin Fresnel. These scientists exploited the analogy between light and sound to develop and defend a wave theory of light.

6. Planet/projectile Toward the end of his celebrated *Principia* (1687), Isaac Newton used an analogy to help bring planetary motion within the scope of his theory of gravitation. He compared a planet to a stone thrown upward from the earth with greater and greater force. He presented a diagram to show how with a great enough force the path of the stone would become the path of an object in orbit around the earth. Newton used this analogy to support his hypothesis that the orbits of the planets are governed by gravitational force.

7. Lightning/electricity We have already described Benjamin Franklin's famous analogy leading to the hypothesis that lightning was a form of electricity. Like the earth/small magnet example, this comparison became more than an analogy. Following Franklin's work, the definition of electricity has expanded to include the natural phenomenon of lightning.

8. Respiration/combustion During the 1770s when Antoine Lavoisier was developing his oxygen theory of combustion, he also developed a theory of the role of oxygen in animal respiration. Much of his thinking was guided by an analogy between respiration and combustion, both of which involve a change of oxygen into carbon dioxide and a provision of heat.

9. Heat/water In 1824, Nicholas Léonard Sadi Carnot provided a thorough discussion of the motive power of heat, drawing heavily on an analogy between heat and waterfalls. He argued that heat acts on substances, just as water acts on waterfalls, with the power depending in the former case on the amount of caloric (heat substance) and in the latter on the height of the waterfall. The idea of heat as a fluid was already well established by this time, but Carnot put it to much more systematic use.

10. Animal and plant competition/human population growth Charles Darwin reported that he arrived at the basic idea of natural selection in 1838 by fortuitous reading of Malthus's tract on human population growth. Darwin had been searching for a mechanism that could produce the evolution of species, and he realized from Malthus that rapid population growth in the face of limited food and land could lead to a struggle for existence. Darwin noticed the analogy between potential human strife (produced by population growth's outstripping resources) and competition among animals and plants for survival.

11. Natural selection/artificial selection A different analogy played a much greater role in the development and evaluation of Darwin's theory of evolution by natural selection. He often compared natural selection to the artificial selection performed by breeders, who exploited the inherent variability in animals and plants to choose desired features. Natural selection leads to different species, Darwin argued, just as artificial selection leads to different breeds. Darwin used this analogy in the *Origin of Species* (1859) and elsewhere, both in developing explanations and in arguing for the acceptability of his overall theory.

12. Electromagnetic forces/continuum mechanics James Clerk Maxwell was explicit and enthusiastic about the use of mechanical and mathematical analogies. The most important application in his own thinking was the construction in the 1860s of a diagrammed mechanical model for electrical and mechanical forces, consisting of a fluid medium with vortices and stresses. He was able to abstract from this mechanical analog a general mathematical description that could be applied directly to electromagnetism.

13. Benzene/snake As we mentioned in chapter 1, Friedrich Kekulé proposed in 1865 a new theory of the molecular structure of benzene. According to Kekulé, he was led to the hypothesis that the carbon atoms in benzene are arranged in a ring by a reverie in which he saw a snake biting its own tail. This example, like those of Maxwell, Newton, and Morgan, illustrates how visual representations can contribute to creative thinking using analogy.

14. Chromosome/beaded string In 1915, Thomas Morgan and his colleagues explained complex phenomena of inheritance by comparing chromosomes to a string containing beads corresponding to the various factors leading to inheritance. Within a few years, those factors had come to be called "genes." The beaded-string analogy was most useful for describing how novel linkages could arise from crossover of chromosomes, just as new patterns of beads could arise from breaking and recombining the string.

15. Bacterial mutation/slot machine In 1943, Salvador Luria was trying to find experimental support for his view that phage-resistant cultures of bacteria arise because of gene mutations, not because of action of the phage on the bacteria. (A phage is a viral organism that destroys bacteria.) None of his experiments worked, but at a faculty dance at Indiana University he happened to watch a colleague putting dimes into a slot machine. He realized that slot machines pay out money in a very uneven distribution, with most trials yielding nothing, some yielding small amounts, and rare trials providing jackpots. He then reasoned that if bacteria become resistant because of gene mutations, then the numbers of resistant bacteria in different bacterial cultures should vary like the expected returns from different kinds of slot machines. This reasoning led to an experiment and theoretical model, for which he was awarded a Nobel prize.

16. Mind/computer Numerous analogies have been used over the centuries in attempts to understand the nature of mind and thinking. By far the most fertile has been the use since the 1950s, by Alan Turing and many others, of comparisons between thinking and computation. Computational ideas have suggested hypotheses about the nature of mind that have led to much psychological and computational experimentation. As we will discuss below, this analogy is very dynamic and complex; ideas about computation have influenced conceptions of the mind, which have in turn had an impact on the evolution of new types of computers.

But there are not "lesser" analogies

Notably absent from this list are two well-known analogies that have often been used in teaching. Molecules of gases are often compared to billiard balls in motion, but we have not been able to find any use of this analogy by the developers of the kinetic theory of gases. Another famous analogy is the comparison of the Rutherford-Bohr model of the atom with the solar system, but the analogy does not seem to have played a role in the creation of their model.

These examples of scientific analogies vary along several important dimensions. Let us look in particular at the purposes served by the analogies and at the cognitive mechanisms involved in their construction and application.

Purposes

Scientific analogies have at least four distinguishable uses: discovery, development, evaluation, and exposition. The most exciting is discovery, when analogy contributes to the formation of a new hypothesis. After a hypothesis has been invented, analogy may contribute to its further theoretical or experimental development. In addition, analogy can play a role in the evaluation of a hypothesis, as revealed in the arguments given for or against its acceptance. Finally, analogies are often used in the exposition of science, when new ideas are conveyed to other people by comparing them with old ones. We shall see that an analogy can have more than one use.

Of the uses of analogy, discovery is the hardest to document, since records are far less frequently kept of the very beginnings of hypotheses than of their development and evaluation. Nevertheless, three of the above analogies can clearly be seen as contributing to discoveries: Darwin's animal and plant competition/human population growth, Maxwell's electromagnetic forces/continuum mechanics, and Kekulé's benzene/snake. The cognitive mechanisms for producing the discoveries were quite different in these cases, as we will see in the next section, but all the analogies played a crucial role in forming the hypotheses that were developed.

We can conjecture that several other analogies may have played a role in discovery. Chrysippus may well have been inspired to conjecture that sound moves in waves, by noticing water waves and forming the sound/water wave analogy. And perhaps Franklin derived not only the idea for his experiment but also the basic hypothesis that lightning is electricity by grasping the lightning/electricity analogy. The famous story about Newton's theory of gravitation being inspired by a falling apple is not known to be false, so it is possible that the planet/projectile analogy played a role in the discovery of his theory as well as in the later argument for it. Lavoisier may have first understood the role of oxygen in respiration by developing the respiration/combustion analogy. Perhaps further historical research will bring to light evidence that these and additional analogies played important roles in scientific discoveries.

Even if an analogy does not initially form a hypothesis, it can aid greatly in its development. Two kinds of development are relevant: theoretical, in which a hypothesis is refined and linked with other hypotheses; and experimental, in which the empirical consequences of a hypothesis are worked out and translated into feasible experiments. The light/sound analogy contributed to developments of both these kinds. The diffraction properties of light were suggested in part by the ability of sound and water waves to go around corners. The analogy suggested Young's landmark experiments in which coherent light from two pinholes was shown to exhibit interference, and it contributed to Fresnel's counterintuitive but confirmed prediction that the central point in a shadow may be bright. Franklin's electricity/lightning analogy provides another clear case of how analogy can serve to develop experiments. Carnot's heat/water analogy led both to new hypotheses about the properties of heat and to experimental tests of these hypotheses. Finally, Luria conceived of his breakthrough genetic experiment by using his bacterial mutation/slot machine analogy.

On the more theoretical side, Darwin stressed how useful the natural selection/artificial selection analogy was to him in constructing explanations and dealing with objections to his theory. The respiration/combustion analogy also seems to have played a strong role in the development of Lavoisier's respiration theory.

As we saw in the discussion of gods and other minds (chapter 7), analogy is a risky form of argument, often apt to lead to false conclusions. One might therefore suggest restricting its use to the discovery and development of hypotheses, keeping evaluation free of analogical taint. This restriction would, however, contravene the practice of several scientists of unquestioned reputation. Darwin was explicit in listing the natural selection/artificial selection analogy as one of the grounds for belief in his theory. Gilbert intended his earth/small magnet analogy to be of more than heuristic use; it is part of his argument that the earth *is* magnetic. Similarly, when Galileo made the earth/moon and earth/ship comparisons, the analogies were in the service of his conclusion that the earth does in fact move. In addition, Newton's planet/projectile analogy is part of an argument for extending his gravitational theory to planetary phenomena.

In none of these cases is the argument *purely* analogical. Darwin primarily advocated accepting evolution by natural selection on the basis of its ability to unite and explain a very broad range of facts. The analogy between artificial and natural selection contributed to his inference to the best explanation, by virtue of a system mapping that can be crudely schematized as:

Source	*Target*
select (breeders, organisms) *name*: select-1	select (nature, organisms) *name*: select-2
develop (breeds) *name*: develop-1	develop (species) *name*: develop-2
cause (select-1, develop-1)	cause (select-2, develop-2)

Just as artificial selection by breeders using the natural variability of organisms explains how new breeds of plants and animals can arise, so variability and natural selection explain how new species arise. Thus analogy contributes to the explanatory coherence of Darwin's theory, just as it contributes to the explanatory coherence of the hypothesis that other people have minds. Gilbert and Newton also had substantial nonanalogical considerations in support of their views, but analogy nevertheless played a partial role in evaluation in these important cases of scientific thinking. Similarly, psychological theories of how the mind works derive some of their nonexperimental force from computational analogies.

In sum, the greatest scientific analogies have played roles in discovery, development, and evaluation. Many seem to have been used for more than one purpose: discovery and development or development and evaluation. We have not been able to document any analogy used for all three purposes. The key question now is how analogical thinking can have these diverse functions.

Cognitive Mechanisms

Two fundamental processes underlie the use of scientific analogies: selection of a source and application of that source to its target. These processes give rise to two questions. First, given the target domain to be understood, how can a source be found or constructed to provide what is required for the target? Second, given a possible source, how can it be applied to provide a model for understanding the target? Examination

[handwritten marginalia: Four ways: noticing, retrieving, compiling, constructing]

of scientific analogies reveals that the answers to these questions are somewhat more complicated than we have so far suggested.

Here is a simple story about how analogy works, based on the stages of analogy use we discussed in chapter 5 and elsewhere. In trying to solve a target problem, a scientist notices or remembers a source problem and then transfers over to the target the relevant aspects of the source. Selection of a source analog is a matter of retrieving a plausible source from a store of previously solved problems, and transfer involves creating a mapping between the target and the source that shows how to apply insights from the source to answer the relevant questions about the target. Examination of the great scientific analogies reveals, however, that this description is overly simple. In particular, selecting a source analog is not always simply a matter of retrieving one from memory. We need to distinguish at least four ways in which sources can originate: noticing, retrieving, compiling, and constructing.

What we call "noticing" occurs when serendipity provides a source to apply to a target currently under consideration. We can imagine, for example, Chrysippus pondering the phenomena of sound, absentmindedly throwing a pebble into a pond and being struck by the motion of the waves produced. Similarly, Franklin may have thought of his lightning/electricity analogy contemplating the behavior of lightning while he happened to be creating sparks. Noticing a source may also occur when the target is not already in mind, in which case it is the target, not the source, that has to be retrieved. This is different from the simple story of problem solving we started with, in which a source is retrieved from memory to be applied to a target. Darwin's discovery of natural selection came about because the source (human population growth) that he noticed in Malthus reminded him of the target problem on which he had long been working; the target, not the source, was retrieved from memory. Similarly, Luria serendipitously encountered a source, the slot machine, that reminded him of the target, his problem of designing a genetics experiment.

Although difficult to identify because of limitations in the historical record, there are undoubtedly cases from science in which a source is retrieved from memory in order to deal with a target. Some of the more straightforward analogies probably arose when a source was remembered to help with a target. When Huygens thought about light; for example, he may often have been reminded of similar sound phenomena. Similarly, Carnot's investigations of heat may well have prompted him to think of waterfalls. The role of memory, however, is not always confined to retrieving a source as a complete and ready-made complex that can be applied to the target. Memory may be called on to compile a complex of information that was not previously connected in any tight way. Instead of retrieving a single source, the scientist recalls various pieces of information that can be melded together to form a source analog. Franklin's list of electrical properties presented above was surely not retrieved as a whole, but rather was compiled over time as a result of reflection and recollection. Similarly, Galileo compiled a list of respects in which the earth and moon are similar. Darwin devoted much study to gathering information about artificial selection to use in his deliberations about natural selection.

The most cognitively complex origin of a source comes when it is not noticed, retrieved, or compiled, but must be constructed. Construction may involve aspects of the other three processes but goes beyond them in the extent to which the source is different from anything that was previously known to the scientist. For example, Kekulé's unconscious thought processes did not simply produce recollection of a snake biting its tail; he may never have encountered such an image (although it is common in mythology). He nevertheless generated a complex source that drew on the target problem (benzene structure) and a great deal of biochemical knowledge stored in his memory. The new source went beyond both the target and what he knew, by providing a structure—the snake rendered circular—that could inspire the hypothesis of benzene's ring structure. Similarly, Maxwell could not simply use an existing mechanical system to generate answers to his problems about electromagnetism. Rather, he used his deep knowledge of the source domain to build a new mechanical model that could be used to generate mathematical understanding of electromagnetism. Newton's analogy involved creating the thought experiment of throwing a stone harder and harder until it went into orbit. Obviously, he had no memory of such an occurrence but rather constructed the complex source analog involving projectiles to serve his purpose of understanding the target, planetary motion. When Morgan and his colleagues talked about beads on a string, they were not remembering any particular string they had encountered but rather were constructing a new source involving a special kind of organization and transformation designed to help understand the mechanism of crossing over. In cognitive science, computer programs are not simply taken over directly to produce psychological theories but instead involve constructing complex processing systems that are then used as analogs for thought. To understand the uses of analogy in science, then, it is important to realize that selection of source analogs often involves very complex designs and constructions that go beyond simple recall of past cases.

Construction of productive source analogs sometimes makes use of visual representations. Source representations can involve mental images, diagrams on paper, or both. Kekulé's analogy seems to have been visual: the image of the coiled snake directly suggested a similar image of the structure of benzene. The texts of published works by Newton, Maxwell, and Morgan involved diagrams representing their analogical constructions of, respectively, projectile motion, a mechanical system, and beads on a string. In all these cases, the structural correspondences between the source and the target are enhanced by the use of visual representations, which allow the correspondences to actually be seen.

Now let us consider how scientific analogies are used after a source has been in some way selected. Strikingly, the uses of scientific analogy do not conform at all well to the familiar schema for proportional analogy,

A:B::C:?

or A is to B as C is to what? The proportional format suggests that something needs to be filled in for the target, which is known to involve C, and the relation between A and B in the source is intended to provide the clue. In other words, standard proportional analogies involve mappings only at the relational rather than the system level. Perhaps the scientific example that comes closest to a proportional analogy is Kekulé's, encoded as

snake:circle::benzene:?

Putting the analogy this way is misleading, however, since it suggests that Kekulé first constructed the proportion and then filled in the answer, whereas getting an answer was part and parcel of constructing the analogy. Similarly, Darwin did not reason

human population growth:conflict::animal survival:?

and then replace the question mark with "the struggle for existence." Rather, what mattered about the analogy was grasping that this struggle could lead to evolution of different species. The proportion had no point outside the explanatory context of Darwin's trying to figure out a mechanism for evolution.

Some scientific analogies have a structure that can be schematized:

1. Why does T have properties A, B, C, etc.? (target)
2. S is like T in having properties P, Q, R that are like A, B, C. (source)
3. S has P, Q, R because of X. (source)
4. So maybe T has A, B, C because of X', which is a modification of X. (target)

Thus we explain why sound spreads, reflects, and diffracts by noting that it is like water, which spreads, reflects, and diffracts through wave action. The presence of the "cause" relation in (3) and (4) signals the existence of a system mapping and makes analogical explanation possible.

In other analogies, such as earth/moon, earth/ship, and lightning/electricity, the aim of the analogy is not so directly a matter of explanation. Galileo wanted simply to infer that the earth moves, and Franklin wanted to suggest that lightning might be attracted by points. The aim of Maxwell's mechanical analogy was much more complex, since its main use was to enable him to construct a mathematical framework for electromagnetism. As in the case of Galileo, the use of the analogy was indirectly explanatory, since Maxwell's general aim was to explain the electromagnetic phenomena. Maxwell's immediate goal, however, was to work out the mathematics, just as Galileo's local goal was to construct and rebut arguments concerning the motion of the earth. The diverse purposes for which analogies are used confound simplistic general theories of how aspects of a source can be transferred to a target.

Nevertheless, we can notice several interesting features of the mechanisms of transfer in the great scientific analogies. We saw that sources can originate through processes of varying complexity, and target completion can similarly range from virtually automatic to very complex. Inferring that the earth moves like the moon and that lightning may be attracted by points are instances of the simpler sorts of transfer. Often, however, transfer is not so straightforward, particularly when the source deviates unproductively from the target in some respects. Vitruvius did not assume, for example, that sound waves are *just like* water waves: sound waves spread in many planes, water waves in just one. Similarly, Fresnel and later proponents of a wave theory of light realized that to explain polarization, light waves had to be transverse, whereas sound waves are longitudinal. Darwin had to struggle to explain how natural selection produces new species, whereas breeders practicing artificial selection succeed only in producing new breeds. All of these are examples in which major adaptations were required before the target could be understood.

bidirectional

We have been writing as if transfer is always a matter of going from source to target, tacitly assuming that analogies are always used unidirectionally. And indeed, we do not use benzene to help understand snakes, chromosomes to help understand beads, or atomic structure to help understand the solar system. Many scientific analogies, however, are to some degree bidirectional. Sometimes similar phenomena can be used to shed light on each other. For example, in the use of the analogy between mind and computer, accessible aspects of mind have been used to suggest new ways of doing computation, just as computation has provided new ways of understanding thinking. Planets can help us think about projectiles, just as projectiles can help us think about planets, and we can learn something about electricity by studying lightning. In these cases, we have the achievement or the prospect of achievement of a unifying theory that specifies why two phenomena once thought to be disparate are fundamentally similar. The best example is the unification of projectiles and planets by Newtonian mechanics. Perhaps someday we will have a unified theory of information-processing systems that will establish the depth of the analogy between mind and computer. We conjecture that such a theory will only arise through a process of coevolution of theories of mind and of computation, with analogies among mind, brain, and computers going in various possible directions depending on how the state of knowledge about each domain develops.

Our collection and analysis of great scientific analogies has shown that analogy has played an important role in scientific development in many epochs and fields. Analogy has contributed to various stages of science, from discovery to evaluation, and served various explanatory and inferential ends. Scientific analogies require complex representations and processes. To fully understand them will require new projects in cognitive science, with methodologies that range from computational modeling to historical analysis to empirical investigation of analogy in action. Cognitive psychologist Kevin Dunbar has used the last of these methodologies to study analogical thinking in four laboratories doing research on molecular biology. He found that analogies were frequently and creatively used in three of the four laboratories; the exception was the least successful laboratory. Most of the analogies were either *local,* from the same experimental domain, or *regional,* involving a whole system of relationships from a similar domain. Dunbar found few *long-distance* analogies (ones that required mapping across very different domains) in the day-to-day biological research, except ones used for educational purposes. The absence of long-distance analogies in everyday work in a mature field is compatible with our finding of great scientific analogies that leap across domains, a kind of leap that naturally is rarer than those that guide more routine conceptual developments.

Social Sciences

Except for the mind/computer analogy, our collection has been drawn from the natural sciences, but analogies have also played an important role in the social sciences. In psychology, there have been many influential analogies besides the computational one. The mind has at various times been compared with containers, hydraulic devices, telephone switchboards, and complex, chaotic, dynamic systems.

Many economists have employed analogies in their theorizing. Adam Smith compared what he saw as the confluence of individual self-interest and social well-being to the operation of an invisible hand. In nineteenth- and twentieth-century economics, the concept of equilibrium, which was borrowed from physics, has been important for theorizing. Economies are assumed to move naturally toward equilibria, just as thermodynamic systems do.

Sociologists have often assumed an analogy between a society and a biological organism with parts that have identifiable functions. Similarly, political scientists have compared the state to an organism, and also to a machine and to a family. The state/family analogy is also commonly used in everyday discourse. For example, in the United States, George Washington is known as the father of his country, and in Canada the founders of the country are known as the fathers of confederation.

Archaeologists frequently resort to ethnographic analogies when trying to interpret the very fragmentary evidence about ancient peoples. Lauren Talalay, for example, argued for an original interpretation of separated clay-figurine legs in Neolithic Greece by comparing them to similarly split objects, such as bronze figurines used in much more recent cultures for economic transactions. In chapter 6, we discussed the role of historical analogies in decision making. Analogy also plays a role in historical explanation when two situations are compared with a goal of understanding rather than action. For example, in the history of science, the concept of a scientific revolution was introduced by analogy with political revolutions.

Unfortunately, social science analogies are not always benign. Nancy Leys Stepan has described how the analogy between race and gender has occupied a strategic place in scientific theorizing about human variation. In the nineteenth century, it was claimed that women's low brain weights and deficient brain structures were analogous to those of "lower" races; similar explanations of intellectual inferiority were applied in both cases. In this example, inferences about both the source and the target analogs were fundamentally erroneous, and the race/gender analogy contributed to mismeasurement and misinterpretation in both domains. *also subjugation*

Invention and Design

Science blends into technology and engineering, so it is not surprising that analogies have contributed to the development of new inventions. *visual + verbal* The goals of invention and design are somewhat different from the scientific goal of finding explanations for puzzling phenomena, but the connections are clear. Inventors are typically concerned with figuring out how to create a new piece of technology, but to do so they often must acquire a better understanding of how and why things work.

For example, when Alexander Graham Bell was inventing the telephone, he explicitly used an analogy: "Make transmitting instrument after the model of the human ear. Make armature the shape of the ossicles. Follow out the analogy of nature." He drew diagrams that made explicit the structure of the ear and then drew analogous diagrams of physical devices that could transmit vibrations the way the ear does. His analogy thus employed visual as well as verbal representations.

Another technological breakthrough based on visual analogy was the development of Velcro. In 1948, Georges de Mestral noticed that burdock burrs stuck to his dog's fur by virtue of tiny hooks. He figured out how to produce the same effect artificially, so that now shoes and many other objects can be fastened using burrlike hooks and clothlike loops. Velcro, which was originally a target analog for the burr source, has in turn become a source for further analogical designs and explanations, with targets drawn from medicine, biology, and chemistry. These new domains for analogical transfer include abdominal closure in surgery, epidermal structure, molecular bonding, antigen recognition, and hydrogen bonding. Like the development of the telephone, the development of Velcro was a case of technology drawing on a natural analog, but with Velcro the technology was then used as a source analog to understand nature.

Even in computer science, natural analogs have led to technological progress. John Holland developed his influential idea of genetic algorithms for learning by working out how to implement computationally the mutation and crossover operations that occur in chromosomes. Biology thus suggested ways to make computer programs modify and adapt themselves to be able to perform complex tasks.

Of course, biological analogs are not always the most successful, especially when the analogies are not deep, as was the case for Icarus's technique of strapping birdlike wings onto human arms to produce flight. When the Wright brothers produced the first working airplane, they used aerodynamic principles concerning lift and drag, although the analogy with birds was occasionally helpful. Wilbur Wright noticed that soaring birds often twist their wings to restore balance, and he tried warping the wings of the aircraft to achieve the same effect.

Technological invention can be thought of as a design problem, and many other kinds of design employ analogies. Architects sometimes model both the aesthetic and the structural features of new buildings after previously successful ones, with visual analogies being particularly important. For example, the Crystal Palace, built in London in 1850, served as a source analog for buildings in New York and Munich, and Thomas Jefferson took the general scheme for the Virginia State Capitol from Maison Carrée at Nîmes. Graphical computer interfaces have been compared with desktops. Designing a meal can be accomplished analogically, by thinking of previous dishes that worked well and modifying them for the dinner at hand. Artificial intelligence systems that use analogy have been developed for modeling the task of meal planning, as well as for circuit design and automatic programming.

Educating Scientists

Teaching science and technology, as well as other advanced topics, is a challenging endeavor. One basic reason is that the material being taught will often be very unfamiliar to students and may even contradict erroneous beliefs they have acquired in everyday life. Analogy provides a potential tool for "jump starting" students by introducing unfamiliar target domains in terms of more familiar source analogs. Good teachers frequently use analogies to render unfamiliar matters comprehensible to their students. What are the cognitive processes of the teachers and students that make such instruction possible? What kinds of analogies are likely to be most effective in increasing students' understanding? Our theory of analogical thinking as satisfaction of multiple constraints applies to the use of analogies in instruction. The strengths of particularly good analogies and the weaknesses of particularly bad ones can be understood in terms of the constraints of similarity, structure, and purpose. Our claims about the importance of these constraints for analogy have implications for how teachers do and should use analogies in providing explanations to their students. As good teachers are well aware, there are many potential pitfalls in using analogies in instruction. We will attempt to identify these pitfalls and suggest ways of avoiding and overcoming them.

Analogical thinking is sensitive to the purpose for which the analogy is being used. The main purpose of educational analogies is to convey to students a basic understanding of unfamiliar material. Students sometimes also use analogies in solving problems, for instance, when they use examples in textbooks to figure out how to solve new problems. That sort of problem solving involves analogies within one domain, with students using given problems to solve quite similar ones. In contrast, analogical explanation often involves cross-domain analogies, as teachers struggle to impart to students understanding of a domain that is new to them. For example, science writer Edward Dolnick explains why pandas, which are inefficient at both eating and reproducing, have managed to survive for millions of years: "In evolution, as in television, it's not necessary to be good. You just have to be better than the competition." Moving outside the domain of biology to a highly familiar source domain serves the pedagogical purpose of overcoming a common misconception about evolution, that survival implies optimality.

But there is much more to analogy than purpose: our ability to use a source analog to help understand or solve a target analog depends on there being natural correspondences between the two analogs. These correspondences involve the other two types of constraints: similarity, based on semantic or perceptual overlap between components of the two analogs, and structure, based on isomorphic configurations of objects and the relations among them. For example, we can schematize the panda/television analogy as follows, with the panda case as the target analog and television as the intended source of understanding.

Target

T1 Pandas are poor at eating and reproducing.

T2 There have been few organisms (before humans) that compete with pandas.

T3 Pandas have survived.

T4 T2 explains why T3 is true despite T1.

cross - domain analogies

Source

S1 Television programs are poor at informing and entertaining.

S2 There have been few better television programs to compete with them.

S3 Poor television programs continue.

S4 S2 explains why S3 is true despite S1.

As is typically the case with cross-domain analogies, not all components can be paired on the basis of object similarity: pandas are not in general much like television, even in black and white. But there are two respects in which the target and source are semantically similar: both involve relations of competition and survival (that is, competing to stay in existence as a species and competing to stay in existence on television).

Equally important to the effectiveness of this analogy is the structural correspondences between them. At the propositional level, the similarity between S4 and T4 shows that the overall structure of the analogs is the same. If we break T2 and S2 down further, then correspondences at a lower level become evident:

Target

breaking down

T2a Pandas live in areas of China.

T2b Other organisms live in these areas of China.

T2c These other organisms are no better than pandas in competing for food and territory.

Source

S2a Television programs occur in the television industry.

S2b Other television programs are devised.

S2c The other programs are no better than the dominant ones in the competition to be shown on television.

Obviously, there are many differences between the source and the target, since the competition, the competitors, and the locations are not at all similar, but the point is made nevertheless. Note that this is a system analogy, since it puts in correspondence the explanatory structure of the source and target, not just the first-order relations and objects.

Ideally, therefore, an educational analogy should satisfy the constraints of similarity, structure, and purpose and provide a deep system mapping rather than a mere comparison of low-level attributes and relations. Although our theory claims that all three constraints are used in all stages of analogy, the relative importance of each constraint varies across the stages. Both psychological experiments (chapter 5) and com-

system analogy

putational simulations (chapter 10) suggest that for retrieving a potential source from memory the most important constraint is semantic or perceptual similarity. In contrast, if students do not have to recall the analog but are presented with both the source and the target and merely have to determine the mapping between them, then structure is paramount. Finally, when the stage of evaluation and adaptation is reached, what matters is whether the source analog can actually be used to understand or solve the target, so that questions of purpose dominate.

When students are trying to understand a complex, new domain, a superficial analogy can be seriously misleading. Medical students often compare a failing heart to a stretched-out, sagging balloon. And indeed both a heart and a balloon will increase in size as they fail. However, despite this perceptual similarity, the underlying causal relationships are not analogous at all. Students using the balloon analogy are likely to infer that tension in the heart wall decreases as it fails, just as the tension in a balloon decreases as it leaks air. But in fact, tension increases in the heart walls. Inferences based on this superficial analogy simply promote serious misconceptions about how the heart actually operates.

Even useful analogies are often imperfect. For example, students often think of the "flow" of electricity as being analogous to the flow of water through a pipe. The water-flow analogy can be quite helpful in gaining a basic understanding of the concepts of current, voltage, and resistance. Water flows through a pipe because of a pressure difference produced by a reservoir; analogously, electrons move through a circuit because of a voltage difference produced by a battery. The water-flow analogy is particularly good in providing insight into the effects of combining batteries in different ways. Consider what happens if two identical reservoirs are connected, one above the other, by a pipe. Because the pressure produced by the reservoirs is determined by the height of the water, and the height has been doubled, it follows that the two reservoirs will double the pressure and hence double the rate of water flow. Analogously, two batteries connected in series will increase the current relative to a single battery. Now suppose that the two reservoirs are instead placed side by side, flowing into a single pipe. Because the height of the water will be the same as for a single reservoir, the water pressure and flow rate will not increase (although the water from the two reservoirs will flow for a longer time before the reservoirs are exhausted). Analogously, two batteries connected in parallel provide the same current as a single battery but will last a longer time.

problem, with analogies

However, the water-flow analogy for electricity seems less helpful in deriving inferences about how resistors affect electrical current. Novices generally think of resistors as being like constrictions in a water pipe, which limit the flow. The more resistors, then, the less flow. Although this inference is correct for resistors connected in series, it is wrong for resistors connected in parallel. If multiple resistors are connected in parallel, the current will pass through each of them at the same rate it would pass through a circuit with that corresponding resistor alone. The total current passing through two identical resistors connected in parallel will therefore be twice as great as that passing through a circuit with only one of them. (In fact, parallel pipes each with an identical constriction also permit more flow than does a single pipe with that constriction, just as parallel resistors permit more current to pass through; however, students apparently have difficulty understanding this aspect of the water-flow source analog.)

There is another possible analogy for electricity that can help to understand parallel resistors. This is the analogy to people moving in a crowd along a corridor. A resistor is then like a narrow gate that restricts the movement of the crowd, slowing it down. But if two gates are placed side by side, people can move through both gates, doubling the number who will be able to pass in a given time, relative to a situation in which only one gate was available.

But although the moving-crowd analogy provides a good model of resistors, it does not really provide any useful way of thinking about how batteries combine. When Gentner and Gentner tested high school and college students, screened to be naive about physical science, they found that students who used the water-flow analogy did better on battery than on resistor problems, while those who used the moving-crowd analogy did better on resistor than on battery problems. Each analogy proved more beneficial in solving problems involving electrical concepts for which the analogy allowed students to generate a coherent mapping that yielded correct inferences.

One way to aid students in adapting analogical inferences may be explicitly to teach them multiple analogies and to explain to them when each analogy is appropriate. It is also important to remember that the main value of analogies is usually to help the novice start to understand the target domain, not to provide expertise directly. Students need to appreciate that although analogies can be useful tools for learning, they are no substitute for critical thinking.

Unfortunately, novices are by definition ill equipped with the kind of direct knowledge of the target domain required to evaluate analogical inferences. Students learning topics in mathematics will often solve a new word problem by mapping it to a previous example. If the two problems are in fact isomorphic and involve similar first-order relations, the students are very likely to generate the correct solution by analogy. However, if the new problem requires calculating a quantity in a different way or taking account of an additional constraint—in other words, if the isomorphism is imperfect—then novice students generally are unable to adapt the analogous solution to take account of the unique requirements of the new problem. Novices will often fail to represent and map crucial higher-order relations that convey *why* a solution is appropriate. They may succeed in transferring a solution by relational mapping yet fail to find the more fundamental system mapping that is based on the causal structure of the analogs. Without guidance from a teacher, analogy is often a trap for the unwary novice, rather than a stepping stone to expertise.

Lessons

The panda/television analogy is far from perfect, but it is very effective. In contrast, consider our choice for the Worst Analogy Ever Made, used in an advertisement for Merit cigarettes that appeared in *Psychology Today* and other magazines in the summer of 1989. The analogy is so terrible that charity requires the assumption that its atrociousness was intended to draw attention to the ad: "Enriched Flavor™ explained: It's sort of like the Theory of Relativity. With relativity, it's like this: If you go fast enough, time slows down. With Enriched Flavor™, it's like this: The taste stays just as rich as you like even though the tar goes down. What could be simpler?"

This analogy seems to violate every constraint. The purpose of the advertisement is presumably to get people to buy Merit cigarettes by making them understand the surprising relation between having both enriched flavor and low tar. Accomplishing the purpose of increasing understanding of the target always requires that the source analog be more familiar than the target. But even the trivialized implication of relativity theory used here is likely to be less familiar to the readers than are flavor and tar, so the purpose of the analogy is unlikely to be accomplished. Even for readers who know a little about relativity, the analogy is defective, since the semantic and structural correspondences are so weak. There is no semantic similarity between flavor and relativity, time and smoking, going fast and rich taste, or time slowing and tar going down. Moreover, the structure of the analogs is different. Going fast causes time to slow down, whereas taste staying rich happens despite tar going down. Because the causal relations in the two analogs are so different, no consistent system mapping is possible.

Good teachers are well aware of the pragmatic importance of using analogies to matters that are familiar to their students. In science education, chemistry teachers seem to be particularly fond of making analogies to the everyday lives of students, as in the regular feature of the *Journal of Chemical Education* called "Applications and Analogies." For example, the chemical bonds that hold atoms together can be compared to the rope that holds two people together in a tug-of-war. Physics teachers, in contrast, seem more inclined to explain physical phenomena in terms of other physical phenomena, for example heat flow in terms of water flow. Both strategies have strengths and weaknesses: comparisons to aspects of students' everyday lives have the advantage that the students at least know the source analogs, but they carry the risk of being not very similar to the target. On the other hand, physical phenomena may be less familiar to students but may map better to their intended targets. Thus in analogical explanation there can be a tension between the purpose constraint and the other two. The teacher wants to help the students use what they already know to understand something new, but the old and the new may differ in important ways.

In teaching history, it can be valuable to compare historical events to similar ones that the students already know about, but students' ignorance can obviously short-circuit the explanation. Comparing Hitler's failed invasion of Russia during the Second World War to Napoleon's failed invasion of Russia in 1812 may be illuminating, but not to someone who knows nothing of Napoleon. Tolstoy's brilliant description in *War and Peace* of Napoleon's invasion often makes use of cross-domain analogies, such as comparing the marauding French army to a herd of cattle trampling underfoot the fodder that might have saved it from starvation.

For an analogy to be useful, the teacher must ensure that students find the appropriate correspondences between the analogs. All three constraints are relevant. As novices, students will often be unsure exactly what aspects of the source and target are important to the analogy. The teacher can help students avoid mismappings by clarifying which components of the analogs are actually relevant to the comparison. The similarity and structure constraints can also guide the mapping process. In the analogy between chemical bonding and tug-of-war, there is at least some semantic similarity to work with, since bonding and holding together are related. Where there is no semantic similarity evident, as with atoms and people, finding the correspondences requires sensitivity to structure. Structural correspondences are especially important for mappings at the system level, since the causal relations that appear in the analogs may be crucial to the explanation. In the chemical bond case, the competition of atoms for electrons is what keeps them together, just as the competition for the rope keeps the people together.

For the students to see the correspondences, the chunks of material presented to them must not be too large or too little. If the two analogs are presented too cryptically, the correspondences may not be apparent. As we saw in chapter 5, finding similarities based on corresponding higher-order relations is encouraged by having people map at least three objects at once, so that they process relations, and relations between relations. But it is important to have students focus on the important components, so that the intended correspondences are not buried in irrelevant detail.

Careful guidance from a teacher will be especially important when analogies are used to teach young children, as the work we described in chapter 4 suggests. In addition to simply being novices in the target domain, children may lack important concepts required to build useful representations of the analogs. Special concerns arise for preschool children. In a system mapping, understanding the source analog, just as much as the target, requires the ability to represent higher-order relations, which preschool children may not yet be ready to cope with. Such limitations would make it difficult for very young children to gain understanding through analogies that require system mapping, even if the source analog would be highly effective for older children.

It is useful to distinguish two kinds of analogical explanations relevant to education. These are *why-answering* explanations, which use similar causal relations to tell why something happens in the target, and *clarifying* explanations, in which the point of the analogy is merely to display systematic correspondences. Most of the examples we have considered, such as chemical bonding/tug-of-war, involve why-answering explanations. An example of a clarifying explanation would be explaining the British parliamentary system to an American by comparing the prime minister to the president, Parliament to Congress, the House of Lords to the Senate, and the House of Commons to the House of Representatives. The analogy is imperfect, since the British prime minister is a member of Parliament, whereas the American president is not a member of Congress, but nonetheless it can serve to get someone ignorant about the British system started. For the analogy to work, it is necessary for each of the two analogs (as well as the correspondences between them) to be clearly described.

Since teachers often present a source and target analog directly, it might seem that the most important process in instructional analogies is mapping, in which case structural correspondence would presumably be the most important constraint. But for students to make full use of a source analog, they may have to retrieve it later from memory on their own. This means that the kinds of semantic cues that play a major role in analog retrieval can be important for subsequent usability of a source analog. Retrieval of the source analog by the students may be different from retrieval by a teacher, who has a more detailed knowledge base and conceptual system. Of course, if students succeed in grasping the deep connections between the source and the target, they will begin to construct a more abstract schema linking the two domains. Such a schema should make retrieval less dependent on low-level similarities and also make it more likely that the students will notice new cases that share the relevant structure.

In sum, teachers should take pains to use analogies based on domains already familiar to the students and should make clear the semantic and structural correspondences between the analogs that are important for providing the desired explanation. Even then, however, problems can arise, and we shall now consider some ways of overcoming them.

Even if the teacher tries to use analogies to situations that are familiar to the students, failures can arise because the students' knowledge is not in fact organized the way the teacher thinks it is. Good teaching requires a model of the students, what they think and what they care about. How can one find out what students know prior to being shocked by their exams?

One useful strategy may be to have students generate analogies themselves. Often, if the students have little knowledge of the domain of instruction, their proposed analogs will be very bad; however, pointing out the misunderstandings can be a useful way of correcting their misconceptions. By doing a sort of "analogy therapy" the students can be led toward more effective analogies, and the bad analogies may even help to serve as a bridge toward much more illuminating ones. For example, consider what people might take as analogous to analogy.

Someone once suggested to Thagard that analogy is like using a figure in a geometry proof. Certainly there are correspondences between the figure and the general geometrical proposition one is trying to prove, but this case is importantly different from analogical mapping, in which you have two cases to put in correspondence. In geometrical proof, the figure is an instantiation of the geometrical situation, not an analog of it. Distinguishing analogizing (comparing two cases represented at roughly the same level of generality) from exemplifying (providing a specific example of a more general concept or category) should help to increase understanding of analogy. As described in chapter 9, some forms of analogy therapy serve cultural purposes.

By far the greatest danger with using analogies to familiar domains is that students can be misled by unnoticed differences between the source and the target. Many people, for example, think that thermostats are like valves and so suppose that setting the temperature at maximum will make their house heat faster than simply setting it at the level they want it to reach. Politicians discuss governmental finances as if these were the same as those of ordinary people, even though "living within our means" is very different in the two cases.

There are at least two ways of overcoming the effects of source/target differences in analogical explanations, and hence to aid students in adaptation. The first is to point out explicitly to students the places where the analogy breaks down, as in the example of the United States president's not being elected to Congress. A more complicated strategy is to use multiple analogs, comparing the target to sources with different characteristics. The idea of the earth's molten core might best be conveyed by comparing the earth to an egg, which has a yolk, but further comparison with a peach might prevent the student from thinking that the earth has a hard shell.

Related to the problem of differences is the danger that worn-out analogies may interfere with the acquisition of new ones. For example, beginning physics students are taught the Rutherford-Bohr model of the atom by analogy to the solar system, but the model of orbits fostered by this analogy can get in the way of later acquisition of quantum-mechanical notions. Thus teaching a new model may require the kind of analogy therapy that we suggested for student-provided analogs, pointing out the defects in old analogies. Another problem that can arise is that students might think of other analogies and alternative explanations. Then it is necessary to guide students in the evaluation of the different hypotheses, perhaps using principles of explanatory coherence.

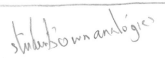

If analogy has all these pitfalls, why use it? Maybe teachers should try to get by with simply presenting the basic material to the students without analogizing. We are reminded of the remark that democracy is the worst system of government except for all the others. Similarly, analogy is often indispensable for providing students with the beginnings of understanding in a strange domain. Like pandas and television, analogical thinking survives despite its imperfections, because it often performs its cognitive role better than any available competitor. Advanced as well as beginning students may profit from well-chosen analogies, just as Darwin and Maxwell successfully exploited analogies in developing their famous theories. Analogical explanation will continue to be an important part of educational practice, and we hope that attention to the constraints of similarity, structure, and purpose will promote improved use of instructional analogies.

Summary

Analogies have made substantial contributions to the discovery, development, evaluation, and exposition of scientific ideas. System mappings, such as that found in Darwin's analogy between natural and artificial selection, can contribute to the acceptability as well as the development of hypotheses, while analogies involving simpler mappings can contribute to discovery and development. The cognitive mechanisms used in scientific analogies are more complex than straightforward retrieval and mapping, since useful source analogs may be noticed, compiled, or constructed rather than remembered. Analogies have also been used in the social sciences and in the development of technology. The constraints of similarity, structure, and purpose apply also to education, where they can be used to understand the difference between effective and ineffective instructional analogies. Like decision making and explanation, education often benefits from the use of multiple analogs. Another pedagogic technique is analogy therapy, in which the analogies underlying students' misconceptions are identified and contrasted with more insightful analogies.

9

The Web of Culture

The Japanese Tea Ceremony

The web of culture that holds people together in social groups is constructed from shared beliefs and feelings, knowledge of a common history, and a sense of place in the natural and social world. These strands provide the connections by which members of a society can communicate with one another. Myth and magic, rites and ceremonies, poetry and everyday conversation all form part of the web. A culture is built and maintained in large part by symbolic stories and rituals, in which objects and events are given meanings that in various ways go beyond themselves. Analogy plays a prominent role in providing these extended meanings and thus in building and maintaining the web of culture. We will discuss several overlapping cultural purposes of analogy: promoting social cohesion, allowing indirect communication, evoking amusement and other emotions, and helping with social and psychological problems.

Consider the tea ceremony, which evolved over centuries and is often regarded as an embodiment of Japanese culture. Benjamin Colby has described how the everyday social act of serving and drinking green tea is given a deeper set of meanings as the focus of a symbolic activity, one that imposes order on the natural and social world. The ceremony takes place in a tea hut in a garden. This context is itself the basis of an analogy, as a Japanese garden is designed as an idealization of nature. As the guests walk through the garden to the tea house, pausing along the way to wash at a small spring or basin, they leave the bustle of everyday life and its attendant stresses and anxieties, arriving at a physical place of retreat and a mental state of contemplation. The intended analogy has been described by the tea master Soshitsu Sen XV: "As the garden suggests a mountain trail, the tea hut suggests a simple mountain hermitage. Everyday materials, unpainted wooden posts and lintels, wattle walls, and thatched or bark roofs allow the structure to blend unobtrusively into the surroundings." When the guests arrive inside the tea room, the tea making itself builds on the analogy to nature. Kakuzo Okakura writes, "The kettle sings well, for pieces of iron are so arranged in the bottom as to produce a peculiar melody in which one may hear the echoes of a cataract muffled by clouds, of a distant sea breaking among the rocks, a rainstorm sweeping through a bamboo forest, or of the soughing of the pines on some faraway hill." The tea itself has qualities that resonate with those of the garden outside, further connecting the entire ceremony with nature. Its color is green, like the green plants, trees, and moss outside. It is made of pure water, like both a pool in a mountain stream and the washing place in the garden. And the herbal scent of the tea connects with the smell of the wet leaves and earth in the garden. In the words of Soshitsu Sen, "In my own hands I hold a bowl of tea; I see all of nature represented in its green color. Closing my eyes I find green mountains and pure water within my own heart. Silently sitting alone and drinking tea, I feel these become part of me." The tea is thus the focal symbol for nature; in drinking the tea, the participants in the ceremony symbolically make themselves one with the natural world.

Even as it evokes oneness with nature, the tea ceremony is also intended to create what Shoshitsu Sen calls "oneness of host and guest." The ritual elevates etiquette to an art form. The positions of the guests, the placement of the bowls of tea on the mats, even the manner in which the lips touch the bowl are subject to exacting prescriptions. At the same time, the host, much like an artist working in a formal style, has creative scope in such details as the selection of tea instruments and the decoration of the tea house, all of which aim to stimulate aesthetic appreciation by the guests. In everyday Japanese life, rigorous etiquette functions to maintain social relationships, emphasizing distinctions based on rank and social distance. In the tea ceremony, however, the usual differences in social power are suppressed; all the guests, regardless of rank, maintain an attitude of humility as they accept the offerings of their host. Taken out of the context of its ordinary functions in the Japanese culture, etiquette becomes a vehicle for artistry, linked to the order inherent in the Japanese idealization of nature. The result is a sense of coherence between the natural and social worlds of the Japanese. The fundamental simplicity of drinking tea, the key symbolic act, is in keeping with a general Asian emphasis on tasteful restraint and brevity, also exhibited in calligraphy, proverbs, and poetry.

metaphor + metonymy

The tea ceremony provides a sophisticated example of a symbolic act that in its cultural context takes on an extended meaning. We can recognize elements of the ceremony that if used in language would be called figures of speech. But the tea ceremony illustrates how these symbolic modes can be expressed in nonverbal acts, so it is more apt to call them figurative devices. Two such devices are basic to symbolic expression. The first is *metaphor*, which uses cross-domain analogies. The analogy between the setting of the tea ceremony and that of a mountain hermitage metaphorically links the intimacy of the garden to nature on a larger scale. The second device is *metonymy*, which allows elements that are in some way associated to substitute for one another. Metonymy is a looser connection than metaphor and provides a way to extend meanings within a domain. Thus tea metonymically stands for food and drink in general, because tea is strongly associated with Japanese meals. In the context of the tea ceremony, and indeed in everyday Japanese life, drinking tea also is closely associated with interactions between people. More generally, many different types of relations can provide a basis for metonymy, including part-whole (a top student may be called a "brain"), cause-effect (to read a poem written by Keats is to "read Keats"), and simple contiguity.

Our focus will be on metaphor, the figurative device most directly linked to analogy. But we need to pay attention to metonymy as well, because the two devices often work together. A metonym can in turn be extended by its use in a metaphor. The tea ceremony establishes a metaphorical connection between drinking tea and appreciating nature; by metonymy, the connection is extended to partaking of food and drink in general, and indeed to the entire social order on which Japanese etiquette is based. As another example, after reading a lyric poem by the eighth-century Chinese poet Li Po, one might exclaim, "I have read the Chinese Keats!" thus building a metaphor on top of a metonymy. Even more generally, finding an analogical connection between two domains can itself foster a metonymic relation between them. The analogy between the setting of the tea ceremony and that of a mountain retreat creates a kind of mental contiguity between the two domains, which helps to create cross-domain associations. When elements are connected by some salient property viewed in isolation, such as the greenness of tea, trees, and moss, the distinction between metonymy and the simplest form of metaphor (that based on attribute mapping) blurs. The looser process of metonymy often serves to create a kind of associative aura around a poetic metaphor.

Star Trek and the Hidden Paths

In an episode of a science-fiction television program, *Star Trek: The Next Generation,* the starship Enterprise from earth makes contact with the Tamarians, the inhabitants of a planet in a distant star system. The Enterprise crew wants to communicate with the new species to establish peaceful relations. But the initial encounter ends abruptly in mutual confusion when neither the humans nor the Tamarians are able to understand what the other is saying. The crew's problem is not in understanding the words and sentences of the language, as the Tamarians actually speak in English. The trouble is that what they say seems to be gibberish, a muddle of strange names and places, such as "Darmok and Gilad, at Tenagra." Later the crew members realize that the Tamarians speak entirely in metaphors, which are couched in the terms of mythological events familiar in their own culture. It turns out, for example, that Darmok was a hunter who met Gilad on the island of Tenagra, where they were forced to confront a common enemy, a beast who lived there. In the course of fighting and eventually vanquishing the beast, the two warriors overcame their initial suspicion of each other and learned to cooperate, becoming friends in the process. The captain of the Tamarian space vessel arranges a parallel adventure for himself and the captain of the Enterprise, hoping to achieve the analogous outcome—mutual understanding between the two peoples.

This fanciful story of the pitfalls of interstellar communication nicely illustrates a basic point about the role of analogy in communication—success depends on shared knowledge of the relevant source analogs. Without knowledge of earth history and culture, such remarks as "The team finally met its Waterloo" or "I'm afraid this takeover bid could be our company's Vietnam" would be as meaningless to us as Tamarian metaphors were to the crew of the Enterprise. Because communication by analogy depends on shared knowledge, analogy and cultural experiences are inextricably linked.

By its very nature, metaphor, which involves speaking of one thing to say something about another, lends itself to calculated ambiguity. As we pointed out in chapter 1, a political writer living in a repressive society may be able criticize the government under the protective cover of satire. People who share privileged knowledge may be able to create a private language based on metaphor, one difficult to penetrate for those who do not share the requisite knowledge of the source analog and its mappings.

Indirect, metaphorical speech has been documented in a number of societies and cultures. Anthropologist William McKellin has studied the use of allegories—extended metaphorical stories—as a negotiating device among the Managalese people of Papua New Guinea. This allegorical style is called *ha'a*. The Managalese compare metaphorical communication to a circuitous, hidden path through the forest, in contrast to using the more direct and open public walking paths. A seasoned Managalese politician uses metaphors in situations that require extreme politeness and evasion, or trickery and subterfuge. They are used to negotiate marriages, inform relatives of deaths, warn allies of possible attacks by enemies, and reprove kinsfolk for their shortcomings. When performed in public, a *ha'a* allows the speaker to demonstrate cleverness superior to that of an adversary who is less competent in the metaphorical style of discussion. Orators will deliberately select metaphors to direct their message to specific listeners and to place responsibility on the intended audience for the interpretation (correct or mistaken) of the story, as well as for the acceptance or rejection of the proposed offer. The very nature of the speech is open to alternative interpretations. If the negotiation is acceptable, then the narrative will be interpreted as an allegory; if not, it may be treated as a slightly odd or irrelevant story—a literal description of events, devoid of metaphorical meaning. The interpretation of a story is highly dependent on the context, including the identities of the speaker and listeners.

Here is a *ha'a* told by a mother while standing in the middle of the village in which she lived: "When I was a young woman and visited people's houses people gave me fresh juicy young betel nuts to chew. Now I am older. When I visit I am given old, hard betel nut. When I chew it my teeth and gums hurt and bleed. This makes me unhappy and upset." Only some of her listeners could understand the allegorical significance of the woman's story. It turned out that earlier that day the woman's son, who had never been married, had run off with a widow. This violated the tradition that single people should marry other single people and only widowers should marry widows. The key to the intended interpretation is a conventional metaphorical motif—betel nut represents a woman. The mother was voicing her displeasure at her son's action, which brought into the family an "old, hard betel nut" (the widow) rather than the "fresh juicy young betel nut" that tradition led the mother to expect. But even as she used her story to complain about her son's choice of a bride, in telling it the mother was also polling her kin to see whether they intended to support or reject the marriage.

Managalese ha'a

As this example illustrates, a *ha'a* is a constructed analogy, not simply a story retrieved from memory. The story is molded in part by conventional symbols, but even these are often ambiguous. Betel nuts, for example, do not always represent women—they can also signify pigs. The disasters that might befall someone who misconstrued such ambiguities are self-evident. In fact, the Managalese style of indirect negotiation can be used to set traps for the unwary. One man told how when he was single, he failed to recognize an allegory told him by his father's brother. As a result, he was tricked into giving this relative his small string bag. When he returned to his parents' house, he found a girl waiting there with his string bag, now full of betel nuts, hanging around her neck—the sign of a publicly recognized betrothal.

McKellin reports that expert composers of *ha'a* are able to invent new metaphors in the traditional style. For example, in a request for food it is conventional to use betel nut to stand for food. So if a man tells another that he has some betel nut for a feast but needs more, this is likely to be interpreted as a request for an extra pig to add to those already available for the feast. (McKellin notes that the Managalese are monogamous and therefore unlikely to interpret the story as a request for an extra wife! The ambiguity of the betel nut symbol reflects the fact that wives and pigs both figure prominently in exchange negotiations within the Managalese society.) With the changes in society that took place in the twentieth century, experts in *ha'a* incorporated new symbols within the narrative form, such as the goods found in the new trade stores.

A simple version based on trade-store goods is the following *ha'a*. Korahare was the guardian of a young man who wished to marry, and Arasa was the brother of the mother of an eligible girl, whose permission was required for her to marry. Arasa owned and operated a trade store. One day Korahare went into the store and asked for a tin of fish. Then he said to Arasa, "I would like a tin of fish, but the price is 1.50 kina, and all I have is one kina. Is that enough?" It was indeed—Korahare left the store with the tin of fish and Arasa's consent for a marriage. Besides illustrating the incorporation of a new symbol into the traditional discourse style, this example shows that it is possible for a *ha'a* to have a meaningful interpretation at both literal and metaphorical levels.

What Is Metaphor?

We need to look more carefully at what metaphor is and how we understand metaphorical expressions. It is often noted that a metaphor says one thing to mean another, which has a paradoxical ring. Of course, that is close to what analogy accomplishes—understanding the target in terms of the source. A metaphor always connects two domains in a way that goes beyond our ordinary category structure. "Socrates was a man" is literally true, whereas "Socrates was a lion" is a metaphor. This simple metaphor is based on attribute mapping, which transfers an attribute conventionally ascribed to lions, courage, to a human. Many metaphors are based on deeper relational and system mappings. "Socrates was a midwife of ideas" (see chapter 7), despite its syntactic resemblance to "Socrates was a lion," is actually a system mapping, one which relates the role of the philosopher in helping his students develop ideas to that of an ancient Greek midwife aiding in matchmaking and childbirth. The overt words used in the metaphorical expression serve as cues that activate a wide range of knowledge about the source and target domains. The connection between the two domains need not be directly asserted, as it is in the above examples. The source domain can instead be suggested more indirectly, by describing the target in terms appropriate to the source, as in "His career stumbled into quicksand" or Carl Sandberg's famous line, "The fog comes on little cat feet."

Although metaphor is often expressed in language, it is more fundamentally a way of thinking. Even literal meanings can often be traced to metaphorical roots. In some cases the source analog is so basic to human experience that it shows its influence in many unrelated languages. For example, in both Chinese and English the "foot" of a mountain and the "mouth" of a river draw their names from human body parts. Of course, we do not expect a mountain to walk or a river to eat, despite the metaphorical origins of the terms. Other "literalized" metaphors appear as idioms or clichés, such as "putting one's cards on the table" (derived from card games) and "beating around the bush" (from a method for hunting birds by flushing them out of the bush into nets). People may often use familiar expressions of this sort without being aware of their metaphorical origins. However, the underlying analogy can sometimes be brought to the foreground by a creative extension, as in this example from Hemingway: "They say the seeds of what we will do are in all of us, but it always seemed to me that in those who make jokes in life the seeds are covered with better soil and with a higher grade of manure."

George Lakoff and his colleagues have argued that much of human experience, especially its abstract aspects, is grasped in terms of broad conceptual metaphors. Time, for example, is understood in terms of objects in motion through space, as in expressions like "Christmas is fast approaching" and "The time for decision has arrived." As we noted in chapter 1, life is often conceptualized as a journey. Lakoff and Mark Turner quote from Robert Frost's poem, "The Road Not Taken":

Two roads diverged in a wood, and I—
I took the one less traveled by,
And that has made all the difference.

Our comprehension of this poem, they say, depends on our implicit knowledge of the metaphor that life is a journey. This knowledge includes understanding several interrelated correspondences: a person is a traveler, purposes are destinations, actions are routes, difficulties in life are impediments to travel, counselors are guides, and progress is the distance traveled. A large number of such metaphors guide our understanding of ordinary life and speech, as well as poetry. The metaphoric correspondences are not fundamentally between words, but rather between systems of concepts. Often words are mapped onto mental images of things of which we have a bodily understanding.

Another indication of how fundamental metaphor is to human thought is provided by studies of how figurative language is understood. There is an obvious idea about how people understand metaphors: they might first try to find a true literal meaning, and if that fails then go on to look for a metaphorical interpretation. For example, we might look for a metaphorical interpretation of "Socrates was a lion" only after noticing that the literal interpretation is false. However, the idea that metaphorical processing is only invoked as a kind of fallback strategy turns out to be erroneous. John Donne's statement "No man is an island" is, of course, literally true—no man is a body of land surrounded by water. But this literal truth does not deter us from finding a metaphorical meaning, one that denies the independence of individuals from each other.

Moreover, Sam Glucksberg, Boaz Keysar, and their colleagues have shown that people find metaphorical meanings even when instructed to find literal meanings. In one study, college students were asked to decide whether or not sentences like "Some desks are junkyards" were literally true. The students were slower to correctly respond "no" to a sentence that was literally false when it also had a metaphorical interpretation, as in the above example, than to respond to literally false sentences, such as "Some desks are roads," that lack a metaphorical interpretation. Similar findings have been obtained for sentences that can be interpreted *both* literally and metaphorically. Keysar presented students with sentences like "My son is a baby" in contexts that manipulated whether the sentence was true or false, literally or metaphorically. The students were instructed to press a key as quickly as possible to indicate the *literal* truth value of the sentence. If the sentence was literally false in the context, the decision was made more quickly if it was also metaphorically false; if the sentence was literally true, the decision was made more quickly if it was also metaphorically true. Such findings imply that literal and metaphorical processing interact with each other. Metaphorical interpretation appears to be an obligatory process that accompanies literal processing, rather than an optional process that occurs after literal processing.

If people typically seek both literal and metaphoric interpretations, what determines their selection of a preferred meaning? Max Black suggests a simple answer: people choose the meaning that makes the most sense in the given context. For example, suppose you know a man who criticizes others for faults that he himself exhibits. You might say, "That's somebody who lives in a glass house and shouldn't be throwing stones." The metaphorical meaning of this expression could be conveyed perfectly well even if it turned out that the man in question really did live in a house made of glass—even, in fact, if he had the habit of tossing stones about the house. Just as the constraints provided by the overall context can select the most sensible of two literal meanings (for example, the "star" in "The astronomer married the star" is finally interpreted as a movie star rather than a celestial sphere), the context can select a metaphorical meaning as more sensible than any literal alternative. The preferred interpretation is the one most relevant in the context.

The erroneous idea that metaphorical interpretation is a fallback strategy, rather than an integral part of normal comprehension, is often accompanied by attempts to eliminate metaphor by reducing it to something else. The "something else" is usually either some hypothetical set of equivalent literal statements or a simple comparison statement. It might be claimed, for example, that "Socrates was a lion" simply means "Socrates was courageous" (literal equivalent) or else "Socrates was like a lion" (an explicit cross-domain comparison statement called a "simile"). However, neither of these approaches is adequate. Attempts to translate metaphors into literal sentences fail, because for any interesting metaphor it is impossible to find a precise literal equivalent that captures all of its nuances. Consider again "Socrates was a midwife of ideas." One could make up a set of sentences that attempt to describe literally some of what this metaphor means, such as "He helped his students develop ideas," "He introduced them to intellectual partners," "He was more experienced than his students," and so on, but the list would not be clearly circumscribed. How does one capture such subtleties as the possible suggestion that having ideas can be dangerous (like childbirth), or the resemblances between the emotional connections between philosopher and student and those between midwife and mother? The problem is that a set of analogical correspondences, accompanied by metonymic associations, is richer and more flexible than any list of sentences. And of course such a list would lose the aesthetic impact produced by the very brevity of the original metaphor.

The idea that metaphors can be reduced to comparison statements also fails to offer any real answer to the question of what metaphors mean. Simply saying that "Socrates was like a midwife of ideas" does not in itself convey how the source and target resemble each other. And of course it is unlikely that many people would still admire Carl Sandberg's poem had it begun, "The fog comes like a cat."

The Analogical Basis

If metaphor is not a shorthand for either literal statements or simple comparisons, what is it? As we have already suggested, metaphor uses many of the same mental processes as analogical thinking. The basis for metaphor can therefore be understood in terms of our multiconstraint theory of analogy, which can remove some of the mystery that metaphor often seems to carry with it. The key idea is one that by now should be very familiar: a metaphor is understood by finding a mapping between the target domain (the topic of the metaphor) and the source domain. The degree to which an analogy is viewed as metaphorical will tend to increase the more remote the target and source domains are from each other. Thus the analogy between the problem of treating a stomach tumor and the story about a general capturing a fortress, discussed in chapter 5, is quite metaphorical, whereas an analogy between treating stomach tumors and treating brain tumors would seem nonmetaphorical. The mapping can be used to enrich understanding of the target by generating new inferences, and it can lead to formation of a schema based on the relational structure common to the target and the source. All the constraints that guide the use of analogy—similarity, structure, and purpose—guide the comprehension of metaphors.

Our view of metaphor is closely related to proposals by such metaphor theorists as Black, Lakoff and his colleagues, and Glucksberg and

Can create new knowledge about the target

Keysar. Black was the first to emphasize that a metaphor involves an interaction between the source and the target (in our terms, this is the mapping between them), an interaction that can change our understanding of both the target and the source. Some have found it mysterious that a metaphor can actually create new knowledge about the target, rather than simply emphasizing existing similarities between the source and target. However, as we saw in chapter 5, the entire process of analogy, especially the generation of inferences, is geared toward the construction of similarities. In addition, analogy goes hand in hand with the formation of schemas—new categories that embrace both the source and the target, thus changing our understanding of both.

Glucksberg and Keysar have argued that metaphorical expressions are actually understood as categorization statements. They suggest, for example, that "My job is a jail" is understood as asserting that my job is a member of a category something like "confining things." Since this category has no established name, a prototypical example of a confining thing, namely "jail," is used as a name for the abstract category. Glucksberg and Keysar point out that category relations are more structured than simple comparisons, so that "My job is a jail" is a stronger claim than "My job is like a jail." The metaphor is an invitation to conceive of a category that embraces both my job and jails, while the simile only implies that my job has some similarity to the specific concept of a jail.

schemas categories

In our terms, a metaphorical category is simply the schema that, as we described in chapter 5, can be generated from the mapping between the source and target analogs. Glucksberg and Keysar's account, while insightful, does not in itself explain exactly what category will be understood as the appropriate abstraction. Why should "jail" be generalized to "confining thing," rather than "room with bars," "place where people sleep," "building," or any other of the indefinitely large number of possibilities? The multiconstraint theory provides a way of understanding how an analogical mapping can constrain formation of a schema. Our theory can explain how metaphorical categories can be formed "on the fly" as people encounter novel metaphors: people can map the target onto the source and use the resulting correspondences to guide construction of a schema that embraces both analogs. We do not need to assume that people already know that "jail" can mean not only a place to hold prisoners but also any sort of confining thing; rather, in the process of using analogy to understand "My job is a jail," this schema can actually emerge.

Of course, if an expression is commonly used metaphorically, the more abstract meaning can become literal. Presumably this is what happened when "mouth" was repeatedly applied to outlets of inanimate tube-like objects that widen toward their ends, such as rivers. In chapter 6 we pointed out that the Vietnam analog, after it had become a familiar schema for a type of debacle resulting from a foreign military incursion, eventually yielded the ironic observation that Cambodia was "Vietnam's Vietnam." Here the topic is the specific country of Vietnam, with respect to which Cambodia is claimed to be a Vietnam in the sense of the abstract schema.

Schema formation is more general than simple category formation in that schemas can be formed even from metaphors that do not directly express a category relation. For example, "His career stumbled into quicksand" does not mean that his career belongs to some abstract category named by "quicksand." But it does mean that the progress of a career is the kind of thing that may play a role in a schema for sudden encounters with unforeseen and potentially catastrophic dangers from which it is difficult to escape. The words in the metaphorical expression provide cues to the broader source and target domains on which the schema is based.

The link between analogy and schema formation makes it clear how metaphor involves an interaction between the source and the target, which can change our understanding of both. In fact, the source may sometimes undergo the more radical change. If I tell you that "my job is a jail," you may alter your conception of the target, my job, by adding such analogical inferences as the idea that my job is unpleasant, confining, and not easy to quit. But at the same time the source concept, jail, may begin to take on a new and more abstract meaning as the name of a schema for confining things. Notice that in a metaphor the source domain is the one that has to "give" in fitting it to the target. We understand that "my job" refers quite literally to my job, but "jail" has to be extended in a way that loses specific attributes of real jails that do not apply to the target, such as having four walls and iron bars.

This asymmetry between the target and the source contributes to the radical asymmetry of metaphorical statements. For example, "The acrobat is a hippopotamus" describes a clumsy acrobat, whereas "The hippopotamus is an acrobat" describes an agile hippopotamus. Verbs, which in metaphors are usually taken from the source domain, are especially likely to yield part of their most common literal meaning when placed in a metaphorical context. For example, the expression "Chuck stole a plumber" is often understood as meaning that Chuck hired a plumber away from another employer. Here "stole" retains its basic structure of "causing transfer of something from another to oneself by aggressive action" but loses aspects incompatible with the target, such as the presumption that anyone owned the thing that was transferred. As Gentner and French noted, "[I]n a sense verbs are institutionalized analogies. They are devices for conveying relational structures independently of the concrete objects to which the structures are applied."

The analogical core of metaphor, the basis of creative mental leaps, depends on a symbiotic relationship between the source and the target. The source provides the basic relational structure, without which the expression would be meaningless. This structure provides a mapping to the target, yielding new inferences about the target. However, these inferences are immediately screened for conformity with what is known about the target. In the aftermath of understanding the metaphor, the mapping may be generalized to form a schema, which may ultimately create a new literal meaning for the source.

Metaphorical Extensions

We do not mean to imply, however, that the multiconstraint theory provides a full account of metaphor comprehension. Analogy may be the cognitive basis of metaphor, but, as we pointed out earlier, metaphor is often extended by an associative aura created by metonymy and other figurative devices. Hence the meaning of a poetic metaphor is not fully captured by the kind of analysis that would suffice for a more rigorous scientific analogy. A theory of metaphor requires extensions that go beyond what is required to account for how analogy is used in problem solving and explanation. Some metaphors are analogies colored by metonymy—analogy seen through a soft-focus lens.

To see some of the complex issues that arise in understanding poetic metaphors, consider a passage in which Ernest Hemingway talks about F. Scott Fitzgerald:

His talent was as natural as the pattern that was made by the dust on a butterfly's wings. At one time he understood it no more than the butterfly did and he did not know when it was brushed or marred. Later he became conscious of his damaged wings and of their construction and he learned to think and could not fly anymore because the love of flight was gone and he could only remember when it had been effortless.

Notice the progressive deepening of the metaphorical identification between the target domain, the writer's talent, and the source domain, a butterfly's flight. In the first two sentences explicit comparatives ("as natural as," "no more than") point out key correspondences. Then in the second clause of the second sentence the passage becomes overtly metaphorical, as the writer's talent is directly described as "brushed" and "marred"—verbs appropriate for a butterfly. Finally, by the third sentence the two domains have been completely identified. The pronoun "he" indicates that the writer is the topic, but the sentence directly describes a personified butterfly.

Although the passage expresses an analogy, it is quite different from a problem analogy, in which the two analogs are compared but not identified with each other. These differences in form reflect differences in purpose. A problem analogy is intended to help provide a solution to the target, whereas this metaphorical passage simply makes a statement about the target. The analogical inferences might include the idea that a writer's talent is very fragile and that memory of past abilities can add to a writer's sense of loss. A more general schema for the pathos of natural skills that diminish as they are overintellectualized is also suggested.

But as is often the case for literary metaphors, the mappings are loose and shifting. The writer's talent is first mapped with the pattern on a butterfly's wings and later with the wings themselves. Indeed, one could argue that the analogy becomes incoherent when analyzed in detail. A butterfly's pattern is not causally related to its flight, so if talent is mapped to the pattern, then there is no reason why consciousness of the talent/pattern should interfere with the ability to exercise it. This analogical inconsistency is a side effect of a metonymy—because strong associations link the concepts of pattern, wings, and flight, these can be interchanged quite freely. As a result, talent can be mapped with any of them. In fact, the apparently inconsistent mapping between talent and the pattern provides a clue that the passage has a broader meaning. The phrase "pattern made by the dust on a butterfly's wings" suggests painting, which in turn encourages thinking of a more general interpretation of the passage as a statement about any mode of creative expression, not just writing.

In fact, this short passage has several levels of interpretation: it is about Fitzgerald, about writing, about artistic skills, and about creative skills in general. When we seek a deeper meaning in an artistic work, this often requires noticing one or more covert target domains. In reading literature, we often confront a problem that is quite the reverse of the standard difficulty that arises in solving problems by analogy. The problem solver faces an inadequately understood target and must find a useful source analog. The reader, on the other hand, encounters a text that may provide a metaphorical source and often has to discover the target domain that is the underlying topic.

Lakoff and Turner discuss a number of Asian proverbs in the form of brief poems, such as

Big thunder
Little rain.

This proverb directly states only the source analog, weather in which loud thunder is heard but little rain falls. But it easily conveys a more general schema: a sign that ought to be predictive of a powerful effect occurs, but the expected effect does not materialize. Most readers can probably think of one or more target analogs that fit this schema, such as a person who brags about results that they fail to achieve, or a dog who barks loudly but then runs away from an intruder. (In fact, the Asian proverb has much the same meaning as the Western expression, "His bark was worse than his bite.") The brevity and concreteness of the proverb make it much more likely to "stick" in memory than would an abstract description of the general schema.

An important point to remember is that communicating a nonliteral interpretation depends on shared background knowledge. Another passage considered by Lakoff and Turner is a Sanskrit poem:

There where the reeds are tall
is the best place to cross the river
she told the traveler
with her eye on him.

You are unlikely to find much meaning in this poem unless you know that in India at the time the poem was written it was common knowledge that illicit sexual encounters often took advantage of the hiding places provided by the tall, thick reeds found along river banks.

Laughter and Love

What purposes are served by metaphors? Why do people use analogies rather than directly saying what they mean? One reason is that analogies are sometimes the most effective way to communicate information. There may be no simple literal equivalent that could replace the metaphor; the source domain is generally more familiar and concrete than the less-understood target; the metaphor may be pithy and memorable;

Purposes of metaphor

and the juxtaposition of the source and target may help create a more abstract schema that highlights the shared relations.

However, analogies can indirectly communicate much more than information and advice. A sportscaster once wrote that trying to explain baseball to a nonfan is like trying to explain sex to an eight-year-old: no matter how much detail you go into, the response is still "But why?" The purpose of this analogy is partly to convey the futility of talking about baseball to the uninterested, but also to make us laugh.

Another example of humor in analogy was provided by a feminist poster that read, "A woman without a man is like a fish without a bicycle." This analogy was intended both to make a statement about women's autonomy and to be amusing. The cynical analogy, "Life is like a sewer: you get back from it just what you put into it," evokes both amusement and disgust, as does the quip that psychologists would rather use each other's toothbrushes than use each other's terminology. Violating the basic distinction between source and target can also provoke humor. An American television advertisement intended to discourage use of illegal drugs showed a picture of an egg ("This is your brain") and then a picture of an egg frying in a pan ("This is your brain on drugs"). Someone put out a poster that added a picture of eggs frying with bacon ("This is your brain with a side of bacon"), bizarrely mixing source and target to achieve a humorous effect.

Another function of analogies is to foster emotions that help to maintain peace and solidarity in social groups. For example, managers of a business may inspire their workers by describing both managers and workers as members of a team or a family, suggesting that the relations among them go beyond that of employer and employee.

As we have already seen, poetic analogies and metaphors have communicative purposes that go beyond mere information passing. Shakespeare wrote,

Shall I compare thee to a summer's day?
Thou art more lovely and more temperate:
Rough winds do shake the darling buds of May,
And summer's lease hath all too short a date.

The point of the comparison—the analogy between the addressed lover and a summer's day—is not merely to say something about constancy, but also to evoke romantic emotions in the reader. As we saw in chapter 7, in the discussion of other minds and empathy, analogy can have emotional as well as cognitive effects. Another of Shakespeare's famous analogies has a negative emotional effect:

All the world's a stage,
And all the men and women merely players,
They have their exits and their entrances;
And one man in his time plays many parts.

The final part "is second childishness, and mere oblivion, sans teeth, sans eyes, sans taste, sans everything." Analogy can convey not only laughter and love, but loss.

In addition to providing amusement and evoking emotions, analogy can be used to avoid embarrassment. As we suggested in chapter 1, people often find it advantageous to be slow or indirect about coming out with the truth. In Tolstoy's poignant story "Happy Ever After," Sergei is the guardian of Katya, and the two fall in love, but neither is able to express it to the other. To avoid the painful situation that is developing, Sergei decides to go away, but Katya confronts him and extracts from him an explanation:

Although it is silly, and impossible to put into words, although it's painful even, I will try and explain to you . . . Imagine there was a certain Monsieur A., shall we say, and that he was old and finished; and a Mademoiselle B., young and happy, and having seen nothing as yet of life or of the world. Family circumstances of various kinds brought them together, and he grew to love her as a daughter, and had no fear of loving her in any other way. But he forgot that B. was so young that life for her was still a game . . . and that he might easily fall in love with her in a different way, and that would seem amusing to her. And he made a mistake, and was suddenly aware of another feeling, as heavy as remorse, creeping into his heart, and he was afraid. He was afraid that their old friendly relations would be destroyed, and he made up his mind to go away before that could happen.

After agonizingly discussing what might become of Monsieur A. and Mademoiselle B., Katya and Sergei are finally able to disclose their love for each other and decide to marry. The analogical mapping, of course, is transparent, but what matters much more than the evident isomorphism is that use of the analogy made it possible for the two lovers to overcome the emotional barriers of pride, fear, and embarrassment.

Analogy as Therapy

Psychotherapy is an important type of social interaction in which indirectness is often required for emotional reasons. There is an old joke in which a psychotherapist tells a patient, "I think you're crazy." The patient demands, "I want a second opinion." So the therapist adds, "Okay, you're ugly too." For obvious reasons, therapy is rarely so direct, and many therapists find analogies and metaphors useful in indirectly communicating with their patients. Psychiatrist Philip Barker describes several clinical situations in which communication by metaphor may be useful. First, pessimistic clients who are doubtful that their problems are soluble can be given anecdotes about people in similar situations who were able to become motivated to recover. Second, when clients resist what the therapist is trying to say to them, the therapist may introduce metaphors to get the message across indirectly. Third, if the direct expression of ideas would upset a client and damage the relationship with the therapist, the therapist can attempt to use indirect communication by means of anecdotes concerning situations analogous to that of the client. Fourth, metaphor can make clients, particularly children, more interested in the course of therapy than they would be in a direct discussion. Finally, Barker advocates use of multiple anecdotes during hypnosis, when clients are particularly susceptible to learning from analogs.

In family therapy, for example, the target analog is the troubled family under treatment, consisting of the members of the family and the complex relationships among them. The source analog is a real or imaginary family with similar relationships and problems. Barker describes how a story might be constructed to deal with a family consisting of a father (Harold), a mother (Jane), a seventeen-year-old son (Lance), a twelve-year-old daughter (Nancy), and a six-year-old adopted daughter (Pamela). Problems arise because Jane favors Lance, who orders Nancy around; the two daughters fight, and the parents do not know how to handle it. The constructed or remembered analogous family consists of a father (Ivan), a mother (Karen), a sixteen-year-old daughter (Mary), a thirteen-year-old son (Oscar), and a five-year-old foster son (Quentin). The therapist can describe how this family worked out their problems so that, for example, Oscar and Quentin learned how to get along with each other, and the parents developed a common strategy for dealing with their children. The hope is that the members of the family under treatment will be able to recognize the connections between the anecdotal family and themselves and transfer their solutions over to their own case. The analogy can serve in a nonthreatening way to make clearer the complex causal relationships in the family and suggest ways of altering them in the direction of family happiness.

Part of what therapists need to do to understand their clients' problems is to appreciate the metaphors with which the clients understand their own lives. Anthropologist Naomi Quinn has identified sev-

eral metaphors that have a large affect on how couples think about their marriage. Some people think of marriage as a manufactured product, with strengths and weaknesses, good parts and bad parts, and things to work on. In another metaphor, marriage is an ongoing journey, with good and bad stages and the open questions of where to head and when to stop. A third metaphor is marriage as a durable bond between people who are tied to each other but are at risk of being driven apart. Finally, Quinn describes how some people see marriage as an investment into which people put effort and expect a return. Another financial metaphor views marriage as a merger, as in the Broomhilda cartoon in which someone says that in marriage two people live as one, and Broomhilda asks, "Which one?" A more positive metaphor for marriage that Quinn does not mention compares a couple to a partnership that shares work and rewards. In all these cases, there is a complex analogical mapping between the various sources and the target, marriage.

In chapter 8 we suggested using analogy therapy in science education by identifying students' naive analogies and proposing better explanatory alternatives. Marital therapy might use a similar technique, identifying couples' use of problem-causing analogies for marriage, such as *merger,* and proposing more productive analogies, such as *partnership.* Both the elicited and the replacing analogies would have to be developed beyond attribute and relational mappings: system mappings should highlight how aspects of both problematic and helpful analogies affect the difficulties in the marriage. Clinical psychologist Donald Meichenbaum has used a related technique to treat victims of post-traumatic stress disorder and found that clients whose thinking is dominated by positive metaphors and analogies have a higher recovery rate. Personal-development "guru" Anthony Robbins urges people to identify the central metaphors they use to view life, for example, life as a test, a game, a gamble, or a battle; then more positive metaphors can be sought. Just as multiple analogies are often useful in decision making and explanation, so multiple metaphors can enhance one's life. Jobs may sometimes be usefully thought of in terms of battles and competitions, but these are poor metaphors for desirable interpersonal relationships.

Management consultant Gareth Morgan uses analogy therapy to help understand and change organizations, such as businesses. Many different metaphors affect how workers and managers view their companies, for example, the company as machine, organism, brain, culture, prison, or instrument of domination. Morgan works with companies to identify how personnel conceive of their company and to help personnel

reframe their approach to the work environment using more cooperative metaphors. In analogy therapy, analogies and metaphors are used not just for communicative purposes but also as tools to help overcome personal and social problems.

Making Magic   *Lévi-Strauss / structuralism*

Analogies have also served social purposes in nonliterate cultures. Many anthropologists have argued that various forms of analogy have been central to the development of basic social phenomena that arose around the world. Claude Lévi-Strauss suggested that many social groups, including the aboriginal Australians and the natives of North America, divided themselves into distinct caste-like clans analogous to the divisions apparent among natural species. That is, just as it is evident that birds differ from bears, which differ from fish, and so on, many cultures developed analogous divisions among clans. In addition to transferring the basic relation of "different from" (which sometimes was associated with prohibitions on interclan marriage), the people of each clan were often believed to share the stereotypical characteristics of an associated animal. Lévi-Strauss reports that among the Chippewa of North America, for example, people of the Crane clan had loud ringing voices and provided the clan with its orators, those of the Cassowary clan were supposed to have long legs and be fast runners, and people of the Bear clan were believed to have thick, coarse hair that never turned white and to be ill tempered and quick to fight.

Lévi-Strauss claimed that one of the most prevalent of all analogies linking humans and animal species is the analogy with birds. In many cultures, the bird world was seen as "a metaphorical human society." It might seem surprising that birds would be considered analogs of people so frequently, since birds are in many ways less physically similar to people than are many mammals, such as monkeys or dogs. But, as Lévi-Strauss argued, people are prone to notice the relational parallels between birds and people:

Birds . . . can be permitted to resemble men for the very reason that they are so different. They are feathered, winged, oviparous and they are also physically separated from human society by the element in which it is their privilege to move. As a result of this fact, they form a community which is independent of our own but, precisely because of this independence, appears to us like another society, homologous to that in which we live: birds love freedom; they build themselves homes in which they live a family life and nurture their young; they often engage in social relations with other members of their species; and they communicate with them by acoustic means recalling articulated language.

Was it some implicit sense of these relational parallels that led Neil (chapter 1) to consider what would be a bird's backyard?

In many cultures, people in some way made use of the parts of animals to aid in acquiring their desired characteristics. Wearing a necklace of bear claws, for example, might be considered a way to acquire the strength and courage of a bear. In such practices we can see connections between analogy and magic. Writing more than a hundred years ago, Sir James Frazer proposed two fundamental principles of what he termed "sympathetic magic." The first principle, which he called the Law of Similarity, is "that like produces like, or that an effect resembles its cause." The second principle, called the Law of Contact, is "that things which have once been in contact with each other continue to act on each other at a distance after the physical contact has been severed." The Law of Similarity leads to what Frazer called "homeopathic magic." For example, the Ojibwa of North America would make a little wooden image of an enemy and then jab a needle into its head or heart, believing that this would cause a sharp pain in the corresponding part of the foe's body. The Law of Contact leads to "contagious magic," an example of which comes from Australian aborigines, who believed that any harm befalling an extracted tooth would be passed on to the person who lost the tooth, because the tooth had once been in contact with the person's gums.

The contrast between homeopathic and contagious magic is related to that between metaphor and metonymy: the first is based on resemblance across domains, the second on a relation (often that of part to whole) within a single domain. As they do in other aspects of culture, the two figurative devices can interact in magical thinking. In wearing a necklace of bear claws to acquire courage, we see both the Law of Similarity (the metaphorical identification of the person and the bear) and the Law of Contact (the metonymic use of the claws of the bear to convey the power of the entire animal). Similarly, a witch might cast a piece of her lover's clothing into the fire, so that he would melt with love for her. Here the Law of Contact is assumed to make the action on the fragment of cloth affect the person it once touched, while the Law of Similarity is supposed to transform the dissolution of the cloth in the fire into a metaphorical melting with love.

Homeopathic magic, the variety most directly related to analogy, appears to have been practiced in every part of the world. In ancient India, Babylon, Egypt, Greece, and Rome, and in more recent peoples of Australia, Africa, and America, sorcerers have attempted to injure or destroy their enemies by injuring or destroying images of them, as in the above example from the North American Ojibwa tribe. Homeopathic magic is also used positively, for example, to help women conceive and deliver children, to win or restore love, and to heal and prevent illness. Frazer provided dozens of examples from many cultures in which magical similarity suggests what to do, and sometimes even what not to do. For example, natives of Baffin Island were forbidden to play the string game of cat's cradle, lest their fingers later be caught in a harpoon line.

The anthropologist Edward Evans-Pritchard found many instances of such magical analogies among the Azande people of Africa. The Azande prick the stalks of bananas with crocodile teeth so that the bananas will be prolific like crocodile teeth. To keep the sun from being quick to set, they place a stone in the fork of a tree. Because ringworm resembles fowl's excrement, they view the excrement as both cause and cure of ringworm. One of the remedies for epilepsy is to eat ashes of the burnt skull of the red monkey, which is thought to display movements similar to epileptic fits. As S. J. Tambiah points out, the purpose of these analogical actions is not to explain or communicate but to bring about some desirable state of affairs, such as a cure.

The cognitive complexity of homeopathic magic can vary in ways that parallel the levels of complexity in analogical mapping. In cases like the use of fowl's excrement as a cure for ringworm, the hypothesized cause and effect seem to be linked by a relatively simple attribute mapping. In contrast, the sorcerer's use of an effigy in an attempt to harm a person depends on similarities between relations as well as attributes: the action (sticking needles in the doll) does not directly resemble the desired effect (pain in the enemy). However, the doll and the person resemble each other, and the action of sticking needles in the doll resembles sticking a spear in the person. When the sorcerer constructs and mutilates a doll to attack an enemy, the basic mapping goes something like this:

Source	*Target*
jab (needle, doll) *name*: jab-1	stab (spear, enemy) *name*: stab-2
mutilated (doll) *name*: mutilated-1	injured (enemy) *name*: injured-2
cause (jab-1, mutilated-1)	cause (stab-2, injured-2)

The evident mappings of objects are

needle ↔ spear
doll ↔ enemy,

and the mappings of attributes and relations are

jab ↔ stab
mutilated ↔ injured
cause ↔ cause.

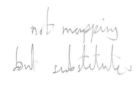
(handwritten margin note) not mapping but substitute

So far this is a perfectly sensible mapping based on the usual constraints. But homeopathic magic then makes a dangerous mental leap: rather than resting content with the mappings between the elements of the source and target, it assumes that a source element can actually substitute for the corresponding element of the target. The result is that an action on the source (the doll) is believed to cause an effect on the target (the person):

cause (jab-1, injured-2).

Whereas system mappings of the sort we have discussed in previous chapters provide mappings between causal relations within the source to causal relations within the target, the Law of Similarity can create the belief that actions performed on the source analog have a causal effect on the objects in the target analog. Homeopathic magic sidesteps the usual requirements for a causal connection, such as contiguity in space, and takes advantage of the fact that it easier to act with impunity on the source than on the target.

Before we sneer at the Azande and other nonliterate peoples for such magical thinking, we should reflect on some of the beliefs to be found in Western culture. Psychologists have shown that people have a tendency to overrate the significance of similarity. For example, Daniel Kahneman and Amos Tversky have conducted experiments that show that people neglect relevant statistical information when resemblances are salient. Richard Nisbett and Lee Ross discuss some of the parallels between common errors in assessing causality and the homeopathic magic of prescientific cultures. Like the Azande, educated Western adults generally expect causes to resemble their effects and may assume without evidence of covariation that spicy food causes heartburn, that people's handwriting tells you something about their personality, and that dramatic effects, such as a presidential assassination, must have dramatic causes, such as a conspiracy. Homeopathy is still widely practiced in alternative medicine; a recent guide explicitly advocates the "law of

cancer with wickedness

similars," that "likes are to be cured with likes." Homeopathy and what Kahneman and Tversky call the "representativeness heuristic" are like analogy in that they involve judgments of similarity, but they nonetheless differ markedly from analogy based on system mappings, in which the causal relations are internal to each analog and there is no assumption that like causes like.

Magical thinking, as Frazer suggested, may well have been a precursor to scientific reasoning, representing an attempt by humans to gain some understanding and control of their complex environment. However, Frazer correctly stressed that magical thinking uses analogy erroneously when it finds causal links between source and target. More generally, while analogies and metaphors can greatly enrich human communication and culture, their effects are not always benign. In her book *Illness as Metaphor,* Susan Sontag describes the emotional pain that has been caused by systems of metaphors associated with the diseases of cancer and tuberculosis. We too easily describe a political event or structure as "a cancer in the body politic," not thinking of the effect that associating cancer with wickedness has on those who are ill. As we noted earlier, metaphor can set the stage for metonymy—once the source and target are associated by analogy, they are in "mental contact" so that their properties become interchangeable in a very loose way. Like tuberculosis before it, cancer becomes an evil to be feared and hidden. Erroneous beliefs about the illness, such as that cancer is somehow contagious, may be encouraged by ill-considered analogies, such as talking about urban blight as "a cancer on the city." Personal development can be hindered by toxic metaphors like "life is a dead-end street."

Just as analogical problem solutions and explanations can fix us into rigid and unproductive ways of thinking, so unexamined metaphors can stifle communication and cultural change. Lakoff and Turner describe how the metaphor of the Great Chain of Being, which assumes that animals and humans are cosmically ordered in hierarchies (often with white, Western males at the top), has interfered with attempts to introduce new ways of thinking about the relations between different human societies and between humans and animals. Acceptance of magical analogies and causal conclusions based on resemblance can impede us from using richer and more creative analogies to achieve better understanding and communication. Like the king of Liang in chapter 7, we have to grant Hui Tzu and others the freedom to talk to us in analogies, but we have to be wary of the use and value of each one. In the web of culture, analogies should be powerful connecting strands, not devouring spiders.

Summary

Cultural practices like the Japanese tea ceremony and the Managalese allegories exhibit the importance of metaphor in promoting social cohesion and indirect communication. Metaphor is not the same as analogy, but metaphorical thinking is based on the same mental processes as analogy and therefore can in part be understood in terms of the constraints of similarity, structure, and purpose. Metaphors range from simple statements like "My job is a jail" that involve a mapping between a target and a schematic source, to much more complex correspondences based on system mappings. Like analogies, metaphors serve to create complex similarities, not merely to apply them. Analogy and metaphor can have diverse emotional applications, serving to evoke amusement, disgust, love, and other reactions. Analogy can be put to use in many therapeutic situations, helping to overcome problems with families, individuals, and organizations. The technique of analogy therapy involves identifying toxic analogies and replacing them with ones that enable people to overcome their personal and social problems. People in some cultures illegitimately use analogy as a device to solve problems based on the magical assumption of a causal relation between source and target.

← toxic metaphors

The Analogical Computer

Looking Backward

We have seen analogy at work in the thinking of organisms as diverse as apes, politicians, scientists, and poets. Our aim has been to show how numerous aspects of the use and misuse of analogies, involving the processes of selection, mapping, evaluation, and learning, can be understood from the perspective of our multiconstraint theory. This theory, laid out in chapter 2, proposes that analogical thinking fundamentally involves the simultaneous satisfaction of the constraints of similarity, structure, and purpose. In accord with the proposals of Genter and Halford, the theory distinguishes three levels of complexity in analogical thinking, each of which is tied to an increasingly abstract form of explicit knowledge: attribute mapping (based on attributes of objects), relational mapping (based on relations between objects), and system mapping (based on higher-order relations between relations). Each increase in complexity is coupled with a deeper basis for finding similarities, a greater sensitivity to structure, and an expanded capacity to think explicitly about the purposes of analogies.

In chapter 3, we provided a sketch of how analogical thinking evolved. We reviewed evidence suggesting that monkeys are capable of attribute mapping and that chimpanzees, at least after special training in the use of symbols for "same" and "different," are capable of relational mapping as well. The similarity, structure, and purpose constraints are all present in some form in the thinking of the chimpanzee. It seems, however, that the analogical capacities of these animals are limited by their inability to perform system mapping based on higher-order relations. Similarly, we found in chapter 4 that the major difference in analogical ability between preschool children and those slightly older is that the latter are able to perform system mapping, which allows them to put more complex analogs to fuller use in problem solving. In chapter 5 we showed how adult problem solvers can use the three interacting constraints of similarity, structure, and purpose to impose coherent interpretations on complex and ambiguous analogies. The evidence we reviewed supports our claim that all three constraints play a role in each of the stages of analogy use, from selection to mapping to evaluation to learning.

Chapter 6 described how analogy can be useful for decision making, provided that system mappings are used to assess whether complex situations are alike with respect to higher-order relations between actions and goals. Similarly, chapter 7 distinguished between strong and weak explanatory philosophical analogies, the strong ones involving system mappings that enable them to contribute to the coherence of explanations. In chapter 8 we saw that the most powerful scientific uses of analogy, such as Darwin's comparison of natural and artificial selection, have made use of the same coalescence of structure and purpose through system mappings. Moreover, attention to the cognitive constraints on analogy can help educators distinguish good analogies for teaching from poor ones. Finally, we showed in chapter 9 how interactions of similarity, structure, and purpose contribute to understanding metaphor, which is involved in diverse cultural uses of analogy, ranging from tea ceremonies to magic.

Except for our brief remarks at the end of chapter 2, we have so far only sketched the nature of the cognitive processes by which the multiple constraints get satisfied. To be more precise requires that we describe how analogical thinking can be performed by computers.

The Computational Mind

The development of computers and computational ideas since the 1950s has provided a way of thinking about thought that is much more powerful than any that had been previously available. Since the workings of the mind are not directly observable, theorizing about them is necessarily analogical: we form hypotheses about mental operations by comparing them to processes that we can more directly observe. Computer programs are fully inspectable by us, so we know the data structures they use to represent information, as well as the algorithms that process information by operating on those structures. For example, a computer program that does arithmetic will have data structures for representing numbers and algorithms for performing operations, such as addition and multiplication. Cognitive theories inspired by the computational analogy hypothesize first a set of representational structures and second a set of computational processes that operate on those structures to produce intelligent behavior. Regrettably, this analogy can be of only limited use to readers who do not already have some understanding of computation. But, in contrast to our technical papers on computational models of analogy, we will try here to present the computational ideas as simply and intuitively as possible. Readers with extensive computational backgrounds may look to our journal articles for fuller detail and rigor.

As we described in chapter 8, analogies can contribute to the development of science at many stages, including initial discovery, development of ideas, and testing and evaluation. In cognitive science, the analogy between computers and the mind has been important for all these purposes. Before the hypothesis of mind as computation arose in its modern form in the 1950s, it was very mysterious how complex thinking could be produced by a physical system, such as the brain. Behaviorists dominated psychology and were also influential in philosophy and other fields; their advice was to restrict psychology to observable behavior, as a way of avoiding unscientific conjectures about the mind. The development of computers that seemed capable of rudimentary reasoning helped to break psychology loose from its behaviorist chains and initiated decades of fruitful research both with people and with computer models. Computational ideas can suggest how the mind might work as well as make it possible to develop detailed models of various kinds of thinking. When implemented in running computer programs, computational theories can be tested by seeing whether the programs have the power that they were supposed to have and whether they perform in ways similar to how humans perform.

It would be a mistake, however, to suppose that there is a monolithic "computational theory of mind," for there are actually many different computational ways of thinking about thinking. Two approaches are especially important for understanding our computer simulations of analogy. One is the "symbolic" approach, which uses symbols that express the structure of predicates and their associated slots. Such symbolic representations are well suited for capturing the structure of explicit knowledge as we described it in chapter 2. The other is the "connectionist" approach, in which models are constructed using networks of neuronlike "units" interconnected by links that allow the units to influence each other. Most connectionist models are only able to represent knowledge implicitly (as the strengths of weights on links) and hence are unable to deal with analogies based on explicit, structured knowledge. Nonetheless, connectionist models are especially well suited for modeling a style of processing called *parallel constraint satisfaction,* in which the units are interpreted as hypotheses of some sort, and the links represent constraints that determine the extent to which sets of hypotheses are mutually coherent. This style of processing turns out to provide a natural way of dealing with the central computational problem facing our multiconstraint theory, which is to specify how the multiple constraints can work together to interpret analogies, even when the constraints conflict to some extent.

Our computer simulations attempt to make use of the strengths of both the symbolic and the connectionist approaches. The multiconstraint theory is implemented as a kind of hybrid, combining symbolic representations of explicit knowledge with connectionist processing. In particular, our computational models of analogical mapping and retrieval (as well as of deliberative and explanatory coherence) depend on parallel constraint satisfaction. We present a general account of computational implementations of parallel constraint satisfaction and then show how mapping and retrieval can be understood in this way. Ours is certainly not the only computational way of approaching analogy, and we will provide pointers to competing views. Finally, we discuss the future of analogy, including its use in human thinking and the study of analogy as a psychological process.

Parallel Constraint Satisfaction

Our theory of analogy is itself in large part a product of analogical thinking, guided by the background source analog of visual perception. The idea that thinking can be understood as a kind of seeing was central to Gestalt psychology, which flourished in Germany early in the twentieth century. The Gestalt psychologists described both problem solving and perception in terms of what we would now call parallel constraint satisfaction. However, the Gestalt movement ended before the advent of computers, and its theoretical ideas were never clearly formulated.

The computational source for the constraint-satisfaction aspect of our theory of analogy originated in the 1970s, when explicit models of parallel constraint satisfaction were developed for computer vision. David Marr and Tomaso Poggio proposed what they called a "cooperative" algorithm for stereoscopic vision. Two eyes form slightly different images of the world: how does the brain match the two images and construct a coherent, combined image? Marr and Poggio noticed that matching is governed by several constraints involving how points in one image can be put into correspondence with those in the other image. Creating a coherent image is then a matter of satisfying the constraints on matching points across the two images. To accomplish this task computationally, Marr and Poggio proposed using a parallel, interconnected network of processors, in which the interconnections represented the constraints. Their model for matching points in two images eventually provided a source analog that suggested ideas about models for the target domain of analogy, which requires mapping the elements of two analogs.

Similar networks were subsequently used by J. A. Feldman to model visual representations in memory and by Jay McClelland and David Rumelhart to model letter perception. Both Feldman and Rumelhart, together with their colleagues, discussed the application of parallel constraint satisfaction to an intriguing demonstration of the way in which the human visual system is able to cope with ambiguity. Figure 10.1 depicts a Necker cube, a peculiar drawing that had been discussed earlier by the Gestalt psychologists. Notice that the drawing is ambiguous—it can be interpreted as either of two distinct three-dimensional cubes. With a little effort you will be able to see either cube, both of which are coherent interpretations but incompatible with each other. One way to see the two views is to concentrate on the top-left corner and "force" it to lie on either the front or the back face of the cube. You will notice that if you switch this corner from front to back or vice versa, the other corners will be reinterpreted so as to be consistent with the switched corner. People can only see one cube at a time (although they can flip

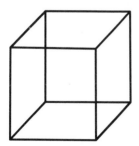

Figure 10.1
An ambiguous Necker cube.

their interpretation back and forth) and almost never see a muddled mixture of the two views.

Parallel constraint satisfaction provides a mechanism for resolving the ambiguity inherent in the Necker cube. The basic insight is that each of the two global interpretations can be defined in terms of a set of more elementary interpretations of the elements of the drawing. For example, under one interpretation, the top-left corner in the drawing is the front-top-left corner of the cube, whereas under the other interpretation the same point is interpreted as the back-top-left corner. Furthermore, the possible local interpretations are highly interdependent, tending either to support or to compete with each other in accord with the structural relations embodied in the canonical cube.

Human interpretations of the Necker cube can be modeled by a simple connectionist network that uses units to represent interpretations of the corners and links between units to represent compatibilities and incompatibilities between interpretations. In this network, parallel constraint satisfaction converges on one or the other of the two possible views, activating a subset of units that collectively represented a coherent interpretation and deactivating the others. Rumelhart and his colleagues argued, moreover, that similar processes underlie the use of schemas in human cognition.

This connection between parallel constraint satisfaction in visual perception and in human thinking set the stage for analogical transfer to our own theory of analogy. By 1986, we had vague ideas that analogy depended on structure, similarity, and purpose, and we had formulated a computational model along these lines. However, this model was unsatisfying in various ways and did not exhibit humanlike capability to cope with the messiness and ambiguity of the analogies used in everyday life. In retrospect, these limitations of the model appear related to the fact that it did not incorporate parallel constraint satisfaction. In April of 1987, after reading Rumelhart's account of how perception of the Necker cube may be related to schemas, Holyoak realized that the two alternative interpretations of the Necker-cube drawing can be seen as two alternative mappings from the two-dimensional picture to a schema for a canonical three-dimensional cube. The resolution of the ambiguity thus depended on a kind of visual analogical mapping.

In the following two months we worked together to figure out how a network could be used to perform analogical mapping by simultaneously satisfying constraints of similarity, structure, and purpose. We quickly succeeded in building and testing a computer program that modeled mapping in this way, called ACME, for Analogical Constraint Mapping Engine. While Thagard was writing ACME, he realized that the same kind of network could be used to model inferences to the best explanation of the sort we discussed in chapters 7 and 8. The result was ECHO, for Explanatory Coherence by Harmany Optimization, a program for modeling the evaluation of hypotheses on the basis of their explanatory coherence. Recognition that analog retrieval is like analogical mapping between a target and many possible sources led us to develop a new model, called Analog Retrieval by Constraint Satisfaction—ARCS. Thus an analogical chain reaction triggered by a model for disambiguating the Necker cube led to analogical mapping (ACME), to explanatory coherence (ECHO), and to analog retrieval (ARCS). Our main purpose in this chapter is to describe how ACME and ARCS operate; however, we also want to convey how parallel constraint satisfaction and its implementation in connectionist networks provide a general way of modeling many complex cognitive phenomena.

As an initial example of a constraint satisfaction problem, consider the task faced by university administrators when they put together a class schedule for each term, semester, or quarter. Some of the constraints they face are inviolable: they cannot put two classes in the same room at the same time, and a student or professor cannot simultaneously be in two different classes. In contrast, many of the constraints are soft ones, involving preferences of professors and students concerning when and where their classes will take place. Coming up with a schedule that takes into account the various constraints imposed by classroom availability and the preferences of professors and students is a daunting task that is rarely accomplished in optimal fashion. Administrators typically take a previous term's schedule and adapt it to handle new problems. But constraint satisfaction problems can be solved in a more general way.

The multiple examples of computational constraint satisfaction models that are now available allow us to abstract their general features to provide a schema. The structures in a parallel constraint satisfaction model consist of elements and various kinds of constraints among them. The elements are hypotheses of various kinds, for example, about what matches what, about what is true in the world, and about what actions should be done and what goals adopted. We can classify constraints as being either internal or external: internal constraints involve only relations among the elements, while external constraints come from outside the system of elements. In addition, constraints can be either positive or

constraints like a tug of war

negative, depending on whether they imply that two elements are compatible or incompatible.

To get a feeling for how parallel constraint satisfaction operates, imagine a game that is something like tug-of-war but that involves pushing as well as pulling and allows many teams instead of just two. Furthermore, the teams can be interlocking in that a single person can be on more than one team. We can call this game "tug-and-shove." Each player tries to help teammates stand up while at the same time trying to make opponents fall down. Players are connected to one another either by ropes that they can use to pull each other, or by sticks that they can use to push each other. Each person is connected to other players in various ways. Two people who are connected by ropes form part of a single team: if one team member falls down, that person will tend to drag down the teammate; but if one gets up, that person will be able to attempt to pull up the other. Both teammates in a connected pair have the same influence on each other. In contrast, two people who are connected by sticks are members of rival teams: if one gets up, that player will tend to push the other one down; and if one falls down, the other will be better able to get up. The interconnected players form the internal part of a constraint satisfaction network.

Now suppose that in addition one other person serves as the master of tug-and-shove. The master is connected to some of the players by ropes that can be pulled and to other players by sticks that can be pushed; but nobody can influence the master, who is always standing. The master, who represents an external input to the constraint network, gets the game started by pulling or pushing some of the players, who then affect each other. Eventually, after a series of interconnected pulls and pushes, some players will be left standing and the others will be knocked over. The players will tend to form clusters, either standing or on the ground: some will be on winning teams, whose members manage to hold each other up, while others will be losers, who end up either holding each other down or being held down by the winners.

The game of tug-and-shove is analogous to an implementation of parallel constraint satisfaction, the players representing elements and the ropes and sticks representing constraints. Once the elements and constraints are specified, implementing this kind of model in a parallel network is very easy. First, elements (here, players) are represented by units. Second, positive internal constraints (ropes) are represented by excitatory connections: if two elements are related by a positive constraint, then the units representing the elements should be linked by an excitatory link. Third, negative internal constraints (sticks) are represented by inhibitory connections: if two elements are related by a negative constraint, then the units representing the elements should be linked by an inhibitory link. (All internal links in the tug-and-shove game, as in our models of analogy, are symmetric.) Fourth, an external constraint can be captured by linking units representing elements that satisfy the external constraint to a special unit (corresponding to the master of tug-and-shove) that constantly affects those units, either positively by virtue of excitatory links or negatively by virtue of inhibitory links. The process by which players push and pull on each other until some are left standing is analogous to the relaxation process by which activation spreads between units until the network settles into a stable state. Some units end up activated, just as some players end up standing, while others are deactivated, just as other players are knocked over, with the result depending on the interconnections among the units (players).

Now let us move from the imaginary game of tug-and-shove to an example of a cognitive model based on parallel constraint satisfaction. An example that is simpler to implement than analogical mapping and retrieval is a model of decision making based on the ideas presented in chapter 6. The elements of a decision are various actions and goals. The positive internal constraints come from facilitation relations: if an action facilitates a goal, then the action and goal tend to go together. The negative internal constraints come from incompatibility relations, when two actions or goals cannot be performed or satisfied together. The external constraint on decision making comes from goal priority: some goals, such as achieving personal happiness, are inherently desirable, providing a positive constraint. Once the elements and constraints have been specified for a particular decision problem, a constraint network can be formed using the same basic method we described for the tug-and-shove game.

Figure 10.2 illustrates a simple network of the sort that is formed by DECO, the computer program that implements the theory of deliberative coherence described in chapter 6. The elements of Howard's dilemma—goals and actions—are represented by units. Positive constraints based on facilitation are represented by excitatory links (solid lines) between units, and negative constraints based on incompatibility are represented by inhibitory links (broken lines). For example, moving to a new job facilitates the goal of attaining prestige, which facilitates the goal of making Howard happy. Staying and moving are incompatible. The external constraint, that some goals have intrinsic priority, is repre-

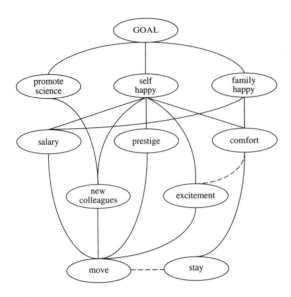

Figure 10.2
A simple DECO network for evaluating the coherence of alternative courses of
action. The solid lines represent excitatory links between the units that represent
goals and actions that cohere with each other. The dashed lines represent inhibitory
links between units representing incompatible actions and goals.

sented by having excitatory links from a special "goal" unit, which is
always active, to each unit that represents a goal that has priority. The
figure assumes that Howard has three intrinsically desirable goals: promoting science, making himself happy, and making his family happy.
Units representing each of these are accordingly linked to the special
goal unit.

All the constraints can then be satisfied in parallel by repeatedly
passing activation among all the units until, after some number of cycles
of activity, all units have reached stable activation levels. This process,
based on the general principles we introduced in discussing tug-and-
shove, is called *relaxation,* by analogy to physical processes that involve
objects gradually achieving a stable shape or temperature. Achieving
stability is called *settling.* Relaxing the network means adjusting the
activation of all units on the basis of the units to which they are
connected until all units have stable high or low activations. A unit with
an excitatory link to an active unit will gain activation from it, while a
unit with an inhibitory link to an active unit will have its own activation
decreased. If a unit settles with high activation, this is interpreted as

acceptance of the goal or action that it represents, whereas deactivation represents rejection. In the network shown in figure 10.2, the unit representing moving has many excitatory links and therefore will get more activation than the unit representing staying, which will be deactivated because of the inhibitory link with the unit for moving.

The models we have used to deal with analogical mapping and retrieval are more complex than either the game of tug-and-shove or decision making in DECO. However, these simpler examples suggest the flavor of how multiple interacting processors linked by excitatory and inhibitory connections can achieve a stable result. We will now describe how our constraint satisfaction models of analogy actually operate.

Mapping

correspondence

As we described in chapter 2, mapping is the process by which the components of two analogs, a source and a target, are put into correspondence with each other. Without any constraints, mapping would be computationally very difficult because of the sheer number of possible mappings. Suppose that the source and the target each involve ten predicates applied to five objects. If we assume that predicates map to predicates and objects to objects and that the mapping is one-to-one, then the number of possible mappings will be in excess of four hundred million! Yet people can quickly spot the correspondences in mapping problems that are considerably larger than this, for example (as described in chapter 5) when comparing the participants in the Persian Gulf War to those in World War II. Not only that, but people do not slavishly require that mappings always be one-to-one, as our calculation of the number of possibilities assumed. (Recall that people sometimes were willing to map the country of Kuwait to more than one of the victims of German aggression in World War II.) People are somehow solving an even harder version of the mapping problem, in which one-to-many mappings are not excluded altogether, but certainly they do not do so by consciously listing and evaluating millions of alternative mappings.

Analogical mapping becomes a tractable task for humans to perform because they are able to bring to bear the three constraints of similarity, structure, and purpose. Development of a computational model requires specification of these constraints in much more detail than does informal description, and makes it possible to test some of the consequences of our multiconstraint theory. The three constraints can all be satisfied together in a single connectionist model. In accord with the general method outlined in the previous section, the first task is to identify what will be the elements that are subject to constraints. Consider a simplified version of the Persian Gulf War analogy that includes only the information that Saddam was president of Iraq, which invaded Kuwait, and Hitler was führer of Germany, which occupied Austria:

Target	*Source*
president-of (Saddam, Iraq)	führer-of (Hitler, Germany)
invade (Iraq, Kuwait)	occupy (Germany, Austria).

For people who understand English, the correspondence is automatic, but how can we program a computer to find the intuitive correspondences? Our ACME model shows how multiple constraints make mapping relatively easy.

Taking structure seriously, it is immediately obvious that we can constrain the mapping problem considerably by mapping predicates only to predicates and objects to objects, so that the correspondence **invade** ↔ **Hitler** will never even be considered. Hence the elements in our constraint satisfaction theory of analogical mapping include only hypotheses that consider mappings between analog components of similar types. The mappings to be considered include only predicate-predicate hypotheses, such as **invade** ↔ **occupy** and **invade** ↔ **führer-of**, and object-object hypotheses, such as **Saddam** ↔ **Hitler** and **Saddam** ↔ **Germany.** Moreover, we can also ignore hypotheses that involve objects that never fill corresponding slots, such as **Saddam** ↔ **Austria.**

Among the hypotheses worth considering, two further kinds of structural constraints can be applied: the positive constraint of structural consistency and the negative constraint of one-to-one mapping. For example, structural consistency requires that the hypothesis **invade** ↔ **occupy** should encourage, and be encouraged by, the mappings **Iraq** ↔ **Germany** and **Kuwait** ↔ **Austria.** Similarly, one-to-one mapping requires that the hypothesis **Iraq** ↔ **Germany** should discourage, and be discouraged by, **Iraq** ↔ **Hitler.** In ACME, structural consistency and one-to-one mappings are both soft constraints, encouraging mappings but not insisting on them, whereas ruling out mappings between objects and predicates is a hard, inviolable constraint.

Similarity and purpose are both external constraints on mapping. We want to favor mappings that involve semantically similar components, such as "invade" and "occupy," not ones involving elements as different as "invade" and "führer-of." Again this is a soft constraint, since we want the system to be able to discover correspondences between elements that were not previously seen to be related to each other. Similarly, the purpose will favor mapping hypotheses that fit with the goals of the analogist: if the point of the analogy is to show that Saddam is evil like Hitler, then the mapping hypothesis **Saddam ↔ Hitler** will be encouraged by the soft constraint that mappings should serve the purpose of the analogy.

Now we can move from the constraint theory to the computational model, in which elements get represented by units, positive and negative constraints get represented respectively by excitatory and inhibitory links, external constraints get represented by links to special units, and parallel constraint satisfaction is achieved by algorithms for updating activations of the units on the basis of their links to other units. In the simple example above, we need eleven units to represent all the mapping hypotheses. (For simplicity, we ignore hypotheses about mappings between propositions.) These units will be interconnected by excitatory and inhibitory links to represent the positive constraint of structural consistency and the negative constraint of one-to-one mapping. To implement the external constraints, we need two special units, one for semantic similarity and the other for purpose. A special unit will be linked with each unit that represents a mapping hypothesis that satisfies the constraints of either semantic similarity or relevance to purpose (or both). For example, ACME produces a link from the special "similarity" unit to the unit representing the **president-of ↔ führer-of** correspondence but not the **president-of ↔ occupy** correspondence. Of course, satisfying a constraint can be a matter of degree. For example, the concept of being a president is somewhat similar to that of being a führer, but perhaps less so than to that of, say, being a prime minister. The magnitude of the positive or negative weight on each link reflects the degree to which the corresponding constraint is satisfied or violated.

Figure 10.3 depicts the network created by ACME when it is given as input the source and target represented above. Once this network is created, a simple algorithm updates the activation of each unit in parallel to determine which mapping hypotheses should be accepted. All units start with activations near 0, except for the special units for semantic similarity and purpose, which start with, and retain full activation of, 1. These units start to activate the units with which they are linked; then activation spreads throughout the system, fostered by excitatory links and suppressed by inhibitory links. We will not give the full details here, but

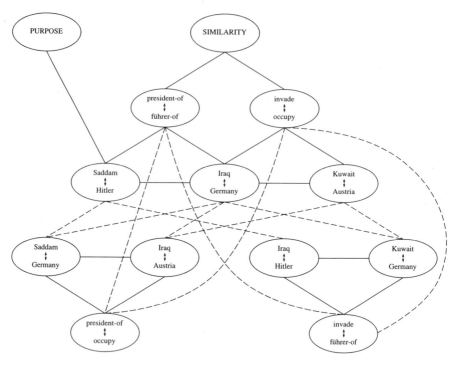

Figure 10.3
The structure of the network created by ACME for the simplified Saddam example.
Solid lines indicate excitatory links and dashed lines indicate inhibitory links. We
have simplified by not showing the units representing mappings between whole
propositions.

anyone interested in programming ACME can find a full description of
the algorithms for creating and relaxing networks in our 1989 paper in
the journal *Cognitive Science*.

ACME is capable of exploiting higher-order relations to provide
much deeper mappings. An enhanced representation of our Persian Gulf
War target and World War II source might include the information that
Saddam's being president of Iraq was a *cause* of Iraq's invading Kuwait,
just as Hitler's being führer of Germany was a cause of Germany's
occupying Austria. ACME would then map the two "cause" relations
together and create additional mapping hypotheses, treating the related
propositions as fillers of slots in each "cause" relation and therefore
putting entire propositions into correspondence with each other. In this
way ACME can exploit the use of causal and other higher-order relations

that contribute to effective problem solving as well as to deliberative and explanatory coherence.

How does one decide that a model such as ACME is a good representation of human analogical mapping? Computationally, the first test is to show that the model is in fact able to find sensible mappings for analogies of varying sizes. We have tested ACME on dozens of examples, with analogs that require over one hundred propositions to describe, and also with target analogs that have severely impoverished representations. But computational power is not the only criterion by which a cognitive model must be evaluated, since we need evidence that the model captures aspects of human performance. In our 1989 paper and in subsequent work, we showed how ACME can closely mimic mapping behavior in a variety of psychological experiments, many of which were described in chapters 4 and 5. For example, ACME can find humanlike mappings between the Persian Gulf War and World War II analogs when given propositions that capture an elaborate summary of each. Like humans, ACME is sensitive to the "Necker-cube" quality of this ambiguous analogy, settling into one of two sets of coherent but mutually exclusive correspondences: President Bush and the United Sates tend to be mapped to Roosevelt and the United States, or to Churchill and Britain, but not to a mixed combination of a leader and a country, such as Churchill and the United States. Also like people, ACME occasionally will tolerate a one-to-many mapping, such as that between Kuwait and Austria/Poland. ACME is able to account for the intricate interplay among the constraints of structure, similarity, and purpose that have been revealed in psychological experiments. We were also able to apply the model to complex metaphors, such as Socrates' metaphor of a philosopher as a midwife of ideas (chapter 7). In general, the model seems to capture the human ability to find coherent relationships among complex and imperfectly understood situations, on the basis of the interplay among the same three constraints.

Retrieval

The mapping problem is computationally difficult, due to the huge number of possible mappings, but it pales in comparison to the problem of retrieving an interesting and useful source analog from memory in response to a novel target analog. People have a vast amount of knowledge stored in their long-term memory, including many thousands of episodes. The problem of retrieving relevant analogs from memory is therefore even more formidable than the problem of finding a mapping between a single source analog and a target analog. Given a target problem to solve, we need to be able to match it against many potential source analogs stored in memory. The constraints of similarity, structure, and purpose are once again needed to solve this matching problem, but the increased difficulty of retrieval compared to mapping requires them to be implemented somewhat differently.

In our ACME model, structure is the main constraint used to restrict the number of mapping hypotheses considered, allowing us to ignore mappings between predicates and objects and between objects that never fill corresponding slots. Semantic similarity served as an external constraint, aiding mappings between components with similar meanings but not proscribing mappings between components with dissimilar meanings. For retrieval, however, a semantic screen is necessary to avoid having to consider every episode stored in memory. Hence our ARCS model only considers matching a given structure to those structures stored in memory that have some semantic overlap with it.

In ACME, the semantic similarity of attributes and relations was provided by the programmer, but ARCS needed a built-in way of associating semantically similar components. We therefore borrowed information from WordNet, an electronic thesaurus developed by George Miller and his colleagues. WordNet is an ambitious attempt to encode a large proportion of English words in a plausible form, on the basis of what is known about human language understanding. Words are stored in ways designed to correspond to how concepts are organized in human memory. WordNet is thus an elaborate version of the kind of semantic network of concepts we introduced in chapter 2. For nouns, WordNet notes how words are related to each other by "kind-of" and "part-of" relations. For example, the word "dog" has an entry that indicates that it is a kind of canine, which is a kind of carnivore, which is a kind of mammal, and so on. In addition, the entry for dog reveals many subkinds, such as terrier and collie, and parts, such as tail and fur. For ARCS, we associated each predicate with pointers to semantically relevant concepts. So if ARCS is presented with a story about dogs and a probe is initiated to retrieve related stories from its memory, then the program will search for structures concerned with such related concepts as canines, terriers, and collies.

Considering only semantically related structures narrows the search through memory considerably but still leaves a huge problem of selecting the overall best matches for a structure. Let us complicate the simple

Saddam example from the last section by supposing that memory includes other related examples, and the task is to pick the most relevant ones. So in addition to the Hitler source, we might have:

Source 2	Source 3
leader-of (Ho Chi Minh, North Vietnam)	prime-minister-of (Trudeau, Canada)
invade (North Vietnam, South Vietnam)	visit (Trudeau, United States).

If ARCS is given the Saddam structure, with Saddam as president of Iraq and Iraq invading Kuwait, it probes into memory looking for related structures. All three of the sources we have described—concerning Germany, Vietnam, and Canada—will be considered by ARCS as potentially relevant sources, so a constraint network needs to be constructed to determine which is the most relevant.

Figure 10.4 shows part of the network that would be created by ARCS to choose the best source by parallel constraint satisfaction. In

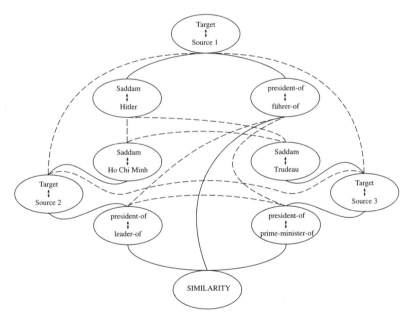

Figure 10.4
Portion of a constraint network created by ARCS for retrieval. Only a few of the units and links created are shown. In particular, we have simplified by not showing the units representing mappings between whole propositions. Solid lines indicate excitatory links and dashed lines indicate inhibitory links.

addition to the mapping hypotheses concerning correspondences between attributes, relations, objects, and propositions used by ACME, ARCS also forms mapping hypotheses concerning whole structures that comprise a target and potential sources. As in ACME, structural consistency provides a positive constraint represented by excitatory links, and one-to-one mapping provides a negative constraint represented by inhibitory links. Again, the external constraints of semantic similarity and purpose are implemented by links from special units to units representing mapping hypotheses that satisfy those constraints. (Only the special "similarity" unit is shown in figure 10.4.) After the network has settled, the activations of the top-level hypotheses that have the form **Target** ↔ **Source** will reveal which source is most active and therefore apparently most relevant to the target. Retrieval is competitive: as a unit representing one target-source mapping becomes active, it tends to suppress the activation of units representing alternative target-source mappings because of the inhibitory links between units representing incompatible mappings. In addition to finding the strongest top-level mappings of the target to the alternative sources, ARCS will also find mappings for some of the predicates and objects in the target. The output of the retrieval process thus provides part of the mapping for the components of the target. If this information is passed on to ACME, that program can then go on to elaborate the mapping between the target and whatever source analogs ARCS retrieved.

In sum, ARCS proceeds in three stages. First, it uses semantic similarity as encoded in WordNet to select sources that are potentially relevant to a target. Second, it creates a constraint network that takes into account structure and purpose as well as similarity. Finally, it uses relaxation to identify which of the possible source analogs are most relevant to the target with respect to all three constraints.

To evaluate ARCS computationally, we constructed two large databases consisting of representations of one hundred of Aesop's fables and twenty-five synopses of Shakespeare's plays. ARCS performed reasonably well with both databases, showing that it could retrieve appropriate structures from among many complex ones in storage. For example, a story about a person who tried to get a job but failed and then said the job would have been boring anyhow tended to activate Aesop's fable about the fox who decided the grapes he could not reach were sour. When ARCS was probed with a synopsis of Hamlet, it tended to activate the other Shakespearean tragedies in its memory, such as Othello and King Lear.

Using the database of Aesop's fables, we performed a computational experiment to see how the program would perform as the size of its store of examples in memory increased. We were particularly interested in the number of cycles of activation updating that would be required for the program to settle into a stable state. Accordingly, we varied the number of fables in ARCS's memory over the range from ten to ninety-nine to determine how the number of fables in memory would affect the number of cycles of activity required to achieve settling. The results are depicted in figure 10.5. The number of required cycles increased by a factor of only two as the number of stored fables was increased from ten to sixty, and then leveled off as the number was further increased to ninety-nine. The program was thus able to determine the best match to the target with a roughly constant number of cycles of activation updating, even as the number of stored examples varied over a substantial range. This result illustrates the power of parallel processing in memory retrieval: rather than evaluating each alternative case in memory one at time in a serial fashion, ARCS in effect evaluates all of them at once as it performs parallel constraint satisfaction. Such parallel processing also characterizes human memory retrieval, allowing people to continue to retrieve information efficiently as their store of knowledge increases.

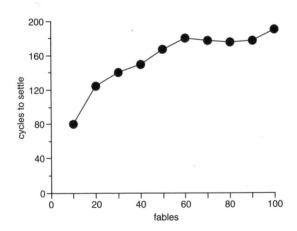

Figure 10.5
The average number of cycles of activation updating required for ARCS to settle into a stable state, as a function of the number of fables stored in its memory. Adapted from Thagard et al. (1990). Adapted by permission.

ARCS has also been used to simulate the performance of people in some of the psychological experiments on analog retrieval we described in chapter 5. We generally found a good fit between how often people retrieve particular cases from memory in response to a case provided as a cue and the degree to which structures representing those stored cases were activated by ARCS. The leading role of semantic similarity as a constraint on analog retrieval, which is central to ARCS, allows the model to capture the general finding from psychological research that semantic similarity is the most important constraint affecting human recall of analogs. At the same time, ARCS (like people) is not totally dependent on superficial similarity in retrieving cases from memory. A cue can activate stored cases not only by links from simple attributes, such as "grape" or "sour," but also by links from first-order relations, such as "get," and higher-order relations, such as "cause" and "decide." The model leads to the prediction that greater expertise in a domain, when accompanied by richer encodings of cases in terms of important abstract relations, will foster the ability to access remote analogs in memory.

One of the most important predictions that was derived from ARCS is that retrieval of analogs is fundamentally competitive: the best matching source in memory tends to suppress the others. It follows that a source that satisfies the structural constraints will be accessed more often than one that does not, but only when both potential sources are available in memory, competing with each other. As we saw in chapter 5, this prediction has been tested and confirmed in several experiments. ARCS thus has passed one of the most important tests of a scientific theory—it has generated new and correct predictions. More generally, ARCS predicts that human retrieval of analogs, while certainly heavily constrained by semantic similarity, will also be guided by the constraints of structure and purpose.

The Competition

In our earlier account of the origins of our models, we emphasized the role of cross-domain analogies, especially between the source provided by constraint satisfaction models of perception and the target domain of models of analogical mapping and retrieval. However, computational models of analogy have their own history. Our models are neither the first nor the only current contenders as simulations of human use of analogy. Here we will briefly describe the competition to our own multiconstraint theory. It might be more accurate to describe the array of alternative models as the ecology in which theories of analogy have developed. For the competition among alternative approaches to analogy has helped to shape each of them. Different theorists have emphasized different aspects of analogy use, thereby providing distinct pieces of the solution to the overall puzzle of understanding how people use analogies. As we will see, the most prominent current computational models have actually converged in stressing the importance of the three basic constraints on which we have focused throughout this book: structure, similarity, and purpose.

The first computational model of analogical inference was developed by Thomas Evans in the 1960s. He wrote a program that could solve analogy problems involving geometric figures, where the problems had the general form of proportional analogies, A:B::C:? Many of the ideas embodied in his model were carried over to the field of psychology in a mathematical model proposed by Robert Sternberg in 1977, which was applied to the solution of proportional analogy problems by children and adults. Because proportional analogies do not tap many important aspects of analogical thinking, such as the role of purpose, these early models did not address many of the issues with which we have been concerned in this book.

Beginning in the late 1970s, a number of researchers in both psychology and artificial intelligence began to investigate the use of analogy in more complex tasks, such as understanding stories and solving novel problems. This new focus led theorists to break away from the limitations of proportional analogies and encouraged greater attention to the more general constraints of structure and purpose. The first major computational model to arise from this line of work was developed by Patrick Winston in 1980. His model provided a number of key contributions, such as the use of structured representations based on predicates with slots to represent analogs, and an emphasis on the importance of both semantic similarity and purpose. However, his model lacked the flexibility provided by parallel constraint satisfaction and therefore was limited in its ability to find mappings between dissimilar concepts.

Since 1980 dozens of other computational models of analogy have been proposed. We will review only those that are most similar to our own ACME and ARCS models of mapping and retrieval, describing their relation to our multiconstraint theory. From a psychological perspective, the most impressive alternative models of analogical mapping are the Structure-Mapping Engine (SME), developed by Brian Falkenhainer, Kenneth Forbus, and Dedre Gentner; the Copycat model, developed by Douglas Hofstadter and Melanie Mitchell; and the class of artificial-intelligence models that perform case-based reasoning. Of these, SME had the most direct influence on the development of ACME. SME performs mapping between two analogs by using structural constraints to determine possible matches and then selecting the best match according to how well different matches preserve relational structure. It incorporates Gentner's insight, which she calls the "systematicity principle," that systems of interconnected relations, especially higher-order relations like "cause," contribute more to analogy than do isolated first-order relations or attributes.

The similarities and differences between ACME and SME can be related to the three constraints postulated by the multiconstraint theory. With respect to the constraint of structure, ACME incorporates SME's powerful use of structural constraints but in a more flexible manner. For SME, one-to-one mapping and structural consistency are hard constraints: the model automatically excludes any mapping that violates them. ACME certainly displays a preference for one-to-one mappings, using inhibitory links to discourage multiple mappings, but it can find one-to-many or many-to-one mappings when appropriate. For example, suppose one wants to map the hydrogen atom with a nucleus and one electron to the solar system with the sun and nine planets. Like SME, ACME will map the nucleus to the sun, but it will also map the electron equally to the nine planets. ACME, like SME, gives greater weight to interconnected systems of relations than to isolated relations or attributes. This preference is a natural consequence of the way in which ACME produces excitatory links: mappings for more complex relational structures end up with more interconnected links that support one another.

With respect to the similarity constraint, the two models differ in several important ways. Unlike SME, ACME does not simply discard attributes that describe objects; ACME will use mapped attributes as well as relations to generate analogical inferences. Unlike ACME, SME will match relations (except for functions) only if they are identical. Because of this limitation, SME would be unable to match the relations "invade" and "occupy" in our example based on the Persian Gulf War/World War II analogy. ACME displays a preference for matching identical relations but treats this as a limiting case of semantic similarity. With its emphasis on structure to the exclusion of other constraints, SME does not simply discourage mappings between nonidentical but semantically similar items; it does not even permit them.

The most dramatic differences between the models relate to the constraint of purpose. SME does not incorporate any impact of purpose, which it assumes is relevant only to analogical reasoning before or after the mapping stage. However, as we saw in chapter 5, experimental evidence indicates that purpose does in fact make a difference to what mappings people compute.

The Copycat model of Hofstadter and Mitchell differs in numerous respects from both SME and ACME. It is restricted so far to a single domain, proportional analogies using letter strings, which we discussed in chapter 5. For example, given a problem that asks "If the string *abc* is changed into *abd*, then how could *kji* be changed in the same way?" Copycat can potentially produce a variety of answers. The program operates with a degree of randomness, so that running the program multiple times may allow it to find different answers to the same problem. Because each term in such proportional analogies has an internal structure (for example, *abc* is an ascending triple), Copycat's domain includes solutions based on system mapping, rather than merely on relational mapping. To solve letter-string problems, Copycat relies on many small "codelets" interacting in parallel to build representations of the analogs, perform mapping, and construct a completion. Copycat uses a network of concepts, called a Slipnet, to find correspondences between nonidentical objects, just as ARCS uses WordNet-style semantic information to find similar concepts. Like ACME, Copycat achieves its answers by using soft constraints, which Hofstadter and Mitchell call "pressures."

Copycat has many points of agreement with ACME; indeed, its treatment of letter-string analogies involves versions of all three of the basic constraints hypothesized by our multiconstraint theory. Mitchell writes, referring to ACME,

Copycat has counterparts to Holyoak and Thagard's three classes of constraint: structural consistency (Copycat's pressure toward compatible correspondences), semantic similarity (in Copycat, correspondences involving close concept mappings are strong), and pragmatic centrality [i. e., purpose] (Copycat has certain *a priori* assumptions—e.g., string-position descriptions such as *left-of* are assumed *a priori* to be relevant—that affect the importance values of certain objects).

But Copycat also has features that ACME does not share. The codelets are chosen nondeterministically from a constantly changing pool, so Copycat can display much flexibility in representing the analogs and in constructing alternative solutions. Moreover, Copycat's parallel search for correspondences varies in speed according to moment-to-moment evaluations of the promise of each map, so that Copycat's selection of preferred mappings is incremental as well as parallel. Both these features are psychologically interesting and deserve to be tested experimentally, both with letter-string analogies and in more complex domains.

A number of computational models have also been developed for the retrieval of analogs from memory. Gentner and Forbus have produced MAC/FAC (Many Are Called but Few Are Chosen), which uses two stages of processing to retrieve analogs. The first stage (MAC) uses a computationally simple nonstructural matcher to filter candidates from a pool of memory items. The second stage (FAC) uses SME to compute a true structural match between the probe and output from the first stage. MAC/FAC is thus quite similar to ARCS, which also has an initial stage, in which semantic information is used to select a set of potential source analogs, and a second stage, in which a constraint network is used to select the best analogs from memory. However, MAC does not make use of a semantic network, such as WordNet, and hence is less flexible than ARCS in accessing analogs that do not include concepts identical to those in the representation of the cue provided to the program. Also, MAC is much more selective than the first stage of ARCS in that it picks only a small subset of the semantically relevant structures to be considered by FAC, whereas ARCS can produce a large constraint network, allowing its second stage to select from among all the semantically related structures those that are most relevant, taking into account constraints of purpose and structure as well as similarity. The danger for MAC/FAC is that it may prematurely discard possible analogs that human memory might retrieve by using a combination of structural and semantic constraints. In addition, MAC/FAC is not well suited for modeling the competitive aspects of human memory retrieval that we discussed in chapter 5 and at the end of the section on retrieval in this chapter.

Whereas Gentner and Forbus's account of analog retrieval puts more emphasis than ours does on the constraint of semantic similarity, proponents of case-based reasoning in artificial intelligence (following Roger Schank) have preferred to emphasize the constraint of purpose. They claim that structures are indexed in memory based on their causal relevance to the accomplishment of goals and avoidance of failures. Such detailed indexing can indeed be useful for special-purpose systems in narrow domains, such as areas of law as described in chapter 6, for which Ashley's program Hypo uses a detailed indexing scheme to pick the previous legal cases that are most on point. But human memory is much more flexible, as it needs to be if previous episodes are to be used for many different kinds of future uses, and especially if cross-domain analog retrieval is to be possible.

Some models in the style associated with case-based reasoning programs tend to rely heavily on single "smart" retrieval cues for accessing cases that are analogous to one another. For example, the Aesop's fable about the fox and grapes might be indexed by a cue such as "failed-goal-attainment-causes-goal-devaluation." A story about a disgruntled job seeker might be coded using the same cue, which would then serve to trigger access to the sour grapes fable in memory. But using such cues requires careful coding when the source analog is initially stored in memory. Moreover, because such "smart" cues are highly specific, they will fail to access analogs that deviate even slightly from the crucial description. ARCS, by contrast, does not require such specific retrieval cues (although it could certainly make use of them if they were included in its semantic network). Instead, ARCS makes use of multiple semantic cues and structural correspondences to find the optimal match in memory. Using parallel constraint satisfaction, the job-seeker story could evoke the sour grapes fable, because both analogs involve an actor that tries to attain something, fails to do so, and as a result devalues what was previously desired. The connection between the stories is provided not by a single specific index but by the pattern of interrelated concepts. This style of reminding, which integrates the constraints of structure, similarity, and purpose, seems to better capture the flexibility of human memory retrieval. In her textbook on case-based reasoning, Janet Kolodner surveys numerous retrieval techniques used in current case-based systems and remarks that there have been few implementations of systems using hierarchical memory and parallel search. ARCS is just such a system, and so, we would argue, is the human mind. We must note, however, that case-based reasoning systems have implemented more sophisticated methods of adapting cases than are found in our models.

The differences among the various alternative models of analogy should not obscure their commonalities. In particular, all of the models make some use of the three classes of constraints we have emphasized. The multiconstraint theory reflects the convergence of theoretical developments in the field. Analogy is undoubtedly one of the success stories of cognitive science. Only a few decades ago, it was almost entirely a mystery how people use analogies. In the past fifteen years or so, the explosion of work on analogy in several interrelated fields has led to great progress, as researchers from psychology, artificial intelligence, philoso-

phy, and linguistics have drawn on each other's work to move understanding along. In our own research, psychological, philosophical, and
computational ideas and methods have been closely entwined, and other
research groups have similarly benefited by the kind of interdisciplinary
approach that defines cognitive science.

The Future of Analogy

Where does analogy go from here? This is really two questions. First, to
what extent and for what purposes will people use analogy in the future?
And second, what more is required to have a complete scientific theory
of human use of analogy?

The first question has a ready answer: people will continue to use
analogy freely for all the purposes we have described in this book, and
others as well. Various "enemies of analogy" have pointed out that
analogies often get people into cognitive difficulties. People under the
influence of analogies are liable to make errors in solving problems and
making decisions, to accept specious arguments and faulty explanations,
and to be trapped by false insights. These pitfalls are real, but the solution
is not to abandon analogical thinking altogether. This would be far too
high a price to pay given the power of analogy to contribute to creativity.
As Samuel Butler once said, "Though analogy is often misleading, it is
the least misleading thing we have." Indeed, it is not only undesirable
to proscribe the use of analogy; it is simply impossible. Comparing novel
situations to familiar ones and finding correspondences between them,
and then using these correspondences to generate inferences about the
new cases, is integral to human thinking. Admonishing people to refrain
from analogy would have about as much chance of success as telling
them to abstain from sex: although a few may manage to achieve a
lifetime of chastity, they will be little envied by the rest of us.

The use of analogy must, however, be accompanied by critical
analysis. Analogists need to be careful that their analogies really do
contribute to productive reasoning and do not serve merely as a lazy
alternative to hard thinking. Chapters 6, 7, and 8, especially, offer
suggestions for how the evaluation of analogies might be improved.
There are important questions one can ask oneself when thinking
through an analogy: What is my purpose in using this analogy? What
aspects of the source caused the outcome it exhibited? Are these same
aspects present in the target? Are there alternative source analogs that
should be considered? Are the inferences generated by analogy plausible,

given what I already know about the target? More generally, understanding the cognitive structures and processes involved in analogical thought should help people to think more explicitly about their own use of analogy.

The second and more open-ended question concerns what remains to be learned before we could claim to have a complete scientific theory of analogical thinking. The limitations of current understanding are evident if one compares the scope of the computational models described in this chapter with that of analogy itself. The key processes of retrieval and mapping have been modeled with sufficient success that we can at least claim to be on the way to understanding them. But as we mentioned in chapter 5 and discussed in more detail in chapter 8, analogies are not always simply retrieved as whole cases from memory. Sometimes analogies must be creatively constructed (as we attempted in adapting tug-of-war to come up with the game of tug-and-shove, which then served as a source analog for parallel constraint satisfaction). We still have little idea how these constructive aspects of analog selection actually operate. Notably, many constructed analogs are visual, so it would be desirable to apply principles of creative visualization to the development of analogies. But cognitive science still lacks a good general theory of the structures and processes that make human visual reasoning so powerful. Similarly, we lack a way of capturing the nature of emotional states that contribute to empathic understanding based on analogy. A full-fledged model of analogy will have to be multimodal, encompassing verbal, visual, emotional, and other sorts of representations. We have not even touched on how analogies can contribute to art forms, such as painting and music. The interconnections among visual, auditory, and tactile analogies provide a potential source of mental leaps. We often use cross-sensory metaphors, such as "bitter cold" and "loud colors," and some creative individuals claim that they get their best ideas from the interaction of representations tied to different senses.

Creative construction of source analogs can also be aided by using multiple analogs. More generally, the use of multiple analogs has been suggested as an antidote to fixation on a single misleading one. But there are at least two aspects of the use of multiple analogs that are not well understood. First, when multiple source analogs are competing to determine how the target should be understood, as in the comparison of Iraq with both Germany and Vietnam, how can the most relevant and useful analog be determined? Answering this question will require a general theory of how analogical coherence can be integrated with deliberative and explanatory coherence. Second, when multiple analogs are potentially combinable rather than competing, how can they both be put to work? For example, it might well have been fruitful to use several historical precedents in deciding how to deal with Iraq, but little is understood about how source analogs can be combined to help with a complex target without producing an incoherent mess. Complex reorganization and revision of knowledge will therefore be part of the process of using multiple analogs. In addition, the process of forming schemas from at least two similar and successful source/target pairs is understood only for simple cases. Human use of analogies can involve operations of chunking, reorganization, and transformation that are only hinted at in current models.

We also know little about how analogy is performed by the human brain. In chapter 3 we considered the possible evolutionary course of the development of analogy, and in chapter 4 we examined its development in children. Both the evolution of explicit thought and its maturation during childhood are accompanied by massive changes in the brain and nervous system, such as increased size of the frontal cortex, but we do not know in any precise way how analogical reasoning is performed at a neural level. This direction for future research may soon be opened up, as more sophisticated methods become available for localizing brain activity during thinking. Neurological research will likely go hand in hand with work on improved computational models. We can hope to see the development of new types of connectionist models that are both neurologically plausible and rich enough in representational power to model how human analogy relies on explicit representations of relations, including higher-order ones.

In the area of education, it remains an open question whether more effective use of analogies can be taught. Many courses on critical thinking include a component on analogy use and misuse, but it would be surprising if such instruction were very effective, given the impoverished views of analogy that are usually presupposed. The multiconstraint theory appears to provide a basis for instructing people about how to avoid abuses of analogy. It remains unknown, however, whether any effective method can be devised for improving creative uses of analogy.

Finally, much more needs to be known about the social context of analogy use. In chapter 9 we described how analogy contributes to many social purposes, but we have not considered how the use of good analogies can be furthered by social as well as cognitive means. Kevin Dunbar has described how the social structure of different laboratory situations can greatly affect the use of scientific analogies. Labs that consist of diversely trained researchers frequently have productive analogies emerge in group meetings. A target problem that has stumped one researcher can be approached by applying a source problem provided by another researcher with a different background. Like human culture in general, science is the product of social interaction as well as individual cognition, and much more needs to be known about how the mental and the social blend in analogy use.

Our current understanding of analogy is the product of a confluence of psychological, computational, philosophical, and linguistic investigations. We predict that new progress will depend not only on additional contributions from these sources but also on contributions from research on the neural substrates of thinking and on its social context. Of course, the future of analogy extends well beyond the limited horizon we can hope to see even hazily from our present-day vantage point. We feel secure, however, in one prediction: analogy in the future, as in its past, will provide a springboard for mental leaps.

Notes

Although no references are cited in the text, the following notes provide extensive documentation of sources. They consist of a page number and quote from that page, followed by additional discussion or citation of articles and books listed in the references section.

Chapter 1

Page 2 *Consider the following discussion between a mother* We thank Neil Holyoak and his mother, cognitive psychologist Patricia Cheng, for providing us with the analogy of a bird's backyard.

Page 2 *The child's everyday world is the source analog* Some discussions of analogy use the term "base" or "analog" instead of "source." In the study of metaphor, the source is usually called the "vehicle," and the target is called the "tenor." We use the term "analog" (which is sometimes spelled "analogue") to refer to either of the cases (source or target) being compared. The term "analogy" is used to refer to the overall relationship between the source and the target (i.e., the representations of the source, the target, and the mapping between them). We also use "analogy" to refer to the cognitive mechanism by which cases are compared (as in the subtitle of this book).

Page 3 *Personification means to treat something* Mark Turner (1987) provides an illuminating discussion of the cognitive basis for the uses of personification, and particularly kinship metaphors, in literature.

Page 5 *We can see in Neil's analogy the three basic kinds of constraints on analogical thinking* Gentner (1982, 1983) formulated constraints based on structure, and Holyoak (1985) highlighted the constraint of purpose. Holyoak and Thagard (1989a) describe in somewhat different terminology the constraints that guide human understanding of analogies.

Page 6 *There is a common thread* The analogies of Socrates are discussed in chapter 7, the invention of Velcro and also Ben Franklin's experiment in chapter 8, Vietnam analogies in chapter 6, and the use of analogy by family therapists and by marriage negotiators in chapter 9.

Page 8 *In some cultures, such delicate social negotiations* McKellin (1994). See chapter 9.

Page 9   *Consider the opening lines of Dante's* Divine Comedy   This translation of
Dante Alighieri's poem is from Dante (1904), 17.

Page 9   *George Lakoff and Mark Turner*   Lakoff and Turner's (1989) insightful
analysis of poetic metaphor is based on earlier work by Lakoff and Johnson (1980),
which examines the metaphors that mold our understanding of such basic concepts
as life, death, and time.

Page 11   *In his discussion of the acoustic*   Vitruvius (1960).

Page 12   *According to Kekulé*   Benfey (1958).

Page 13   *George Polya, who wrote extensively*   Polya (1957), 37.

Page 13   *Although we do not believe that analogy is the only cognitive mechanism*   Other
mechanisms for producing new ideas that have been discussed in cognitive science
include abduction and conceptual combination. See Holland, Holyoak, Nisbett, and
Thagard (1986) and Thagard (1988, 1992).

Page 13   *The mathematician Jules Henri Poincaré*   Poincaré (1913) 387 and 386.

Page 13   *Arthur Koestler developed this idea*   Koestler (1964), 200.

Page 14   *As Margaret Boden has observed*   Boden (1990), 25. Boden provides a
detailed discussion of Poincaré's and Koestler's views on creativity in chapter 1 of
her book. The expression "creative connections" comes from the title of her chapter
6. In chapter 8 Boden provides a fine overview of our own analogy models.

Page 15   *We call it a multiconstraint theory*   The multiconstraint theory described in
this book has its roots in a paper by Holyoak (1985), which focused on the use of
analogies in solving problems as revealed by the studies by Gick and Holyoak (1980,
1983). See chapter 10 for a historical sketch of our subsequent work.

Many other models of analogy have been proposed by researchers in cognitive
science. Relative to the multiconstraint theory, most other models have been more
limited in the scope of the content domains and of the stages of analogy to which
they apply, or have been less well specified as computational procedures. The
approach most similar to our own, and the most comparable in scope and computational specificity, is the structure-mapping theory developed by Dedre Gentner
and her colleagues (Falkenhainer, Forbus, and Gentner 1989; Gentner, 1983, 1989;
Gentner and Forbus, 1991). The multiconstraint theory and structure mapping
theory are in general agreement that the core of analogical thinking involves finding
mappings between relational structures, and that the use of analogy depends on
sensitivity to structure, semantic similarity of concepts, and the purpose of analogy.
However, the theories formulate the constraints in different ways. The multiconstraint theory, as we will see in chapter 10, integrates all three types of constraints
within a process of parallel constraint satisfaction. One implication of this approach
is that any of the constraints can potentially be overridden if it conflicts with others.
This aspect of the theory provides an explanation of how people can deal with messy
and ambiguous analogies that violate structural constraints (see chapter 5). In addition, the theory explains how mappings can be made between dissimilar relations
(as well as dissimilar objects). For a comparison of our computational models with
those of Gentner and her colleagues, see chapter 10.

The differences between the theories should not obscure their basic areas of agreement. In particular, Gentner's emphasis on the importance of higher-order relations in guiding analogical mapping has greatly influenced our own thinking about system mapping, as we discuss in chapter 2. We view the presentation of the multiconstraint theory in this book as a step toward a unified view of analogy, borrowing and integrating ideas that many cognitive scientists have helped to develop.

Page 15   *The use of analogy typically involves several steps*   Although there is general agreement that what we term selection, mapping, evaluation, and learning are major components of the use of analogy (for example, see Carbonell, 1983; Gick and Holyoak, 1980; Gentner, 1983; Hall, 1989), it is possible to make more fine-grained distinctions. In chapter 8, for example, we describe multiple ways in which analogs can be selected, ranging from retrieval of whole cases from memory to active generation of a hypothetical source analog. The stage we call "mapping" has two substages: the initial generation of a mapping based on the source and target representations and the subsequent generation of new inferences about the target to fill gaps in the initial mapping. Because there is evidence that these two substages are more closely linked to each other than to post-mapping evaluation and adaptation (Holyoak, Novick, and Melz, 1994; Novick and Holyoak, 1991), we will generally treat mapping/inference together to simplify our discussion.

Chapter 2

Page 19   *It is difficult to conceive*   Borges (1964), quotation from p. 65. This story was originally published in Spanish in 1956 in the volume *Ficciones*. Although Funes is a fictional character, the general syndrome that Borges describes—phenomenal memory for detail that impedes abstract thought—bears a striking resemblance to an actual case study later reported by the Russian neuropsychologist Aleksandr Luria (1968).

Page 20   *This judgment is based on the recognition of some important similarities*   Rips (1975) demonstrated that college students who are taught a novel fact about one type of bird are often willing to infer that the same fact will hold true for other types of birds. Susan Carey (1985) showed that adults who are told either that a dog or a person has an omentum (an unfamiliar internal organ) often infer that mammals and birds also have one, but less often expect it to be present in bugs or worms. Their willingness to infer that other animals have this novel property roughly parallels adults' willingness to say that the various types of animals have a heart. For a survey and discussion of different philosophical and psychological views of the nature of concepts, see Thagard (1992), chapter 2. "Concepts and conceptual systems"

Page 21   *This advance is closely related*   A good discussion of the distinction between implicit and explicit knowledge is provided by Karmiloff-Smith (1992). For reviews of work on implicit thinking and implicit learning, see Holyoak and Spellman (1993), Reber (1993), and Seger (1994).

Page 22   *The very notion of similarity poses many problems*   Goodman (1972). A good discussion of the problems involved in understanding how similarity is related to the way people understand categories is offered by Medin (1989).

Page 23   *We will refer to the representations*   Schemas have a long history in psychological theories of representation. One of the best introductions to the concept is provided by Rumelhart (1980).

Page 25   *So the proposition that Hercules is brown*   In logic and computer science, the formal language that uses the kind of "predicate plus arguments" structure we employ is called *predicate calculus*. See, for example, Copi (1979). We employ it here not because we see logic as a universal representation language, but because it provides a convenient way to display the structure of relations. For simplicity we will ignore such complexities as representing propositions that require quantifiers (e.g., "Some dogs are brown" versus "All dogs are brown").

Page 26   *We will call this type of mapping*   Our taxonomy of attribute, relational, and system mappings is based on those proposed by Gentner (1982, 1983; Gentner and Rattermann, 1991), Halford (1992, 1993), and Premack (1983). All of these types of mappings depend on explicit representations of attributes and relations, and hence are more cognitively complex than reacting to global similarity of objects. Halford uses the term "element mapping" to refer to what we call "attribute mapping." Rather than defining system mapping in terms of mappings based on higher-order relations (as proposed by Gentner, 1983), he uses a definition based on mappings between triples of slots considered together. It can be argued that higher-order relations between propositions involve (at least) three independent slots. Halford also includes a yet more complex level of "multiple system mappings" based on quadruples of independent slots, but this level is not necessary for understanding the basic constraints on analogy. A formal presentation of the underlying mathematical framework for Halford's taxonomy is provided by Halford and Wilson (1980), who extend the analysis of relations to include additional classes of ordered sets of objects—functions and operations. Since these distinctions do not change the basic analysis in any important way, we confine our own discussion to relations. The relationship between types of mappings and analogies is discussed in Halford et al. (1994). Halford has argued that some of the basic changes in cognitive abilities that occur over the course of a child's development from infancy to about age twelve can be related to quantum increments in the number of interrelated elements that can be held in working memory.

Page 28   *Such analogy problems are often called* proportional analogies   Analogy was understood by the Greeks in terms of proportions (the Greek *analogia* meant "proportion"), but their actual use of analogy clearly included examples of the more complex level of system mappings (see chapter 7).

Page 28   *Predicates such as "cause" and "implies" that allow*   Gentner (1983, 1989) outlines a theory of analogical mapping and transfer that stresses the importance of higher-order relations. Her theory provided the first general account of the role played by interlocking relational propositions that give analogs their systematic internal structure.

Page 29 *That is, satisfying these constraints* Holyoak (1985) and Holyoak and Thagard (1989a) discussed the role of isomorphism in understanding analogies.

Page 30 *The basic device for generating inferences by analogy* Some variation of the "copying with substitution" (CWS) procedure for generating inferences by analogy has been suggested by virtually all theorists who have addressed the problem. One of the earliest computer simulations of analogical transfer based on CWS was developed by Winston (1980). A more sophisticated version forms part of a simulation called SME (Structure-Mapping Engine), which is based on Gentner's (1983) structure-mapping theory of mapping and transfer (see Falkenhainer et al., 1989). Our own simulations of analogical transfer also include a CWS procedure (Holyoak and Thagard 1989a, Holyoak et al., 1994). Although all of these different simulations use some form of CWS, the term itself was introduced only recently in Holyoak et al. (1994). The versions differ mainly in terms of how abstract the substitution can be, especially whether different but mapped relations can be substituted for one another, and whether new concepts can be *generated* in the target if no mapped element has already been identified.

Page 32 *Isomorphism is fundamental to all forms of measurement* One of the best introductions to the idea that mental representation is based on establishing isomorphisms is a paper by Palmer (1978). He later related his analysis of representation to analogy in Palmer (1989). Halford (1993, Halford and Wilson, 1980) also describes mental representation in terms of types of isomorphisms.

Page 32 *Many cognitive scientists agree* These scientists include Johnson-Laird (1983) and Gentner and Stevens (1983). In our own previous work we have characterized both mental models and analogies as *approximations* to isomorphisms; see Holland et al. (1986).

Page 33 *Early in the twentieth century, the psychologist Edward Thorndike* Thorndike (1913).

Page 34 *In real-life uses of analogy, the purpose and context* Holyoak (1985) describes the roles that goals and causal understanding play in guiding the use of analogy, and how these factors interact with the structural constraint of isomorphism. The idea that causal relations within each analog establish the basis for deciding which elements need to be mapped was discussed in Holyoak (1984). The centrality of causal relations in scientific analogies was stressed by Hesse (1966). Winston (1980) gave causal relations special importance in his simulation model of mapping.

Gentner (1989) has correctly pointed out that some analogies are based on other relations besides causal connections, such as "implies" (in its mathematical sense). The more general claim we wish to make, however, is that information believed to be relevant to goal attainment is given greatest emphasis. In a mathematical problem, functional relations between quantities needed to calculate the answer will indeed be the focus. But although relations other than causality can certainly be important to analogy, we believe that in everyday use of analogy to solve problems and build explanations, causal relations are generally central. In fact, we suspect that people often use their commonsense understanding of causality as a source analog in trying to understand less familiar types of dependencies, such as mathematical functional relations.

Page 35   *Causality is not easy to pin down*   For a discussion of the information that people and other animals use to make causal judgments, see Cheng (1993).

Page 36   *Even six-month-old infants can perceive and react to basic physical causal connections*   Leslie (1988) reviews the elegant experiments that he and other developmental psychologists have performed to show that young infants recognize basic causal connections. These studies use a "habituation" paradigm, in which the time that infants choose to look at each event in a series is measured. If six-month-old infants watch a series of film clips in which one ball strikes another and appears to launch it, they eventually lose interest in it, as assessed by a reduction in the length of succeeding unbroken looks. But if the film is then run backwards, which destroys the appearance of a causal connection between the balls, the infants show renewed interest in it. The effect of reversing a film of a causal event produces more recovery of sustained looking than does a comparable reversal of a sequence that is not perceived as causal in either direction. This pattern of behavior is taken to indicate that the infants are sensitive to the difference between causal and noncausal event sequences. It is likely that infants' knowledge of causal relations is implicit rather than explicit.

Chapter 3

Page 40   *For example, pigeons can be trained to peck a key for food in response to photographs*   Herrnstein (1979) reports an elegant series of experiments that reveal the remarkable ability that pigeons have to learn to respond to diverse examples of natural categories. Equally interesting are the limits of what pigeons can learn. They fail, for example, to recognize simple cartoon figures as people. Other evidence, reviewed by Mackintosh (1988), suggests that pigeons' performance on categorization tasks depends more on excellent rote memory for training examples that on any ability to learn abstract rules. Interestingly, other species of birds, such as crows, appear to be much more successful at learning rules than are pigeons.

Page 40   *Many difficulties arise in discussing the evolution of thinking*   Mackintosh (1988) provides a useful discussion of these difficulties, as well as evidence for cross-species differences in ability to learn abstractions. Premack (1988) argued that comparisons between different species of primates can be especially informative with respect to the evolution of abstract thought.

Page 40   *The evidence indicates strongly that all mammals have such capabilities*   Much of our discussion of cross-species differences and similarities in relational processing is based on the survey and analysis by Premack (1983). Gentner and Rattermann (1991) compared Premack's account of the use of analogy in chimpanzees to developmental patterns observed in human children.

In his paper, Premack provides a theoretical discussion of isomorphism. A possible source of confusion that could arise in relating Premack's analysis to our own discussion in chapter 2 is that he reserves the term "isomorphism" for representations of the spatial properties of objects, such as their topological relations and the distances and angles between objects. Such representations correspond to mental images of the sort that Shepard (1975) termed "second-order isomorphisms." The latter term was an unfortunate choice in our view, since there is nothing that makes such isomorphisms second-order in any formal sense. Rather, they are isomorphisms of the standard sort—systems of relations in consistent one-to-one correspondence—but restricted to the representation of the spatial (and perhaps other sensory) relations among physical objects and their parts. In contrast, we use the term "isomorphism" in its broader sense, which applies to mappings based on *any* types of relations. From our point of view, the change from representation by mental imagery to general propositional representation does not eliminate isomorphism as a representational principle, but rather increases its generality.

Part of the confusion about what counts as an isomorphism is because an isomorphism is defined relative to whatever relations are being represented (see Palmer, 1978). If topological or other spatial relations are *not* being represented within a certain representation, that representation will not be isomorphic with respect to those relations (even though it may still be isomorphic with respect to other relations that *are* being represented.) It may well be the case that animals (including humans) make use of at least two separate representational systems: one based on imagery (spatial isomorphisms, in which representations of certain spatial relations are obligatory) and another based on general propositions (unrestricted isomorphisms, in which representations of spatial relations are optional). For an introduction to imagery as isomorphism, see Shepard (1975). It is possible that the imagery system has special properties that aid in processing visual analogies.

Page 40   *In 1954, Lawrence and DeRivera*   The classic study described here is that of Lawrence and DeRivera (1954).

Page 45   *Pigeons generally perform poorly on such generalized transfer tests*   Our discussion may have slighted the pigeon, which is in fact capable of some degree of success in generalized transfer on the match-to-sample task. All that really matters to our story, however, is that there was an evolutionary progression from animals that are capable of reacting only to physical similarity to those that are also capable of relational mapping based on O-sameness. Of course, the exact evolutionary history is unknown, and in any case we certainly do not mean to imply that the present-day pigeon evolved into the present-day chimpanzee! The evolutionary tree involved is considerably more complex. However, birds and primates provide convenient labels for the ends of this particular intellectual progression.

Page 47   *Sarah's life was very different*   This section is based heavily on the discussion by Premack (1983). A more recent review and assessment of how language training influences performance on the pairwise match-to-sample task is provided by Thompson and Oden (1993). Sarah's early training in manipulating tokens is described by Premack (1976).

Page 51   *David Oden, Roger Thompson, and Premack*   Oden, Thompson, and Premack (1990) found evidence that infant chimpanzees spontaneously react to R-sameness.

Page 52   *Further experiments with monkeys*   Roger Thompson (personal communication, August 1992).

Page 52   *Human infants, on the other hand, also react to R-sameness*   Tyrell, Stauffer, and Snowman (1991) have shown that R-sameness influences the preferences of human infants for looking at successive pairs of identical or different toys.

Page 55   *The full power of the strategy lies in its call to "repeat"*   The technical name for the style of a strategy like this, in which the output of a procedure can be fed back in as its input, is "recursion." Recursion is a common device used in computer programming.

Page 58   *Premack and his colleagues were able to test Sarah on analogies*   These experiments were performed by Gillan et al. (1981).

Page 60   *Sarah's success on the proportions test*   The careful reader may notice that the concept of a proportion itself involves a relation, suggesting that mapping proportions would require representing a relation between relations and hence would constitute system rather than relational mapping. As we will see later in this chapter, other evidence suggests that Sarah is not generally capable of system mapping. We therefore conjecture that her success on the proportions test is revealing her ability to directly perceive relations like "halfness," rather than an ability to form such concepts by explicitly relating a part to a whole. A similar interpretive issue arises in chapter 4 in interpreting the performance of young children in solving analogies between proportions.

Page 61   *The crucial event appeared to be the introduction of plastic words for "same" and "different"*   This conclusion is based on experiments summarized by Premack (1988).

Page 61   *In fact, studies that Premack has performed*   See Premack (1988).

Page 63   *While spending the period of the First World War*   Köhler (1925).

Page 66   *When shown a videotape of a human actor*   Premack and Woodruff (1978) report a series of studies of Sarah's ability to interpret videotaped scenes as problems facing a human actor. She was able to consistently select photographs corresponding to appropriate solutions. Studies of Sarah's ability to understand causal sequences and problems are reported by Premack (1983).

Page 68   *One striking failure that Sarah exhibited*   Premack (1988) describes this and other examples in which Sarah failed to acquire abstract causal and functional concepts. As he notes, these training attempts were limited, and therefore the failures cannot be considered definitive.

Page 69   *Most of the increased size of the human brain*   The possible role of the frontal cortex in processing relations is discussed by Robin and Holyoak (1994).

Page 72   *As far as we can tell, neither Sarah nor any other chimpanzee could ever be this insightful*   Premack (1983) describes some of the basic cognitive limitations of chimpanzees. Although we do not feel the evidence available shows that Sarah is capable of system mappings, it should be acknowledged that a number of her performances come tantalizingly close. One property of system mappings is that the fillers of at least three independent slots are mapped at once. Sarah appears to process three slot fillers together both in her judgments of causal sequences and in her judgments of orderings. However, in these cases it seems possible that her success may hinge on the use of simpler strategies than system mapping. In the causal tasks, one object—the instrument, such as a pencil—fills a slot that is very distinct from those for the initial and final states (filled by blank and marked paper, respectively). In the transitive same-different judgments, the items were always directly presented as an ordered triple, rather than as the three possible pairs, thus allowing a simpler strategy to be used. For discussion of the basis for transitivity judgments in young children, in which similar interpretive issues arise, see Halford and Kelley (1984).

Page 72 *Rather than being satisfied by having solved* Karmiloff-Smith (1983), in a commentary on Premack (1983), argues for the importance of spontaneous, internally driven reorganization as a force in human cognitive development. She views this as a process that forms increasingly explicit representations of skills. Although her ideas are derived from evidence that would appear far removed from analogy, her conception of explicit thinking converges nicely with the view we have been presenting. Karmiloff-Smith (1992) provides a more extensive discussion of her views on the development of explicit representations in children.

Chapter 4

Page 75 *A little girl named Lori* Lori was a subject in an experiment performed by Holyoak, Junn, and Billman (1984). The other results described in this section are taken from the same paper.

Page 78 *However, the overall success rate of four- and five-year-olds* In addition to this finding of Holyoak et al. (1984), other work by Brown, Kane, and Echols (1986) shows that transfer is enhanced for this age group if the children are asked questions that highlight the goal structure of the source problem ("Who has a problem?" "What does the genie need to do?" "What is stopping him?" "How does he solve his problem?") Such questions presumably encourage encoding of higher-order relations, which may facilitate system mapping. However, as Halford (1993) has noted, Brown et al. had the children roll the same piece of paper both to enact the genie's solution and to solve two additional transfer problems. This variation in the task introduced a highly specific common element shared by the solution for all the analogs, which might have obviated the need to actually perform a system mapping at all. Indeed, one four-year-old was reported to predict, "All you need to do is to get this thing [the paper] rolled up," *before* he even heard the third problem in the series (Brown and Kane, 1988, 517). Other studies that have shown improved transfer of the "rolling" solution have involved either such repeated rolling of a single piece of paper or else rolling of such similar objects as a toy carpet, rug, and blanket (Brown, Kane, and Long, 1989). In contrast, the Holyoak et al. (1984) version of the task required transfer across objects that were more dissimilar (the magic carpet and the sheet of paper).

Page 81 *At age six months* See Premack (1988).

Page 82 *Suppose an infant eleven months of age is given a novel toy* This study was performed by Baldwin, Markman, and Melartin (1993).

Page 82 *As we mentioned in chapter 2, six-month-old infants are already sensitive* See Leslie (1988).

Page 82 *Ann Brown had one- and two-year-old children solve a problem* See Brown (1989).

Page 84 *Judy DeLoache performed an intriguing series of studies* See DeLoache (1987, 1989; DeLoache, Miller, Rosengren, and Bryant, 1993).

Page 87   *One example came about when a father was reading a book*   We thank Daniel
Thagard for supplying his father, Paul, with this example.

Page 87   *Experimental work has revealed that by about age four*   See Goswami and
Brown (1989) and Gentner, Rattermann, and Campbell (1994). Gentner et al.
identified some methodological problems with the earlier study by Goswami and
Brown, which had led to an underestimate of the younger children's tendency to
respond on the basis of perceptual similarity of objects. However, both studies found
that four-year-olds are well above chance in selecting the analogical completion.

Page 88   *Other studies have shown that the majority of four-year-olds*   See Goswami and
Brown (1990). Goswami (1992) provides a good survey of her own research and
other work on analogical reasoning in children. Vosniadou (1989) and Gentner and
Ratterman (1991) also provide useful reviews.

Page 88   *Ann Brown and Mary Jo Kane found evidence*   This study was reported by
Brown and Kane (1988). Also see Brown et al. (1986, 1989).

Page 89   *Michael Waldmann gave children ranging from four*   This experiment was
reported by Waldmann (1989).

Page 90   *Dedre Gentner asked four-year-olds*   This seminal study of young children's
understanding of relational analogies was reported by Gentner (1977).

Page 90   *Personification—the use of knowledge*   See Turner (1987).

Page 90   *The developmental psychologist Jean Piaget*   The classic study is that of Piaget
(1929). A large-scale replication was performed by Laurendeau and Pinard (1962).
Carey (1985) provides a more recent critical discussion of Piaget's theory of animism, as well as new experimental findings.

Page 91   *Even three-year-olds know that a person, a cat, and a doll have eyes*   See
Gelman, Spelke, and Meck (1983).

Page 91   *Susan Carey taught children of various ages*   See Carey (1985, chap. 4). "The
projection of spleen (omentum)"

Page 92   *For example, Kayoko Inagaki found*   Inagaki (1990).

Page 92   *Kayoko Inagaki and Giyoo Hatano asked Japanese kindergarten children*   This
experiment was performed by Inagaki and Hatano (1987); also see Hatano and
Inagaki (1987).

Page 93   *A young child is likely to view death as a kind of sleep*   See discussion by
Carey (1985, "What is alive?" chap. 1).

Page 93   *In one study for example, about 15 percent*   This experiment was performed
by Inagaki and Sugiyama (1988).

Page 95   *Here, for example, is how a five-year-old Japanese girl explained why flowers*
This example was reported by Motoyoshi (1979) and is discussed by Hatano and
Inagaki (1994).

Page 95   *In general, the only possible basis for establishing these mappings is the similarity*
The conception of mapping based on the multiconstraint theory should not be
confused with notions of mapping that have been discussed in previous theories of

the component processes involved in solving proportional analogy problems (for example, Sternberg, 1977; Sternberg and Rifkin, 1979). Two alternative definitions of mapping have been previously offered; these contradict each other and neither is equivalent to our own definition. The first alternative is that mapping requires explicitly representing the relationships between the A and the C terms. It is apparent that mapping in this sense is not required to solve analogy problems. For simple proportional analogies, the mapping A ↔ C is trivially established by the "rules of the game," according to which the terms in the first and third positions play parallel roles. There is no need to represent explicitly how A and C are similar. This definition of mapping differs from our own in that it makes no reference to the mapping of the relation between A and B to that between C and D, which is the actual key to generating the appropriate D term.

The second contradictory definition of mapping that has been offered is, "The use of mapping requires recognition of a higher-order relation between two relations: that which relates the A and B terms to the C and D terms" (Sternberg and Rifkin, 1979, 226). This definition, like our own, does refer to the mapping of the relation between the A and the B terms. However, it is misleading to call this process "recognition of a higher-order relation between two relations," at least in the sense of requiring an explicit higher-order predicate to represent the mapping between relations. In a standard proportional analogy, the "higher-order relation" between the A:B relation and the C:D relation is always R-sameness. Because no other higher-order relation is permitted, analogy problems can be solved without explicitly forming the proposition

R-same (A:B-relation, C:D-relation).

Rather, it is enough to represent the mapping between the two relations implicitly,

A:B-relation ↔ **C:D-relation.**

In the multiconstraint theory, semantic similarity at **any** level, including similarity of relations, can be used to form a mapping. In human development, we assume that children will first be able to solve analogy problems by implicitly mapping relations. The key to relational mapping, as it operates when young children solve simple proportional analogies, is neither explicitly relating the A term to the C term nor extracting an explicit higher-order relation of R-sameness between the A:B and C:D relations. Rather, the crucial requirement is to implicitly map the A:B and C:D relations on the basis of their perceived similarity. We will see, however, that more complex analogies in which each term is represented as multiple elements *do* involve mapping higher-order relations and hence pose great difficulty for four-year-old children.

Page 96 *As figure 4.7 indicates, this problem is complex* You may recall from chapter 3 that one of Sarah's tasks required her to respond on the basis of R-sameness of proportional relations. For example, she was able to match a sample of a half-filled glass cylinder to half of an apple. But since the proportion in the sample and the alternative that matched it were in fact the same (that is, the relations were similar), Sarah's task only required relational mapping. In contrast, the analogy in figure 4.8 requires mapping proportions in the source and target that are different from each other, necessitating a system mapping.

Also beware of the possible confusion between analogy problems based on the relation of "proportion" and what we have termed "proportional analogies." As we noted in chapter 2, the latter term is generally applied to *all* analogy problems in the standard A:B::C:D format, because in a loose sense the A:B relation is proportional to the C:D relation. The problem in figure 4.8 is thus a proportional analogy in which one of the relations being mapped happens to be "proportion." The term "proportional analogy" has unfortunately contributed to the widespread belief among psychologists that solving analogy problems always requires explicit representations of some higher-order relation much like "sameness of proportions," which is simply not the case. (See the note for page 95 concerning alternative definitions of "mapping.")

Page 97   *If children are usually not capable*   This experiment was reported by Goswami (1989). She interprets the difficulty of the "proportion" analogies as reflecting young children's lack of understanding of the concept of proportion. And indeed the four-year-olds also had difficulty in a task in which they had to match differing shapes according to the proportion that was shaded (although twice as many children in this age group achieved above-chance accuracy in the proportion-matching task than in the corresponding analogy task). But even though the proportion-matching task did not strictly require mapping a higher-order relation, any children who could in fact explicitly represent sameness of proportions (a relation between relations) would likely have an advantage. Goswami's findings highlight a tricky interpretive issue: do children have trouble solving analogies involving complex relations because they cannot understand the relations, or are they unable to understand the relations because they cannot do complex analogical mapping? We suspect the answer is "both."

Page 98   *More generally, as Dedre Gentner and Graeme Halford have argued*   Gentner (1988; Gentner and Rattermann, 1991) and Halford (1993) describe specific versions of the relational-shift hypothesis.

Page 98   *Dedre Gentner and Cecile Toupin performed an experiment*   See Gentner and Toupin (1986).

Page 99   *The younger children, however, did not seem to be helped as much by higher-order relations*   We must be cautious in interpreting this finding because Gentner and Toupin did not demonstrate that the younger children actually understood the causal and motivational relations introduced in the systematic versions of the stories. This is another example of the tricky interpretive issue noted above in connection with the interpretation of Goswami's (1989) findings about the difficulty of analogies based on the concept of proportion.

Chapter 5

Page 103   *During the first two days of the counterattack*   This study was reported by Spellman and Holyoak (1992).

Page 106   *Four decades earlier, President Harry Truman discussed how the events*   Truman is quoted by historian Ernest May (1973), 81–82.

Page 107   *In 1981, social psychologist Thomas Gilovich*   See Gilovich (1981).

Page 109   *George W. Ball (a knowledgeable commentator*   This quotation is from an article written in 1992 by Ball, who served as American undersecretary of state 1961–66.

Page 110   *In this "tumor problem"*   The tumor problem was first used to study problem solving early in the twentieth century by the German psychologist Karl Duncker, whose best-known work was published in English in 1945. Gick and Holyoak (1980, 1983) adapted the problem for use as a target analog in a series of experiments on the use of analogy in problem solving. Many later studies of analogy use have also used the tumor problem (e.g., Beveridge and Parkins, 1987; Catrambone and Holyoak, 1989; Holyoak and Koh, 1987; Keane, 1988; Spencer and Weisberg, 1986). Moreover, as Gick and Holyoak discovered after publishing their papers, a half century earlier Duncker himself had performed a preliminary study of analogical problem solving using the tumor problem as the target (Duncker, 1926). The tumor problem has figured so prominently in psychological studies of analogical problem solving that it might be called the "drosophila of analogy" (by analogy to the insect that was a laboratory favorite of geneticists).

Page 112   *Some of the students were asked to talk out loud*   These protocols of people solving the tumor problem by analogy were collected by Gick and Holyoak (1980), 327–28. The gap between spontaneous transfer and transfer after a hint to use the source analog was also first observed in the experiments reported in this paper.

Page 113   *The source analog need not be presented verbally*   Gick and Holyoak (1983) performed this experiment, in which the source analog was a diagram. Beveridge and Parkins (1987) used a visual analog that was even more effective as a source analog for the tumor problem. Their display consisted of transparent colored strips of plastic. These were fanned out so that they intersected to form a star shape. People could see that the color was darker at the center of the star where the strips intersected, visually conveying the summation of multiple forces at their point of convergence.

Page 115   *Suppose, for example, that the lightbulb-repair scenario*   This experiment, using both the fragile-glass and insufficient-intensity versions of the lightbulb story, was performed by Holyoak and Koh (1987). Using problems in probability, Ross (1989) obtained additional evidence that both structure and similarity influence access to source analogs in memory.

Page 115   *In an extreme demonstration of the impact on retrieval*   This experiment was performed by Keane (1988).

Page 117   *Charles Wharton and his colleagues performed a series of experiments*   The experiments described here were reported by Wharton (1993). The first study that investigated the impact of competition on analog retrieval was performed by Wharton et al. (1994). Earlier work by Seifert and her colleagues (Seifert, McKoon, Abelson, and Ratcliff, 1986) demonstrated that reading one story can activate a story with a similar theme that had been read earlier, at least when readers study the first story extensively. The importance of the similarity constraint in story reminding was established in experiments by Gentner and her colleagues, first reported in 1985 and described in detail by Gentner, Rattermann, and Forbus (1993).

Page 121   *What object in the bottom picture best goes with the woman in the top picture?*   This experiment was performed by Markman and Gentner (1993b).

Page 123   *When people are asked to say how the A and B shapes are similar*   This experiment was performed by Medin et al. (1993).

Page 124   *Douglas Hofstadter and Melanie Mitchell have placed particular emphasis*   Hofstadter and Mitchell (1988) and Mitchell (1993) describe their theory of analogy and its implementation in the Copycat program. Burns and Schreiner (1992) presented the "change *kji*" problem to a large group of college students and have reported the wide range of answers that people are able to generate. See chapter 10 for further discussion of Copycat.

Page 125   *Spellman and Holyoak performed an experiment*   This experiment was reported by Spellman and Holyoak (1993).

Page 129   *For example, Brian Ross gave college students examples*   These experiments are reported by Ross (1987, 1989).

Page 129   *People with greater expertise in a domain*   Laura Novick (1988) showed that students who were more expert in mathematics were better able to cope with misleading superficial similarities when solving a novel arithmetic word problem by analogy.

Page 130   *Miriam Bassok taught high school students how to solve problems*   This experiment was performed by Bassok (1990), who extended earlier work by Bassok and Holyoak (1989). A review of this line of research has been provided by Bassok and Holyoak (1993).

Page 132   *Markman and Gentner asked students to list differences*   This study was performed by Markman and Gentner (1993a), who refer to mapped versus unmapped differences as "alignable" versus "nonalignable." Holyoak (1984) made a similar distinction between "structure-preserving differences" and "indeterminate correspondences."

Page 133   *Operation Desert Storm, the successful attack*   Woodward (1991), 348.

Page 133   *Artificial-intelligence researchers have identified*   For surveys, see Riesbeck and Schank (1989), 41–51, and Kolodner (1993).

Page 133   *One of the most powerful is Jaime Carbonell's idea of* derivational *adaptation*   Carbonell (1986).

Page 134   *For example, the CHEF meal-planning system*   Hammond (1989).

Page 134   *Gick and Holyoak used this technique*   Much of the work described in this section was reported by Gick and Holyoak (1983). The quotations of students' descriptions of analog similarities appear on p. 23 of that paper.

Page 135   *Schemas can be learned not only from multiple initial examples*   For illustrations of how people appear to learn schemas as they solve mathematical word problems by analogy, see Bassok and Holyoak (1989) and Novick and Holyoak (1991).

Page 136   *Even with multiple examples that allow novices*   Spencer and Weisberg (1986) demonstrated the difficulty of obtaining transfer of the convergence solution after a delay or context change, even when students had an opportunity to learn a schema from two examples.

Page 136 *Richard Catrambone and Keith Holyoak gave students* This experiment was reported by Catrambone and Holyoak (1989).

Chapter 6

Page 139 *What Is to Be Done?* Our title is borrowed from political essays by Leo Tolstoy and V. I. Lenin.

Page 141 *Thagard and Millgram have proposed* See Thagard and Millgram (in press) and Millgram and Thagard (forthcoming).

Page 145 *Informal logic books* For example, see Copi (1982).

Page 147 *Steve Mann describes the case* Mann (1992).

Page 149 *According to law professor Cass Sunstein* Sunstein (1993), 741.

Page 149 *Kevin Ashley, a law professor and artificial intelligence researcher* Ashley (1990), 3–4. Ashley and Sunstein cite various proponents and opponents of the use of analogical reasoning in the law.

Page 149 *Sunstein poses the basic problem* Sunstein (1993), 774. Sunstein's objection to the explanatory power of similarity in the context of the law is a special case of the arguments against similarity raised by Goodman (1972), which we discussed in chapter 2.

Page 152 *The political philosopher John Rawls* Rawls (1971).

Page 152 *Someone who actually reaches reflective equilibrium may find it difficult to adapt* It should be noted, however, that Rawls did not believe the reflective equilibrium is necessarily stable. Rather, it may be upset by consideration of new cases. See Rawls (1971), 20–21.

Page 152 *At one time, for example, an American legal principle held* Relevant legal precedents include *Pennoyer v Neff* (1877) and *International Shoe v Washington* (1945). In fact, the physical-presence versus minimum-contact criteria are still debated. For example, service of process on an airplane was upheld in *Grace v MacArthur* (1959). However, it is unclear whether the current Supreme Court would uphold that decision (which was based on the rule of physical presence stated in Pennoyer), or overturn it on the basis of the rule of minimum contact stated in International Shoe (see the various opinions in *Burnham v Superior Court*, 1990). We thank Bobbie Spellman, Esq., for providing this example of the evolution of a legal principle. A classic treatment of the use of precedents in legal reasoning is that of Levi (1949).

Page 153 *A similar example of the reexamination* This example, including the quotation, is taken from a newspaper article by Amy Harmon (1993).

Page 154 *As the legal philosopher H. L. A. Hart* This quotation is from Hart (1961), 131.

Page 155 *Richard Neustadt and Ernest May* The examples listed are taken from Neustadt and May (1986) and May (1973). The title of the latter book is *"Lessons" of the Past,* where the quotation marks reflect May's assessment that politicians have often extracted lessons of a highly dubious nature from the analogies they have used.

Page 155   *Moreover, in 1938 Britain was militarily unprepared*   For a brief summary of alternatives to the conventional view of the Munich Agreement as appeasement—including the possibility that Hitler may actually have viewed it as a setback for his plan to provoke an early war—see Khong (1992), 184.

Page 157   *May says that "when thinking*   May (1973), 118.

Page 157   *According to historian James Banner*   Banner (1993), 47. Banner's proposal for an analogy police (p. 49) was widely reported in the popular press.

Page 157   *In any case, there is reason to heed the warning of Gilovich*   Gilovich (1981), 807–8.

Page 158   *Yuen Foong Khong has made a careful historical analysis*   See Khong (1992). The historical details of the Vietnam War in this section are taken from Khong's book, which provides the citations to original sources.

Page 160   *As Eisenhower had done in justifying the Korean War*   The quotation is from Khong (1992), 49.

Page 162   *Such a "controlled commitment," Ball argued*   This quotation is taken from Khong (1992), 153, who provides the original source. Khong conducted the later interview with Ball that is mentioned at the end of this paragraph. George Ball died in 1994, at the age of 84.

Page 163   *In such situations, the human apparatus*   For reviews of psychological research on the sorts of errors that tend to arise when decisions are made under conditions of high uncertainty and ambiguity, see Holland et al. (1986); Kahneman, Slovic, and Tversky (1982); and Nisbett and Ross (1980).

Chapter 7

Page 168   *G. E. R. Lloyd remarks that "the world*   Lloyd (1966), 193–94. This work contains a great many examples of the Greeks' use of analogy.

Page 168   *Lloyd reports, "not only are the Olympians*   Lloyd (1966), 194.

Page 168   *The Greek philosopher Xenophanes*   Kirk and Raven (1964), 169.

Page 169   *Writing in the thirteenth century A.D., St. Thomas Aquinas*   Aquinas (1969). For much more on medieval uses of analogy, see Ashworth (1992). Recent theological uses of analogy include Swinburne's (1992) discussion of revelation and Simons's (1988) consideration of God as a computer programmer.

Page 169   *In book 7 of the* Republic, *Plato*   Plato (1961), 747–49.

Page 170   *In the dialogue* Theaetetus, *Socrates*   Plato (1961), 855. Kittay (1987) provides a thorough analysis of the midwife analogy. For our own formalization of it, see Holyoak and Thagard (1989a), 345.

Page 170   *In the same dialogue, Socrates compares memory*   Plato (1961), 897 (wax analogy) and 904 (aviary analogy). Once the science of psychology developed in the late nineteenth century, a great variety of analogies for memory and other mental concepts influenced psychological theories. A review of these is provided by Gentner and Grudin (1985).

Page 170   *Plato's student Aristotle compared the impact of the senses*   Aristotle (1984), 674.

Page 170   *Centuries later, John Locke took experience to be the sole source*   For the white-paper analogy, see Locke (1961), 77. Locke also compared the operation of the mind to a camera obscura.

Page 170   *Gottfried Leibniz countered empiricist analogies with another*   For the veined-marble analogy see Leibniz (1981), 52.

Page 170   *He claimed that learning a language is like undergoing puberty*   Chomsky (1988), 174. The analogies between teaching and filling a bottle versus letting a flower grow are described on p. 135. Supporters of Chomsky sometimes compare the human innate conceptual system to the body's immune system.

Page 170   *Francis Bacon rejected this dichotomy*   Bacon (1960), 93.

Page 171   *W. V. O. Quine, following Otto Neurath*   Quine (1960), 3; Neurath (1959), 201.

Page 171   *The lore of our fathers is a fabric of sentences*   Quine (1966), 125.

Page 171   *Other contemporary theorists*   See, for example, Campbell (1988) and Hahlweg and Hooker (1989).

Page 171   *Thagard has argued that biological analogies*   Thagard (1988), chap. 6. Thagard (1992), 154–56. "The Darwinian revolution"

Page 172   *This line of argument hit its peak*   Paley (1963).

Page 172   *David Hume had already argued in his* Dialogues   Hume (1964).

Page 173   *The situation changed dramatically*   Darwin (1964).

Page 173   *Unlike pure analogical reasoning, inference to the best explanation*   For a much fuller discussion of this kind of reasoning and its scientific applications, see Thagard (1988). The term originated with Gilbert Harman (1965, 1973).

Page 174   *According to Thagard's account, hypotheses gain explanatory coherence*   See Thagard (1989, 1992) and Harman (1986). There is no circularity in supposing that explanatory coherence depends on analogy at the same time that analogies are evaluated in terms of explanatory coherence. In chapter 10 we describe how both evaluations can be done in parallel by connectionist networks, and simultaneous evaluation simply requires joining the networks.

Page 175   *Since David Hume, at least, many philosophers*   Hume (1888), 176. Plantinga (1967), 191–92, provides numerous references to arguments about other minds.

Page 176   *Alvin Plantinga argued that the analogical*   Plantinga (1967), chap. 10. "God and analogy?

Page 177   *According to Deborah Tannen, men and women*   Tannen (1990).

Page 177   *Alvin Goldman has argued*   Goldman (1992).

Page 177   *As Allison Barnes has argued, empathy*   Barnes and Thagard (forthcoming).

Page 178   *Ideally, people should employ analogies*   Analogy could thus contribute to motivated inference (Kunda, 1990).

Page 178   *John Searle attacked the view that computers*   Searle (1980).

Page 179   *Intuition pumps*   This term is from Dennett (1980).

Page 179   *Judith Jarvis Thomson defended the permissibility*   Thomson (1971).

Page 180   *James Humber proposed that you imagine yourself*   Humber (1975).

Page 181   *As we saw in chapter 6, John Rawls employs a kind of coherence criterion*   Rawls (1971).

Page 181   *Consider two passages from the Upanishads*   These passages were translated by Easwaran (1987). The quotations are from pp. 217–18 and p. 38.

Page 182   *The Chinese philosopher Mencius*   Mencius (1970). The analogies quoted are from p. 160. Volkov (1992) provides a detailed analysis of these analogies, making explicit the analogical mappings. He also describes the use of analogy in Chinese mathematics.

Page 183   *Writing a bit later than Mencius, the Taoist thinker Chuang Tzu*   Chuang Tzu (1964), 59.

Page 183   *Someone said to the King of Liang*   Quoted by D. C. Lau in appendix to Mencius (1970), 262.

Page 184   *The development of theories in logic*   Boole (1951). On Peirce, see Van Evra (1994). This chapter has been concerned with philosophers' use of analogies, not with what they have written about analogy. For examples of the latter, see Mill (1970), Keynes (1921), Burbidge (1990), the philosophers of science cited in chapter 8, and the metaphor theorists cited in chapter 9.

Chapter 8

Page 185   *Several years after he carried out*   Franklin (1941), 334.

Page 185   *It would be easy to compile a list of hundreds*   In addition to the sources given below for particular analogies, see Biela (1991), Hesse (1966), Leary (1990), Leatherdale (1974), and numerous sources that they cite.

Page 186   *In the first century A.D., the Roman architect Vitruvius*   (Vitruvius, 1960). This example, the many ancient Greek examples in Lloyd (1966), and the Asian analogies in chapter 7 refute the claim of Gentner and Jeziorski (1989) that rigorous analogical thinking only emerged in the seventeenth century. Their claim is based on the oddness of the analogies offered by early alchemists such as Paracelsus, which should be attributed to the peculiarity of alchemy rather than to any premodern lack of analogical sophistication.

Page 186   *In his landmark work* De Magnete   Gilbert (1958).

Page 186   *Galileo's* Dialogue   Galileo (1967). The earth/ship analogy was discussed by Gentner (1982).

Page 187   *In his 1678* Treatise on Light   Huygens (1962).

Page 187   *Toward the end of his celebrated* Principia   Newton (1934).

Page 187   *During the 1770s when Antoine Lavoisier was developing his oxygen theory*
Holmes (1989); Lavoisier (1862).

Page 187   *In 1824, Nicholas Léonard Sadi Carnot*   Carnot (1977); see Gentner and
Jeziorski (1989).

Page 187   *Charles Darwin reported*   Darwin (1958).

Page 188   *Darwin used this analogy in the* Origin of Species   Darwin (1859). See
also Thagard (1992), chap. 6. "The Darwinian revolution"

Page 188   *James Clerk Maxwell was explicit*   Nersessian (1992).

Page 188   *As we mentioned in chapter 1, Friedrich Kekulé*   Benfey (1958). Noe and
Bader (1993) contend that the circular structure of benzene was actually proposed
several years earlier by Josef Lofschmidt in a book that Kekulé had read. (See also
Wotiz, 1993.) While it is possible that Kekulé's dream was partly inspired by
Lofschmidt and conceivable that Kekulé made up the story of the dream to exag-
gerate his own originality, the historical evidence is not sufficient to overturn
Kekulé's own account.

Page 188   *Thomas Morgan and his colleagues*   Darden (1991).

Page 188   *In 1943, Salvador Luria was trying*   Luria (1984), 75–77.

Page 188   *By far the most fertile has been*   See, for example, Johnson-Laird (1988).

Page 189   *Another famous analogy is the comparison of the Rutherford-Bohr model*   Wilson (1983). For an analysis of the analogy, see Gentner (1983).

Page 191   *Thus analogy contributes to the explanatory coherence of Darwin's theory*   See
Thagard (1992) for a much more detailed account.

Page 193   *Construction may involve*   Clement (1988) provides an analysis of the
construction of source analogs by experts solving physics problems.

Page 194   *Construction of productive source analogs*   For recent discussions of visual
representations and visual analogies, see Glasgow and Papadias (1992) and Thagard,
Gochfeld, and Hardy (1992).

Page 196   *Cognitive psychologist Kevin Dunbar*   Dunbar (1994).

Page 197   *In psychology, there have been many influential analogies*   See Gentner and
Grudin (1985), Leary (1990), and Sternberg (1990).

Page 197   *Many economists have employed analogies*   See Smith (1937), 423;
McCloskey (1985); and Mirowski (1989).

Page 197   *Similarly, political scientists have compared the state*   Landau (1972).

Page 197   *Lauren Talalay, for example, argued*   Talalay (1987). See also Wylie (1985).

Page 197   *For example, in the history of science, the concept of a scientific revolution*   See
Kuhn (1970) and Cohen (1985).

Page 197   *Nancy Leys Stepan has described*   Stepan (1986).

Page 198   *For example, when Alexander Graham Bell was inventing*   Gorman (1992), 203. The quote is reproduced by Gorman from Bell's papers.

Page 198   *Another technological breakthrough*   Hill (1978) describes the development of Velcro.

Page 198   *John Holland developed his influential idea*   Holland (1975); Holland et al. (1986).

Page 199   *Wilbur Wright noticed that soaring birds*   Bradshaw (1992), 246.

Page 199   *Architects sometimes model*   Pevsner (1976).

Page 199   *Artificial intelligence systems*   Hammond (1989), Riesbeck and Schank (1989), Kolodner (1993), Mostow (1990), Bhansali and Harandi (1993).

Page 199   *Our theory of analogical thinking*   Instructional analogies have been discussed by educational psychologists and other cognitive scientists. See, for example Bransford et al. (1989); Brown (1989); Clement (1988); Duit (1991); Glynn (1991); Halford (1993); Ross (1989); Rumelhart and Norman (1981); Schank (1986); Thagard, Cohen, and Holyoak (1989); Treagust et al. (1992).

Page 200   *For example, science writer Edward Dolnick explains why pandas*   Dolnick (1989), 72.

Page 202   *Medical students often compare a failing heart*   This and other examples of misleading medical analogies are discussed by Spiro et al. (1989). These authors propose ways of using multiple analogies together to help understand a complex target domain.

Page 203   *When Gentner and Gentner tested high school and college students*   The differences between the inferences about electricity generated by the water-flow and moving-crowds analogies were analyzed and tested by Gentner and Gentner (1983).

Page 204   *However, if the new problem requires*   Reed (1987) and Novick and Holyoak (1991) have reported experiments showing that novices are extremely prone to make errors in solving mathematical word problems by analogy when adaptation of the solution is required. The difficulty of adaptation in using analogy to solve word problems is discussed further by Holyoak et al. (1994).

Page 205   *Tolstoy's brilliant description in* War and Peace *of Napoleon's*   Tolstoy (1982), 1192.

Page 208   *Many people, for example, think that thermostats are like valves*   See Collins and Gentner (1987).

Page 208   *A more complicated strategy*   Ways of using multiple analogies in instruction have been discussed by Burstein (1986) and by Spiro et al. (1989). Spiro et al. provide a catalog of kinds of misconceptions that can be induced by poor analogies.

Page 209   *Maybe teachers should try to get by*   For a skeptical view of educational analogies, see Halasz and Moran (1982).

Chapter 9

Page 211 *Benjamin Colby has described* Our description and interpretation of the tea ceremony is based on the discussion of Colby (1991).

Page 211 *The intended analogy has been described by the tea master Soshitsu Sen XV* Sen (1979), quotations from p. 27 and p. 81.

Page 212 *Kakuzo Okakura writes* Okakura (1912), 85.

Page 213 *But we need to pay attention to metonymy as well, because the two devices often work together* The interplay between different figurative devices used in cultural contexts is a central theme of contributions to a volume edited by Fernandez (1991), as well as in his own earlier writings (1986).

Page 214 *In an episode of a science-fiction television program* The episode "Darmok" from the series *Star Trek: The Next Generation* (Captain's log, star date 45047.2). Produced by Paramount Pictures; first broadcast in 1991.

Page 215 *Anthropologist William McKellin has studied the use of allegories* The most extensive account is provided by McKellin (in press); the quoted *ha'a* is from p. 139 in the manuscript. Also see McKellin (1984, 1990).

Page 217 *A metaphor always connects two domains* Discussions of metaphor in linguistics and philosophy, following Richards (1936), have traditionally referred to the target domain as the "tenor," the source domain as the "vehicle," and the basis for connecting the two domains as the "ground" of the metaphor. Thus for "Socrates was a lion," Socrates is the tenor, lion is the vehicle, and the shared attribute of courage constitutes the ground. (Another set of terms was used by Black [1962], who referred to the target and source as the "principal subject" and "subsidiary subject," respectively, and to the mapping and attendant inferences as the "implicative complex.") Because we view metaphor as based on analogical thinking, we will continue to use the standard terms "target" and "source" rather than "tenor" and "vehicle." The ground of a metaphor is essentially equivalent to the set of mappings between the source and the target. Our terminology agrees with the usage of Lakoff (1994).

Page 217 *The source domain can instead* From Sandberg's poem "Fog."

Page 217 *Other "literalized" metaphors appear as idioms* For an analysis of the metaphorical basis for some idioms, see Gibbs (1992).

Page 217 *However, the underlying analogy can sometimes* Hemingway (1964), 104.

Page 217 *George Lakoff and his colleagues have argued* See Lakoff and Johnson (1980), Lakoff and Turner (1989), and Lakoff (1994).

Page 218 *In one study, college students were asked to decide* This study was reported by Glucksberg, Gildea, and Bookin (1982).

Page 219 *Keysar presented students with sentences* See Keysar (1989).

Page 219 *Max Black suggests a simple answer* See Black (1979).

Page 219 *Just as the constraints provided by* This example is from Waltz and Pollack (1985).

Page 219 *The preferred interpretation is the one most relevant* Sperber and Wilson (1986) have emphasized the general role of relevance in guiding communication.

Page 219 *Attempts to translate metaphors* The earliest discussion of metaphor was provided by Aristotle (1984), 2243. Other philosophical, linguistic, and psychological discussions of alternative approaches to metaphor are provided by Richards (1936), Black (1962, 1979), Davidson (1978), Kittay (1987), Fogelin (1988), Tirrell (1991), Gentner (1982), and Gentner and Jeziorski (1989).

Page 220 *Our view of metaphor is closely related* See, for example, Black (1979), Lakoff and Turner (1989), and Glucksberg and Keysar (1990).

Page 221 *Glucksberg and Keysar have argued* Glucksberg and Keysar (1990).

Page 222 *This asymmetry between the target* Ortony (1979) emphasized the radical semantic asymmetry of metaphorical expressions. The example here is from Gentner and French (1988), who describe a series of experiments demonstrating that in nonliteral sentences, verbs generally alter their meanings more than nouns do. The quotation is from p. 376 of their paper.

Page 223 *To see some of the complex issues* Hemingway (1964), 147. Holyoak (1982) discussed this and other examples illustrating the roles that analogy plays in literary interpretation, and Gentner (1982) pointed out some of the differences between literary metaphors and scientific analogies. Lakoff and Turner provide the most thorough analysis of the role of metaphor in poetry, including the interplay between metaphor and metonymy.

Page 225 *Lakoff and Turner discuss a number of* See Lakoff and Turner (1989). The translation is from Merwin (1973).

Page 225 *Another passage considered by Lakoff and Turner* This Sanskrit poem was translated by Merwin and Masson (1981), 155.

Page 226 *Shall I compare thee to a summer's day?* Shakespeare, Sonnet 18.

Page 227 *All the world's a stage* Shakespeare, *As You Like It,* act 2, scene 7.

Page 227 *In Tolstoy's poignant story "Happy Ever After"* Tolstoy (1960); the quotation is from p. 45.

Page 228 *Psychiatrist Philip Barker describes several clinical situations* Barker (1985), 53.

Page 228 *Anthropologist Naomi Quinn has identified several metaphors* Quinn (1987).

Page 229 *Clinical psychologist Donald Meichenbaum* Personal communication.

Page 229 *Personal-development "guru" Anthony Robbins* Robbins (1991), chap. 10 "Destroy the blocks, break down the walls, let go of the rope, and dance your way to success: The power of life metaphors."

Page 229 *Management consultant Gareth Morgan* Morgan (1993).

Page 230 *Claude Lévi-Strauss suggested that many social groups* See Lévi-Strauss (1966); quotation from p. 204.

Page 231 *Writing more than a hundred years ago, Sir James Frazer* The abridged version of the third edition of *The Golden Bough,* made by Frazer himself, is Frazer (1922); the quotations are from p. 11 of this version. The first edition of the work was published in 1890. It should be noted that Frazer related his two varieties of sympathetic magic to the misapplication of two general ways in which ideas can be associated, first suggested by the philosopher David Hume. The Law of Similarity is related to association by "resemblance," and the Law of Contact is related to association by "contiguity." The basic error in sympathetic magic is to suppose in these cases that the association of ideas in the mind reflects a connection between cause and effect in the world.

Page 232 *The anthropologist Edward Evans-Pritchard* Evans-Pritchard (1937).

Page 232 *As S. J. Tambiah points out* Tambiah (1973).

Page 233 *For example, Daniel Kahneman and Amos Tversky* Kahneman and Tversky (1972).

Page 233 *Richard Nisbett and Lee Ross* Nisbett and Ross (1980).

Page 233 *Homeopathy is still widely practiced in alternative* Garion-Hutchings and Garion-Hutchings (1993).

Page 234 *In her book* Illness as Metaphor, *Susan Sontag* Sontag (1979).

Page 234 *Lakoff and Turner describe how the metaphor of the Great Chain of Being* Lakoff and Turner (1989), chap. 4. "The Great Chain of Being"

Chapter 10

Page 237 *In accord with the proposals of Gentner and Halford* See Gentner (1983) and Halford (1993).

Page 239 *Computational ideas can suggest how the mind might work* For a brief history of cognitive science, see Thagard (1992), chap. 9. "Revolutions in Psychology?" For more detail, see Gardner (1985).

Page 239 *The other is the "connectionist" approach* A thorough introduction to connectionism (and especially to the type of connectionist modeling termed "parallel distributed processing") is provided by Rumelhart and McClelland (1986).

Page 239 *Most connectionist models are only able to represent knowledge implicitly* Clark and Karmiloff-Smith (1994) describe a variety of limitations in the performance of some types of connectionist models (in particular, those based on "distributed" representations of concepts) that result from their lack of explicit knowledge. They do not include analogy in their discussion; however, Barnden (1994) provides an analysis of some of the problems that arise in attempting to construct connectionist models capable of analogical thinking.

Page 240 *The multiconstraint theory is implemented as a kind of hybrid* Holyoak (1991) and Holyoak and Spellman (1993) discuss hybrid "symbolic–connectionist" models of thinking.

Page 240   *The idea that thinking can be understood as a kind of seeing was central to Gestalt psychology*   For a sketch of the relationship between Gestalt ideas and the multiconstraint theory of analogy, see Holyoak and Barnden (1994).

Page 240   *David Marr and Tomaso Poggio*   Marr and Poggio (1976). See also Marr (1982), 115–19.

Page 241   *Similar networks were subsequently used*   See Feldman (1981), Feldman and Ballard (1982), and McClelland and Rumelhart (1981). For more systematic discussion of parallel constraint satisfaction using networks, see Rumelhart and McClelland (1986). Especially relevant is the chapter by Rumelhart, Smolensky, McClelland, and Hinton (1986), which presents a network model of how a Necker cube can be disambiguated and relates parallel constraint satisfaction to the use of schemas. McClelland and Rumelhart (1989) provide details on how to program models of this sort. Note that in other types of artificial-intelligence research, "constraint satisfaction" typically refers to a very different approach that uses hard Boolean constraints and nonconnectionist algorithms for satisfying them. See Mackworth (1990) for a survey.

Page 242   *However, this model was unsatisfying in various ways*   The application of our earlier model, PI ("Processes of Induction") to analogy is described by Holyoak and Thagard (1989b). To be fair to PI, it attempted to deal with multiple stages in analogy use, including learning, and therefore in some respects went beyond the later ACME and ARCS models.

Page 242   *In April of 1987, after reading Rumelhart's account*   Holyoak (1987) wrote a review of the book in which this account appeared, which provided the occasion for noticing the potential connection to analogy.

Page 243   *Thus an analogical chain reaction*   For ACME, see Holyoak and Thagard (1989a); for ECHO, see Thagard (1989); for ARCS, see Thagard et al. (1990). The story is actually longer than this. A model of visual analogical mapping, VAMP.2, was developed partly on the basis of ACME (Thagard, Gochfeld, and Hardy, 1992), as was a model of mapping called IMM that uses a different style of connectionist processing (Hummel and Holyoak, 1992; Hummel et al., 1994), as well as a model of how people judge similarity between structured representations, called SIAM (Goldstone and Medin, 1994). CARE, an integrated model of analogical and rule-based reasoning, was modeled partly on ARCS and partly on ECHO, a case of using multiple analogies (Nelson, Thagard, and Hardy, 1994). Finally, Elijah Millgram noticed similarities between theoretical reasoning as modeled by ECHO and practical reasoning (that is, everyday decision making), so the theory of deliberative coherence and the program DECO were developed by close analogy to explanatory coherence and to ECHO (Thagard and Millgram, in press; Millgram and Thagard, forthcoming).

Page 244   *We can call this game "tug-and-shove"*   Note that this analogy for explaining relaxation is a dynamic visual analogy, which uses a system mapping to compensate for the fact that there is no direct similarity between units and people. Kosslyn and Koenig (1992) on p. 18, provide a vivid connectionist analogy in which units are represented by octopuses, whose tentacles squeeze each other; however, their analogy illustrates feed-forward networks rather than ones that perform parallel constraint satisfaction with feedback. Boden (1988) has explained various kinds of networks by analogy with children passing messages to each other. Networks of roughly the sort we use for modeling analogy are sometimes called "Hopfield nets" because of the theoretical analysis provided by Hopfield (1982).

Page 247 *Without any constraints, mapping would be* More generally, if the source and target each have *m* predicates relating *n* objects, then under the stated assumptions *m!n!* represents the number of possible mappings.

Page 248 *Taking structure seriously* In more detail, ACME only considers mappings between predicates with the same number of slots (i.e., one-place predicates to one-place predicates, two-place predicates to two-place predicates, and so on).

Page 249 *To implement the external constraints* The links from the special unit for semantic similarity are always excitatory. The special unit for purpose can have inhibitory links to suppress elements unrelated to the goal, as well as excitatory links to activate mappings that are supported by prior knowledge (see Spellman and Holyoak, 1993).

Page 249 *We will not give the full details here* See Holyoak and Thagard (1989a).

Page 251 *We have tested ACME on dozens of examples* See Holyoak and Thagard (1989a); Thagard, Cohen, and Holyoak (1989); Spellman and Holyoak (1992, 1993); and Holyoak et al. (1994).

Page 251 *In our 1989 paper, and in subsequent work* The psychological studies mentioned in chapters 4 and 5 that ACME has been used to simulate are those of Gentner and Toupin (1986), Holyoak and Koh (1987), Reed (1987), Novick and Holyoak (1991), and Spellman and Holyoak (1992, 1993).

Page 251 *For example, ACME can find humanlike mappings* See Spellman and Holyoak (1992).

Page 251 *ACME is able to account for the intricate interplay among the constraints* See especially Spellman and Holyoak (1993).

Page 251 *We were also able to apply the model to complex metaphors* Holyoak and Thagard (1989a); cf. Kittay (1987).

Page 252 *Hence our ARCS model only considers* See Thagard et al. (1990) for a full account, including detailed specification of all algorithms. Our description here is highly simplified and is meant only to give the flavor of how ARCS works.

Page 252 *We therefore borrowed information from WordNet* See Miller et al. (1990).

Page 256 *ARCS has also been used to simulate the performance of people* ARCS has been used to model experimental results obtained by Holyoak and Koh (1987), Gentner et al. (1993), and Wharton et al. (1994). These simulations are reported by Thagard et al. (1990) and Wharton et al. (1994).

Page 256 *A cue can activate stored cases* In our initial applications of ARCS (Thagard et al., 1990), "cause" and a small number of other very common predicates were not used as search cues. However, this restriction was dropped in later simulation work (Wharton et al., 1994).

Page 256   *As we saw in chapter 5, this prediction has been tested*   Wharton et al. (1994); Wharton (1993).

Page 257   *The first computational model*   Evans (1968).

Page 257   *Many of the ideas embodied in his model*   Sternberg (1977).

Page 257   *The first major computational model to arise*   Winston (1980).

Page 257   *Since 1980 dozens of other computational models*   For a comprehensive review of computational models of analogy prior to ACME, see Hall (1989).

Page 257   *From a psychological perspective*   See Falkenhainer et al. (1989). SME was originally described in a conference paper published in 1986. This program can be used to implement a variety of mapping models. The version we describe and compare to ACME is based on the structure-mapping theory of Gentner (1983, 1989).

Page 258   *The Copycat model, developed by Douglas Hofstadter and Melanie Mitchell*   Hofstadter (1984), Hofstadter and Mitchell (1988), Mitchell (1993).

Page 258   *Unlike ACME, SME will match relations (except for functions) only if they are identical*   The identicality restriction was relaxed by Forbus and Oblinger (1990).

Page 259   *However, as we saw in chapter 5, experimental evidence*   Spellman and Holyoak (1993).

Page 259   *Mitchell writes, referring to ACME*   Mitchell (1993), 210.

Page 259   *Copycat has many points of agreement with ACME*   Burns and Holyoak (1994) illustrate how ACME can be applied to some of the letter-string analogies for which Copycat was developed.

Page 260   *Gentner and Forbus have produced MAC/FAC*   Gentner and Forbus (1991).

Page 260   *Whereas Gentner and Forbus's account*   Case-based reasoning models are described by Schank (1982), Hammond (1989), Kolodner and Simpson (1989), and Kolodner (1993).

Page 261   *In her textbook on case-based reasoning*   Kolodner (1993).

Page 262   *As Samuel Butler once said*   Bartlett (1955), 671.

Page 263   *Notably, many constructed analogs*   See Finke, Ward, and Smith (1992).

Page 263   *We often use cross-sensory metaphors, such as "bitter cold" and "loud colors"*   Marks, Hammeal, and Bornstein (1987).

Page 264   *Kevin Dunbar has described how the social structure*   Dunbar (1993).

References

Aquinas, S. T. (1969). *Summa theologiae.* Garden City, N.Y.: Image Books.

Aristotle (1984). *The complete works of Aristotle.* Princeton: Princeton University Press.

Ashley, K. (1990). *Modeling legal argument.* Cambridge, Mass.: MIT Press.

Ashworth, E. J. (1992). Analogical concepts: The fourteenth century background to Cajetan. *Dialogue* 31:399–413.

Bacon, F. (1960). *The New Organon and related writings.* Indianapolis: Bobbs-Merrill.

Baldwin, D. A., E. M. Markman, and R. L. Melartin (1993). Infants' ability to draw inferences about nonobvious object properties: Evidence from exploratory play. *Child Development* 64:711–28.

Ball, G. W. (August 2, 1992). The tyrant who refuses to die. *Los Angeles Times.*

Banner, J. M. (1993). The history watch: A proposal. *The Public Historian* 15:47–54.

Barker, P. (1985). *Using metaphors in psychotherapy.* New York: Brunner/Mazel.

Barnden, J. A. (1994). On the connectionist implementation of analogy and working memory matching. In *Analogy, metaphor, and reminding.* Advances in Connectionist and Neural Computation Theory, edited by J. A. Barnden and K. J. Holyoak, Vol. 3, 327–74. Norwood, N.J.: Ablex.

Barnes, A., and P. Thagard (forthcoming). Empathy and analogy.

Bartlett, J. (1955). *Familiar quotations.* 13th ed. Boston: Little, Brown.

Bassok, M. (1990). Transfer of domain-specific problem-solving procedures. *Journal of Experimental Psychology: Learning, Memory, and Cognition* 16:522–33.

Bassok, M., and K. J. Holyoak (1989). Interdomain transfer between isomorphic topics in algebra and physics. *Journal of Experimental Psychology: Learning, Memory, and Cognition* 15:153–66.

Bassok, M., and K. J. Holyoak (1993). Pragmatic knowledge and conceptual structure: Determinants of transfer between quantitative domains. In *Transfer on trial: Intelligence, cognition, and instruction,* edited by D. K. Detterman and R. J. Sternberg, 68–98. Norwood, N.J.: Ablex.

Benfey, O. T. (1958). August Kekulé and the birth of the structural theory of organic chemistry in 1858. *Journal of Chemical Education* 35, no. 1:21–23.

Beveridge, M., and E. Parkins (1987). Visual representation in analogical problem solving. *Memory & Cognition* 15:230–37.

Bhansali, S., and M. T. Harandi (1993). Synthesis of UNIX programs using derivational analogy. *Machine Learning* 10:7–55.

Biela, A. (1991). *Analogy in science.* Frankfurt: Peter Lang.

Black, M. (1962). *Models and metaphors.* Ithaca, N.Y.: Cornell University Press.

Black, M. (1979). More about metaphor. In *Metaphor and thought,* edited by A. Ortony, 10–43. Cambridge: Cambridge University Press.

Boden, M. (1988). *Computer models of mind.* Cambridge: Cambridge University Press.

Boden, M. A. (1990). *The creative mind: Myths and mechanisms.* New York: Basic Books.

Boole, G. (1951). *An investigation of the laws of thought.* New York: Dover.

Borges, J. L. (1964). Funes the memorious. In *Labyrinths: Selected stories and other writings,* 59–66. New York: New Directions.

Bradshaw, G. (1992). The airplane and the logic of invention. In *Cognitive models of science,* edited by R. Giere, 239–50. Minneapolis: University of Minnesota Press.

Bransford, J. D., J. J. Franks, N. J. Vye, and R. D. Sherwood (1989). New approaches to instruction: Because wisdom can't be told. In *Similarity and analogical reasoning,* edited by S. Vosniadou and A. Ortony, 470–97. New York: Cambridge University Press.

Brown, A. (1989). Analogical learning and transfer: What develops? In *Similarity and analogical reasoning,* edited by S. Vosniadou and A. Ortony, 369–412. Cambridge: Cambridge University Press.

Brown, A. L., and M. J. Kane (1988). Preschool children can learn to transfer: Learning to learn and learning from example. *Cognitive Psychology* 20:493–523.

Brown, A. L., M. J. Kane, and C. H. Echols (1986). Young children's mental models determine analogical transfer across problems with a common goal structure. *Cognitive Development* 1:103–21.

Brown, A. L., M. J. Kane, and C. Long (1989). Analogical transfer in young children: Analogies as tools for communication and exposition. *Applied Cognitive Psychology* 3:275–93.

Buchanan, L., S. Joordens, R. Fleck, and P. Thagard (1993). Orientation and complexity effects: Implications for computational models of visual analogical reasoning. In *Proceedings of the Fifteenth Annual Conference of the Cognitive Science Society,* 272–76. Hillsdale, N.J.: Erlbaum.

Burbidge, J. (1990). *Within reason: A guide to non-deductive reasoning.* Peterborough, Ont.: Broadview Press.

Burnham v Superior Court, 110 S. Ct. 2105 (1990).

Burns, B. D., and K. J. Holyoak (1994). Competing models of analogy: ACME versus Copycat. In *Proceedings of the Sixteenth Annual Conference of the Cognitive Science Society.* Hillsdale, N.J.: Erlbaum.

Burns, B. D., and M. E. Schreiner (1992). Analogy and representation: Support for the Copycat model. In *Proceedings of the Fourteenth Annual Conference of the Cognitive Science Society,* 737–42. Hillsdale, N.J.: Erlbaum.

Burstein, M. (1986). Concept formation by incremental analogical reasoning and debugging. In *Machine learning: An artificial intelligence approach,* edited by R. S. Michalski, J. G. Carbonell, and T. M. Mitchell, 351–69. Vol. 2. Los Altos, Calif.: Morgan Kaufman.

Campbell, D. (1988). *Methodology and epistemology for social science: Selected papers.* Chicago: University of Chicago Press.

Carbonell, J. G. (1983). Learning by analogy: Formulating and generalizing plans from past experience. In *Machine learning: An artificial intelligence approach,* edited by R. S. Michalski, J. G. Carbonell, and T. M. Mitchell, 137–61. Palo Alto, Calif.: Tioga Publishing Co.

Carbonell, J. G. (1986). Derivational analogy: A theory of reconstructive problem solving and expertise acquisition. In *Machine learning: An artificial intelligence approach,* edited by R. S. Michalski, J. G. Carbonell, and T. M. Mitchell, 371–92. Vol. 2. Los Altos, Calif.: Morgan Kaufman.

Carey, S. (1985). *Conceptual change in childhood.* Cambridge, Mass.: MIT Press/Bradford Books.

Carnot, S. (1977). *Reflections on the motive power of fire,* translated by R. Thurston. Gloucester, Mass.: Peter Smith.

Catrambone, R., and K. J. Holyoak (1989). Overcoming contextual limitations on problem-solving transfer. *Journal of Experimental Psychology: Learning, Memory, and Cognition* 15:1147–56.

Cheng, P. W. (1993). Separating causal laws from casual facts. In *The psychology of learning and motivation,* edited by D. L. Medin, 215–63. San Diego: Academic Press.

Chomsky, N. (1988). *Language and problems of knowledge.* Cambridge, Mass.: MIT Press.

Chuang T. (1964). *Chuang Tzu: Basic writings,* translated by B. Watson. New York: Columbia University Press.

Clark, A., and A. Karmiloff-Smith (1994). The cognizer's innards: A psychological and philosophical perspective on the development of thought. *Mind and Language*, 8:487–568.

Clement, J. (1988). Observed methods for generating analogies in scientific problem solving. *Cognitive Science* 12:563–86.

Clement, J. J. (1989). Generation of spontaneous analogies by students solving science problems. In *Thinking across cultures: The third international conference on thinking*, edited by D. M. Topping, D. C. Crowel, and V. N. Kobayashi, 303–8. Hillsdale, N.J.: Erlbaum.

Cohen, I. (1985). *Revolution in science*. Cambridge, Mass.: Harvard University Press.

Colby, B. N. (1991). The Japanese tea ceremony: Coherence theory and metaphor in social adaptation. In *Beyond metaphor: The theory of tropes in anthropology*, edited by J. W. Fernandez, 244–60. Stanford, Calif.: Stanford University Press.

Collins, A., and D. Gentner (1987). How people construct mental models. In *Cultural models of language and thought*, edited by N. Quinn and D. Holland, 243–65. Cambridge: Cambridge University Press.

Copi, I. (1979). *Symbolic logic*. 5th ed. New York: Macmillan.

Copi, I. (1982). *Introduction to logic*. 6th ed. New York: Macmillan.

Dante A. (1904). *The Divine Comedy of Dante: The Inferno*, translated by M. R. Vincent. New York: Charles Scribner's Sons.

Darden, L. (1991). *Theory change in science: Strategies from Mendelian genetics*. Oxford: Oxford University Press.

Darwin, C. (1859). *The origin of species*. London: Murray.

Darwin, C. (1958). *The autobiography of Charles Darwin and selected letters*. New York: Dover.

Darwin, C. (1964). *On the origin of species. Facsimile of first edition of 1859*. Cambridge, Mass.: Harvard University Press.

Davidson, D. (1978). What metaphors mean. *Critical Inquiry*, 5:31–47.

DeLoache, J. S. (1987). Rapid change in the symbolic functioning of very young children. *Science* 238:1556–57.

DeLoache, J. S. (1989). Young children's understanding of the correspondence between a scale model and a larger space. *Cognitive Development* 4:121–39.

DeLoache, J. S., K. F. Miller, K. Rosengren, and N. Bryant (1993). Symbolic development in young children: Honey, I shrunk the room. Paper presented at the Thirty-fourth Annual Meeting of the Psychonomic Society, Washington, D.C.

Dennett, D. (1980). The milk of human intentionality. *Behavioral and Brain Sciences* 3:428–30.

Dolnick, E. (1989). Panda paradox. *Discover Magazine* (September):71–2.

Duit, R. (1991). On the role of analogies and metaphors in learning science. *Science Education* 75:649–72.

Dunbar, K. (1994). How scientists really reason: Scientific reasoning in real-world laboratories. In *Mechanisms of insight,* edited by R. J. Sternberg and J. Davidson. Cambridge, Mass.: MIT Press.

Duncker, K. (1926). A qualitative (experimental and theoretical) study of productive thinking (solving of comprehensible problems). *Journal of Genetic Psychology* 33:642–708.

Duncker, K. (1945). On problem solving. *Psychological Monographs* 58, no. 270.

Easwaran, E. (1987). *The Upanishads.* Tomales, Calif.: Nilgiri Press.

Evans, T. (1968). A program for the solution of a class of geometric analogy intelligence test questions. In *Semantic information processing,* edited by M. Minsky, 271–353. Cambridge Mass.: MIT Press.

Evans-Pritchard, E. (1937). *Witchcraft, oracles, and magic among the Azande.* Oxford: Clarendon Press.

Falkenhainer, B. (1990). A unified approach to explanation and theory formation. In *Computational models of discovery and theory formation,* edited by J. Shrager and P. Langley, 157–96. San Mateo, Calif.: Morgan Kaufman.

Falkenhainer, B., K. D. Forbus, and D. Gentner (1989). The structure-mapping engine: Algorithm and examples. *Artificial Intelligence* 41:1–63.

Feldman, J. A. (1981). A connectionist model of visual memory. In *Parallel models of associative memory,* edited by G. E. Hinton and J. A. Anderson, 49–81. Hillsdale, N.J.: Erlbaum.

Feldman, J. A., and D. Ballard (1982). Connectionist models and their properties. *Cognitive Science* 6:205–54.

Fernandez, J. W. (1986). *Persuasions and performances: The play of tropes in culture.* Bloomington: Indiana University Press.

Fernandez, J. W. (1991). *Beyond metaphor: The theory of tropes in anthropology.* Stanford, Calif.: Stanford University Press.

Finke, R., T. B. Ward, and S. M. Smith (1992). *Creative cognition.* Cambridge, Mass.: MIT Press/Bradford Books.

Fogelin, R. J. (1988). *Figuratively speaking.* New Haven: Yale University Press.

Forbus, K. D., and D. Oblinger (1990). Making SME greedy and pragmatic. *Proceedings of the Twelfth Annual Conference of the Cognitive Science Society,* 61–68. Hillsdale, N.J.: Erlbaum.

Franklin, B. (1941). *Benjamin Franklin's experiments.* Cambridge, Mass.: Harvard University Press.

Frazer, J. G. (1922). *The golden bough: A study in magic and religion.* Abridged edition. New York: Macmillan.

Galileo (1967). *Dialogue concerning the two chief world systems,* translated by S. Drake. Berkeley: University of California Press.

Gardner, H. (1985). *The mind's new science.* New York: Basic Books.

Garion-Hutchings, N., and S. Garion-Hutchings (1993). *The concise guide to homeopathy.* Shaftesbury, Dorset: Element.

Gelman, R., E. Spelke, and E. Meck (1983). What preschoolers know about animate and inanimate objects. In *The acquisition of symbolic skills,* edited by D. Rogers and J. A. Sloboda, 297–326. New York: Plenum.

Gentner, D. (1977). If a tree had a knee, where would it be? Children's performance on simple spatial metaphors. *Papers and Reports on Child Language Development* 13:157–64.

Gentner, D. (1982). Are scientific analogies metaphors? In *Metaphor: Problems and perspectives,* edited by D. S. Miall, 106–32. Brighton, Sussex: Harvester Press.

Gentner, D. (1983). Structure-mapping: A theoretical framework. *Cognitive Science* 7:155–70.

Gentner, D. (1988). Metaphor as structure mapping: The relational shift. *Child Development* 59:47–59.

Gentner, D. (1989). Mechanisms of analogical learning. *Similarity and analogical reasoning,* edited by S. Vosniadou and A. Ortony, 199–241. Cambridge: Cambridge University Press.

Gentner, D., and K. D. Forbus (1991). MAC/FAC: A model of similarity-based retrieval. *Proceedings of the Thirteenth Annual Conference of the Cognitive Science Society,* 504–9. Hillsdale, N.J.: Lawrence Erlbaum.

Gentner, D., and I. M. French (1988). The verb mutability effect: Studies of the combinatorial semantics of nouns and verbs. In *Lexical ambiguity resolution in the comprehension of human language,* edited by S. L. Small, G. W. Cottrell, and M. K. Tanenhaus, 343–82. Los Altos, Calif.: Morgan Kaufman.

Gentner, D., and D. R. Gentner (1983). Flowing waters or teeming crowds: Mental models of electricity. In *Mental models,* edited by D. Gentner and A. L. Stevens, 99–129. Hillsdale, N.J.: Erlbaum.

Gentner, D., and J. Grudin (1985). The evolution of mental metaphors in psychology: A ninety-year perspective. *American Psychologist* 40:181–92.

Gentner, D., and M. Jeziorski (1989). Historical shifts in the use of analogy in science. In *The psychology of science: Contributions to metascience,* edited by B. Gholson, W. Shadish, R. Beimeyer, and A. Houts, 296–325. Cambridge: Cambridge University Press.

Gentner, D., and M. J. Ratterman (1991). Language and the career of similarity. In *Perspectives on language and thought: Interrelations in development,* edited by S. A. Gelman and J. P. Byrnes, 225–77. Cambridge: Cambridge University Press.

Gentner, D., M. J. Ratterman, and R. Campbell (1994). Evidence for a relational shift in the development of analogy: A reply to Goswami and Brown. Manuscript in preparation, Department of Psychology, Northwestern University.

Gentner, D., M. J. Rattermann, and K. D. Forbus (1993). The role of similarity in transfer. *Cognitive Psychology* 25:524–75.

Gentner, D., and A. L. Stevens, eds. (1983). *Mental models.* Hillsdale, N.J.: Erlbaum.

Gentner, D., and C. Toupin (1986). Systematicity and surface similarity in the development of analogy. *Cognitive Science* 10:277–300.

Gibbs, R. (1992). What do idioms really mean? *Journal of Memory and Language* 31:485–506.

Gick, M. L., and K. J. Holyoak (1980). Analogical problem solving. *Cognitive Psychology* 12:306–55.

Gick, M. L., and K. J. Holyoak (1983). Schema induction and analogical transfer. *Cognitive Psychology* 15:1–38.

Gilbert, W. (1958). *De magnete,* translated by P. Fleury Mottelay. New York: Dover.

Gillan, D. J., D. Premack, and G. Woodruff (1981). Reasoning in the chimpanzee: I. Analogical reasoning. *Journal of Experimental Psychology: Animal Behavior Processes* 7:1–17.

Gilovich, T. (1981). Seeing the past in the present: The effect of associations to familiar events on judgments and decisions. *Journal of Personality and Social Psychology* 40:797–808.

Glasgow, J. I., and D. Papadias (1992). Computational imagery. *Cognitive Science* 16:355–94.

Glucksberg, S., P. Gildea, and H. Bookin (1982). On understanding nonliteral speech: Can people ignore metaphors? *Journal of Verbal Learning and Verbal Behaviour* 21:85–98.

Glucksberg, S., and B. Keysar (1990). Understanding metaphorical comparisons: Beyond similarity. *Psychological Review* 97:3–18.

Glynn, S. M. (1991). Explaining science concepts: A teaching-with-analogies model. In *The psychology of learning science,* edited by S. M. Glynn, R. H. Yeany, and B. K. Britton, 219–40. Hillsdale, N.J.: Erlbaum.

Goldman, A. I. (1992). Empathy, mind, and morals. *Proceedings and Addresses of the American Philosophical Association* 66 no. 3:17–39.

Goldstone, R. L., and D. L. Medin (1993). Similarity, interactive activation, and mapping. In *Analogical connections.* Advances in Connectionist and Neural Computation Theory, edited by K. J. Holyoak and J. A. Barnden, Vol. 2, 321–61. Norwood, N.J.: Ablex.

Goodman, N. (1972). Seven strictures on similarity. In *Problems and projects,* 437–47. Indianapolis: Bobbs-Merrill.

Gorman, M. E. (1992). *Simulating science.* Bloomington: Indiana University Press.

Goswami, U. (1989). Relational complexity and the development of analogical reasoning. *Cognitive Development* 4:251–68.

Goswami, U. (1992). *Analogical reasoning in children.* Hillsdale, N.J.: Erlbaum.

Goswami, U., and A. Brown (1989). Melting chocolate and melting snowmen: Analogical reasoning and causal relations. *Cognition* 35:69–95.

Goswami, U., and A. Brown (1990). Higher-order structure and relational reasoning: Contrasting analogical and thematic relations. *Cognition* 36:207–26.

Grace v MacArthur, 170 F. Supp. 442 (E.D. Ark 1959).

Hahlweg, K., and C. A. Hooker, eds. (1989). *Issues in evolutionary epistemology.* Albany: State University of New York Press.

Halasz, F., and T. Moran (1982). Analogy considered harmful. In *Conference on Human Factors in Computer Systems. Association for Computing Machinery.*

Halford, G. S. (1987). A structure-mapping approach to cognitive development. *International Journal of Psychology* 22:609–42.

Halford, G. S. (1992). Analogical reasoning and conceptual complexity in cognitive development. *Human Development* 35:193–217.

Halford, G. S. (1993). *Children's understanding: The development of mental models.* Hillsdale, N.J.: Erlbaum.

Halford, G. S., and M. E. Kelley (1984). On the basis of early transitivity judgements. *Journal of Experimental Child Psychology* 38:42–63.

Halford, G. S., and W. H. Wilson (1980). A category theory approach to cognitive development. *Cognitive Psychology* 12:356–411.

Halford, G. S., W. H. Wilson, J. Guo, R. W. Gayler, G. Wiles, and J. E. M. Stewart (1994). Connectionist implications for processing capacity limitations in analogies. In *Analogical connections.* Advances in Connectionist and Neural Computation Theory, edited by K. J. Holyoak and J. A. Barnden, Vol. 2, 363–415. Norwood, N.J.: Ablex.

Hall, R. (1989). Computational approaches to analogical reasoning: A comparative analysis. *Artificial Intelligence* 39:39–120.

Hammond, K. (1989). *Case-based planning: Viewing planning as a memory task.* New York: Academic Press.

Harman, G. (1965). The inference to the best explanation. *Philosophical Review* 74:88–95.

Harman, G. (1973). *Thought.* Princeton: Princeton University Press.

Harman, G. (1986). *Change in view: Principles of reasoning.* Cambridge, Mass.: MIT Press/Bradford Books.

Harmon, A. (March 19, 1993). New legal frontier: Cyberspace. *Los Angeles Times.*

Hart, H. L. A. (1961). *The concept of law.* Oxford: Oxford University Press.

Hatano, G., and K. Inagaki (1987). Everyday biology and school biology: How do they interact? *Quarterly Newsletter of the Laboratory of Comparative Human Cognition* 9:120–28.

Hatano, G., and K. Inagaki (1994). Young children's naive theory of biology. *Cognition* 50:171–88

Hemingway, E. (1964). *A moveable feast.* New York: Charles Scribners' Sons.

Herrnstein, R. J. (1979). Acquisition, generalization, and discrimination reversal of a natural concept. *Journal of Experimental Psychology: Animal Behavior Processes* 5:116–29.

Hesse, M. (1966). *Models and analogies in science.* Notre Dame, Ind.: Notre Dame University Press.

Hill, R. (1978). Dozens of uses for Velcro fasteners. *Popular Science* 213 (July):110–12.

Hofstadter, D. (1984). The Copycat project: An experiment in nondeterminism and creative analogies. AI Memo 755. Cambridge, Mass.: MIT Artificial Intelligence Laboratory.

Hofstadter, D. R., and M. Mitchell (1988). Conceptual slippage and mapping: A report of the Copycat project. In *Proceedings of the Tenth Annual Conference of the Cognitive Science Society,* 601–7. Hillsdale, N.J.: Erlbaum.

Holland, J. H. (1975). *Adaptation in natural and artificial systems.* Ann Arbor: University of Michigan Press.

Holland, J. H., K. J. Holyoak, R. E. Nisbett, and P. R. Thagard (1986). *Induction: Processes of inference, learning, and discovery.* Cambridge, Mass.: MIT Press.

Holmes, F. (1985). *Lavoisier and the chemistry of life.* Madison: University of Wisconsin Press.

Holmes, F. (1989). Antoine Lavoisier and Hans Krebs: Two styles of scientific creativity. In *Creative people at work,* edited by D. Wallace and H. Gruber, 44–68. Oxford: Oxford University Press.

Holyoak, K. J. (1982). An analogical framework for literary interpretation. *Poetics* 11:105–26.

Holyoak, K. J. (1984). Analogical thinking and human intelligence. In *Advances in the psychology of human intelligence,* edited by R. J. Sternberg. Vol. 2, 199–230. Hillsdale, N.J.: Erlbaum.

Holyoak, K. J. (1985). The pragmatics of analogical transfer. In *The psychology of learning and motivation,* edited by G. H. Bower. Vol. 19, 59–87. New York: Academic Press.

Holyoak, K. J. (1987). A connectionist view of cognition. Review of *Parallel distributed processing,* by D. E. Rumelhart, J. L. McClelland, and the PDP Research Group. *Science* 236:992–96.

Holyoak, K. J. (1991). Symbolic connectionism: Toward third-generation theories of expertise. In *Toward a general theory of expertise: Prospects and limits,* edited by K. A. Ericsson and J. Smith, 301–35. Cambridge: Cambridge University Press.

Holyoak, K. J., and J. A. Barnden (1994). Introduction. In *Analogical connections. Advances in Connectionist and Neural Computation Theory,* edited by K. J. Holyoak and J. A. Barnden, Vol. 2, 321–61. Norwood, N.J.: Ablex.

Holyoak, K. J., E. N. Junn, and D. Billman (1984). Development of analogical problem-solving skill. *Child Development* 55:2042–55.

Holyoak, K. J., and K. Koh (1987). Surface and structural similarity in analogical transfer. *Memory & Cognition* 15:332–40.

Holyoak, K. J., L. R. Novick, and E. R. Melz (1994). Component processes in analogical transfer: Mapping, pattern completion, and adaptation. In *Analogical connections.* Advances in Connectionist and Neural Computation Theory, edited by K. J. Holyoak and J. A. Barnden, Vol. 2, 113–80. Norwood, N.J.: Ablex.

Holyoak, K. J., and B. A. Spellman. (1993). Thinking. *Annual Review of Psychology* 44:265–315.

Holyoak, K. J., and P. Thagard (1989a). A computational model of analogical problem solving. In *Similarity and analogical reasoning,* edited by S. Vosniadou and A. Ortony, 242–66. Cambridge: Cambridge University Press.

Holyoak, K. J., and P. Thagard (1989b). A computational model of analogical problem solving. In *Similarity and analogical reasoning,* edited by S. Vosniadou and A. Ortony, 242–66. Cambridge: Cambridge University Press.

Hopfield, J. J. (1982). Neural networks and physical systems with emergent collective computational abilities. *Proceedings of the National Academy of Sciences* 79:2554–58.

Humber, J. M. (1975). Abortion: The avoidable moral dilemma. *The Journal of Value Inquiry* 9:284–302.

Hume, D. (1888). *A treatise of human nature.* Oxford: Clarendon Press.

Hume, D. (1964). *Dialogues concerning natural religion.* Indianapolis: Bobbs-Merrill.

Hummel, J. E., and K. J. Holyoak (1992). Indirect analogical mapping. In *Proceedings of the Fourteenth Annual Conference of the Cognitive Science Society,* 516–21. Hillsdale, N.J.: Erlbaum.

Hummel, J. E., E. R. Melz, J. Thompson, and K. J. Holyoak (1994). Mapping hierarchical structures with synchrony for binding: Preliminary investigations. In *Proceedings of the Sixteenth Annual Conference of the Cognitive Science Society.* Hillsdale, N.J.: Erlbaum.

Huygens, C. (1962). *Treatise on light,* translated by S. Thompson. New York: Dover.

Inagaki, K. (1990). The effects of raising animals on children's biological knowledge. *British Journal of Developmental Psychology* 8:119–29.

Inagaki, K., and G. Hatano (1987). Young children's spontaneous personification as analogy. *Child Development* 58:1013–20.

Inagaki, K., and K. Sugiyama (1988). Attributing human characteristics: Developmental changes in over- and underattribution. *Cognitive Development* 3:55–70.

International Shoe v Washington, 326 U.S. 310 (1945).

Johnson-Laird, P. N. (1983). *Mental models.* Cambridge, Mass.: Harvard University Press.

Johnson-Laird, P. N. (1988). *The computer and the mind.* Cambridge, Mass.: Harvard University Press.

Kahneman, D., P. Slovic, and A. Tversky (1982). *Judgment under uncertainty: Heuristics and biases.* New York: Cambridge University Press.

Kahneman, D., and A. Tversky (1972). Subjective probability: A judgment of representativeness. *Cognitive Psychology* 3:430–54.

Karmiloff-Smith, A. (1983). A new abstract code or the new possibility of multiple codes? *Behavioral and Brain Sciences* 6:149–50.

Karmiloff-Smith, A. (1990). Constraints on representational change: Evidence from children's drawing. *Cognition* 34:57–83.

Karmiloff-Smith, A. (1992). *Beyond modularity: A developmental perspective on cognitive science.* Cambridge, Mass.: MIT Press.

Keane, M. (1988). *Analogical problem solving.* Chichester, Eng.: Ellis Horwood.

Keynes, J. M. (1921). *A treatise on probability.* London: Macmillan.

Keysar, B. (1989). On the functional equivalence of literal and metaphorical interpretations in discourse. *Journal of Memory and Language* 28:375–85.

Khong, Y. F. (1992). *Analogies at war.* Princeton: Princeton University Press.

Kirk, G. S., and J. E. Raven (1964). *The presocratic philosophers.* Cambridge: Cambridge University Press.

Kittay, E. F. (1987). *Metaphor: Its cognitive force and linguistic structure.* Oxford: Clarendon Press.

Koestler, A. (1964). *The act of creation.* New York: Macmillan.

Köhler, W. (1925). *The mentality of apes.* New York: Harcourt.

Kolodner, J. (1993). *Case-based reasoning.* San Mateo, Calif.: Morgan Kaufmann.

Kolodner, J., and R. Simpson (1989). The MEDIATOR: Analysis of an early case-based problem solver. *Cognitive Science* 13:507–49.

Kosslyn, S., and O. Koenig, (1992). *Wet mind: The new cognitive neuroscience.* New York: Free Press.

Kuhn, T. (1970). *Structure of scientific revolutions* 2 ed. Chicago: University of Chicago Press.

Kunda, Z. (1990). The case for motivated inference. *Psychological Bulletin* 108:480–98.

Lakoff, G. (1994). What is metaphor? In *Analogy, metaphor, and reminding.* Advances in Connectionist and Neural Computation Theory, edited by J. A. Barnden and K. J. Holyoak, Vol. 3, 203–57). Norwood, N.J.: Ablex.

Lakoff, G., and M. Johnson (1980). *Metaphors we live by.* Chicago: University of Chicago Press.

Lakeoff, G., and M. Turner (1989). *More than cool reason: A field guide to poetic metaphor.* Chicago: University of Chicago Press.

Landau, M. (1972). *Political theory and political science.* New York: Macmillan.

Laurendeau, M., and A. Pinard (1962). *Causal thinking in the child: A genetic and experimental approach.* New York: International Universities Press.

Lavoisier, A. (1862). *Oeuvres.* Paris: Imprimerie Impériale.

Lawrence, D. H., and J. DeRivera (1954). Evidence for relational transposition. *Journal of Comparative and Physiological Psychology* 47:465–71.

Leary, D. E. (1990). *Metaphors in the history of psychology.* Cambridge: Cambridge University Press.

Leatherdale, W. H. (1974). *The role of analogy, model, and metaphor in science.* Amsterdam: North-Holland.

Leibniz, G. (1981). *New essays on human understanding,* translated by P. Remnant and J. Bennett. Cambridge: Cambridge University Press.

Leslie, A. M. (1988). The necessity of illusion: Perception and thought in infancy. In *Thought without language,* edited by L. Weiskrantz, 185–210. Oxford: Oxford University Press.

Levi, E. H. (1949). *An introduction to legal reasoning.* Chicago: University of Chicago Press.

Lévi-Strauss, C. (1966). *The savage mind.* Chicago: University of Chicago Press.

Lloyd, G. E. R. (1966). *Polarity and analogy: Two types of argumentation in early Greek thought.* Cambridge: Cambridge University Press.

Locke, J. (1961). *An essay concerning human understanding.* London: Dent.

Luria, A. R. (1968). *The mind of a mnemonist.* New York: Basic Books.

Luria, S. (1984). *A slot machine, a broken test tube*. New York: Harper and Row.

McClelland, J. L., and D. E. Rumelhart (1981). An interactive activation model of context effects in letter perception: Part 1: An account of basic findings. *Psychological Review* 88:375–407.

McClelland, J. L., and D. E. Rumelhart (1989). *Explorations in parallel distributed processing*. Cambridge, Mass.: MIT Press.

McCloskey, D. N. (1985). *The rhetoric of economics*. Brighton, Sussex: Wheatsheaf.

McKellin, W. H. (1984). Putting down roots: Information in the language of Managalese exchange. In *Dangerous words: Language and politics in the Pacific*, edited by D. L. Brenneis and F. R. Myers, 108–27. New York: New York University Press.

McKellin, W. H. (1990). Allegory and inference: Intentional ambiguity in Managalese negotiations. In *Disentangling: Conflict discourse in Pacific societies*, edited by K. A. Watson-Gegeo and G. M. White, 335–70. Stanford, Calif.: Stanford University Press.

McKellin, W. H. (1995). *Hidden paths in the forest: Distributed culture, communication, and cognition among the Managalese of Papua New Guinea*. Toronto: University of Toronto Press. In press.

Mackintosh, N. J. (1988). Approaches to the study of animal intelligence. *British Journal of Psychology* 79:509–25.

Mackworth, A. K. (1990). Constraint satisfaction. In *Encyclopedia of artificial intelligence*, edited by S. C. Shapiro, 205–11. New York: John Wiley.

Mann, S. (January 29, 1992). The gloves come off at arbitration table. *USA Today*.

Markman, A. B., and D. Gentner (1993a). All differences are not created equal: A structural alignment view of similarity. In *Proceedings of the Fifteenth Annual Conference of the Cognitive Science Society*, 682–86. Hillsdale, N.J.: Erlbaum.

Markman, A. B., and D. Gentner (1993b). Structural alignment during similarity comparisons. *Cognitive Psychology* 25:431–67.

Marks, L. E., R. J. Hammeal, and M. H. Bornstein (1987). Perceiving similarity and comprehending metaphor. *Monographs of the Society for Research in Child Development* No. 215, 52(1).

Marr, D. (1982). *Vision*. San Francisco: Freeman.

Marr, D., and T. Poggio (1976). Cooperative computation of stereo disparity. *Science* 194:283–87.

May, E. R. (1973). *"Lessons" of the past: The use and misuse of history in American foreign policy*. New York: Oxford University Press.

Medin, D. (1989). Concepts and conceptual structure. *American Psychologist* 44:1469–81.

Medin, D., R. Goldstone, and D. Gentner (1993). Respects for similarity. *Psychological Review* 100:254–78.

Mencius (1970). *Mencius,* translated by D. C. Lau. Harmondsworth, Eng.: Penguin.

Merwin, W. S. (1973). *Asian figures.* New York: Atheneum.

Merwin, W. S., and J. M. Masson (1981). *The peacock's egg.* San Francisco: North Point Press.

Mill, J. S. (1970). *A system of logic* 8th ed. London: Longman.

Miller, G. (1956). The magical number seven, plus or minus two: Some limits on our capacity for processing information. *Psychological Review* 63:81–97.

Miller, G., R. Beckwith, C. Fellbaum, G. Gross, and K. Miller (1990). Introduction to WordNet: An on-line lexical database. *International Journal of Lexicography* 3:235–44.

Millgram, E., and P. Thagard (forthcoming). Deliberative coherence.

Mirowski, P. (1989). *More heat than light.* Cambridge: Cambridge University Press.

Mitchell, M. (1993). *Analogy-making as perception.* Cambridge, Mass.: MIT Press.

Morgan, G. (1993). *Imaginization: The art of creative management.* Newbury Park, Calif.: Sage.

Mostow, J. (1990). Design by derivational analogy: Issues in the automated replay of design plans. In *Machine learning: Paradigms and methods,* edited by J. Carbonell, 119–84. Cambridge, Mass.: MIT Press.

Motoyoshi, M. (1979). *Watashino Seikatuhoikuron. (Essays on education for day care children: Emphasizing daily life activities.)* In Japanese. Tokyo: Froebei-kan.

Nelson, G., P. Thagard, and S. Hardy (1994). Integrating analogies with rules and explanations. In *Analogical connections.* Advances in Connectionist and Neural Computational Theory, edited by J. A. Barnden and K. J. Holyoak, Vol. 2, 181–205). Norwood, N.J.: Ablex.

Nersessian, N. (1992). How do scientists think? Capturing the dynamics of conceptual change in science. In *Cognitive models of science,* edited by R. Giere, 3–44. Minneapolis: University of Minnesota Press.

Neurath, O. (1959). Protocol sentences. In *Logical positivism,* edited by A. J. Ayer, 199–208. Glencoe, Ill.: The Free Press.

Neustadt, R., and E. May (1986). *Thinking in time: The uses of history for decision makers.* New York: The Free Press.

Newton, I. (1934). *Mathematical principles of natural philosophy,* translated by A. Motte and F. Cojou. Berkeley: University of California Press.

Nisbett, R. E., and L. Ross (1980). *Human inference: Strategies and shortcomings of social judgement.* Englewood Cliffs, N.J.: Prentice Hall.

Noe, C. R., and A. Bader (1993). Facts are better than dreams. *Chemistry in Britain* (February):126–28.

Novick, L. R. (1988). Analogical transfer, problem similarity, and expertise. *Journal of Experimental Psychology: Learning, Memory, and Cognition* 14:510–20.

Novick, L. R., and K. J. Holyoak (1991). Mathematical problem solving by analogy. *Journal of Experimental Psychology, Learning, Memory, and Cognition* 17:398–415.

Oden, D. L., R. K. R. Thompson, and D. Premack (1990). Infant chimpanzees spontaneously perceive both concrete and abstract same/different relations. *Child Development* 61:621–31.

Okakura, K. (1912). *The book of tea.* New York: Duffield.

Ortony, A. (1979). Beyond literal similarity. *Psychological Review* 87:161–80.

Paley, W. (1963). *Natural theology: Selections.* Indianapolis: Bobbs-Merrill.

Palmer, S. E. (1978). Fundamental aspects of cognitive representation. In *Cognition and categorization,* edited by E. Rosch and B. B. Lloyd, 259–303. Hillsdale, N.J.: Erlbaum.

Palmer, S. E. (1989). Levels of description in information processing theories of analogy. In *Similarity and analogical reasoning,* edited by S. Vosniadou and A. Ortony, 332–45. London: Cambridge University Press.

Pennoyer v Neff, 95 U.S. 714 (1877).

Pevsner, N. (1976). *A history of building types.* Princeton: Princeton University Press.

Piaget, J. (1929). *The child's conception of the world.* London: Routledge and Kegan Paul.

Plantinga, A. (1967). *God and other minds.* Ithaca, N.Y.: Cornell University Press.

Plato (1961). *The collected dialogues.* Princeton: Princeton University Press.

Poincaré, H. (1913). *The foundations of science,* translated by G. Halsted, New York: Science Press.

Polya, G. (1957). *How to solve it.* Princeton: University Press.

Premack, D. (1976). *Intelligence in ape and man.* Hillsdale, N.J.: Erlbaum.

Premack, D. (1983). The codes of man and beasts. *Behavioral and Brain Sciences* 6:125–67.

Premack, D. (1988). Minds with and without language. In *Thought without language,* edited by L. Weiskrantz, 46–65. Oxford: Oxford University Press.

Premack, D., and G. Woodruff (1978). Does the chimpanzee have a theory of mind? *Behavioral and Brain Sciences* 4:515–26.

Quine, W. V. O. (1960). *Word and object.* Cambridge, Mass.: MIT Press.

Quine, W. V. O. (1966). *The ways of paradox and other essays.* New York: Random House.

Quinn, N. (1987). Convergent evidence for a cultural model of American marriage. In *Cultural models in language and thought,* edited by D. Holland and N. Quinn, 173–92. Cambridge: Cambridge University Press.

Rawls, J. (1971). *A theory of justice.* Cambridge, Mass.: Harvard University Press.

Reber, A. S. (1993). *Implicit learning and tacit knowledge.* New York: Oxford University Press.

Reed, S. K. (1987). A structure-mapping model for word problems. *Journal of Experimental Psychology, Learning, Memory, and Cognition* 13:124–39.

Richards, I. A. (1936). *The philosophy of rhetoric.* London: Oxford University Press.

Riesbeck, C., and R. Schank (1989). *Inside case-based reasoning.* Hillsdale, N.J.: Erlbaum.

Rips, L. J. (1975). Induction about natural categories. *Journal of Verbal Learning and Verbal Behavior* 14:665–81.

Robbins, A. (1991). *Awaken the giant within.* New York: Simon and Schuster.

Robin, N., and K. J. Holyoak (1994). Relational complexity and the functions of prefrontal cortex. In *The cognitive neurosciences,* edited by M. S. Gazzaniga, 987–97. Cambridge, Mass.: MIT Press.

Ross, B. (1987). This is like that: The use of earlier problems and the separation of similarity effects. *Journal of Experimental Psychology: Learning, Memory, and Cognition,* 13:371–416.

Ross, B. (1989). Distinguishing types of superficial similarities: Different effects on the access and use of earlier problems. *Journal of Experimental Psychology: Learning, Memory, and Cognition* 15:456–68.

Rumelhart, D. E. (1980). Schemata: The building blocks of cognition. In *Theoretical issues in reading comprehension,* edited by R. Spiro, B. Bruce, and W. Brewer, 33–58. Hillsdale, NJ: Erlbaum.

Rumelhart, D. E., and D. Norman (1981). Analogical processes in learning. In *Cognitive skills and their acquisition,* edited by J. R. Anderson, 335–59. Hillsdale, N.J.: Erlbaum.

Rumelhart, D. E., and J. L. McClelland, eds. (1986). *Parallel distributed processing: Explorations in the microstructure of cognition.* Cambridge Mass.: MIT Press.

Rumelhart, D. E., P. Smolensky, G. Hinton, and J. McClelland, J. (1986). Schemata and sequential thought processes in PDP models. In *Parallel distributed processing: Explorations in the microstructure of cognition,* edited by J. McClelland and D. E. Rumelhart, 7–57. Cambridge Mass.: MIT Press.

Schank, R. C. (1982). *Dynamic memory: A theory of reminding and learning in computers and people.* New York: Cambridge University Press.

Schank, R. C. (1986). *Explanation patterns: Understanding mechanically and creatively.* Hillsdale, N.J.: Erlbaum.

Searle, J. (1980). Minds, brains, and programs. *Behavioral and Brain Sciences* 3:417–24.

Seger, C. A. (1994). Implicit learning. *Psychological Bulletin.*

Seifert, C. M., G. McKoon, R. Abelson, and R. Ratcliff (1986). Memory connections between thematically similar episodes. *Journal of Experimental Psychology: Learning, Memory, and Cognition* 12:220–31.

Sen, S., XV (1979). *Tea life, tea mind.* New York: Weatherhill.

Shepard, R. N. (1975). Form, formation, and transformation of internal representations. In *Information processing and cognition: The Loyola Symposium,* edited by R. Solso, 87–122. Hillsdale, N.J.: Erlbaum.

Simons, G. (1988). *Is God a programmer?* Brighton, Sussex: Harvester Press.

Smith, A. (1937). *The wealth of nations.* New York: Modern Library.

Sontag, S. (1979). *Illness as metaphor.* New York: Vintage.

Spellman, B. A., and K. J. Holyoak (1992). If Saddam is Hitler then who is George Bush? Analogical mapping between systems of social roles. *Journal of Personality and Social Psychology* 62:913–33.

Spellman, B. A., and K. J. Holyoak (1993). An inhibitory mechanism for goal-directed analogical mapping. In *Proceedings of the Fifteenth Annual Conference of the Cognitive Science Society,* 947–52. Hillsdale, N.J.: Erlbaum.

Spencer, R. M., and R. W. Weisberg (1986). Context-dependent effects on analogical transfer. *Memory & Cognition* 14:442–49.

Sperber, D., and D. Wilson (1986). *Relevance: Communication and cognition.* Cambridge: Cambridge University Press.

Spiro, R. J., P. J. Feltovich, R. L. Coulson, and D. K. Anderson (1989). Multiple analogies for complex concepts: Antidotes for analogy-induced misconception in advanced knowledge acquisition. In *Similarity and analogical reasoning,* edited by S. Vosniadou and A. Ortony, 498–531. Cambridge: Cambridge University Press.

Stepan, N. L. (1986). Race and gender: The role of analogy in science. *Isis* 77:261–77.

Sternberg, R. J. (1977). Component processes in analogical reasoning. *Psychological Review* 84:353–78.

Sternberg, R. J. (1990). *Metaphors of mind.* Cambridge: Cambridge University Press.

Sternberg, R. J., and B. Rifkin (1979). The development of analogical reasoning processes. *Journal of Experimental Child Psychology* 27:195–232.

Sunstein, C. R. (1993). On analogical reasoning. *Harvard Law Review* 106:741–91.

Swinburne, R. (1992). *Revelation: From metaphor to analogy.* Oxford: Clarendon Press.

Talalay, L. E. (1987). Rethinking the function of clay figurine legs from Neolithic Greece: An argument from analogy. *American Journal of Archaeology* 91:161–69.

Tambiah, S. J. (1973). Form and meaning of magical acts: A point of view. In *Modes of thought,* edited by R. Horton and R. Finnegan, 199–229. London: Faber and Faber.

Tannen, D. (1990). *You just don't understand: Women and men in conversation.* New York: Morrow.

Thagard, P. (1988). *Computational philosophy of science.* Cambridge, Mass.: MIT Press.

Thagard, P. (1989). Explanatory coherence. *Behavioral and Brain Sciences* 12:435–67.

Thagard, P. (1992). *Conceptual revolutions.* Princeton: Princeton University Press.

Thagard, P., D. Cohen, and K. Holyoak (1989). Chemical analogies: Two kinds of explanation. In *Eleventh International Joint Conference on Artificial Intelligence,* 819–24. San Mateo, Calif.: Morgan Kaufmann.

Thagard, P., D. Gochfeld, and S. Hardy (1992). Visual analogical mapping. In *Proceedings of the Fourteenth Annual Conference of the Cognitive Science Society,* 522–27. Hillsdale, N.J.: Erlbaum.

Thagard, P., and S. Hardy (1992). Visual thinking in the development of Dalton's atomic theory. In *Proceedings of the Ninth Canadian Conference on Artificial Intelligence,* 30–37. Vancouver: Canadian Society for Computational Studies of Intelligence.

Thagard, P., K. J. Holyoak, G. Nelson, and D. Gochfeld (1990). Analog retrieval by constraint satisfaction. *Artificial Intelligence,* 46:259–310.

Thagard, P., and E. Millgram (1995). Inference to the best plan: A coherence theory of decision. In *Goal-directed learning,* edited by A. Ram and D. B. Leake. Cambridge, Mass.: MIT Press. In press.

Thompson, R. K. R., and D. L. Oden (1993). "Language training" and its role in the expression of tacit propositional knowledge by chimpanzees (*Pan troglodytes*). In *Advances in the study of animal language,* edited by H. S. Roitblat, L. M. Herman, and P. Nachtigall, 365–84. Hillsdale, N.J.: Erlbaum.

Thomson, J. J. (1971). A defense of abortion. *Philosophy and Public Affairs* 1:47–66.

Thorndike, E. (1913). *Educational psychology.* New York: Columbia University Press.

Tirrell, L. (1991). Reductive and nonreductive simile theories of metaphor. *Journal of Philosophy* 88:337–58.

Tolstoy, L. (1960). *The death of Ivan Ilyich and other stories,* translated by R. Edmonds. Harmondsworth, Eng.: Penguin.

Tolstoy, L. (1982). *War and peace,* translated by R. Edmonds. London: Penguin.

Treagust, D. F., R. Duit, P. Joslin, and I. Lindauer (1992). Science teachers' use of analogies: Observations from classroom practice. *International Journal of Science Education* 14:413–22.

Turner, M. (1987). *Death is the mother of beauty: Mind, metaphor, criticism.* Chicago: University of Chicago Press.

Tyrell, D. J., L. B. Stauffer, and L. G. Snowman (1991). Perception of abstract identity/difference relationships by infants. *Infant Behavior and Development* 14:125–29.

Van Evra, J. (1994). Logic and mathematics in Charles Sanders Peirce's description of a notation for the logic of relatives. In *Studies in the logic of Charles Sanders Peirce,* edited by N. Houser, D. Roberts, and J. Van Evra. Indianapolis: Indiana University Press.

Vitruvius (1960). *The ten books on architecture,* translated by M. H. Morgan. New York: Dover.

Volkov, A. (1992). Analogical reasoning in ancient China: Some examples. *Extrême Orient–Extrême Occident: Cahiers de recherches comparatives* 14:15–48.

Vosniadou, S. (1989). Analogical reasoning as a mechanism in knowledge acquisition: A development perspective. In *Similarity and analogical reasoning,* edited by S. Vosniadou and A. Ortony, 413–37. Cambridge: Cambridge University Press.

Waldmann, M. R. (1989). Children's understanding of inadequate transfer in jokes. Poster. Kansas City, Mo.: Society for Research in Child Development.

Waltz, D. L., and J. B. Pollack (1985). Massively parallel processing: A strongly interactive model of natural language interpretation. *Cognitive Science* 9:51–74.

Wharton, C. M. (1993) *Direct and indirect measures of the roles of thematic and situational knowledge in reminding.* Ph.D. dissertation, Department of Psychology, University of California, Los Angeles.

Wharton, C. M., K. J. Holyoak, P. E. Downing, T. E. Lange, T. D. Wickens, and E. R. Melz (1994). Below the surface: Analogical similarity and retrieval competition in reminding. *Cognitive Psychology* 26:64–101.

Wilson, D. (1983). *Rutherford, simple genius.* Cambridge, Mass.: MIT Press.

Winston, P. H. (1980). Learning and reasoning by analogy. *Communications of the ACM* 23:689–703.

Woodward, B. (1991). *The commanders.* New York: Simon and Schuster.

Wotiz, J. H. (Ed.). (1993). *The Kekulé riddle: A challenge for chemists and psychologists.* Clearwater, Fla.: Cache River Press.

Wylie, A. (1985). The reaction against analogy. *Advances in Archaeological Theory and Method* 8:63–111.

Index